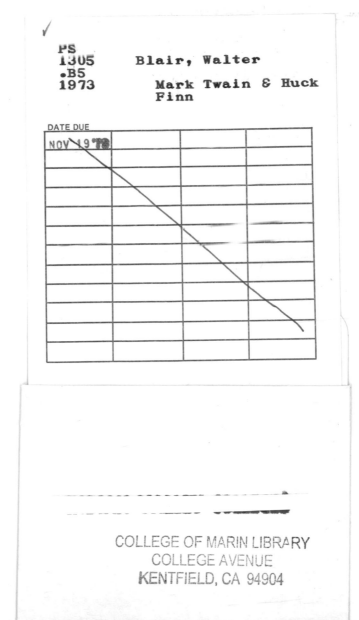

MARK TWAIN & *HUCK FINN*

Mark Twain, ca. 1874

Walter Blair

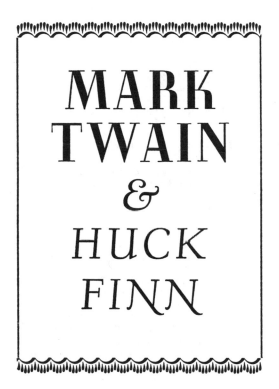

MARK TWAIN

& HUCK FINN

UNIVERSITY OF CALIFORNIA PRESS
BERKELEY, LOS ANGELES, LONDON

University of California Press
Berkeley and Los Angeles, California

University of California Press, Ltd.
London, England

© *1960 by The Regents of the University of California*

Published with the assistance of a grant
from the Ford Foundation

California Library Reprint Series Edition, 1973
ISBN: 0-520-02521-0

Library of Congress
Catalog Card Number: 73-87552

Designed by Ward Ritchie
Printed in the United States of America

FOR CAROL AND PAULA

"THEY ENDURED."

PREFACE

This is a study of an American novel unique in being held in the highest esteem by critics and at the same time prodigiously popular in the United States and throughout the world. More specifically, I attempt to define the forces which gave Adventures of Huckleberry Finn *its substance and its form.*

Like many, including Mark Twain, I consider contributions which the author's boyhood in Hannibal and his piloting years on the Mississippi made to this novel. But I believe that even more important than Twain's remembered experiences were ways he manipulated and augmented them when he transmuted them into fiction. Therefore I discuss in greater detail the forces shaping such modifications—the man's life, his reading, his thinking, and his writing between 1874 and 1884.

In the autumn of 1874 Samuel L. Clemens and his family occupied the house in Hartford which was his home during the period of this study. Because it represented his achievements and his ambitions and because it proved to be his delight and his despair, this teeming mansion loomed large in his consciousness. So did the quiet farm near Elmira, New York, to which he fled in summer to do much of his writing, and Europe, where he sought refuge in 1878–1879. In 1882 he paid a visit to the river and the town of his youth which moved him profoundly. Throughout the decade he lived expensively and expansively; he engaged in bitterly partisan politics; he toiled feverishly to outwit cheats (as he conceived them) and to win success in the world of publishing and business; he had more trouble with a nagging conscience than most men have. All these elements in his life palpably shaped his novel.

From his youth Clemens had loved books. Acutely conscious, thanks in part to persistent critics, of the meagerness of his cultural background, he hoped to improve himself by reading. He had a greedy curiosity about history, human nature, and philosophy which books helped appease. So in Hartford, Elmira, and Europe he read much in several areas—in history, biography, philosophy, humor, and (though he believed he disliked it) fiction. His familiarity with contemporary literature helped him write a book which became a best seller. And in portraying more characters and incidents than students heretofore have noticed, consciously or unconsciously he echoed his wide-ranging reading.

Much of the reading was thoughtful, for this man with little formal education was fiercely determined to wrest from books and from life a philosophy. Ancient problems obsessed this incorrigible moralist: What is the nature of man? How does he distinguish evil from good? What are the wellsprings of human action? From 1874 on he was stimulated by a book which concerned his most absorbing problem, Lecky's History of European Morals. *For Lecky discriminated two types of moralists and traced their stories: those holding with Lecky that man has intuitive powers which enable him to act virtuously, and those holding that uncontrollable exterior forces shape man's character and selfish interests his actions. In bellicose marginalia, in notebooks, in works published and unpublished, Mark Twain worked steadily to build up a strong case against Lecky. Shortly before he wrote the major and concluding portion of* Huckleberry Finn *he delivered a paper in which he championed determinism and selfish motivation. A few months after completing his manuscript (so he implies) he became a pessimist, which in his way of thinking meant a determinist. Nevertheless, while writing his novel he wavered between a logical conviction that Lecky's position was untenable and a pathetic hope that some men at least might live as Lecky held all could. This vacillation—and indeed a host of others—made possible, even necessary, his writing a humorous novel. And it had much to do with the picture of humanity which the book in the end presented.*

Mark Twain's literary activity during these years (and to a lesser extent before) also was influential. Self-trained as he was, the author chiefly learned to write by writing, and though falteringly, he moved perceptibly to the acquisition of the technique which entered into the writing of his masterpiece. Narratives closely allied to it, such as "Old Times on the Mississippi," The Adventures of Tom Sawyer, *and Part II of* Life on the Mississippi, *and narratives seemingly remote from it, such as the playfully obscene sketch* 1601, *the travel book* A Tramp Abroad, *and the historical romance for children* The Prince and the Pauper, *helped him discover subject matter and form. Writings completed before he started* Huck *helped him consciously select a fictional point of view important for the novel's achievement; even those written after he began the novel helped him infuse meaning into his narrative, not sporadically and tentatively as at its start but consistently and surely.*

Having considered how these forces brought Huckleberry Finn *into being I turn in my final two chapters to aftermaths of its composition—first, its publication; second, its achievement of world-wide popularity.*

It is a pleasure to express my gratitude to the following publishers who have permitted me to quote at length from copyrighted works: the President and Fellows of Harvard College and Harvard University Press, publishers of Kenneth R. Andrews, Nook Farm: Mark Twain's Hartford Circle, *and of Bernard De-Voto,* Mark Twain at Work; *Harper and Brothers, publishers of* The Writings of Mark Twain (*Definitive Edition*); *Clara Clemens,* My Father Mark Twain; *William Dean Howells,* My Mark Twain; The Love Letters of Mark Twain, *ed. Dixon Wecter;* Mark Twain's Notebook, *ed. Albert Bigelow Paine;* Mark Twain's Autobiography, *ed. Albert Bigelow Paine;* Mark Twain in Eruption, *ed. Bernard DeVoto;* Mark Twain's Letters, *ar. Albert Bigelow Paine; and Albert Bigelow Paine,* Mark Twain: A Biography. *To avoid* *excessive documentation, I have not cited in my notes specific references to the last four of these, basic for any study of Mark Twain.* I also am pleased to thank Houghton Mifflin Company for permission to quote from Bernard DeVoto,* Mark Twain's America, *and Dixon Wecter,* Sam Clemens of Hannibal. *The latter of these, though not specifically cited in the notes, is a definitive treatment of the author's Hannibal years.*

The illustration by Eberhard Binder-Stassfurt from Die Abenteuer des Huckleberry Finn *(Berlin, 1955, 1957) on page 378 is reproduced with the permission of the publisher, Verlag Neues Leben.*

Libraries which have consented to my study and citation of unpublished letters and manuscripts include: the Houghton Library, Harvard University, custodian of the William Dean Howells Collection and the Rogers Theatrical Collection; the Rutherford B. Hayes Memorial Library, Fremont, Ohio; the New York Public Library, custodian of the Henry W. and Albert A. Berg Collection; the Yale University Library, custodian of the Willard S. Morse Collection; the Buffalo and Erie County Public Library, Buffalo, New York, which has made available for study and reproduction its partial manuscript of Huckleberry Finn *and illustrations in its collection of foreign editions. To all these, my thanks. To the University of California Library, Berkeley, California, in which the greatest body of useful materials, the Mark Twain Papers, is housed, I am particularly indebted.*

I am particularly indebted also to the Mark Twain Company for giving me access to this collection for its study and for allowing me to quote unpublished and published material at length. The

---

* To enable readers to locate numerous but often important quotations, however, I list here citations from the last two. From *Mark Twain's Letters,* arranged by Albert Bigelow Paine, I reprint, with the permission of Harper and Brothers, quotations on the following pages: 16, 24, 26, 35, 36, 37, 38, 39, 43, 50, 51, 53, 64, 78, 80, 90, 91, 98, 99, 111, 145, 158, 160, 166, 167, 168, 179, 186–187, 194–195, 199, 200, 222, 224, 255, 257, 264, 269, 273, 287, 289, 317, 323, 334, 339, 350, 357, 360, 371, 372, 403. From Albert Bigelow Paine, *Mark Twain: A Biography,* I reprint, with the permission of Harper and Brothers, quotations on the following pages: 10, 31, 41, 88, 107, 138, 154, 165, 168, 169, 177–178, 222, 228, 249, 254, 263, 271, 323, 324, 359.

photograph of Samuel L. Clemens, that of Olivia Clemens, the working note, and the circular are reproduced through the courtesy of the Mark Twain Company.

My writing of a large share of this book was made possible when the University of Chicago, in 1958, freed me from academic duties by generously granting a leave of absence.

During the more than two decades when I carried on research and wrote this study, I have been helped by collectors, students, scholars, and colleagues in countless ways. To all of these I am most thankful, no less warmly because limitations of space allow me to mention specifically only a few. Clifton Waller Barrett gave me access to his fine collection of letters, manuscripts, and printed material, and allowed me to quote them. Samuel C. Webster has permitted me to quote from letters in the Moffett Collection, University of California, previously not utilized by scholars, and to quote extensively from his book, Mark Twain, Business Man. *Over the years the late Bernard DeVoto exchanged letters and engaged in discussions and arguments which were of inestimable value. Franklin J. Meine has been constantly eager to discuss problems at length, to give me access to his collection, and to share his great learning. Henry Nash Smith, literary executor of the Mark Twain Estate, and his assistant Frederick Anderson have been endlessly patient and helpful. By preserving me from errors, presenting me with valuable ideas, helping me track down facts, and even battling to give my study a degree of lucidity, they have helped me more than anyone is likely to imagine.*

W. B.

CONTENTS

ILLUSTRATIONS

HIS HUMOR'S WILDEST EXTRAVAGANCE IS THE
BREAK AND FLING FROM A DEEP FEELING, A
WRATH WITH SOME FOLLY WHICH DISQUIETS
HIM WORSE THAN OTHER MEN, A PERSONAL
HATRED FOR SOME HUMBUG OR PRETENSION
THAT EMBITTERS HIM BEYOND ANYTHING BUT
LAUGHTER.

William Dean Howells

1

"THE END. YOURS TRULY, HUCK FINN."

There ain't no more to write about, and I am rotten glad of it, because if I'd 'a' knowed what a trouble it was to make a book I wouldn't 'a' tackled it. . . . THE END. YOURS TRULY, HUCK FINN.—Final paragraph, manuscript, Adventures of Huckleberry Finn.

Late in August, 1883, Samuel L. Clemens—more accurately Mark Twain, since that was his *nom de plume*—wrote the last page of *Adventures of Huckleberry Finn.* He was on a farm near Elmira, New York, where he worked in a one-room house built as his study nine years before. Photographs show a room cluttered with a sofa, assorted chairs, and the two little antique statues which stood on the fireplace mantel. There he sat writing on a small round table heaped with books and papers.

These photographs and others, and friends' descriptions, picture a presence which was impressive even in that era of majestically bearded authors. Three months short of his forty-eighth birthday, he looked years younger, in part because he was wiry and tautly alert, in part because he was enjoying his usual vibrant health (thanks, he would have claimed, to his steady smoking and his habit of drinking malt or spirituous liquor each morning and evening). He was slightly above average height, but his thin figure and small delicate hands and feet made a few who saw him briefly consider him small. His arresting head, however, was disproportionately large, or perhaps its features gave that impression—the great cockatoo swirl of dense gray hair, the high forehead, the feathery eyebrows, the long aquiline nose, and the big drooping moustache. Many have mentioned the piercing quality of his eyes, which glinted sternly or quizzically from beneath lowered lids. His dress for the time was dazzling; though other American men wore dark suits the year round, in summer he wore suits of spotless white.

As he finished each page his habit was to drop it to the floor to join others written that day. Late in the afternoon he gathered and stacked the pages, probably counted them (since he was always interested in the day's output), and carried them over to the farmhouse where his wife and daughters awaited his arrival.

On the last page of the novel Huck in his role of narrator expressed vast relief upon finishing his story. His creator must have shared this sentiment as he did many others of this character, for he had composed the novel haltingly and slowly. He had started it rather more than seven years before, had written about four hundred pages, and had wavered between burning and pigeonholing them. Luckily he had put them aside. On returning to them now and then he had found that he could add pages. Finally that summer in a great spurt of creation he had completed the manuscript.

There is no evidence that he felt that the moment was an unusually important one. In retrospect, however, it is possible to see that it was a climax in Mark Twain's long career and also in American literary history.

"In retrospect." The words need emphasis. For students recounting the zigzags of the author's reputation have found that for some time many critics were cool toward his masterpiece. A month after the book was issued in America the Boston *Transcript* held that it was "so flat, as well as coarse, that nobody wants to read it after a taste of it . . ."; and *Life*, in those days a comic magazine by intention, after "a search expedition for the humorous qualities of the book," reported that far from being amusing it contained one bloodcurdling scene after another. Charges of coarseness and flatness were repeated over the years, often supplemented with the charge that the novel proved that its author was "absolutely unconscious of almost all canons of literary art." [1]

At intervals, alerted by hostile critics to the possibility that *Huck* might corrupt morals, upright citizens banned it from libraries and schoolrooms. Ink was scarcely dry on the first edition when the Library Committee of Concord, Massachusetts, pulled it from their shelves for "dealing with a series of experiences not elevating." Disturbed by news of this, soon the librarian of the New York State Reformatory contemplated saving his customers from contamination by confiscating the book. He was prevented only by the report of a visiting Professor Sanborn that, after reading it, he felt that it might safely "go into your Reference Library, at least." [2] In August, 1902, a Denver preacher persuaded the city's library managers to exclude the book as "immoral and sacrilegious." The same month the Omaha Public Library Board, unfortunately confusing *Huckleberry Finn* with *Tom Sawyer*, snaked it out of the juvenile department "on the ground it puts wrong ideas in youngsters' heads, teaching them to desire the life of a pirate rather than a sedate good citizen." [3] In 1905 the novel was snatched from the children's room of the Brooklyn Public Library because it was deemed "a bad example for ingenuous youth," and in 1907 E. L. Pearson reported that *Tom* and *Huck* were being "turned out of some library every year" since "word has gone forth that these two books are to be condemned." [4] For about half a century thereafter, if additional young readers were saved from the book their good luck was not publicized. Then in 1957 New York City's board of education suddenly roused itself and excised *Huck* from approved textbook lists (though not the library lists) of elementary and junior high schools. [5]

Nevertheless from the start there were influential critics who expressed great admiration for the novel. And as time passed the number of these proportionately increased. Even before the book was completed it was inordinately praised. In 1881 William Livingston Alden, editorial writer and columnist on the New York *Times*, the author of several humorous books and the founder of

'Gee, Huck — Teacher Says I Shouldn't Play With You'

(JACOB BURCK, CARTOON IN CHICAGO *Sun-Times*, SEPTEMBER 15, 1957)

the Lotos Club, which Clemens frequently visited while in New York, wrote at the end of a business note a brief but impressive testimonial: "I have just read Huck through in course. It is the best book ever written." Before filing this, Clemens wrote on the envelope, with no sign of excitement: "from Alden 'best book ever written.'" [6] And just about the time he was finishing the manuscript a reviewer in the *Atlantic* enthusiastically praised a chapter which had been removed from it and published: "Rude, sturdy, unflinching though the picture is, it is likely to stand a long while as a transcript from nature, and as a memorial of the phase of existence which it describes will not easily be surpassed in the future." [7] Before the book was issued in America, though after it was published in England, in the earliest review I have found, a critic praised it for British readers as the wonderfully rich achievement of "a literary artist of the highest order." [8]

The anonymous reviewer was Professor Brander Matthews of Columbia University, a scholar held in high esteem who for years was a persistent champion of the novel. And though thereafter some academics sneered at *Huck* or even ignored it, within less than two decades such leading critics as William Dean Howells, Barrett Wendell of Harvard, Sir Walter Besant of England, and Andrew Lang and Robert Louis Stevenson of Scotland called it one of America's—or even one of the world's—greatest. Within another two decades two men who as boys had read *Huckleberry Finn* soon after its publication had become the critics most influential in shaping American taste. Professor William Lyon Phelps of Yale called it America's greatest novel. H. L. Mencken, like Phelps only in being ebullient, a male, and a powerful literary force, called his discovery of the novel at the age of nine "probably the most stupendous event of my whole life" and set forth in his "Credo" of 1913: "I believe that *Huckleberry Finn* is one of the great masterpieces of the world. . . . I believe that [Twain] wrote better English, in the sense of cleaner, straighter, vivider, saner English, than either Irving or Hawthorne. . . . I believe that he was the true father of our national literature, the first genuinely American artist of the blood royal." Even the Van Wyck Brooks of 1920, who gave Mark Twain a stern post-mortem scolding because he had not had the good taste to be Jonathan Swift, spoke of "the beauty, the eternal freshness" of *Huck,* and admitted that "it flies like a gay, bright, shining arrow through the tepid atmosphere of American literature."

During recent decades the number of critics praising *Huck* has steadily grown and the number dispraising it has steadily shrunk. When, about two decades ago, "the Heritage Press asked fifty literary critics to name the ten leading American books, thirty-eight out of the forty-two who replied merged *Tom Sawyer* and *Huckleberry Finn* and the book thus rather violently created appeared on five more lists than its leading rival." [9] "Everyone," as Leo Marx says, "seems to agree that [*Huck*] is a great book, or even one of the great American books. But we are less certain about what makes it great." [10] The eagerness of critics to decide this question is shown by the scores of articles in critical and learned journals, of chapters in books, and of long introductions to new editions which offer answers, often supporting them with the formidable artillery of the New Critics.[11] At the moment no other American book is so often discussed. And arrayed against the adulations of *Huck* the lonely article arguing that *Huck* has been overpraised stands out like a very sore finger.[12]

Creative writers, too, speak highly of it, and often proclaim that the novel has been very influential in shaping their art. Nobel prize winner T. S. Eliot, poet, critic, and literary historian, offers a summary:

Twain, at least in *Huckleberry Finn,* reveals himself to be one of those writers of whom there are not a great many in any literature, who have discovered a new way of writing, valid not only for themselves, but for others. I should place him, in this respect, even with Dryden and Swift, as one of those rare writers who have brought their language up to date and in so doing, "purified the dialect of the tribe." In this respect, I should place him above Hawthorne.[13]

Eliot himself could not have been influenced by *Huck* since he did not read it until he was an established author. Besides, to imagine what would have happened to Eliot's work if he had been influenced by Mark Twain boggles the imagination. But elsewhere influence is clear.

In 1956 Herman Wouk, who was much praised—probably over-praised—for his Pulitzer prize novel, *The Caine Mutiny,* and for *Marjorie Morningstar,* called Mark Twain "the commanding figure in our literature" and *Huck* "the crown of our literature." In this book, he says, Twain "established at a stroke the colloquial style which has swept American literature, and indeed spilled over into world literature." Wouk then gives a long list of authors who "with their disciples and imitators, are hardly conceivable except coming after Twain"—Jack London, O. Henry, Sherwood Anderson, Theodore Dreiser, F. Scott Fitzgerald, Sinclair Lewis, H. L. Mencken, Booth Tarkington, Ernest Hemingway, J. P. Marquand, Ring Lardner, William Faulkner, "as well as many major writers who have not yet generated trains of followers" (probably including one whom Wouk is too modest to mention). Critic George Mayberry adds to a similar list two names which Wouk missed—John Dos Passos and Erskine Caldwell. Whether major writers or not, such diverse authors as Ben Hecht, Henry Miller, and William Saroyan have personally testified that they have worked under Mark Twain's tutelage and benefited by it.[14] I cannot believe that anyone who knows *Huck* and who reads *Catcher in the Rye* and *Adventures of Augie March* will hesitate to add the names of J. D. Salinger and Saul Bellow, much admired by the young literati of the 1950's, to this census. And in 1958 Robert Lewis Taylor so obviously imitated Huck's mode of writing in *The Travels of Jamie McPheeters* that even booksellers noticed the fact. The novel was awarded a Pulitzer prize.

Two Nobel prize winners have justified the claim that Mark Twain shaped their work. Hemingway's statement, written with his laconic pen, has the quality of a rhapsody: "All American literature comes from one book by Mark Twain called *Huckleberry Finn* . . . the best book we've had. All American writing comes from that. There was nothing before. There has been nothing as good since." As one interested in ancestry William Faulkner naturally has worked out a more elaborate line of descent, but traces back to the same forebear: "[Sherwood Anderson] was the father of my generation of American writers and the tradition which our successors will carry on. . . . Dreiser is his older brother and Mark Twain the father of them both." [15]

Though scholars, critics, and novelists took several decades to agree on the great merit of *Huck*, the vast reading public has been strong for it from the start. "A classic," Mark Twain once said, "is something that everybody wants to have read and nobody wants to read." What the public could do to disqualify this novel as a classic in this sense it did. It made *Huck* on its publication a best seller and during the author's lifetime the best paying of all his highly remunerative books. Over the decades children learned that, though like *Silas Marner* and *Julius Caesar* it was on reading lists, this book, even in school, they could enjoy. That mythical character, the Man on the Street, traditionally allergic to anything more literary than a well-turned dirty limerick, a vivid sports report, or a red-blooded adventure story, either remembered the novel from childhood and on occasion reread it or discovered it and delighted in it. It went into hundreds of editions, sold millions of copies in the United States and abroad, winning a place among the most popular novels by American authors of all times. In the 1950's, seventy years and more after its appearance, it was selling more briskly in both deluxe and inexpensive editions than it had in its initial printings. Television writers and producers at intervals were capitalizing on its fame with purported dramatizations, and in 1959 two motion picture companies were racing to complete new versions.

American novels competing with its popularity—*Gone with the Wind, Peyton Place, God's Little Acre,* Spillane's sadistic thrillers—had not an iota of *Huck's* critical reputation. American novels considered by critics to be equally "great"—*The Scarlet Letter, Moby Dick,* and *Portrait of a Lady*—had but a fraction of its fame or its influence. The unique combination of appeals— to discerning critics, to practicing novelists, and to masses of readers—would seem to justify writing in detail of what might be called its "biography." An account of its writing, its publication, and its dissemination should cast light upon the times which shaped it, the extraordinary personality, the life and career of its author, popular taste, and finally the book itself.

Adventures of Huckleberry Finn, like Mark Twain's other best works, recreates scenes, characters, and events in the author's boyhood and youth. Mark once wrote:

I confine myself to life with which I am familiar, when pretending to portray life. But I confine myself to the boy-life out on the Mississippi because that had a peculiar charm for me and not because I was not familiar with other phases of life. . . . *Now* then: as the most valuable capital, or culture, or education usable in the building of novels is personal experience, I ought to be well equipped. . . . [And yet I can't get away from the boyhood period and write novels because capital is not sufficient by itself and I lack the other essential: interest in handling the men and experiences of later times.] [16]

This is shrewd self-analysis: as Dixon Wecter remarks in his fine study of the author's youth, "Mark Twain's genius always swung like a compass toward his fourteen years' childhood and adolescence in Hannibal. . . . Mark himself told the story of those days, repeatedly, in fiction, semi-fiction, and purported fact. . . ." The settings of *Huck* are the riverside town which was Sam Clemens' boyhood home, the farm he visited during vacations, and another background that greatly appealed to him—the river upon which he was a pilot during his young manhood. He often said that his experiences in youth were the chief (sometimes the *only*) sources of happenings in the novel. Understandably, therefore, many readers, biographers, and critics have come to believe that literal transcripts of reality gave it and Mark Twain's other finest writings their merit and their power.

"But," Wecter continues the statement just quoted, "Mark had a habit that grew with the years of forgetting or changing anything he did not like. It was a mythmaking process. . . . All his days he wrote fiction under the cloak of autobiography, and autobiography under the trappings of fiction." This biography of *Huckleberry Finn* will show that the novel which Mark Twain completed that summer afternoon in 1883 was something very different from a simple recording of scenes, personalities, and events. It will show many forces transforming actualities into fiction which differs greatly from them—the author's fallible memory, his manipulation of facts for artistic purposes, his sharp recollections of recent experiences and emotions, his extraordinarily varied and influential reading, his philosophizing about moral motivation and the nature of depravity.

"Memory, of course," Ernest Hemingway once wrote, "is never true." A creative writer's memory probably is less true than others because as an artist he often consciously or unconsciously improves upon it. Albert Bigelow Paine, Mark Twain's official biographer, and other students of the author have found his inaccuracies awe-inspiring even in his *Autobiography*, where he was making a great effort to be truthful. Wecter once called his memory "almost perversely fallacious." And Mark himself knew about this foible. "When I was younger," he said, "I could remember anything, whether it happened or not, but I am getting old, and soon I shall remember only the latter."

His manipulation of facts in his writings often helped the process. On April 16, 1867, for instance, as a traveling correspondent for the San Francisco *Alta California,* he reported reminiscences evoked by a recent visit to Hannibal. The facts were that the author's father, not a "professional reformer" but a "spasmodic" one, had tried to reform Hannibal's town drunkard, Jimmy Finn, and much later Jimmy "died a natural death in a tan vat, of a combination of delirium tremens and spontaneous combustion." [17] Compare the news story:

Hannibal has had a hard time of it ever since I can recollect. . . . First, it had me for a citizen, but I was too young then to really hurt the place. Next, Jimmy Finn, the town drunkard, reformed, and that broke up the only saloon in the village. But the temperance people liked it; they were willing enough to sacrifice public prosperity to public morality. And so they made much of Jimmy Finn—dressed him up in new clothes, and had him out to breakfast and dinner, and so forth, and showed him off as a great living curiosity—a shining example of the power of temperance doctrines when earnestly and eloquently set forth.

Which was all very well, you know, and sounded well, and looked well in print, but Jimmy Finn couldn't stand it. He got remorseful about the loss of his liberty; and then he got melancholy from thinking about it so much; and after that, he got drunk. He got awfully drunk in the chief citizen's house, and the next morning that house was as if the swine had tarried in it. That outraged the temperance people and delighted the opposite faction. The former rallied and reformed Jim once more, but in an evil hour temptation came upon him, and he sold his body to a doctor for a quart of whiskey, and that ended all his earthly troubles. He drank it all in one sitting, and his soul went to its long account, and his body went to Doctor Grant. This was another blow to Hannibal. Jimmy Finn had always kept the town in a sweat about something or other, and now it nearly died from utter inanition.

Here, as Mark admitted a little later in the same dispatch, he was exaggerating "the ups and downs" of Hannibal. Not his father, therefore, but "the temperance people," one of the two factions comprising Hannibal, reform Finn. Hannibal at the time actually had three distilleries and at least six saloons, but to emphasize the town's misfortune Twain has Jimmy's reform close the only saloon in the village. When Jimmy backslides and gets drunk, he messes up not John Clemens' house but the chief citizen's house. And Jimmy's way of dying is changed for comic effect.

This, as it turned out, was a practice run, "a literary rehearsal," for an incident in *Huckleberry Finn*, chapter v, written about nine years later. There Pap Finn is reformed by a new judge who does not know Pap's history. The judge takes the old reprobate home, dresses him handsomely, and feeds him. After an orgy of preaching, confessing, praying, and weeping, Pap Finn makes an eloquent speech promising reform, holds out his hand, and asks the family to shake it. Says Huck:

So they shook it, one after the other, all around, and cried. The judge's wife she kissed it. Then the old man signed—made his mark. The judge said it was the holiest thing on record, or something like that. Then they tucked the old man into a beautiful room . . . and in the night some time he got powerful thirsty and clumb out . . . and traded his new coat for a jug of forty-rod, and clumb back again and had a good old time. . . . And when they come to look at that spare room they had to take soundings before they could navigate it.

The judge he felt kind of sore. He said he reckoned a body could reform the old man with a shotgun, maybe, but he didn't know no other way.

The town has dropped out of this, since Mark is no longer making a point about the town. He is making a point about the silly sentimentalism of "professional reformers" which has long annoyed him; so he has the judge and his family shed torrents of tears and manifest unwarranted emotion in other ways. Pap, an unsympathetic character, is shown to be a hypocrite as well as a drunkard. And Huck, who tells the whole story, reveals his character and his objective attitude throughout the account.[18]

Based though they are upon actuality, several other scenes had been similarly rehearsed before they were incorporated in the novel. Superimposed upon the actualities as the author's fallible memory recalled them were recollections of literary recountings in which he had made changes to suit his purposes at the time.

Actualities were modified in other ways. During the decades since he had left Hannibal and the river, Clemens had had experiences, he had read books, and he had acquired attitudes and ideas that were bound to color what he wrote. The nickname he assigned the chief character of his novel, always used in lieu of the first name, for instance, had not derived from a common usage he recalled from boyhood but from one encountered decades later. In August, 1868, he had mentioned in another *Alta California* travel letter from Hartford, "The huckleberries are in season, now. They are a new beverage to me. This is my first acquaintance with them. . . ." [19] The indication is plain that Huck's name originated not in the Hannibal of the 1840's but in the New England of the 1860's. Again, the animus against sentimentalism—especially in dealing with rascals or criminals—originated in the 1870's, but it led the writer to invent several details in telling of the judge's effort to reform Pap Finn so as to give it satirical expression. Clemens' attempts to storm the citadels of culture and high society in New England, his discoveries about mankind while visiting Germany, France, and England, his passionate involvements in hot political battles of the postwar era, his hectic adventures in the world of business, all shaped the novel in vital ways which heretofore have gone unnoticed.

Clemens' reading, too, was echoed in *Huckleberry Finn*. Nothing could be more inaccurate than the popular belief that the humorist was a simple homespun philosopher all of whose insights came from natural-born wit and experience rather than from book learning. Actually he ranged avidly and widely through literature of many sorts, constantly garnering material. He read enough French, English, and American history to become a really impressive (though opinionated) specialist in certain periods. He read books and even documents written in French; he read novels in German. He read English and American histories, memoirs, biographies, philosophical treatises, travel books, dramas, humorous stories, and novels—old and new, bad, indifferent, and great. A far larger amount of such reading than anyone seems to have suspected influenced *Huck*, often in surprising ways.

Sometimes this varied reading provided incidents in character for personages in the novel: the mundane Huck's lack of enthusiasm about a heaven wherein the most exciting pastime was playing a harp, Jim's naïve operations as a "speculator," or the king's befooling the pious folk at a camp meeting. Sometimes it gave substance to the author's ideas—about man's moral motivation, say —and thus gave substance to the inner struggles of Huck or the speeches and actions of this ragamuffin hero and of others.

The beginnings of *Huckleberry Finn*, then, were far back in the author's boyhood. But the years just before he started to write it and the years of its sporadic composition were as important, perhaps more important. Those were the years when he lived in the great mansion in Hartford, when he summered in Elmira and did most of his writing there, when he made the experiment of living and writing in Europe, when he tried his hand at big business. These were the years when he wrote "Old Times on the Mississippi" (1875), *The Adventures of Tom Sawyer* (1876), *A Tramp Abroad* (1880), *The Prince and the Pauper* (1882), and *Life on the Mississippi* (1883). Of these narratives, immediately preceding *Huck* or sandwiched between spells of its composition, three made use of similar materials and all helped shape the novel.

It was during those years that the fruitful memories came to him, that he read most of the books and had the moods and ideas which the novel echoed. It was during those years that he learned how best to transmute his recollections, his feelings, and his beliefs into fiction.

An account of *Adventures of Huckleberry Finn,* therefore, may appropriately begin with the fall of 1874, when he and his family moved into the new mansion in Hartford. The mansion was not only a symbol of his achievements and aspirations but his bliss and his bane during the next ten years. This also was when Mark Twain in imagination revisited the town and the river of his youth and wrote "Old Times on the Mississippi."

2

THE HANDSOMEST MANSION
IN HARTFORD

*It is of brick, three stories high. Length of building 105
feet 4 inches, extreme width 63 feet 4 inches. On west
side, octagonal tower 62 feet 4 inches in height; on extreme ends, north and south towers of less height. . . .
On the first floor will be reception room, parlor, library,
dining-room, bedroom; on the second floor a study, nursery, sewing-room, boudoir, housekeeper's room, servants'
bedroom, numerous bathrooms. On the third floor, billiard room, artist friend's room, two servants' rooms . . .
no less than five balconies, beside that of the east tower
. . . veranda . . . around the south end and the east
front of the ground floor . . . with an extensive porte co-
chere. . . . —Hartford* Times, *March 23, 1874.*

Clemens, his wife Olivia, their two daughters, and the German
nursemaid Rosa moved into the new house in Hartford, September 19, 1874. Although swarming workmen had started it in the
spring of 1873, and had toiled on it ever since, it was not completed. For days the family were cooped on the second floor.
They put down some old carpets and installed furniture destined
for other parts of the house, slept in a guest room and Mrs. Clemens' private sitting room, ate in the nursery, and used the study
for a parlor. Carpenters still worked elsewhere, their jobs com-

plicated now and then by the delivery of furnishings from New York.[1]

Getting settled was a trial for Clemens, who had a temper of the sort popularly believed to go with red hair. "I have been bully-ragged all day," he wrote, "by the builder, by his foreman, by the architect, by the tapestry devil who is to upholster the furniture, by the idiot who is putting down the carpets, by the scoundrel who is setting up the billiard-table (and has left the balls in New York), by the wildcat who is sodding the ground and finishing the driveway. . . , by a book *agent* . . ." But for all his groaning, the author was basking in splendor. The rooms, almost without exception, were huge. The over-all dimensions of the structure were large, but the many towers and balconies and the varicolored designs on the walls made them seem even larger.

It was a house that attracted attention. Clemens casually mentions, in one letter, sitting on the west balcony and noticing that "the customary Sunday assemblage of strangers is gathered together on the grounds discussing the house." Sidewalk superintendents had been active ever since the previous March, when a Hartford *Times* reporter who had nudged his way through the crowd to interview the builder found himself viewing "one of the oddest looking buildings in the State ever designed for a dwelling, if not in the whole country." This was an impressive statement in an era when the homes of the very rich were in their way almost as peculiar as they are today. (In Hartford itself, Colonel Samuel Colt, of firearms fame, was living in "Armsmere," an overgrown Italian villa with a high tower in front and an Oriental glass dome in the rear.) One viewer managed to discern "a deck and pilot-house effect in front in recollection of Clemens' steamboat days"; [2] a British visitor saw an example of "quaint old English architecture"; [3] and the architect Edward T. Potter told a puzzled inquirer that his was "the English violet order of architecture." [4] The coloration was unusual, at least for America: the specifications called for "dark red brick with brown stone trimmings, interspersed with inlaid devices of scarlet painted brick and black Greek patterns in mosaic" [5] in the walls, and for intricate patterns in the tiled roofs.

The furnishings, imported from many countries, were showy and obviously expensive. Oriental draperies hung at windows and on walls. Persian rugs dotted the hallway floor. Above each library door stood a Biblical or mythical figure which had been carved in Europe, and sphinxes and griffins, also carved abroad, draped their bodies and spread their wings around chairs and sofas. Italy and France supplied statues, paintings, hand-carved tables, and beds.[6]

THE CLEMENS MANSION IN HARTFORD
(*Harper's*, LXVI, OCTOBER, 1885, 724)

Luxuriating in his new surroundings, Clemens must have recalled his first visits to Hartford six years before when he had been a journalist with only a few dollars in his pocket. For his newspaper he had written: "The dwelling houses are the amplest in size, the shapeliest, and have the most capacious ornamental grounds." [7] Now he had erected and outfitted a mansion of his own which shone brilliantly even among the splendid dwellings of the opulent city. With the grounds and furnishings, it cost $122,000 in a depression year and in a period when dollars were dollars. Economists say that an exact translation of this sum into modern dollars would be impossible; but $350,000 to $400,000 would hardly seem excessive.

The Clemens family was to live in a style appropriate for such a mansion. They would employ six servants—a nursemaid, a housemaid, a laundress, a cook, a butler, and a coachman. (Their total salaries in the 1870's would be $1,650 annually, with some living in and the coachman ensconced in a four-room apartment above the stable.) The family would enjoy all the luxuries, including travel in private railway cars and lengthy stays (often with friends as guests) abroad. They would give generously to charity, and entertain on a lavish scale.

The mansion and the Clemens' way of life betokened the place in the world which its builder had made for himself. There was a side of the writer's nature which gloried in the showy, in the theatrical. Like his character Tom Sawyer, he loved to "throw style" into what he did—to "spread himself." Like his other character, Hank Morgan, he could be "immensely satisfied" with achieving "one of the gaudiest effects I ever instigated."

"The assemblage of strangers" gathered on the lawn that fall afternoon in 1874 had been attracted not only by the great house but also by the fame of its occupant. Those who glimpsed the fierce eagle-like features with the unruly mop of red hair glowing above them as the author peered out from the balcony probably were as excited about seeing him as they were about seeing the mansion. For despite his relative youth (he was thirty-nine), his life and his achievements had made him as renowned in the United States and even in England and Europe as, say, the most promiscuous motion picture actresses and the most ubiquitous American comedians are today.

Clemens' life story, which was constantly being retold more or less accurately in newspapers, magazines, and his own writings, was of wide interest because of the variety and color of its details and the leap to fortune it recorded. In 1873 Charles Dudley Warner, who had collaborated with him in writing the novel *The Gilded Age,* had written, in chapter xii: "To the young American . . . the paths to fortune are innumerable and all open; there is invitation in the air and success in all his wide horizon. He is embarrassed which to choose, and not unlikely to waste years dallying with his chances, before giving himself to the serious tug and strain of a single object. He has no traditions to bind or guide him, and his impulse is to . . . make a new way for himself." Warner may or may not have thought of his collaborator when he wrote this; it was the American Success Story, already a fictional cliché. But it summarized Clemens' biography: unhampered by tradition, he had spent years dallying with various chances before he found his open pathway to fortune.

Born on the Missouri frontier in 1835 into a family with a proud past and a poverty-bedeviled present, he had lived in Hannibal from the end of his fourth year to the middle of his eighteenth. After a little schooling he became a printer on his brother Orion's floundering country newspaper ("One Dollar, if paid in advance; if not paid within Six Months, One Dollar and Fifty Cents; if not paid within Twelve Months, TWO DOLLARS"). In 1853 he wandered eastward, stopping to see the sights and to work as a tramp printer in St. Louis, Philadelphia, New York, and Washington, D.C., before returning to the Midwest. Much of his education, like that of Walt Whitman, Artemus Ward, E. W. Howe, and William Dean Howells, was obtained informally from travel, and from work at the printer's case.

Beginning in 1857 during the span of one brief decade he was a cub and a licensed pilot on the Mississippi; a Confederate soldier in Missouri; a speculator in timber and mining stock, a quartz tail shovelman, a pocket miner and prospector in Nevada and California; a feature writer and reporter on Virginia City and San Francisco newspapers; a traveling correspondent in the Sandwich Islands, New York City, Europe, and the Holy Land; a political reporter and a senator's secretary in Washington; a Buffalo newspaper editor; and a lecturer in the Far West, the Midwest, the East, and London.

The ascent to fame began in 1864—a steep one since within eight years he reached great heights. He started by publishing in an obscure New York magazine "Jim Smiley and His Jumping Frog," a retelling of a yarn he had heard in a dingy bar in Angel's Camp, California; it was reprinted in many newspapers and relished throughout the country. Similarly his travel letters were widely reprinted, and when he recast some of them into *Innocents Abroad* (1869) the book became a best seller to the tune of 70,000 copies the first year—equivalent, if population is taken into account, to about 323,400 today—though it sold for high prices for those uninflated times, $3.50 to $5.00. *Roughing It* (1872), an account of his life in the Far West, sold nearly 59,000 copies at similar prices within half a year (modern equivalent, 273,000). And even after the first flurry these books continued to sell briskly.[8]

By 1872 he was firmly established, and his subsequent writings added to his fame and his income. *The Gilded Age* (1873) sold 44,000 copies in four months (modern equivalent, 203,000). Rewritten by Mark Twain in the summer of 1874 as a drama, with John T. Raymond in the leading role, it played to large audiences across the continent, bringing royalties of $150 to $500 a week.

Lecturing further swelled Clemens' income and made him famous from the Far West to New England. Of the gloomy-visaged "Phunny Phellows" flourishing in that Golden Age of humorous lecturers [9]—Petroleum V. Nasby, Josh Billings, and Bill Nye, to name only a few—he was probably the most in demand. Any year he chose, he could allow his manager to arrange a full season. Back in 1864 he had set down the formula which he and other comic lecturers followed with fine results, naming as "the first virtue of a comedian" the ability to "do humorous things with grave decorum and without seeming to know that they are funny," [10] a skill which he employed in writing as well as in speaking. His leonine head, drooping moustache, and somber black costume—comically contrasting with his outrageous tall tales, shaky logic, and feckless sentences—and his deep-voiced Pike County drawl (greatly exaggerated on the platform) helped make his meandering discourses succeed. British approval of lectures in London in 1873 did no harm, despite the lore about the English lack of humor, as prevalent then as now. Long before, Americans had formed the habit of being more impressed by England's praise for an American author than by their own countrymen's praise, and had allowed the British to "discover" such diverse geniuses as Washington Irving, Herman Melville, Artemus Ward, and Walt Whitman.

Accounts of Clemens' courtship, marriage, and family life added to his popularity, since by nineteenth century standards these, like his rise from rags to riches, followed the approved pattern.

Olivia Langdon, whom he met in 1867, had the sort of poor health which qualified her for a role in a nineteenth-century true romance. Newspapers and periodicals told a fascinating story of her illness and recovery. At sixteen, after a fall, she was partly paralyzed. She lay in a darkened room, comfortable only when on her back, unable to sit up without the aid of a pulley rigged on the ceiling; and even when she was slowly lifted to a half-reclining position, she could not sit long without vertigo or nausea. For two years her family spent money profusely but in vain on the best medical care.

Then came a miracle. A breeze blew a sheet of soiled paper through a door and it settled at her mother's feet. Mrs. Langdon read a crudely printed advertisement saying that a Dr. Newton was in Elmira, prepared to make the blind see, the deaf hear, and the lame walk by an old Biblical formula, the laying on of hands. The Langdons decided to try him. He strode into the darkened room and gave a dramatic command: "Have light! Throw up the curtains! Open the windows!" Then he went to the bedside, prayed for the girl, and told her, "Daughter, according to your faith be it unto you. I put my arms about you and tell you to sit up." When, despite family protests, Olivia obeyed for a time without bad results he made his exit, promising to return. He completed the cure in two more visits and said, "Health and strength will abide with you. Sickness and pain are banished." He refused a fee and departed. Such was the popular story—more exciting than the true story [11]—which naturally appealed to readers of the day.

When Clemens met her Olivia was "a slender, girlish figure with the little touch of appeal which long confinement to a sick-room brings." [12] In this period, when bewhiskered males and very feminine females (as women still were sometimes called) were much admired, the appeal was a poignant one. Robert Browning's romance had several counterparts among writing men in America: Washington Irving loved a lady invalid; Edgar Allan Poe, Ralph Waldo Emerson, Nathaniel Hawthorne, James Russell Lowell, and William Dean Howells each married one.

Clemens' courtship had other aspects which were admiringly reported. He lost his heart to Miss Langdon before he met her when her brother showed him her miniature in a ship's cabin off Smyrna during a Holy Land excursion. On meeting her and finding that her cameo features and ethereal aura corresponded to her picture, he began a vigorous courtship, won her consent and her family's only after great difficulties, and married her in Elmira on February 2, 1870.

In popular tales about the poor boy struggling onward and upward as told, for instance, by Horatio Alger, the climax often was the hero's marriage to a lady of wealth. Jervis Langdon was a well-to-do coal dealer in Elmira whose bins were stocked from his own mines. News stories spread the fact that he had set the couple up in a furnished house in Buffalo which (with stable, horse, and carriage) cost $40,000.

The humorist's "Memoranda" in *The Galaxy* and his contributions to the Buffalo *Express* (in which he bought an interest) were widely reprinted and discussed. The move to Hartford in 1871, *Roughing It* in 1872, trips to England in 1872 and 1873, lectures there, *The Gilded Age* in 1873, and the move into his great house in 1874 were reported in newspapers as far away as Nevada and England.

This was a period when the family was venerated, when, if the nauseating word "togetherness" had been invented, it would not have inspired laughter. Not surprisingly, therefore, the press often reported the author's home life with admiration. Except when urgent trips briefly took him away, Clemens was with the family all the time, and usually their wants were law. He joined them at breakfast and dinner and, although he himself ate no lunch, often at lunchtime. As they ate he entertained them with monologues, pacing the dining room and waving a napkin or gesturing wildly. When his handsome study was needed for a nursery-schoolroom he moved, first to a room above the stable, later to the billiard room on the third floor. Habitually he stopped writing at five or five-thirty to play with the children, consume a perambulatory dinner, and tell stories or read aloud until the youngsters were packed off to bed. Then he talked or read with Livy until bedtime.

Besides book sales, lecture attendance figures, and frequent news stories, some of the letters the author received in 1874—those among the Mark Twain Papers—attest to his fame. Well-known men and women, admirers, literary aspirants, and crackpots were writing to him in extraordinary numbers. Already the problem of dealing with the piles of letters was a harassing one. As his fame continued to mount, the task became even more exhausting.[13]

Early in 1874 Clemens boasted in a letter to his Scottish friend John Brown that he was as contented as a man could be. *The Gilded Age,* he said, had

really the largest two-months' sale which any American book has ever achieved (unless one excepts the cheaper editions of Uncle Tom's Cabin). The average price of our book is 16 shillings a copy—Uncle Tom was 2 shillings a copy. But for the panic our sale would have doubled, I verily believe. . . .

Indeed I *am* thankful for the wife and the child—and if there is one individual creature on all this footstool who is more thoroughly and uniformly and unceasingly *happy* than I am I defy the world to produce him and prove him. In my opinion, he doesn't exist.

This was before the birth of his second daughter Clara in the summer of 1874, before the success of his dramatization of *The Gilded Age,* and before he and the family had begun to enjoy the felicities of the wonderful new mansion.

Yet despite his happy home life, prosperity, and fame, Clemens was not satisfied with his position in 1874 and for years thereafter. In the letter bragging to Dr. Brown about his happiness, he glanced at a tribulation: "I was a mighty rough, coarse, unpromising subject when Livy took charge of me 4 years ago, and I may *still* be, to the rest of the world, but not to her. She has made a very creditable job of me." To that part of "the rest of the world" whose judgment Clemens most respected, he knew that he was an uncouth Westerner, as the phrase went "a mere humorist."

In the days of courtship Livy's family had made clear that this slouching frontiersman with his variegated past and shadowy future, his smoking and drinking, seemed an appalling suitor. "When this novel . . . Westerner," said Mrs. Thomas Bailey Aldrich poetically, "wooed . . . this white and fragile flower . . . , the men of her world said, 'We did not dare to speak of love to her, she seemed as if she so lightly touched earth, belonging to another sphere.' " [14] It would be fascinating to hear any group of men chorus such a remark and one doubts that they did; but the fanciful report suggests the contemporary attitude. Jervis Langdon may not have been as stern as Barrett of Wimpole Street, but his firm jaw, grim mouth, and muttonchop whiskers qualified him to play the role without makeup. Sometimes he did act it, when he told Livy that he never would let any man take her from him. He once forbade Clemens to court her; when he finally granted permission he warned Clemens to go slowly; and he and his wife voiced their grave doubts. Olivia helped her suitor see his limitations: she refused him three times and forced him to be "a brother to her" for a period before accepting him. The Langdons still made demands. "When I am permanently *settled,*" the author reported, "—and when I am a Christian—and when I have *demonstrated* that I have a good, steady, reliable character, her parents will withdraw their objections. . . ." [15]

After his marriage he was instructed about his limitations by others and by his family as well. Mrs. Aldrich tells what happened when in 1871 her husband brought home to dinner this stranger wearing his fur-lined coat wrong side out. Removing the coat he revealed other sartorial blasphemies—violet neck-knot, gray coat and waistcoat, buff trousers hanging "well below the coat . . . stockings of the same tawny hue . . . low black shoes . . ." His drawl confirmed her suspicion that he was drunk; so did his demeanor: he "showed marked inability to stand perpendicular, but swayed." Determined not to dine with such a boor, Mrs. Aldrich waited long past the dinner hour without budging until he left, then berated her husband for "bringing a man in that condition to his house." She smugly explained his difficulty: "The years which Mr. Clemens had passed on the Mississippi, and the rough life of California, lacked greatly the refining influence of a different civilization. With that sharp schooling he had become too well acquainted with all the coarser types of human nature . . . In despite Mrs. Clemens's desire for better things, he was still a man untrained and unpolished; the customs of the frontier still held him fast." [16] At this first meeting and later she did not hide her feeling from her keen-eyed visitor. "A strange and vanity-devoured, detestable woman!" he called her long after. "I do not believe that I would ever learn to like her except on a raft at sea with no other provisions in sight. I conceived an aversion for her the first time I saw her. . . ."

Literary critics also stressed the author's limitations. He was first publicized as "The Wild Humorist of the Pacific Slope." When *Innocents Abroad* appeared, although some reviewers said that he ranked a cut above other jokesmiths, [17] many disagreed; according to the New York *Tribune* he showed "an offensive irreverence" toward things "which other men hold sacred." The note recurred for years. On April 6, 1871, *The Nation* noted that he "was sometimes vulgar and low . . . not refined." In September, 1872, *The Southern Magazine* maintained that the huge sale of *Innocents Abroad* had led to the decision "that the person of refined and polished sensibility will not permit the perusal of this vicious school of publications." Though general readers continued, despite this ban, to admire Twain, critics harped on his bad taste. Worse, some felt that his doom was to be a low comedian forever. The Chicago *Tribune*, on February 27, 1871, said that he "has no aspirations or abilities in any other direction." [18]

Support for these criticisms was offered by the most respected authors. Incredible though it may seem to us who are sophisticated enough to leave to advertising agencies the formation of our attitudes, people then left such matters to Harvard professors and literary Bostonians. Their belief (as it turned out, a questionable one) was that education and foreign travel had prepared these gentlemen to be arbiters of taste.

Howells, though an Ohioan, had won the acceptance of New England's literati; and Bret Harte, in Boston on his way back to New York after briefly visiting California, "swept them before him," as Howells said. But Howells had to admit that with Clemens it was different: "In proportion as people thought themselves refined they questioned that quality . . . which was then the inspired knowledge of the simple-hearted multitude. I went with him to see Longfellow, but I do not think Longfellow made much of him . . . Lowell made less. . . . I cannot say why Clemens seemed not to hit the favor of our community of scribes and scholars, . . . but certainly he did not. . . ." Howells tells how once, when the humorist found himself appreciated by "a symposium of Boston illuminati," Bret Harte spluttered, "Why, fellows, this is the dream of Mark's life!" [19] The truth of the comment was somewhat damaged by the fact that actually the group had not included any Brahmin leaders; then and later these generally ignored or condescended to the Westerner.[20]

Clemens reacted to snubs in various ways. Sometimes he grew angry, as when Langdon tried to bribe him to forego smoking and drinking [21] or when a Hartford neighbor "joked him about not caring for a pretty lampshade after he found it so very cheap": "His eyes flashed, and he looked really angry." [22]

Sometimes he used a traditional gambit of frontier humor, answering Eastern charges of vulgarity with exaggerations of Western boorishness.[23] He did so in a letter after Howells and Aldrich had tried to guide his taste: "When I said [to Livy that] you and Aldrich had given me two *new* neckties . . . she was in a fever of happiness until she found I was going to frame them. . . ." When the Aldriches, Osgood, and Howells visited Hartford and Clemens and Warner met them, he greeted them thus: "Well, I reckon I am prodigiously glad to see you-all. I got up this morning and put on a clean shirt, and feel powerful fine. Old Warner there didn't do it, and is darned sorry—said it was a lot of fuss to get himself constructed properly just to show off, and that bit of a red silk handkerchief on the starboard side of his gray coat would make up for it; and I allow it has done it." [24] Granting that Mrs. Aldrich, who reports this, possibly overdoes the rusticity of the diction, the likelihood is that Clemens used some of the terms: "reckon," "you-all," "feel powerful fine," "old Warner," "darned sorry," "lot of fuss," "starboard"—deliberately posing as a vulgarian. He continued in the role. He introduced his butler George as "a gambler. . . . I have trained him so that now he is a proficient liar." In the impeccable Clemens parlor one evening, wearing cowskin slippers wrong side out, he "twisted his angular body into the strange contortions" of a Negro hoedown.[25]

Usually, however, he was less rambunctious. The move to Hartford had been motivated in part by the dissatisfaction of the family with Buffalo, in part by the desire to be in the city of his publisher; but an important reason was the desire of the Clemenses to become members of the Nook Farm community. The Farm was a heavily wooded hundred-acre tract which the owners, the Hookers, parceled out only to cultured folk of whom they approved—distinguished lawyers, businessmen, ministers, savory politicos, and some editors and authors not inclined toward Bohemianism. As Hartford had expanded the area had become a showplace: Farmington Avenue was one of the city's finest streets and the name of the stream running through the Farm had been changed from Meandering Swine Creek to the Riveret so that it would no longer embarrass the impressive mansions.[26]

The Clemenses intended their fine home to be a token not only of opulence but also of good taste. They had chosen as their architect a New Yorker of high repute in Hartford. His handling of materials was an adaptation of "permanent polychrome," which adorned the finest High Victorian Gothic buildings abroad; [27] Clemens probably had seen examples during recent visits to London. When the house was building, he stressed the tastefulness of the structure and the grounds in a letter to his mother: "There is no other place in Hartford (or elsewhere) quite so lovely. . . . There is nothing *flashy* about the grounds, but they are singularly *shapely* and bright and they fit. The house and barn *grew* out of them and were part of them." [28] The former pilot and pocket miner boned up enough on interior decorating to be able to pontificate about it at length in a letter:

One can use colors that "swear at each other"—or colors that don't. One can daub on a fresco that will make a spectator cry—or a fresco that will make him stand and worship. One can cover the walls with chromos that will make a visitor want to go home—or with originals that will make him stay till *you* want him to go home. In a word, one may make a house a gaudy and unrestful Palace of Sham, or he can make it a Home—a refuge, a place where the eye is satisfied, the intellect stimulated, the spirit broadened, the soul surcharged with peace.[29]

Sixty years after his job was finished, Robert Garvie, supervisor of plumbing installation, recalled the splendor of the bathrooms in an interview published in the Hartford *Times*, November 1, 1935. Since at that time toilets only recently had moved indoors and even in mansions some plumbing still was expected to show signs of its disreputable past, he understandably remembered the trouble Mrs. Clemens took to enhance the beauty of the washbowls:

There were seven bathrooms in the house, Mr. Garvie said, and after they all had been installed it occurred to Mrs. Clemens one day that it would be more attractive if the washbowls could be decorated to harmonize with the rugs in adjoining bathrooms and halls. . . . A trip to New York and a consultation with a leading plumber . . . resulted in a design being submitted, accepted, and the bowls being decorated by baking the designs into the porcelain. Mr. Garvie . . . believes these were about the first decorated washbowls in the country.[30]

Mrs. Clemens with equal care selected the furnishings during long shopping tours of Europe and New York City.

And however the mansion may strike one with twentieth-century (instead of nineteenth-century) prejudices, it was admired as its owners hoped it would be. The correspondent for the *English World* set forth that it had "a most pleasing and novel effect, nothing gaudy or glaring, but all arranged with a rare artistic taste and a strict regard for harmony and colour." A member of a distinguished Hartford family who as a child played with the Clemens girls recalled that it was "the height of elegance." [31] Howells spoke of it as "the stately mansion in which Clemens satisfied his love of magnificence." [32] A traveled English visitor said that while the landscaped grounds "were such as one might look for in Surrey, England, as the result of centuries of culture . . . the house . . . represented the consummate American taste and art." [33]

In one of his essays Twain recalls a competition in elegance held by Southern Negroes in olden times—a cakewalk: "One at a time the contestants enter, clothed in the perfection of style and taste, and walk down the vast central space and back [before the spectators]. All that the competitor knows of fine arts and graces he throws into his carriage. . . . He may use all the helps he can devise: watch-chain to twirl . . . cane . . . snowy handkerchief to flourish . . . shiny new stovepipe hat to assist in his courtly bows." [34] The mansion was an architectural cakewalk parading, so the Clemenses hoped, "perfection of style and taste." Ordinarily the writer tried hard to rise to his surroundings Mrs. James T. Fields, a visitor in 1875, got an impression quite different from that of Mrs. Aldrich: "It is curious and interesting to watch this growing man of forty—to see how he studies and how high his aims are." [35]

Clemens had started the self-improvement years before. If he had not begun it he had accelerated it when, on the Holy Land cruise, he met Mrs. Abel W. Fairbanks, who was reporting for her husband's Cleveland newspaper. Plump motherly Mary Fairbanks, Clemens' senior by seven years, had been reared in the East, educated in a seminary, and before her marriage had taught school. She was, he said, "the most refined, intelligent, and cultivated lady on the ship." In a period when (as in some other periods) "good women" enjoyed reforming misguided young men, she immediately spotted Clemens and pounced. Throughout the trip she lectured him about shortcomings and informed him when his copy lacked refinement. For years after the trip they exchanged letters and she continued her instruction. Typical encouragement: "Do you know how . . . time and study and conscience have developed the fineness of your nature? . . . Your latest article has some most delicate touches. . . ." Typical counsel: "Keep doing the nice things. Say nothing that is irreverent—make your own wit exquisite . . . not broad. . . ." [36]

During the dismal period when Livy was being a sister to him and Clemens was trying to improve his status, he urged her to join the Fairbanks' crusade: "If you and mother Fairbanks will only scold me and upbraid me now and then, I shall fight my way through the world." [37] Not only was this shrewd strategy; it was a sincere wish. After marriage, casting Livy as his lifetime "teacher of the Better Way" (capitals his), he had her "plunge her dainty fingers into his affairs as much as she wanted to." [38]

Many guests in Hartford were impressed by Mrs. Clemens' regular features, made cameo-like by the way she pulled her hair tightly from her forehead and coiled it. They talked of her in Victorian superlatives as "an exquisite lily" and "the flower and perfume of ladylikeness." [39] Even after more than two decades as her personal maid, Kate Leary called her "something from another world"—"an angel." [40] Close friends noticed that the quiet serenity was unruffled as she tutored her willing husband. Howells recalled her as "in a way the loveliest person I have seen, the gentlest, the kindest . . . she united wonderful tact with wonderful truth, and Clemens not only accepted her rule implicitly, but he rejoiced, he gloried in it"; and he noticed that among her virtues was "a sense of humor which qualified her to appreciate the self-lawed genius" of her husband. [41] Dixon Wecter ends his study of the pair's relationship:

As his wife she did exercise pressures now and then by tactful suggestion, nudging, patient domestic lobbying, and on rare occasions a mingling of affectionate scolding with prideful concern that he do and say his best before the public. But she also spoiled, petted, shielded him, drudged over his correspondence when he was on lecture tour,

Olivia Clemens, ca. 1872

surrounded him with gracious social life in which he was always cast as the prima donna, worshipped his wit and creative genius with well-grounded confidence and also his business judgment with a faith much less deserved.[42]

The picture is completely incongruous with passages which some biographers cite in Clemens' letters to prove Livy a raging tyrant who roared her husband into servile obedience. Incongruous—that is exactly the point. Both Clemens and Howells had semi-invalid wives who were unusually gentle, and their private joke (not novel in husbandly humor) was to picture them as shrews. Failure of biographers to see this indicates a lack of humor, something of a handicap for students of a humorist's biography.

However she did so, Livy shaped both Clemens' manners and his writings. "Ever since papa and mama were married," wrote his little daughter Susie, "Papa has written his books and then taken them to mama in manuscript, and she has expergated them." After reading to the family, he left suspected sheets with her. These and manuscripts that he did not read aloud she placed at her bedside and lay, pencil in hand, writing suggestions.[43] He considered her judgments sound. "Do you know . . . ," he told her sister, "whenever I have failed to follow the advice of Livy to change this or that sentence or eliminate a page, I have always come to regret it. . . ." Her vision he characterized as "unfailing." [44]

A portrayal of Livy and himself in an unfinished novel of 1898 or 1899 casts light upon his conception of their characters and their relationship. Their fictional counterparts are Susan and David Gridley.[45] He pictures Susan as flawless—

educated, utterly refined, scrupulously high principled, genuine to the marrow, deeply religious . . . firm and strong . . . delicate in her feelings, and modestly shrinking, but when courage was required to back a principle, she had it. She had a sound, practical, business head, and in the next compartment of her skull a large group of brain-cells that had a vivid appreciation of the beautiful in nature, art and literature, and an abiding love of it. She was just and fair in her judgments, leaning—if at all—to the generous side always.[46]

He pictures his own counterpart as a dual personality.

The real David, the inside David, the hidden David, was on an in-
curably low tone, and wedded to low ideals; the outside David, Susan
Gridley's David, the sham David, was of a lofty tone, with ideals which
the angels in heaven might envy. The real David had a native affection
for all vulgarities, and his natural speech was at home and happy only
when it was mephitic with them; the sham David traded in fine and
delicate things only, and delivered them from a tongue aromatic with
chaste fragrance. . . . The real David was a Vesuvius boiling to the
brim with imprisoned profanity; the sham one was a bland and peaceful extinct crater. . . . The real David was born to the gait and manners of a hostler; the sham one was Chesterfield come back. . . . The
real David loathed society and its irksome polish and restraints; the
sham one was the society model.[47]

Susan keeps the real David under control by providing "the
rebel's boiler with a safety valve," allowing "the steam to blow
off at home." She tinkers with David's writings: "Usually they
had fire and brimstone and thunder and lightning in them when
they reached her hands, but they were reserved and courteous
. . . when she got done trimming them. . . . He complained
that he sent his Indians out to the war-path and she ambushed
them and sent them to Sunday school." [48] Working notes for the
novel put this more strongly: David has published in various magazines and the villagers expect that some day he will write a
book, but "they don't know one thing: he has done several, but
as soon as his wife took their devilishness out they were dish-
water." [49]

Based though this is on actuality and revealing though it is, it
is not an accurate picture of Clemens and his wife in the 1870's
and 1880's. The use of the name Susan, that of Livy's pious sister,
suggests that this pictures a composite character. This was written in the misanthropic years of *The Mysterious Stranger*; it was
part of an early version of that dark novel, and was colored by
the author's mood. More important, though it uncannily foreshadows what some biographers would set forth as unadulterated
fact, this is fiction which peppers fictionized realities with invented facts. Never was the author's self-expression curtailed as

David's is. Never in his darkest moments would Clemens have maligned himself by assigning to himself all the boorish qualities or a fraction of the hypocrisy he does to David. Finally, as the story continues, the sympathies of the author shift until eventually he manifests as much sympathy for David as he does for Susan. What is involved here, I suggest, is the ability a humorist must have to tolerate simultaneously two incongruous positions and to exaggerate the contrasts between them. In gayer moods during the 1870's and 1880's he had used practically the same contrasts to produce gentle or hilarious humor, notably in writing of Tom Sawyer and Huckleberry Finn.

In the 1870's and 1880's he knew that he had been "rough, coarse and unpromising" when he had married; and reviewers' sneers, the coolness of genteel Bostonians, the bristlings of the Mrs. Aldriches, and the gentle chidings of Mother Fairbanks reminded him that the rough diamond still needed polishing. But the preponderance of evidence is that he agreed with Mrs. Fairbanks and Livy that essentially he was a fine and sensitive man maligned by picturings of him as no more than an uncouth jester. He longed to win recognition as what he felt he was. The handsome Hartford mansion proclaimed his good taste; he hoped his writings also would. The rough and the polished side of his nature, his ambitions, and Livy's welcome tutelage molded what he wrote during those years in the Hartford mansion, sometimes in unfortunate ways, sometimes—as when he wrote "Old Times on the Mississippi"—in very fortunate ways.

3

A SERIES FOR THE *ATLANTIC MONTHLY*

*When I was a boy, there was but one permanent ambi-
tion among my comrades in our little village on the west
bank of the Mississippi . . . to be a steamboatman. We
had transient ambitions. . . . When a circus came and
went, it left us burning to become clowns; the first negro
minstrel show that came to our section left us all suffering to try that kind of life; now and then we had a hope
that, if we . . . were good, God would permit us to be
pirates. These ambitions faded out, each in its turn; but
the ambition to be a steamboatman always remained.—
"Old Times on the Mississippi" (1875).*

It may seem improbable that Joseph Hopkins Twichell became
Clemens' closest friend. The Westerner, many New Englanders
thought, was a man of no family; Twichell descended from old
Connecticut families. Clemens, profane, irreverent, had lost his
faith; Twichell, a pious man, had cultivated his in theological
schools and his pastor's study. But after the two met in 1868 their
friendship flourished. Clemens had Joe assist at his marriage, and
in Hartford during frequent meetings over the years the pair became increasingly fond of one another.

For years Clemens had consorted with clergymen. Perhaps he
had obscure reasons which may be left (probably with prepos-

terous results) to psychoanalysts to explain, but there were obvious reasons. Like him, some ministers were compassionate; they pondered morality and religion; they enjoyed arguing. And it amused the author to tell his family that he was "thick as thieves" with a man of God in San Francisco or that "I wine, dine and swap lies" with ministers in New York. Finally, ministers were good companions for a man seeking reassurances about his respectability.

Twichell's robust personality attracted many.[1] At Yale he had rowed stroke and had been expelled for his part in a riot; as a Civil War chaplain he had served in tough campaigns; in Hartford he had caused a parishioner to rejoice that heaven had sent his church "a real MAN." Level-eyed, jauntily moustached, square-jawed, with a figure kept lithe by mountain climbing and hiking, he was masculine enough to deserve the capitalized epithet. Vital statistics justified it: he fathered nine children. Humorous, tolerant to the point of appreciating bawdry and forming friendships with priests, profane hostlers, and army officers, he had qualities Clemens greatly appreciated.[2]

So Sam and Joe roved the countryside having high times and warm gesticulatory arguments. The association shaped some of the author's writings. When lounging by the roadside during a pause in a long walk, he read manuscripts for Joe's comments and often made the suggested revisions. And Joe at times gave him ideas for scenes or even books.

A walk in 1874 had important results. In September, Howells as editor had asked the humorist to write within a month an article for the January *Atlantic Monthly* following up his first of the previous summer. This magazine, founded with the aid of eminent New England writers (including a Cabot) and edited at the start by a Lowell, had great prestige. As the historian of American magazines, Frank Luther Mott, puts it, "In the terminology of an older New England, the *Atlantic* may be said to have enjoyed a perpetual state of grace, so that for a large section of the American public, whatever the *Atlantic* printed was literature."[3] Howells felt that in 1874 it was "the most scrupulously cultivated of our periodicals."[4]

Prodded frequently by Livy, the author racked his brain for a subject. But on October 24 he regretfully wrote Howells, "I have delayed this long, hoping I might do something . . . but it's no use—I find I can't." After posting the refusal he joined Twichell for their Saturday walk. Plodding through the crisp leaves, Clemens fell to reminiscing "about old Mississippi days of steamboating glory and grandeur as I saw them (during five years) *from the pilot house*." Said Twichell, "What a virgin subject to hurl into a magazine!"

Clemens wrote Howells a hurried note crediting Twichell for hitting on a subject he "had not thought of before." "I take back that remark that I can't write for the January number . . . would you like a series . . . to run through three months or six or nine —or about four months, say?"

Clemens erred in believing the subject new to him.[5] On January 20, 1866, he had pasted in a letter a clipping from a San Francisco newspaper saying that he had started a book "on an entirely new subject" and the last pages "would have to be written in St. Louis, because the materials for them can only be got there." [6] This sounds like a book on the river. A letter to Livy on October 24, 1874, clearly refers to such a book: "When I come to write the Mississippi book, *then* look out. I will spend two months on the river and make notes, and I bet I will make a standard work." [7] The dredging up, then redredging, of memories as well as the chance spark kindling his enthusiasm prefigure similar haphazard starts on *Tom Sawyer* and *Huckleberry Finn*.

It is said that Howells approved because, coming from a line of pilots, he appreciated the subject; but surely an editor attuned to popular taste had a better reason. Soon after the Civil War John Hay with "Pike County Ballads" and Bret Harte with California stories had discovered gold in Far Western themes. Also, as Mott says, "the sympathetic interpretation of the South" was standard magazine fare in the 1860's. "But the magazine series about the South which attracted the greatest attention was the one written by Edward S. King for *Scribner's Monthly* in 1873–74 . . . 'The Great South' . . . In 1874, *Harper's Monthly* followed this lead with an illustrated series by 'Porte Crayon' called 'The New

South.' George Cary Eggleston's 'A Rebel's Recollections' made the *Atlantic's* gesture of conciliation in the same year." [8] In the mid-seventies, when factual studies of the South and fiction about the Far West were sure-fire, an ex-pilot's story about his Mississippi career which had both Southern and Western aspects was promising. Just as Mark Twain, journalist, had produced *Innocents Abroad* when foreign travel books (some satirizing tourists) were flourishing, and *Roughing It* when the West fascinated readers (he told Livy he feared his subject was "too hackneyed"), he had gravitated toward a popular subject which he was uniquely qualified to treat. The very month of the fateful walk with Twichell, King's installment of "The Great South" contained this paragraph: "The pilots on the Western rivers . . . are men of great energy, of quaint, dry humor, and fond of spinning yarns. The genial 'Mark Twain' served his apprenticeship as a pilot, and one of his old companions and tutors, now on the 'Great Republic,' gave us reminiscences of the humorist. One sees, on a journey down the Mississippi, where Mark found many of his queerest and seemingly impossible types." [9] It is barely possible that this very passage started the author reminiscing. Whether it did or not, it identifies him as a man qualified to treat a topic currently of interest.

Soon after getting Howells' approval, Mark Twain started writing, but he did not send Article I until about a month later. His covering letter showed uneasiness: "Cut it, scarify it, reject it, handle it with entire freedom." Howells called the piece "capital" —evocative enough to muddy water in his ice pitcher—and rushed it to the printer,[10] but Mark was still jittery. Howells, noticing "a hurried and anxious air" and suspecting a reason, said, "Don't write *at* any supposed Atlantic audience, but yarn it off into my sympathetic ear." The not entirely candid reply suggests that Howells' suspicion was valid: "It isn't the Atlantic audience that distresses me: for *it* is the only audience that I sit down before in complete serenity (. . . it doesn't require a 'humorist' to paint himself striped and stand on his head every fifteen minutes)."

The author's evident irritation at being considered a humorist (in quotes) affected his attitude toward piloting, as expressed in the series and in a letter written in 1874. "I have loved the profession," he said in one article, "more than any I have followed since." And he told Howells in a letter (December 8), "I am a person who would quit authorizing any minute to go piloting, if madam would stand it."

Circumstances rather than lasting convictions were responsible for these statements. In 1862 he had written his sister from California, "I never *once* thought of returning home to go on the river again, and I never expect to do any more piloting at any price." [11] After the Civil War and before his marriage he might have returned to the river, but he did not. Bernard DeVoto notices that through the rest of his life Clemens mentioned his piloting years infrequently.[12] But he had hit upon his theme while talking about "steamboating glory and grandeur as I saw them *from the pilot house.*" He was writing about "the official rank and dignity of a pilot." He was teaching Eastern readers that he was not an undignified and untamed Western barbarian but a man who had learned the lore, the craftsmanship, the disciplined artistry of piloting. He was often moved by his own eloquence. Witness his conclusion, in *Roughing It,* of an account of his leaving Virginia City: "I . . . felt that doubtless I was bidding a permanent farewell to a city which had afforded me the most vigorous enjoyment of life I had ever experienced." Now, painting with rainbow tints pictures of his life preceding his Western years, he was similarly moved. As in the idyllic passages of *Huckleberry Finn,* he was evoking a river far finer than any real one in his past.

The series ran to seven articles, the first appearing in January, 1875, the others in the next five months and August. As narrative they were Twain's best work so far published. And not only the mood but also the discovery of materials and methods prepared for *Huck.*

Critics have complained that "Old Times" gives an incomplete picture of steamboating. This unregulated branch of American commerce in an era of rugged individualism was highly profitable whether boats were flimsily built (as they often were) or not, and whether crews and passengers survived wrecks or not (as they often did not). "Everything," says DeVoto, "that chicanery, sabotage, bribery, and malfeasance could devise was part of the . . . trade."[13] DeVoto underrates twentieth-century ingenuity, but operators strove to deserve this high tribute.[14]

The morality of passengers and crews was not impeccable. John Habermehl, who became a steamboatman in 1844, said in *Life on the Western Rivers* that his fellows were "like . . . other men away from home and unknown." Ashore they frequented theaters "which ladies never attend," saloons, dance halls, gambling joints, and bawdyhouses; and afloat or ashore they engaged often in fights and on occasion in rapes. Passengers drank heavily, swindled one another, and had illicit sexual relationships. Some boats had in residence broadminded waitresses and *nymphes de fleuve.* Gambling flourished; *Forty Years a Gambler on the Mississippi* (1887), by George Devol, has an instructive subtitle: "A Cabin Boy in 1839; Could Steal Cards and Cheat the Boys at Eleven; Stack a Deck at Fourteen; . . . Won Thousands of Dollars from Paymasters, Cotton Buyers, Defaulters and Thieves; Fought More Rough-and-Tumble Fights than any Man in America. . . ." Devol was a prodigy and something of a liar, but many others hinted that life on steamboats was lively.

Except in two brief passages, one about being swindled, another about meeting a drunken watchman, Mark skips these aspects. He had both a practical and an artistic reason. He was writing for the *Atlantic Monthly*, and that magazine, which recently had come to regret publishing Mrs. Stowe's announcement that Byron had committed incest,[15] was not hospitable to vivid immorality. The artistic reason is suggested in a letter the author wrote Howells on December 4, 1874, asking that a less "pretentious, broad and general" title be given the series:

I have finished Article No. III and am about to start No. 4 and yet I have spoken of nothing but Piloting as a science so far; and I doubt that I ever get beyond that portion of my subject. And I don't care to. Any muggins can write about Old Times on the Miss. of 500 different kinds; but I am the only man alive that can scribble about the piloting of the day. . . . If I were to write fifty articles they would all be about pilots and piloting—therefore let's get the word Piloting into the heading.

He offered an alternate title, "Steamboating on the Mississippi in Old Times," which would have committed him to treat sordid aspects, but he made it clear that he preferred "Personal Old Times on the Mississippi" or better, "Piloting on the Mississippi in Old Times." So, as the author saw the series, treatises on greedy entrepreneurs, lusty boatmen, immoral women, and tricky gamblers were irrelevant, incompetent, and immaterial.

Conscious selectivity does not jibe with the belief of many critics that Twain's way was simply to dump recollections onto his pages. Robert Spiller suggests that "an image of grandeur" was achieved in "Old Times" by "a sheer massing of details . . . out of Mark Twain's memories and his facts." [16] Yet Howells saw the unity of the first articles well enough to approve a new title: "All right, Piloting it shall be." [17] Although in the end he decided against this, beginning with Article II he provided subtitles containing "Pilot" or "Piloting." These show that until he was well into the next to the last article Mark stuck to the science of piloting. Though at the end he wandered to the treatment of anomalous matters, Articles I–V and the first third of VI unfold a story of a cub's education ranking with those American classics of the 1840's, *Two Years before the Mast, The Oregon Trail,* and *Redburn.* Like these, Mark's is the story of a young man's initiation, purportedly factual but colored and shaped by imagination. His characterization of his "cub," his management of narrative, and his evocation of atmosphere all manipulate facts.

One who compares the apprentice pilot of the series with the real Sam Clemens who learned piloting will see that the former is largely fictional. The boy of the series is so eager to become a pilot that he runs away; his creator never did this. Here is how the youth in the series happens to go down the Mississippi: "I had been reading about the recent exploration of the river Amazon by an expedition sent out by our government. It was said that the expedition, owing to difficulties, had not thoroughly explored a part of the country. . . . It was only about fifteen hundred miles from Cincinnati to New Orleans, where I could doubtless get a ship. I had thirty dollars left; I would go and complete the exploration of the Amazon. . . ." Paine rightly calls this "a literary statement." Young Clemens in 1856 had been reading Lieutenant William Lewis Herndon's *Exploration of the Valley of the Amazon* (Washington, 1853). Its two volumes describe the valley as fabulously rich and salubrious, and urge Americans to exploit it.[18] The report resembles others on new frontiers which for decades had inspired pioneers to move westward. Like his countrymen, who were in the habit of believing that such a report gave sound reasons for making a new start on a new frontier, Sam could be persuaded by it to pull up stakes and migrate. And this, rather than a silly exploration, was what he had in mind. Two friends, one a doctor and a professor, found the report so persuasive that they agreed to join him.[19]

The youth in the story reaches New Orleans and learns there that "a vessel would not be likely to sail for the mouth of the Amazon under ten or twelve years; and the nine or ten dollars left in my pocket would not suffice for so impossible an exploration as I had planned," and therefore he signs as a cub. But Horace E. Bixby, who gave Sam his training, testifies that actually young Clemens abandoned his Amazon project and arranged his apprenticeship nine hundred miles above New Orleans while the boat was still going downstream.[20] Paine mentions another disparity: the fictional cub is "a boy of perhaps seventeen" when he signs, but Sam was, "in reality, considerably more than twenty-one years old." Therefore Mark Twain pictures not the real Sam Clemens but a character younger, more gullible, more naïve.

The author had assumed like roles in "autobiographical" books and sketches all preparatory, as "Old Times" was, for his assuming the very similar role of Huck Finn. A character with such traits was an established figure in American humor, indeed in world humor. Soon after introducing this innocent, Twain exploits his comic possibilities by showing him being fleeced and duped. A bit later other values are evidenced. Early in his apprenticeship the cub is questioned by Bixby about a point above New Orleans: "I was gratified to be able to answer promptly. . . . I said I didn't know." As questions bring similar replies, Bixby's incredulity grows:

"You—you—don't know? . . . What *do* you know?"

"I—I—nothing, for certain."

"By the great Caesar's ghost, I believe you! You're the stupidest dunderhead I ever heard of, so help me Moses! . . ."

Oh, but his wrath was up! . . .

"Look here! What do you suppose I told you the names of those points for?"

I tremblingly considered a moment, and then the devil . . . provoked me to say: "Well to—to—to be entertaining, I thought."

This was a red rag to the bull. He raged and stormed. . . .

The episode has narrative interest as well as humorous appeal, and at the same time it enables Twain to expound the intricacies of piloting to lay readers. The characterization makes the scene possible.

The characterization also makes possible a narrative threading through several articles. After establishing his cub's ignorance, Twain can tell how the youth is initiated into the mysteries of piloting one by one—the shape of the twelve-hundred-mile river seen by day, then by night, then the surface signs of hidden trouble, then menaces of the river when flooded, then those of the river when low, and so on—complications heaped one on another. The pattern is that of the American tall tale with which the humorist had become familiar during his youth and early manhood. Henry James tells in *The American* how Christopher Newman "had sat with Western humorists in circles around a castiron stove, and had seen tall tales grow taller without toppling over." Wherever the fastidious James had observed this formula (and one wonders), he describes it with his usual insight.

A second thread follows the cub's development toward wisdom and maturity, showing how he learned the trade and cultivated its virtues—"good and quick judgment and decision, and a cool, calm courage that no peril could shake." Twain climaxes Article V with a crucial test of courage comparable with ordeals which climax primitive initiations, and in the next article turns to consider "Official Rank and Dignity of a Pilot." Part of the growth is disillusionment—about men,[21] even about the river's glories and the romance of piloting. The account stops as the cub reaches pilothood. This is artistically desirable, since the narrative threads could not have been carried into an account of the pilot's career. But the series shows what lies ahead: by his amused superiority to the starry-eyed callow youth the writer constantly indicates his own disillusionment and sophistication.[22]

The author was concerned with another matter. Explaining the delay of Article I, he wrote: "The trouble was, that I was only bent on 'working up an atmosphere' and that is to me a most fidgety and irksome thing sometimes. I avoid it, usually, but in this case it was absolutely necessary, else every reader would be applying the atmosphere of his own sea experiences, and *that* shirt wouldn't fit, you know." The atmosphere at the start was important in setting the tone of the series. Elsewhere, too, Twain must have taken unusual pains, often one suspects, with the descriptions; for he averaged only five hundred words a day, an output which usually would have humiliated him.

The passage referred to has been quoted again and again by critics—with reason, since it shows Twain invoking a favorite scene and infusing emotion. Compare it with a similar passage in King's "The Great South," published only a month before Twain's article:

The towns on the Kentucky shore, while few of them are large and bustling, have a solid and substantial air. Around the various taverns in each of these are grouped the regulation number of tall gaunt men, with hands in pockets, and slouched hats drawn over their eyes. A vagrant pig roots here and there in the customary sewer. A few cavaliers lightly mount the rough roads into the unimposing hills; a few negroes slouch sullenly on a log at the foot of the levee, and on a wharf boat half a hundred white and black urchins stare, open-mouthed, as if they had never seen strangers before.[23]

This is competent journalism. The generalized description does, indeed, indicate that the towns are not "large and bustling." But if King intends irony here, he has little success since the irony disappears after this fitful phrase. Evidently he is not sure what he wants to say about the towns. He claims they are "exceedingly interesting" and have "a solid and substantial air"; then, for no clear reason, he equips them with "the regulation number of gaunt men," pigs in "the customary sewer," "cavaliers," and sullen Negroes. King shows what a writer achieves by merely heaving in details.

Turn to Mark Twain's "atmospheric" picture of the Hannibal of his boyhood:

After all these years I can picture that old time . . . : the white town drowsing in the sunshine of a summer's morning; the streets empty, or pretty nearly so; one or two clerks sitting in front of the Water Street stores, with their splint-bottomed chairs tilted back against the walls, chins on breasts, hats slouched over their faces, asleep—with shingle-shavings enough around to show what broke them down; a sow and a litter of pigs loafing along the sidewalk, doing a good business in watermelon rinds and seeds; two or three lonely little freight piles scattered about the "levee"; a pile of "skids" on the slope of the stone-paved wharf, and the fragrant town drunkard asleep in the shadow of them; two or three wood flats at the head of the wharf, but nobody to listen to the peaceful lapping of the wavelets against them; the great Mississippi, the majestic, the magnificent Mississippi, rolling its mile-wide tide along, shining in the sun; the dense forest away on the other side; the "point" above the town, and the "point" below, bounding the river-glimpse and turning it into a sort of sea, and withal a very still and brilliant and lonely one.

Twain marshals details which easily surpass King's in local color: John Hay, reared in a river town near Hannibal, called this "perfect" for evocative power. But authentic though the description is, the instant one compares it with a picture painted by the artist Henry Lewis during the very decade Twain is recalling one sees an inaccuracy. This picture shows that though Hannibal contained a number of white frame houses so many buildings were red brick that "the general effect of the town" must have been "much more red than white." [24] The author, I suggest, calls his town "white" because "white" floods the scene with drowsy bright sunlight and therefore initiates an impression of quietude. This is strengthened by lethargic words such as "drowsy," "sitting," "tilted back," "slouched over," "loafing," and "asleep." The exceptions—the sow and her litter "doing a good business," and the river "rolling"—actually augment the impression of lassitude, since the most energetic creatures in the village are swine which are loafing and the only other movement or sound is not in the streets but on the still, brilliant, and lonely river.

This static description is only the first stage in a structuring of contrasts. A steamboat soon arrives with "a film of dark smoke . . . and the scene changes! The town drunkard stirs, the clerks wake up, a furious clatter of drays follows, every house and store pours out a human contribution, and all in a twinkling the dead town is alive and moving. Drays, carts, men, boys, all go hurrying from many quarters to a common center, the wharf. Assembled there, the people fasten their eyes upon the coming boat as upon a wonder they are seeing for the first time." The "sleepy" passage leads the eye slowly across town to the river in a prodigiously long sentence. Here the eye leaps from the river across town in a much shorter sentence and then back to the river again in an even shorter one. The former sentence is five staccato clauses separated by commas. The latter starts with one-syllable words —"drays, carts, men, boys"—which give a jolting effect. Active verbs rush to a climax—"stirs," "wake up," "follows," "pours."

But there is a still greater climax of movement with the arrival of the boat. Contrasted with the white drowsy town the boat is splashed with color and gold paint; contrasted with the silent streets it is violently noisy. This section ends, "Then such a scramble as there is to get aboard, and to get ashore, and to take on freight and to discharge freight, all at one and the same time; and such a yelling and cursing as the mates facilitate it all with!" The final contrast comes as the boat leaves and movement, color, and sound fade away: "Ten minutes later the steamer is under way again, with no flag on the jack-staff and no black smoke issuing from the chimneys. After ten more minutes the town is dead again, and the town drunkard asleep by the skids once more." The dragging sounds appropriately return Hannibal to a deep slumber which will last until another steamboat awakens it.

Pivoting like many of Mark Twain's passages around a contrast, the paragraph achieves humor. It has narrative interest. It helps initiate the series by dramatizing the excitement of steamboats for a Hannibal boy, thus motivating his becoming a cub pilot. And it establishes the tone—a compound of longing and laughter— which will pervade the articles.

LOAFERS IN *The Gilded Age*

Hard work probably involving several revisions helped give this passage its quality. Previous "literary rehearsals" for this paragraph played their part also. In chapters i, iv, and vi of *The Gilded Age*, which he had written the previous year, the author had described lazy towns in old-time Tennessee and Missouri, noticing "the balmy and tranquil" air, the loafers with "canted" hats, aperch a fence rail, "hump-shouldered and grave" or "sitting in front of the store on a dry-goods box, whittling it with their knives . . . and shooting tobacco juice at various marks." "But presently," says one such passage, "there was a dog-fight . . . and the visitors slid off their perch . . . with interest bordering on eagerness." In chapter xvii Twain's collaborator Charles Dudley Warner had attempted a similar vignette, adding details about muddy roads and wallowing hogs which were incorporated in Twain's descriptions thereafter.[25] In early chapters of *Tom Sawyer* written during the summer of 1874, Twain had given St. Petersburg the standard drowsiness, "the balmy summer air," and "the restful quiet."

These passages, the somnolent portion of the paragraph in "Old Times," and similar descriptions were preparatory for picturings in *Huck Finn:* Pokeville, "a little one-horse town . . . nobody stirring; streets empty, and perfectly dead and still"; Bricksville, described in the most detailed passage Twain was to write about such a town, and incorporating the old details and many new ones; the unnamed town of the Wilkses.

The picture of the town awakening would reappear, usually juxtaposed with descriptions of the town asleep. In *Tom Sawyer*, bemused St. Petersburg is awakened again and again by some adventure of Tom or Huck. In *Huckleberry Finn* a description of dreamy Pokeville is followed by one showing Pokevilleites in a fronzy at a camp meeting, after the description of even dreamier Bricksville the townsfolk are shown galvanized into action by a shooting, then becoming even more frenetic as they coalesce into a rampaging mob; the somnolent town of the Wilkses is aroused by the arrival of the alleged heirs to the Wilks fortune.

Article I contained two other passages germinal to passages in *Huck*. The town drunkard slumbering on the wharf was to return as Huck's Pap. The night watchman tells a sad story: "He was a wronged man, a man who had seen trouble. . . . He said he was the son of an English nobleman—either an earl or an alderman, he could not remember which, but believed he was both: his father, the nobleman, loved him, but his mother hated him from the cradle . . . and by and by his father died and his mother seized the property and 'shook' him, as he phrased it." In chapter xix a similar fake joins Huck and Jim on the raft and represents himself as the Duke of Bridgewater, and thereafter plays an important part.

Article IV treats seasonal hazards to navigation, the spring rise which brought heaps of debris along with sundry rafts downstream, and the impenetrable fogs covering the lower river. In the novel a spring rise brings Huck the canoe in which he escapes from Pap, the shack in which Pap's body lies, and the raft fragment on which Huck and Jim travel downstream. A fog causes them to miss Cairo and enables Huck to play a trick on Jim. The article also contains a description of a steamboat bearing down through the murk on a trading scow or raft. In the novel a boat rams the raft under similar circumstances. Like the apprentice pilot escaping when the sounding-boat is stove in, Huck and Jim escape by diving deep beneath the steamboat's paddle wheel.

In addition to such details, "Old Times" helped Mark discover material and patterns of action that he later used in his masterpiece. The narrator had qualities and values as both a character and a storyteller which he would modify and develop in Huck's account of his adventures. Twain had learned something about the possibilities of the subject matter of Hannibal which he would find useful as he wrote about St. Petersburg in *Tom Sawyer* and its sequel.

And the narrative threads in "Old Times" evolved from previous experiments with narrative and predicted future developments. Mark Twain had hit upon—or had had forced upon him —a story structure of sorts when he wrote his first travel series for the Sacramento *Union* in 1866. On his visit to the Sandwich Islands he inevitably wrote about the journey and what he learned while making it. Just as inevitably in 1867 he wrote about similar travels and discoveries during the *Quaker City* excursion. But this time he made a book of his letters—"a record of a pleasure trip," as his preface says, telling what "I have seen with impartial eyes." The full title, *The Innocents Abroad, or The New Pilgrim's Progress*, shows that "an innocent"—"a new pilgrim"—was the chief character. Since the author was debunking tourists, his hero's "progress" took the form of disillusionment concerning

Europe and the East. In the part of *Roughing It* which was a continuous narrative, another sort of innocent—a greenhorn— was disillusioned about the West of romance. "Old Times" follows a similar pattern: journeying on the river, the cub is disillusioned concerning its romance. Such educational journeyings would figure in *The Prince and the Pauper* and in Part II of *Life on the Mississippi*. In *Roughing It* and "Old Times" the author developed another line of narrative—the initiation which turns a tenderfoot or a novice into an old-timer. *Tom Sawyer* and *The Prince and the Pauper* similarly would show an irresponsible boy moving toward responsible maturity. In *Huckleberry Finn*, Mark Twain would again deal with the educational journey leading to disillusionment and with a boy's initiation.

4

TOM SAWYER

You don't know about me without you have read a book by the name of The Adventures of Tom Sawyer. . . . *That book was made by Mr. Mark Twain, and he told the truth, mainly. There was things which he stretched, but mainly he told the truth.*—Adventures of Huckleberry Finn, *opening paragraph.*

The Adventures of Tom Sawyer, to which Mark Twain turned, or rather returned, after "Old Times," carried him into the writing of *Huckleberry Finn.* He composed *Tom Sawyer,* as he would *Huck,* in different places at various times. One version of Tom and Becky's love story he wrote in Buffalo in 1870. His recollection was that he wrote about Tom's whitewashing trick in London in 1872. He started the "final" version of the book in Hartford in 1873 or 1874. During the summer of 1874, in Elmira, he averaged five thousand words a day. September 2, discovering that "that day's chapter was a failure, in conception, moral truth to nature, and execution," he decided "I had worked myself out, pumped myself dry." He was to recall that this was at page 400, and subsequently he made an important discovery:

When the manuscript had lain in a pigeonhole two years I took it out one day and read the last chapter that I had written. It was then that I made the great discovery that when the tank runs dry you've only to leave it alone and it will fill up again in time while you are asleep—also while you are at work at other things and are quite unaware that this unconscious and profitable cerebration is going on. There was plenty of material now, and the book went and finished itself without any trouble.

In this account the writer perhaps was recalling the pigeon-holing of his partial version of 1870 or of 1872; for, after less than a year, he evidently resumed writing in Hartford about mid-May, 1875. By July 5, 1875, he had "finished the story . . . about 900 pages of MS, and maybe 1000 when I have finished 'working out' vague places."

Clemens once told his friend Brander Matthews that his tank refilled because he remembered boyhood happenings:

He began the composition of "Tom Sawyer" with certain of his boyish recollections in mind, writing on and on until he utilized them all, whereupon he put his manuscript aside and ceased to think about it, except in so far as he might recall from time to time, and more or less unconsciously, other recollections of those early days. Sooner or later he would return to his work to make use of the memories he had recaptured in the interval. After he had harvested this second crop, he again put his work away, certain that in time he would be able to call back other scenes and other situations. When at last he became convinced that he had made his profit out of every possible reminiscence, he went over what he had written with great care, adjusting the several instalments one to the other, sometimes transposing a chapter or two and sometimes writing into the earlier chapters the necessary preparation for adventures in the later chapters unforeseen when he was engaged on the beginnings of the book. Thus he was enabled to bestow on the completed story a more obvious coherence than his haphazard procedure would otherwise have attained.[1]

The many details from memory in *Tom Sawyer* offer some support for this simple account. The St. Petersburg of the novel is the Hannibal, "the white town drowsing in the sunshine," of "Old Times." Tom's house is the old Clemens house, Becky Thatcher's house that of a childhood sweetheart. The schoolhouse and the church where Tom undergoes boredom are modeled after identifiable buildings. Cardiff Hill, where Tom reënacts Robin Hood's adventures, is Holliday's Hill; the cemetery where Tom and Huck watch the murder is the Baptist Cemetery; Jackson's Island, scene of the Gang's career as pirates, is Glasscock's Island; the stillhouse branch, scene of the treasure hunt, is part of the actual Hannibal; McDougal's cave, where Tom and Becky are lost and Injun Joe dies, is McDowell's cave downstream to the south.

"Huck Finn is drawn from life," says the preface, "Tom Sawyer also, but not from an individual—he is a combination of the characteristics of three boys whom I knew. . . ." Paine holds that Tom's characteristics came from Sam Clemens himself and from Will Bowen and John Briggs, two Hannibal contemporaries, though other members of Sam's gang have been mentioned for the honor.[2] At any rate, Tom was based on actual characters. And real-life prototypes of all the other leading figures in the book have been identified.

"Most of the adventures recorded in this book," the preface continues, "really occurred; one or two were experiences of my own, the rest those of boys who were schoolmates of mine." The author's jottings over the years substantiate this to some extent. August 5, 1866, on a trip to the Sandwich Islands he wrote, "Superstitions: Wash hands in rainwater standing in old hollow stump to remove warts. . . . Split-bean, bind it on wart—wait until midnight and bury it at cross-roads in dark of the moon." These recipes, recalled from boyhood, are discussed in chapter vi. A few days before, in the same notebook, Clemens had noted, "Cat and Painkiller,"[3] and some years after writing the novel he made a note for his *Autobiography*, "Peter and Davis painkiller" and "Water-cure."[4] In chapter xii Aunt Polly tries a water treatment on Tom ("stood him up in the woodshed and drowned him with a deluge of cold water"). This failing, she hears of a "Pain-Killer . . . simply fire in liquid form." She doses Tom with this, and he feeds some to a cat, Peter, who wrecks the house.

The same notes for the *Autobiography* contain this: "fired cannon to raise drowned bodies of Christ Levering [a boyhood Hannibal contemporary] and me—when I escaped from the ferryboat [and was thought drowned]." [5] In chapter xiii the boys on Jackson's Island watch the ferryboat shooting a cannon over the side:

"I know now!" exclaimed Tom; "somebody's drowned!"

"That's it!" said Huck; "they done that last summer, when Bill Turner got drownded; they shoot a cannon over the water, and that makes him come up to the top."

On January 25, 1868, writing to Will Bowen, Clemens said, "I still remember the louse you bought of poor Arch Fuqua"; in chapter vii Tom and Joe Harper torture a tick in school. The details, Clemens has testified, "are strictly true, as I have reason to remember." [6] February 6, 1870, in another letter to Bowen, Clemens recalled how "we used to undress and play Robin Hood in our shirt-tails, with lath swords, in the woods" [7]—a pastime re-created in chapter viii.

Clemens' testimony and his relating of these real scenes to the book led Paine to decide that "the personal details of this story were essentially nothing more than the various aspects of his own boyhood." DeLancey Ferguson said in his excellent biography, "The atmosphere and incidents of . . . Hannibal boyhood came back to his memory as he wrote; he had only to set them down." [8] In 1954 Jerry Allen, convinced that the novel is literally true, incorporated many of Tom's adventures in her biography, *The Adventures of Mark Twain*, as actual events. It is easy to demonstrate, nevertheless, that here, as in "Old Times," Twain made many changes when he transformed fact into fiction.

Despite recognizable aspects, St. Petersburg is for the most part far lovelier than Hannibal. In chapter i, to dramatize the elegance of a new boy which irritates Tom, Mark calls St. Petersburg a "poor little shabby village"; that is what the old Hannibal really was. But except in a few similar phrases St. Petersburg and its environs are realms of quiet delight bathed in summer air fragrant with the aroma of meadows, woodlands, and flowers. The idyllic setting was one aspect of the book that led Twain to call it "simply a hymn, put into prose to give it a worldly air."

He chose characters which suited his purposes. Unpublished memories of real Hannibal folk prove that the town could have stocked a Spoon River or a Peyton Place. The Ratcliff boy "had to be locked in a small house . . . and chained. . . . Would not wear clothes, winter or summer. . . . Believed his left hand had committed a mortal sin . . . and chopped it off." His brother "became a fine physician in California ventured to marry but went mad. . . ." Dr. Jim Lampton was "captured by Ella Hunter, a loud vulgar beauty from a neighboring town. Young Dr. John McDowell boarded with them; followed them from house to house; an arrant scandal. . . ." Mary Moss, shut in solitude to study so that she would be a credit to her lawyer husband in society, after two years "had become wedded to her seclusion and her melancholy brooding. . . . Saw no company, not even the mates of her childhood." [9] There are no fictional prototypes of characters such as these.

Characters copied from life are modified. In an interview in the Portland *Oregonian,* August 11, 1895, the author indicated that, though he drew Tom and Huck from actuality, he changed their names, and for an interesting reason:

I have always found it difficult to choose just the name that suited my ear. "Tom Sawyer" and "Huckleberry Finn" were both real characters, but "Tom Sawyer" was not the real name of the former, nor the name of any person I ever knew, . . . but the name was an ordinary one—just the sort that seemed to fit the boy, some way, by its sound. . . . No, one doesn't name his characters haphazard. Finn was the real name of the other boy, but I tacked on the "Huckleberry." You see, there was something about the name "Finn" that suited, and "Huck Finn" was all that was needed to somehow describe another kind of a boy than "Tom Sawyer," a boy of lower extraction or degree. Now, "Arthur Van de Vanter Montague" would have sounded ridiculous, applied to characters like either "Tom Sawyer" or "Huck Finn."

Except for the fact that either Clemens or the reporter was inaccurate about the name "Finn" the account is believable. (The character Emmeline Grangerford in *Huckleberry Finn* acquired her name similarly.)

Characters usually had much more than their names changed. Jane Clemens, Aunt Polly's prototype, had willful ways, family pride, a sharp tongue, and a clever mind; Aunt Polly has none of these. The writer testified that though his brother Henry "is Sid . . . Sid was not Henry. Henry was a much finer and better boy. . . ." Tom Blankenship, unlike Huck, who is copied after him, had two sisters, a mother, and a father; he, rather than Sam, led the boy's gang; he, rather than Sam, thought of digging for treasure.[10] Muff Potter was (as Twain said of Tom) "of the composite order of architecture," embodying qualities of several Hannibal ne'er-do-wells. The prototype of Injun Joe was not the villain that Injun Joe of the novel is. Tom Sawyer, like the narrator of *Innocents Abroad* and *Roughing It* and the cub pilot of "Old Times," is probably a much better-read and more romantic lad than any of the characters after whom he is modeled.

True, some incidents had counterparts in actuality. But consider these memorable scenes: the grave robbery, the murder of the doctor, the appearance of the boys at their own funeral, Tom's taking Becky's punishment and being praised for it by her father, Tom's testifying at the trial, Injun Joe's plotting to mutilate Widow Douglas, Huck's rescue of her, Becky's and Tom's tribulations in the cave, Tom's rescue of Becky, the discovery of the treasure, Injun Joe's horrible death.

Some of these, as Booth Tarkington suggests, are not based upon actual happenings but upon "adventures that all boys, in their longing dreams, make believe they have."[11] Others, as De-Voto remarks, are "ghastly stuff . . . murder and starvation, grave robbery and revenge, terror and panic, some of the darkest emotions of men, some of the most terrible fears of children, and the ghosts and demons and death portents of the slaves."[12] These were not as inappropriate to Sam Clemens' Hannibal as modern readers may believe: located on the rough frontier, it had been more violent than most small towns. During his boyhood, Sam three times came close to drowning, and before he was seventeen he witnessed the abortive lynching of an abolitionist, a death by fire, a hanging, an attempted rape, two drownings, two attempted homicides, and four murders. The town's religion stressed hell-fire damnation. Folklore of whites and Negroes featured topics differing from those recommended by authorities on juvenile literature today—witches, ghosts, death, and putrefaction. But however true these episodes were to the atmosphere of Hannibal, careful search has indicated that none was based upon an actual event.

Mark Twain, then, greatly modified settings, characters, and happenings. Three processes brought changes: his shifting memories and moods, the influence of his biography and his reading in the 1870's, and his manipulation of materials.

The author's memory, like most memories, was tricky. One checking his recollections over the years against ascertainable facts finds that, as Dixon Wecter says, sometimes they were surprisingly accurate. But they were at times quite inaccurate. Often, too, moods colored his remembering. Shortly after his marriage he wrote Will Bowen:

Your letter has stirred me . . . and I have rained reminiscences for four and twenty hours. The old life has swept before me like a panorama; the old days have trooped by in their old glory again. . . . Heavens what eternities have swung their hoary cycles about since . . . Jimmy Finn was town drunkard and . . . slept in the vat . . . since we used to go swimming above the still-house branch . . . since . . .

And there followed a long paragraph of savored reminiscences.[13] A process which he has described in chapter lx of *Innocents Abroad* is at work here:

Schoolboy days are no happier than the days of after life, but we look back upon them regretfully because we have forgotten our punishments at school, and how we grieved when our marbles were lost and our kites destroyed—because we have forgotten all the sorrows and privations of that canonized epoch and remember only its orchard robberies, its wooden sword pageants, and its fishing holidays.

In the summer of 1876, in another mood, he wrote Bowen a very different sort of letter about old Hannibal days:

As to the past, there is but one good thing about it, . . . that it *is* the past. . . . I can see by your manner of speech, that for more than twenty years you have stood dead still in the midst of the dreaminess, the melancholy, the romance, the heroics, of sweet but sappy sixteen. Man, do you know that this is simply mental and moral masturbation? It belongs eminently to the period usually devoted to *physical* masturbation, and should be left there and outgrown. . . . You need a dose of salts. . . .[14]

The mood of *Tom Sawyer* is that of the earlier letter. Amateur and professional psychologists will note with interest that the earlier reminiscences followed close upon the writer's marriage. So did the narrative which Paine found in the Papers, labeled " 'Boy's Manuscript,' probably written about 1870," and filed. Long after, Bernard DeVoto saw its significance: it was "the embryo" of *Tom Sawyer*. It develops at length one line of narrative in the novel—a boyish courtship during which the hero suffers much distress.[15] Clemens himself had only recently been as ardent, as despairing—and sometimes almost as gauche—in his courtship of Olivia Langdon: it is fascinating to see how this humorist, soon after his own grim battle, treats similar material in a boy's travesty of grown-up love-making.[16] By the time he rewrote this as part of *Tom Sawyer*, even more remote from his agonizing experiences, he could write of them in an even gayer fashion.

There are other parallels between Clemens' recent situation and that of his boyish characters. "But you," he had written Livy in January, 1869, "will break up all my irregularities when we are married, and *civilize* me, and make of me a model husband and an adornment to society—won't you . . . ?"[17] Billy Rogers, in *Boy's Manuscript*, and Tom, his later embodiment, are likewise subjected to "civilizing" influences in the hope that they will become "model boys"; and their creator, already (as will be shown) able to look back with detachment on his own period of being housebroken, could exploit some of his recent difficulties humorously. More: in chapter vi he could introduce a character whom Tom envies because he is even less restrained:

Huckleberry [Finn] came and went, at his own free will . . . he did not have to go to school or to church, or call any being master or obey anybody . . . he could sit up as late as he pleased . . . he never had to wash, nor put on clean clothes; he could swear wonderfully. In a word, everything that goes to make life precious, that boy had. So thought every harassed, hampered, respectable boy in St. Petersburg.

Interestingly, Huck has the same freedom as quite a different kind of hero whom Twain praised in "Old Times" less than a year later:

> . . . a pilot, in those days, was the only unfettered and entirely independent human being that lived in the earth. Kings are but the hampered servants of parliament and people; parliaments sit in chains forged by their constituency; the editor of a newspaper cannot be independent . . . ; no clergyman is a free man . . . ; writers of all kinds are manacled servants of the public. We write frankly and fearlessly, but then we "modify" before we print. In truth, every man and woman and child has a master, and worries and frets in servitude, but in the day I write of, the Mississippi pilot had *none*.[18]

Thus both memories colored by time and personal attitudes impelled Twain, in the 1870's, to write nostalgically about life in an idyllic Southwestern town in the days before the Civil War.

Literary influences also operated. Dime novels, melodramas, and similar trash are echoed in the sensational courtroom scene, Injun Joe's bloodthirsty schemes for vengeance, his wandering around town unrecognized in a skimpy disguise, and the boys' discovery of Murrel's buried treasure. Respected novels such as those of Dickens, Reade, and Collins encouraged Twain to jam four plots and several unrelated episodes into one book.

And since this was the era of kindly pictures of the past, an idyllic tone was to be expected. Mrs. Stowe's *Oldtown Folks* (1869) and *Sam Lawson's Fireside Stories* (1871), Harte's *The Luck of Roaring Camp and Other Sketches* (1870) about the California of the forty-niners, and Eggleston's *The Hoosier Schoolmaster* (1871) about the Indiana frontier of his youth had started a deluge of fiction about various sections of the country in bygone days. In 1872 Howells remarked that "gradually, but pretty surely, the whole varied field of American life is coming into view in American fiction. . . ." [19] Most writers, like Twain, were trying to be authentic: "I desire," wrote Mrs. Stowe in *Oldtown Folks*, "that you should see the characteristics of those times, and hear them talk. . . . My studies for this object have been . . . taken from real characters, real scenes, and real incidents." But most were nostalgic. Looking back across the chasm which the Civil War had made in American history, writers found the past happier and rosier than the troubled present. There is no evidence that the humorist knew Eggleston at this time; but he knew Harte and his writings well, and annotated a copy of *The Luck of Roaring Camp*. Mrs. Stowe he had recently met as a Nook Farm neighbor. But local-color fiction was everywhere, and any of scores of writers may have acquainted him with it. He, as usual, was apace with literary movements when, happily, he learned that "the boy life out on the Mississippi . . . had a peculiar charm" for him. Reviewing *Tom Sawyer* for the *Atlantic*, in May, 1876, Howells linked it with contemporaneous writings, saying that it "gives incomparably the best picture of life" in the Southwest "as yet known to fiction."

Clemens would have been surprised if other, more specific, literary influences were not operative. In 1869, as he put it, he had "stolen" the dedication of a book by Oliver Wendell Holmes "almost word for word" quite unconsciously, and on apologizing had been reassured by Holmes of the "truth" that "we all unconsciously work over ideas gathered in reading and hearing, imagining they were original with ourselves." [20] Midway in *Tom Sawyer* he again caught himself committing "unconscious plagiarism." [21] In a letter of 1876, the year *Tom Sawyer* appeared, he indicated that he often knowingly transplanted ideas from stories by others into stories of his own. [22]

That same year, after having a bookseller "ransack England"— so his inscription on the flyleaf indicates—he procured a copy of Henry H. Breen's *Modern English Literature: Its Blemishes and Defects* (London, 1857). Clemens showed particular interest in a chapter on plagiarism by marking it up more and making more marginal comments on it than any other part of the book, perhaps while preparing a paper on the topic. [23] His comments strike one as pretty sophisticated. On page 218 Breen scornfully quotes a statement of Alexander Dumas, whom he calls, rather sweepingly, "the most audacious plagiarist of any time or country." Says Dumas: "The man of genius does not steal; he conquers; and what he conquers, he annexes to his empire. He makes laws for it, peoples it with subjects, and extends his golden scepter over it. And where is the man who, in surveying his beautiful kingdom, shall dare to assert that this or that piece of land is no part of his property?" Though Breen calls this a barefaced plea for literary thievery, Clemens agrees with Dumas in a marginal comment: "A good deal of truth in it. Shakespeare took other people's quartz and extracted the gold from it—it was a nearly valueless commodity before."

Breen scolds Dumas for "claiming a place" for plagiarism and citing Shakespeare and Moliere as examples: "They, indeed, were men of genius, while Dumas is little better than 'un habile arrangeur de la pensée d'autrui.'" Clemens notices that Breen has unwittingly granted the truth of Dumas' statement and writes: "Now here *you* are 'claiming a place for it' &c." [24]

On page 224, where Breen cites some of Pope's borrowings from other writers, Clemens writes, "The thought is nothing—it has occurred to everybody; so has every thought that is worth fame. The *expression* of it is the thing to applaud, and there Pope is best." Again, on page 236, where Breen parallels a passage by Gray with one by Milton, Clemens comments: "Here it is the thought rather than the language." On page 251 he writes of another passage quoted, "an old thought"; on page 253, "a common thought"; on pages 262 and 266, "An old thought—no details."

These marginal bickerings indicate that Clemens was more discriminating in his thinking about literary indebtedness than one might expect. With Pope, he realized that writers could be admired for expressing old ideas in a new way. He realized, too, that an author might make materials his own by adapting them to the fictional world he was creating. Clemens' attitude did not change over the years: at sixty-eight he endorsed the belief that "all our phrasings are spiritualized shadows cast multitudinously from our readings." [25]

The readings of Clemens that might cast such shadows were

extensive. He believed that a turning point in his life had been his finding, at fifteen, a page of a biography of Joan of Arc, since this had led to his learning how fascinating history was. During his *Wanderjahren* he was an avid reader, as a tramp printer in Philadelphia and New York, as a printer in Keokuk (where he read Dickens and Poe), as a river pilot, as a San Francisco reporter. Settled down in Hartford, still a lover of books and eager for culture, he had more chances than ever to enjoy this favorite pastime. "For years past," wrote Charles H. Clark in 1885, "he has been an industrious and extensive student in the broad field of general culture. He has a large library and a real familiarity with it, extending . . . into the literature of Germany and France." [26] Any careful study of Clemens' acquaintance with literature supports this claim.[27] Not surprisingly, literary echoes in *Tom Sawyer* are both varied and fairly numerous.

There is the grave-robbing scene in chapter ix. Wecter's search of Hannibal history has revealed no records of grave-robbing there, and Clemens' reminiscences mention no instances. But in a notebook of his for 1885, considering unusual instances of unfunny humorous characters in Charles Dickens, he mentions "the body-snatcher—Tale of 2 Cities." [28] Dickens had been popular since Clemens' boyhood, and evidence proves that Clemens had read his books from 1855 on. Eventually the precise date is not known—*A Tale of Two Cities* (1859) became a favorite book.[29] In Book 2, chapter xiv, of that novel, a boy goes to bed, lies awake until the middle of the night, then sneaks from his house and goes to a graveyard. There, with horror, he watches three men rob a grave. Since exactly this sequence is followed by Tom, it is quite possible that the idea for the scene came from Dickens' novel.

In chapter xxv, after Tom and Huck have failed to find the hidden treasure: " 'Oh,' says Tom, 'I know what the matter is! What a blamed lot of fools we are! You got to find out where the shadow of the tree falls at midnight, and that's where you dig!' " From his reading of Poe in Keokuk days or possibly from a later reading, the author here recalled—and burlesqued—the elaborate procedure used in "The Gold Bug" to find buried treasure.

Back in Clemens' youth, a great school of humorists had flourished in the old Southwest from whom he had learned important skills as a comic writer.[30] A pioneer in the school, Augustus Baldwin Longstreet (1790–1870) was a Georgia lawyer who moved down the scale until he became a humorist and eventually a college president. His *Georgia Scenes* had appeared in Georgia in 1835, then in a more popular edition in New York in 1840, and had gone through eight additional printings by 1860. In 1880, jotting down names of humorous books he recalled, the humorist listed this book twice and Longstreet's pseudonym once; and as an old man he testified that he had known Longstreet's writings for a long time.[31] Longstreet's "Georgia Theatrics" tells at length how an imaginative youngster, with many ferocious cries and blows, felled a completely imaginary opponent. A paragraph in chapter xviii of *Tom Sawyer* tells how, when a fellow student has stolen his sweetheart, Tom has a similar theatrical rehearsal: ". . . he went through the motions of thrashing an imaginary boy—pummeling the air, and kicking and gouging. 'Oh, you do, do you? You holler 'nough, do you? Now, then, let that learn you!' And so the imaginary flogging was finished to his satisfaction." Since the humor and the situation are almost the same as in Longstreet, and since some of the language is close to Longstreet's, this appears to be one of Twain's literary shadows.

Elsewhere, he shows indebtedness to a Yankee humorist, B. P. Shillaber (1814–1890), whose magazine *The Carpet-Bag* the Hannibal *Journal* often quoted when Sam set type for it. Probably Sam contributed to this magazine his first published sketch. By 1870, Shillaber and Clemens had met, and Shillaber had published in the Boston *Post* a poem, "Congratulatory," following Clemens' marriage. *Roughing It* contains a mention of one Ballou's "Partingtonian fashion of loving and using big words for their own sakes, and independent of any bearing they might have upon the thought." The reference is to Shillaber's character in *Life and Sayings of Mrs. Partington* (1854) and *Mrs. Partington's Knitting Work* (1859)—a great user of malapropisms. Mrs. Partington has an uncanny resemblance to Aunt Polly: she looks like her (her portrait turns up as an illustration—presumably picturing Tom's aunt—in the first edition); she has the same enthusiasm for patent medicines; she is a Calvinist restrained from doing her duty by her tender heart. Like Aunt Polly (and unlike Jane Clemens), she is a widow who has taken charge of the rearing of an orphaned nephew, Ike.

AUNT POLLY ALIAS MRS. PARTINGTON
(FRONTISPIECE, *Life and Sayings of Mrs. Partington,* 1854)

And Ike, like Tom, is full of mischief; but a character says of him, "Where there is no malice, mischief is no sin." Aunt Polly, in chapter xv, says of Tom: "he warn't *bad,* so to say, only mischievous . . . warn't any more responsible than a colt." Ike has many adventures similar to Tom's. While listening to his aunt's pious lectures, he swipes doughnuts. He misbehaves in church. ("You have been acting very bad in meeting," says his aunt, "and I declare I could hardly keep from boxing your ears in the midst of the lethargy.") He feigns sickness to avoid school. He plays tricks on cats. He pretends he is a pirate, drawing his inspiration from exactly the same source Tom uses—*The Black Avenger, or The Pirates of the Spanish Main.*[32]

Another probable influence was an extremely popular book by Thomas Bailey Aldrich, *The Story of a Bad Boy* (1869), with which Howells compared *Tom Sawyer* on reviewing it. After meeting Aldrich (and his wife) in 1871, Clemens saw him often. In 1908 he remembered that Aldrich's novel had a connection with *Tom Sawyer*—probably, Paine guesses, because the book came to his attention when "he began discussing his own boy story." Tom Bailey, Aldrich's hero and narrator, anticipates Tom Sawyer: he has a dull time at Sunday school, sneaks out of his bedroom window for night-time adventures, imitates the heroes of books which he has read, camps with other boys on an island where "we played we were . . . Spanish sailors." [33] Particularly interesting is the fact that shortly before *Boy's Manuscript*, Aldrich's novel recounts a love affair during the course of which Tom Bailey acts out a childish burlesque of sentimental lovesickness:

I avoided my playmates. . . . I did not eat as much as was good for me. I took lonely walks. I brooded in solitude. . . . I used to lie in the grass and gloat over the amount and variety of mournful expressions I could throw into my features. . . . I no longer joined the boys on the playground at recess. I stayed at my desk reading some lugubrious volume. . . . A translation of The Sorrows of Werther fell into my hands . . . , and if I could have committed suicide without killing myself, I should certainly have done so. . . . In a quiet way I never enjoyed myself better in my life than when I was a Blighted Being.[34]

Clemens, having had childish love affairs of his own, drew upon memories of them when he wrote fiction about boys in love. But it seems likely that he learned some of the possibilities of such comedy and acquired details from Aldrich. Billy Rogers notes in his diary phenomena very similar to those in Aldrich:

I don't care for apples, I don't care for molasses candy, swinging on the gate don't do me no good, and even sliding on the cellar door. . . . I said the world was a mean, sad place, and had nothing for me to love and care for in it—and life, life was only misery. It was then that it first came into my head to take my life . . . but then she would only be sorry for a little while . . . and I would be dead for always. I did not like that.[35]

Tom Sawyer suffers similarly, and like Aldrich's hero wishes for suicide without death:

He no longer took an interest in war, nor even in piracy. . . . He put his hoop away, and his bat. . . . (chapter xii) The boy's soul was steeped in melancholy; his feelings were in happy accord with his surroundings. It seemed to him that life was but a trouble, at best, and he more than half envied Jimmy Hodges, so lately released. . . . If he only had a clean Sunday school record, he would be willing to go. . . . Ah, if he could only die *temporarily!* (chapter viii)

If, as I suggest, Twain learned from Aldrich how to picture Boy as Blighted Being, we owe him as well as Twain our thanks for these passages.

A number of writings allied to Shillaber's accounts of Ike and Aldrich's book influenced more than occasional incidents in *Tom Sawyer*: they provided the over-all structure (such as it is) of the novel. These were humorous pieces attacking fashionable serious juvenile fiction of the nineteenth century. In this moralizing fiction, two kinds of children clearly labeled "good" and "bad" appeared. Good children—Little Rollos, Little Evas, Alger boys—came to good ends, and their creators urged readers to go and do likewise. Bad children, their foils, came to bad ends—the boy who played hooky, for instance, "grew up to be a very wicked man, and at last committed a murder" [36]—and their creators warned readers not to get into similar messes.

Beginning in the 1840's and well into the 1870's, at least a dozen popular humorists—a group usually antiromantic, antisentimental, and amoral—attacked these misrepresentations of youth by picturing boys in a "more realistic" fashion—as merely mischievous, irresponsible creatures who matured into normal adults. In the 1860's Henry Ward Beecher was attacking from his pulpit the "impossible boys, with incredible goodness," of fiction. "Boys," he said, "have a period of mischief much as they have measles and small-pox." And by the time of *Tom Sawyer*, many humorists had taken pot shots at the "Model Boy." Four in addition to Shillaber and Aldrich were George W. Harris of Tennessee, James M. Bailey of Connecticut, Robert J. Burdette of Iowa, and Charles B. Lewis of Michigan.

In the *Californian*, December 23, 1865, appeared "The Christmas Fireside. For Good Little Girls and Boys, by Grandfather Twain," the author's first contribution to this type of literature— later retitled "The Story of the Bad Little Boy Who Did Not Come to Grief." In a notebook in 1868 Twain wrote an unpublished sketch, "The Story of Mamie Grant, the Child-Missionary," deriding the stories about pious Sunday-school infants. In 1870 he wrote a companion piece to his first, "The Story of the Good Little Boy Who Did Not Prosper." These were burlesques in the mode—inverted fables. During his early months in Hartford, so his neighbor Charles Dudley Warner records, the humorist said facetiously, "I tried a Sunday-school book once; but I made the good boy end in the poorhouse, and the bad boy go to Congress." [37] A contemporary reviewer of *Tom Sawyer* in the San Francisco *Chronicle* said that it was similarly unorthodox: "Twain has run the traditional Sunday-school boy through his literary mangle . . . the skin of that strumous young pietist is now neatly tacked up to view on the Sunday-school door of today as a warning."

Tom Sawyer then is a humorous—though not burlesque—version of "The Story of a Bad Boy Who Did Not Come to Grief." Opening chapters show Tom stealing, lying, playing hooky, and fighting—proving that he is what juvenile fictionists would call a Bad Boy; but the author clearly admires him. Twain soon indicates his contempt and dislike for "the Model Boy of the village," pious Willie Mufferson, and for Tom's goody-goody half-brother Sid. Twain's preachment is that Tom is what a normal boy should be; his mischief is a harmless part of his maturing; and he will become a well-adjusted adult.

Accordingly, each of several lines of action begins with Tom's behaving in an irresponsible childish fashion and ends with an incident signifying his approach to responsible maturity. The love story begins with his fickle desertion of a former sweetheart and his ungainly attempts to win Becky; it ends with his chivalrously undergoing punishment for her and bravely helping her in the cave. The story of Tom and Muff Potter begins with the superstitious trip to the graveyard; it ends with Tom's defiance of boyish superstition and his courageous testimony in court. At the end, in a conversation with Huck, Tom, though still a boy, is talking very much like an adult.

The end of each line of action also departs from conventional patterns in juvenile fiction. Tom and his companions, who have run away to Jackson's Island, have played hooky, and have smoked (all vile sins in Sunday-school stories), are greeted with cheers when they return. Tom becomes a hero because he saves Potter, is compared with George Washington because he takes Becky's punishment, is lionized because he rescues Becky. To top it all, Tom and the even more disreputable Huck at the end acquire a fortune such as traditionally had been reserved only for the best of Alger's little heroes.

Literary influences thus shaped both incidents and the over-all pattern of *Tom Sawyer*.

More important, of course, than Twain's literary dependence was his adaptation of "borrowed" materials into appropriate parts of a narrative which, regardless of its origins, is all of a piece. More than a little artistic skill was required to give such diverse materials the color of Twain's personality and the tone of this book, and to intertwine diverse but similar stories throughout the novel.

Still, Twain's art was probably more noteworthy in individual episodes, many of which readers remember long after the rest of the book has been forgotten. His handling of several of these was the result of "literary rehearsals" like those preparatory for the description of Hannibal in "Old Times."

An instance is the St. Petersburg Sunday-school services in chapter iv. As far back as 1856, young Sam Clemens had written a comic essay for a girl friend, Annie Taylor, describing how a swarm of bugs, attracted by the light overhead, gathered around his printing case one night. By degrees—in accordance with the tall-tale tradition of Southwestern humor—these insects were "humanized" until they became a religious mass meeting "presided over by a venerable beetle" perched on a lock of Sam's hair, "while innumerable lesser dignitaries . . . clustered around . . . keeping order . . . endeavoring to attract attention . . . to their own importance by industriously grating their teeth." [38] In 1873, in chapter liii of *The Gilded Age,* telling about Senator Dilworthy's electioneering in the Cattleville Sunday school, the author remarked similar phenomena and added others, including Dilworthy's pious speech to the children. The *Tom Sawyer* chapter goes over the same ground for a third time, with its superintendent, librarian, teachers, pupils, and visitor (Judge Thatcher here) all "showing off" before the judge delivers his version of the visiting celebrity's speech. The humorist therefore may be said to have practiced twice for the final—and best—rendition of the scene.

Chapter v, the church services which follow, had been similarly rehearsed in a letter of 1871 which Clemens wrote to Livy from Paris, Illinois, after a service there—a compounding of recent notations with some from the past, since "It was as if twenty-five years had fallen away . . . and I was a lad of eleven again in Missouri village church." [39] The second rendition combines details of the practice run with new ones appropriate to the novel.

Similarly a paragraph in a newspaper letter dated April 16, 1867, on Sam Clemens' boyhood experience as a member of Hannibal's Cadets of Temperance was a rehearsal for a better paragraph in chapter xxii ascribing the same experience to Tom.

Another instance is chapter xxi, Examination Day in Tom's school. On January 14, 1864, the author had written for the *Territorial Enterprise* a story about exercises in Miss Clapp's school in Carson City, Nevada. This contained descriptions of recitations by students and a spelling bee, and it quoted a childish composition which was read and commented upon by others.[40] In August, 1868, he sent *Alta California* an account of a burlesque of such exercises staged aboard the *Montana* on a recent ocean voyage. Dressed in boys' costumes, the men had recited poems, declaimed orations; and the humorist had read a composition, "The Cow."

The program was reproduced and performances were described.[41] Before writing the chapter in his novel, therefore, he had twice set down versions of the scene. To see how he retained some details, deleted others, and added still others is to see the scene moving by degrees to its final perfection. It is noteworthy, too, that a visit to a similar exhibition in a young ladies' academy, probably in 1870 or 1871, suggested some of the new matter—the compositions read by several young ladies.[42]

Boy's Manuscript is an earlier handling of incidents in *Tom Sawyer*. In it, as DeVoto has noticed,

a heroine named Amy . . . inflicts on the hero the same agonies and ecstasies that Becky Thatcher was to inflict on Tom. Billy Rogers makes love to her in almost the same terms Tom uses. . . . Like Tom also he does battle for her with a boy called Wart Hopkins. . . .

When we first meet Wart Hopkins he is on his way back from a crossroads where he has buried a bean that has blood on it: from this seed the central action of *Tom Sawyer* was to grow. Before this he has been in the circus business with Billy, and that too was to have its part in the book, together with the sham battle, the tooth, the sore toe, and the posturing and parading before Amy's house. More striking is the louse which is tormented on Bill Bowen's desk. It has become a more seemly tick when we see it again in *Tom Sawyer* and Bill Bowen . . . has become Joe Harper, but the scene is duplicated almost exactly.[43]

Also, Paine believes—though DeVoto disagrees—that there was another rehearsal of much of the novel in the form of a play.

Nor were written rehearsals the only kind. In 1872 Clemens says, in London, "I told Irving and Wills, the playwright, about the whitewashing of the fence by Tom Sawyer, and thereby captured on cheap terms a chapter; for I wrote it out when I got back to the hotel while it was fresh in my mind." [44] And on the opening manuscript page of chapter i Twain wrote: "Put in thing from Boy-lecture." These two bits of evidence suggest that parts of the book, at least, were orally rehearsed.

Passages rehearsed in those ways were for the most part based upon memories of actual happenings. Because of such reworkings, these parts of the book may have been the ones he remembered best. This may explain his frequent claims that most adventures in the novel "really occurred." As a result of their authenticity and the practiced art which shaped them, these memorable episodes contribute much to the impression the book gives of being realistic.

Clearly, though, the merits of the book did not result from a simple recording of remembered facts. Even actual happenings— a study of the rehearsals makes evident—were transmuted into new things. The nostalgic mood, created by the era and by the life the author was living as he wrote, was an important ingredient. So was the fear, a recollection from childhood, which was also part of the mood. DeVoto's point is valid: "Mark is nowhere truer to us, to himself, or to childhood than in the dread which holds this idyl enclosed." [45] The humorist's reading, past and present, contributed episodes, an over-all scheme, and a theme which concerned the true nature of boyhood. And parts of the book and the book as a whole benefited greatly from his skill as an artist.

During the composition of *Tom Sawyer* the author, still a novice at fiction writing, had found material congenial to him. He had learned the advantage of pigeonholing a manuscript while "his tank filled up again." He had learned how to utilize his memories to suit his purposes. These discoveries would be important when he embarked shortly upon the writing of a sequel.

5

TOM AND HUCK

. . . a gray squirrel and a big fellow of the "fox" kind came skurrying along, sitting up at intervals to inspect and chatter at the boys, for the wild things had probably never seen a human being before and scarcely knew whether to be afraid or not. All Nature was wide awake and stirring, now; long lances of sunlight pierced down through the dense foliage far and near, and a few butterflies came fluttering upon the scene.—The Adventures of Tom Sawyer, *chapter xiv.*

I could see the sun out at one or two holes, but mostly it was big trees all about, and gloomy in there amongst them. There was freckled places on the ground where the light sifted down through the leaves, and the freckled places swapped about a little, showing there was a little breeze up there. A couple of squirrels set on a limb and jabbered at me very friendly.—Adventures of Huckleberry Finn, *chapter viii.*

A year after finishing *Tom Sawyer,* while reading chapter proofs for that book, Mark Twain started, as a sequel, *Adventures of Huckleberry Finn,* subtitled "Tom Sawyer's Comrade." Because of juxtapositions in time and subject matter the two books were closely related. One result was that, just as other writings had rehearsed parts of *Tom Sawyer,* that book rehearsed parts of the later novel.

On Jackson's Island, in chapter xiii of the book bearing his name, Tom talks about the superiority of a pirate's life over a hermit's:

> "You see," said Tom, "people don't go much on hermits, now-a-days . . . but a pirate's always respected. And a hermit's got to sleep on the hardest place he can find, and put sack-cloth and ashes on his head, and stand out in the rain, and—"
>
> "What does he put sack-cloth and ashes on his head for?" inquired Huck.
>
> "*I* dono. But they've *got* to do it. Hermits always do. You'd have to do that if you was a hermit."
>
> "Dern'd if I would," said Huck.
>
> "Well what would you do?"
>
> "I dono. But I wouldn't do that."
>
> "Why Huck, you'd *have* to. How'd you get around it?"
>
> "Why I just wouldn't stand it. I'd run away."
>
> "Run away! Well you *would* be a nice old slouch of a hermit. You'd be a disgrace."

Tom's skimpy knowledge and his pedantic acceptance of books as authorities as contrasted with Huck's ignorance, his respect for Tom's learning, and his common sense are ingredients of this passage. The same incongruities occur in chapters xxv, xxxiii, and xxxv, when Tom and Huck discuss robber gangs, and in chapter xxvi, when they consider Robin Hood.

At the start of *Huck,* the same pair have an almost identical talk about robbers, and in chapter iii Tom discourses on genies—"as tall as a tree and as big around as a church":

> "Well," I says, "s'pose we got some genies to help *us*—can't we lick the other crowd then?"
>
> "How you going to get them?"
>
> "I don't know. How do *they* get them?"
>
> "Why, they rub an old tin lamp or an iron ring, and then the genies come tearing in . . . and everything they're told to do they up and do it. . . ."
>
> "Who makes them tear around so?"

"Why, whoever rubs the lamp or the ring. They belong to whoever rubs the lamp or the ring, and they've got to do whatever he says. . . ."

"Well," says I, "I think they are a pack of flat-heads. . . . And what's more—if I was one of them I would see a man in Jericho before I would drop my business and come to him for the rubbing of an old tin lamp. . . ."

"Shucks, it ain't no use to talk to you. . . . You don't seem to know anything, somehow—perfect sap-head."

The humor is essentially the same. At the end of the new novel, Tom again lectures—this time on prisoners' escapes—through a series of chapters.

A prediction made by Huck in chapter xxv of the earlier novel about what would happen if he found a treasure is fulfilled in the sequel; indeed, it may have suggested an inciting force: "Pap would come back to thish-yer town some day and get his claws on it if I didn't hurry up [and get rid of it]." Pap does return and in an attempt to get hold of the treasure seizes his son. To avoid Pap's abuse and being "sivilized" by Widow Douglas, Huck escapes to Jackson's Island.

There, just as he and Tom and Joe Harper do in chapter xiv of *Tom Sawyer*, Huck watches the ferryboat hunt for his drowned body:

Well, I was dozing off again, when I thinks I hears a deep sound of "boom!" away up the river. I rouses up and rests on my elbow and listens; pretty soon I hears it again. I hopped up, and went and looked out at a hole in the leaves, and I see a bunch of smoke laying on the water a long ways up—about abreast the ferry. And there was the ferry-boat full of people, floating along down. I knowed what was the matter now. "Boom!" I see the white smoke squirt out of the ferry-boat's side. You see, they was firing cannon over the water, trying to make my carcass come to the top.

In chapter xxviii of *Tom Sawyer*, Huck plans to sleep in the Rogers' hayloft with the consent of the slave, Uncle Jake:

"I tote water for Uncle Jake whenever he wants me to, and any time I ask him he gives me a little something to eat if he can spare it. That's a mighty good nigger, Tom. He likes me, becuz I don't ever act as if I was above him. Sometimes I've set right down and eat *with* him. But you needn't tell that. A body's got to do things when he's awful hungry he wouldn't want to do as a steady thing."

This is a crude pencil sketch of the escaping slave Jim, who joins Huck on the island and later goes down the river with him. And the vein of satire dealing with moral anomalies in a slaveholding society here briefly exposed was to be brilliantly exploited.

UNCLE JAKE IN
Tom Sawyer

During the journey downstream, Huck does some reading and for a time he is to uneducated but commonsensible Jim what Tom is to Huck in *Tom Sawyer*—an argumentative instructor. The two investigate such topics as King Solomon, the French language, and the ways of royalty and nobility.

These and other repetitions relate the two novels. Nevertheless, there would be tremendous differences between these books, close in time though they were. Comparison of even brief excerpts indicates one great difference—in the styles. The descriptions of daybreak preceding this chapter are an instance. In *Tom*, two squirrels (one in apologetic quotation marks) "skurry along . . . to inspect and to chatter at the boys"; in *Huck*, "a couple of squirrels set on a limb and jabbered at me very friendly." In *Tom*, "All Nature [with a capital N] was awake and stirring, now"; in *Huck*, "I could see the sun out at one or two holes." In *Tom*, "long lances of sunlight pierced down through the dense foliage far and near"; in *Huck*, "it was big trees all about, and gloomy in there," and "there was freckled places on the ground where the light sifted down through the leaves." If the earlier passage misses the contrived "prettiness" and artiness of a Victorian description, it barely does so; but the later passage appears to have no more concern with prettiness or artiness than Huck does. If the earlier passage gets its effect, it does so despite the handicap of its all but trite style. If the latter passage gets its effect, it does so largely because it is in a style which handles the detail naturally and in phrases striking enough to be memorable.

The shift to Huck as narrator would liberate Mark Twain from many limitations which an overweening desire to haul off and be literary in the third person had imposed. Huck's character, of course, would have a great deal to do with this. A boy so sensitive and so shrewd was bound to record scenes and actions with insight; but since he was unabashedly uncouth, he was bound to do this naturally and unpretentiously. Since he was almost completely humorless, he was bound to be incongruously naïve and somber on many laugh-provoking occasions. The author's experience would help him climb into Huck's skin. He too was sensitive and perceptive, and he too had been informed of his lack of manners and culture. And for purposes of both written and oral humor he had often impersonated a similar character, using language homely to him which had given him a freedom that the literary language of the day could not afford.

And the ideas in the new book would be more vital to Twain—and to his readers—than those in the earlier novel. *Tom* is a light book suitable for children and for adults satisfied with a funny story; *Huck* is a funny book suitable for children, too; but grown-ups who read it find depths in its humor and in its meanings which as childish readers they completely missed.

In *Tom Sawyer*, Mark Twain pictures with amusement and sympathy youngsters who were currently labeled Bad Boys, and he concludes by showing such youngsters triumphant. In a sense, therefore, the book was rebellious. But its attack was a playful one. The boys can resist civilization blamelessly and comically—blamelessly because they are not responsible, comically because their innocent insurrections contrast incongruously with the tensions of responsible grownups. Tom and his companions—even Huck—do not question the standards, nor does Mark. In 1875, when he finished this novel, he could make his happy ending a boy's attainment of respectability.

But in the new book, while Tom's character would be greatly simplified, Huck's would be made far more complex, and this outcast would be the narrator and the protagonist. Pap Finn, not on the scene in *Tom Sawyer*, would figure prominently because Huck was to live with him and escape from him. Jim would be pictured at full length because Huck would spend days and nights with him out on Jackson's Island, on the raft drifting downstream or ashore away from everybody else. On his journey, this waif would meet and come to know many other characters who could not have invaded Tom's childhood world except as melodramatic figures. Most of them would be adults. The civilization which they represent would differ greatly from that of godly St. Petersburg. Twain's attitude toward this civilization, moreover, would be very different. Many of its standards he would not accept but would question and reject. Huck would struggle with his own problems not in a childish but in an adult fashion. And whereas the ending of *Tom* shows the boy initiated into society, the new book would show the much more mature Huck fleeing from society.

These changes would come about because of the life the author led, the books he read, his ponderings, and the conclusions he reached about humanity during the seven-year period of the book's composition.

6

"PEACE, QUIET, REST, SECLUSION"

*"Looky here, Tom, being rich ain't what it's cracked up
to be. It's just worry and worry, and sweat and sweat,
and a-wishing you was dead all the time. . . . Tom, I
wouldn't ever got into this trouble if it hadn't 'a' been for
that money. . . ."—Huckleberry Finn in* Tom Sawyer,
chapter xxxv.

In the 1920's, when the flaming issue was frankness in literature
and chic biographers doubled as do-it-yourself psychoanalysts,
several developed a theory that Twain's writings were what they
were because he was constantly restrained from saying and doing
what he wished by the prudish censorship of Livy and Howells.
The humorist's playful statements about Livy's emasculations of
his manuscripts and her dictatorial control over his actions, swal-
lowed literally without a smile, and Howells' report that the
author accepted suggestions, provided documentation.

Since that decade, more specific evidence has become avail-
able and has been carefully studied. Data on the writing of "Old
Times" are incomplete, since no manuscript has been found.
Twain tells of writing the first half of Article V three times at
Livy's insistence; but his report affords no evidence that her ob-
jections were moral rather than artistic, and the subject matter
("Soundings") makes it virtually impossible that they were. The

only deletions by Howells which could have involved censorship were one bit of profanity and a brief passage about sea songs which was irrelevant and probably was neither profane nor sexy.[1]

Two manuscripts of *Tom Sawyer* have survived, however, and have been studied. The original at Georgetown University, Washington, D.C., shows no signs of Livy's censorship, though it does indicate that she took the trouble to remind her husband to have Tom take Becky's spanking for her in chapter xx and to have the cat snatch off the master's wig in chapter xxi. If she suggested bowdlerizations, the manuscript does not show where.[2]

The amanuensis copy now in Jefferson City, Missouri, was made after Livy had offered whatever suggestions she had. But this manuscript contains passages later deleted. Also it shows Howells at work. Clemens had met Howells in 1869, after the latter had favorably reviewed *Innocents Abroad* for the *Atlantic*. Both men were Westerners educated at the printer's case, both were rising to prominence in literature. Since Howells had been accepted by the genteel New Englanders, the humorist delighted in his praise. In 1872, when Howells appreciatively reviewed *Roughing It*, Clemens wrote: "I'm as uplifted and reassured by it as a mother who had given birth to a white baby when she was awfully afraid that it was going to be a mulatto." [3] Howells also won Clemens' gratitude by urging him to write for the *Atlantic*. As their friendship grew, Clemens depended increasingly on Howells' literary judgments. Clemens talked with his friend about *Tom Sawyer* in the summer of 1875 and possibly accepted suggestions. Later, when Howells read the completed manuscript, he suggested it be published "explicitly as a boy's book," and Clemens, as the preface shows, agreed. It must be strongly emphasized that Howells had a juvenile audience in mind, therefore, when he "made some corrections and suggestions in a faltering pencil—almost all in the first third," [4] and that it was with such an audience in mind that the author accepted them.

Most, indisputably, were stylistic.[5] But the humorist "tamed all the obscenities until I judged that they no longer carried offense." Only three passages were involved. The poodle which sat on the pinchbug in church (chapter v) originally "went sailing up the

aisle with his tail shut down like a hasp." Howells, having spotted
an indecency which I have been able to find with the kind help
of a colleague, wrote, "Awfully good but a little too dirty," and
the last eight words were deleted.

A more extensive change was made in chapter xx, where Becky
stole a peek at the schoolmaster's book and found a picture of "a
human figure, stark naked." Howells commented, "I should be
afraid of this picture incident." Twain excised Tom's explanation,
"How could *I* know it wasn't a nice book? I didn't know girls ever
—" He deleted Becky's plaint that she would suffer worse punishments than whipping: "But that isn't anything—it ain't *half*.
You'll tell everybody about this picture, and O,O,O!" Becky's
thought, "He'll tell the scholars about that hateful picture—
maybe he's told some of them before now," was removed. So was
part of Tom's soliloquy on "what a curious kind of a fool a girl is":
"But that picture—is—well, now it ain't so curious she feels bad
about that. . . . No, I reckon it ain't. Suppose she was Mary and
Alf Temple had caught her looking at such a picture as that and
went around telling. She'd feel—well, I'd lick him. I bet I would.
. . . Then Dobbins would tell his wife about the picture." The
third refinement made at Howells' suggestion was the deletion
of one of Huck's less elegant complaints about Widow Douglas'
civilizing him (chapter xxxv): "she'd gag when I spit." These
were the moral improvements which Howells urged, and weep
for them though we may, they do not seem disastrous or very frus-
trating. They made sense in a book for juveniles in a society which
would ban the book from some libraries even after these conces-
sions.

True, Twain at times was irked by these and similar restrictions.
When Mrs. James T. Fields visited Hartford in the spring of 1876,
she reported in her diary:

. . . he proceeded to speak of his "Autobiography," which he intends
to write as fully and simply as possible to leave behind him. His wife
laughingly said she should look it over and leave out objectionable
passages. "No," he said, very earnestly, almost sternly, "*you* are not to
edit it—it is to appear as it was written, with the whole tale told as
truly as I can tell it. I shall take out passages from it, and publish as

I go along in the Atlantic and elsewhere. . . . Every man feels that his experience is unlike that of anybody else, and therefore he should write it down." [6]

There is evidence here of a chafing at the bit.

But there is much reason to doubt that at this time the writer was constantly—even frequently—enraged because he was checked. A noteworthy fact is that he himself initiated the most famous change in *Tom Sawyer*, after Livy, her aunt, her mother, and Howells had approved the passage involved. Should Huck, he asked in a letter, "in a book now professedly and confessedly a boy's and girl's book," use a phrase that never bothered the author "until I had ceased to regard the volume as being for adults"—should he complain that the widow's servants "comb me all to hell?" Howells answered that he supposed he had missed the phrase "because the locution was so familiar to my Western sense, and so exactly what Huck would say." "But," he added, "it won't do for children." Huck was duly combed "all to thunder." Nor was this the only passage Twain himself thought needed softening. "Satan" became "the devil"; "foul slop," "water"; "reeking," "drenched." And in chapter xxix he changed Injun Joe's recipe for revenge on a woman, "you cut her nose off—and her ears," to the more genteel (though still somewhat unmannerly) "You slit her nostrils—you notch her ears like a sow!"

These revisions on the author's own initiative provide the strong possibility that if Livy or Howells had not suggested some changes, he may well have made them on his own. For he not only eagerly sought instruction in matters of taste: whatever the reason, he himself was carefully conventional about many matters, and in writing for publication (though not in private conversations or correspondence) he prudishly limited his treatment of sex. This meant that some important aspects of life would not be treated well or at length in his published works. Several moderns who treat these aspects well, or, at any rate, at length, were destined to scold him for his omissions and to devise ingenious theories about his psychoses.[7] This reticence did not necessarily mean that he would find no important matters to treat or that he had any overwhelming feeling of frustration because his writings had been censored.

By 1876 it must have become clear to Clemens and to Livy that most battles which she had waged to reform him were lost. He had married her determined to be reformed, and for some time made a heroic effort—reading the Bible, praying with ministers, protesting his eagerness to be saved. Joe Goodman, erstwhile employer of Clemens on the Virginia City *Territorial Enterprise,* visited him in Buffalo and was astonished at the sight of Clemens saying grace and reading the Scriptures.[8] Clemens had stopped smoking and drinking, had tried to stop swearing. But as De-Lancey Ferguson observes, "Before long these reforms ceased, and ceased on Mark's terms, not on Livy's. The Bible readings were the first to go. . . . Within a year after her marriage. . . , Livy's crusade against tobacco was as if it had never been." [9] A letter to Livy from London, January 2, 1874, shortly before he sailed for home, shows that by that time he could openly get by with three Old-Fashioneds a day for his stomach's sake: ". . . I want you to . . . have in the bathroom, when I arrive, a bottle of Scotch whisky, a lemon, some crushed sugar, and a bottle of *Angostura bitters.* Ever since I have been in London I have taken in a wine-glass . . . a cock-tail (made with those ingredients) before breakfast, before dinner, and just before going to bed. . . . To this I attribute the fact that up to this day my digestion has been wonderful—simply *perfect.*" [10] In addition to these digestive aids, he often drank wine at the table and lager beer or champagne (to help him sleep) after dinner. The ban on swearing theoretically continued for ten years; but since Clemens often "did his devotions," as he delicately put it, in private, at length and with vehemence, Livy must frequently have had trouble pretending she had not heard him. And either in this period or slightly later (certainly by 1879) Livy lost her fervid religious beliefs.

In Clemens' life, therefore, some forces of civilization which had provided fun in *Tom Sawyer* had been defeated when the book was started, and the rest by the time he started *Huckleberry Finn*. In neither his living nor his writing was Clemens in 1876 unduly harassed by censorship.

There is quite a bit of evidence, however, that family and financial worries and certain aspects of life in Hartford were much on his mind when he started his new novel.

His boyhood had prepared him to appreciate his ties with Livy and his daughters. After becoming irritated with a sweetheart too bashful to propose, Clemens' mother had married his father in a fit of pique. Living in an undemonstrative family, Sam had keenly sensed coolness beneath his parents' politeness. And John Clemens had been a harsh father. Livy had astonished and delighted her husband with the demonstrative warmth of her affection. Clemens' love for her and the children was not weakened but strengthened by his spending a much larger share of his time with them than most men did with their families. He was therefore likely to be greatly concerned about their welfare.

From the spring which followed his marriage Clemens had worried about his family. For a time illness and death had made his life a nightmare. Jervis Langdon became desperately ill in Elmira, and the Clemenses were tortured and exhausted by bedside vigils ending only with his death. Soon after, an old friend of Livy, Emma Nye, visiting in Buffalo, came down with typhoid, and again worry and exhaustion continued until her death. Livy, pregnant during these ordeals, gave premature birth to a son in November, then suffered a long serious illness. In mid-March, 1871, Clemens wrote, "I had rather die twice over than repeat the last six months of my life." [11]

These troubles were partly responsible for the move to Hartford, but similar difficulties continued there. The son, Langdon, sickly from the start, died June 2, 1872, soon after the move. And Livy, never strong, frequently was ill.

Moreover, Clemens was harassed by financial worries during these years. When he sold his interest in the Buffalo *Express* he lost $10,000, and though he had vowed never to lecture again he returned to the circuit to rehabilitate his finances. He dropped out of journalism, which had assured a regular income if his books failed to sell, and he could not be sure that his first successful book would be followed by others. The success of *Roughing It* reassured him, but in 1873 there was a panic. Thereafter a depression lasted several years. The Hartford mansion had cost three times the estimated amount, and expenditures needed to live on the scale of the Hartford household were constant worries. In 1876 he wrote Stoddard: "This recent bust-up in the coal-trade hits *us* pretty hard. My wife's whole fortune is in coal, and so her income utterly ceases for the next five or six months. . . ." [12] About this time, he revealed to Howells later, he and Livy began to "feel poor." [13]

These troubles and worries surely contributed to the pleasure with which Mark Twain escaped, in his writings, to relatively carefree days in the West or the Southwest. It is noteworthy that the first and by far the more nostalgic portion of *Roughing It* was written concurrently with the most woeful period in Buffalo.[14] *Boy's Manuscript* was a product of the same period. *The Gilded Age* in 1873 was relatively more genial in representing life on the old-time Western frontier, more critical in picturing corrupt life in contemporaneous Washington. And early years in the Hartford mansion produced the nostalgic "Old Times" and *Tom Sawyer*.

Other factors in Clemens' situation which influenced *Tom Sawyer* and would influence *Huckleberry Finn* even more are suggested when Clemens' home life as he once foresaw it is compared with that life as it really was. Soon after becoming engaged, the prospective bridegroom had pictured their coming happiness: "And so *you* have been having visions of our future home . . . I have such visions. . . . And they always take one favorite shape— peace, and quiet—rest, and seclusion from the rush and roar and discord of the world.—You and I apart . . . reading and studying when the day's duties are done—in our own castle, by our own fireside. . . ." [15] If in 1875 or 1876 Olivia ever pulled this letter from the box in which she treasured her husband's correspondence, she must have smiled wanly at the ironic contrast between vision and actuality.

Nook Farm was what many would consider a horribly congenial community. "Each of us," said John Hooker, "made free of the other's houses . . . each keeping open house . . . all of us frequently gathering for a social evening or to welcome some friendly visitor. . . ." [16] Howells on his first visit was impressed by the way the Hookers, the Clemenses, the Warners, "and a great many delightful people . . . go in and out of each other's houses without ringing." [17] The delightful people of course included the Twichells, frequent visitors. Reading the letters and diaries of these neighbors, one sometimes feels that the Clemens mansion was less secluded and quiet than a railway station.

Frequently there were guests overnight or for several days—Clemens' mother and sister, perhaps, Olivia's mother and aunt, Mrs. Fairbanks, literary associates such as Moncure Conway, Osgood, or Howells—often with their wives. Howells was the most frequent and welcome guest—a plump jolly man who talked and laughed far into the night with Clemens in the guest room or in Clemens' billiard room. "After two days of this," said Howells, "I would come away hollow, realizing myself best in the image of those locust-shells . . . sticking to the bark of trees. . . ." [18] Such visits must have been a strain on the Clemenses, and visits of less informal friends such as the Fieldses or the Aldriches even more exhausting.

Many "company dinners," as Olivia's personal maid testifies, were of a fairly formidable sort:

. . . at those dinners, . . . we had soup first, of course, and then the [filet of] beef or [canvasback] ducks, you know, and we'd have wine with our cigars, and we'd have sherry, claret, and champagne, maybe. . . . We'd always have creme de menthe and most always charlotte russe, too. Then we'd sometimes have Nesselroade pudding and very often ice cream for the most elegant dinners. No, never plain ordinary ice cream—we always had our ice cream put up in some wonderful shapes—like flowers or cherubs, little angels—all different kinds and shapes and flavors, and colors—oh! everything lovely! And then after the company had eat up all the little ice cream angels, the ladies would all depart into the living-room and the gentlemen would sit (lounge, I think they called it) around the table and have a little more champagne (maybe) while we passed the coffee to the ladies in the drawing-room. . . .

Wonderful people come, . . . no end to them.[19]

Wonderful people or not, such elaborate affairs must have been tiring.

Many uninvited visitors also came—salesmen, celebrity hunters, interviewers. Although George the butler had orders to admit only personal friends and had been instructed in lying tactfully, he often yielded to pathetic pleas. When, as Clemens put it fiercely, George "brought in visiting-cards on a tray, as if he were serving the eucharist," Clemens had tantrums. "You go and tell Mr. Smith," Howells once heard him snarl, "that I wouldn't come down to see the Twelve Apostles." Sometimes when visitors got by George, Clemens hid on the billiard-room balcony which extended into the branches of the trees. But in spite of all precautions, many callers wasted his time.[20]

Letters, plentiful enough to bother Clemens in 1874, greatly increased in 1875 and 1876. There were requests for autographs, pleas for literary advice or financial help, letters of praise or criticism, a few anonymous threats. There were social letters—invitations, exchanges of news. Some he filed after jotting comments on the envelope: "Literary aspirant"; "From a muggins"; "From an unknown idiot in Ireland"; "This is the Orion style of ass." A large proportion had to be answered, or (his endorsements indicate) so he thought.[21] In February, 1876, he wrote Mrs. Fairbanks that his correspondence "grew upon me to such an extent that it stopped all literary labor, nearly. . . ." [22] Despite occasional help from secretaries, his correspondence often curtailed his time for writing.

Clemens expended much time, too, on various meetings. Alternate weeks, the Monday Evening Club met at the house of one of the twenty members—lawyers, preachers, political leaders, businessmen, scholars, and authors. Someone read a paper, members discussed it, and refreshments were served—supper or beer and liquors. Clemens usually read a paper each year.[23] Every Friday night he had friends over for billiards while their wives kept Mrs.

FIREPLACE IN THE CLEMENS MANSION

(PHOTO BY R. S. DE LAMATER, *Harper's*, LXXI, OCTOBER, 1885, 725)

Clemens company in the library—beer and hardtack in the billiard room, tea in the library.[24] The Saturday Morning Club, with fifteen to twenty young girls—and Clemens—as members, gathered in the Clemens' home to read and discuss essays.[25] In 1876 Clemens held forth on "The Life of Lord Macaulay"; later he read to them from manuscripts in progress.[26]

There were many civic activities.[27] Each Christmas Livy wore herself out preparing for the annual distribution of gifts to the poor—fifty large baskets, each filled with flowers, fruit, canned goods, candy, nuts, a turkey, a bottle of wine: these Patrick the coachman delivered while Clemens and his daughters waited in the sleigh.[28] In April, 1876, Clemens acted in "The Loan of a Lover," given by an amateur group. He added impromptu speeches of his own which disconcerted others in the cast, delighted the audience, and so impressed visiting Producer Augustin Daly that Daly invited him to play the part in New York.[29] Now and then he spoke at benefits, political rallies, and school assemblies.

Clemens at times was occupied with business matters. Olivia, who had inherited a quarter of a million dollars, trustfully let him handle investments: on one of several letters from a lawyer, C. E. Perkins, reporting purchases of stocks and bonds, Clemens wrote in the summer of 1876, "The 21st thousand invested."[30] As usual he was alert for opportunities to put his own money to work by purchasing what he considered promising stocks.

He began in 1876 to reap profits from "Mark Twain's Self-Pasting Scrap-Book," which he had invented in 1872 and had manufactured and sold. Books were made with dots of mucilage on their pages so that purchasers could moisten the mucilage and affix clippings or documents. The business was going well,[31] but Clemens constantly offered advice about enlarging sales and profits.

The American Publishing Company, which issued his books, also got attention. The firm was in Hartford, and he must have seen Elisha Bliss, its head, often. But he wrote Bliss many letters —about the best time to publish *Tom Sawyer*, illustrations, marketing the book, copyright problems. As a director of the company he also advised Bliss on ways to economize and to sell books other than his own. He exchanged letters with Moncure Conway, his representative in London, and with Baron Tauchnitz, who was publishing *Tom Sawyer* for continental distribution. When a Canadian firm brought out a pirated edition of "Old Times," he telegraphed the librarian of Congress to ask about his rights. And he wrote letters to Osgood about a copyright infringement.[32]

All these activities—social and business—he carried on with characteristic nervous energy and enthusiasm, but even as energetic a man as he was sometimes found them tiring. About this time, moreover, he had a talk with John Hay which he remembered for years. "A man," Hay told him, "reaches his zenith at forty, the top of the hill. If you have any great undertaking ahead, begin it now. You will never be so capable again." November 30, 1875, Clemens' fortieth birthday, doubtless had even more of an impact upon this sensitive man than the completion of the fourth decade of life has on most people. As DeLancey Ferguson observes: "Hay was wrong . . . but for several years Mark's literary output almost suggested that he was right. The story of the nine years which intervened between the completion of *Tom Sawyer* and the publication of *Huckleberry Finn* . . . is a record of abortive undertakings, half-finished manuscripts and second-best output."[33] This omits, of course, the writing of *The Prince and the Pauper*, of which he had a higher opinion than modern readers, and of *Huck*.

Clemens complained of frustrations in Hartford to Mrs. Fairbanks in April, 1875: "I work *at* work here, but can't accomplish anything worth speaking of. . . . I peg away all the time. I allow myself few privileges, but when one is in the *workaday world*, there's a million interruptions and interferences."[34] Actually, during the past seven months he had managed to write "Old Times on the Mississippi" in Hartford, and he soon completed *Tom Sawyer* there, but he was dissatisfied with his output.

Writing to Mrs. Fairbanks again in June, 1876, he was launched upon gloomy philosophizing by news of the sudden death of Fairbanks' partner, George A. Benedict, and the confinement for insanity of Benedict's son-in-law:

What a curious thing life is. We delve away, through years of hard-ship, wasting toil, despondency; then comes a little butterfly season of wealth, ease, and clustering honors.—Presto! the wife dies, a daughter marries a spendthrift villain, the heir and hope of the house commits suicide, the laurels fade and fall away. Grand result of a hard-fought, successful career and a blameless life. Piles of money, tottering age, and a broken heart. . . . It does seem as if Mr. Bene-dict's case is about the ordinary experience, and must be fairly ex-pected by everybody.

Mrs. Fairbanks' news about the happiness of her son Charles in-spired a brief congratulatory sentence followed immediately by a return to grim brooding:

I rejoice in his happiness and egg him on in his enthusiasms. Let him go it now when he's young! Never mind about that grisly future season when he shall have made a dazzling success and shall sit with folded hands in well-earned ease and look around upon his corpses and mine, and contemplate his daughters and mine in the madhouse, and his sons and mine gone to the devil.

The contrast between youth and old age shows that Clemens in his forty-first year was feeling decrepit. Elsewhere in the letter, perhaps recalling Hay's dismal prophecy, he predicted the end of his literary career: "Two or three years more will see the end of my ability to do acceptable work. . . ." And there was the usual news about his frustrations: "I have written but little lately, be-cause one can *not* work here." [35]

In both letters, though, he spoke of one place where he could work satisfactorily. In the first, "I can write ten chapters in Elmira where I can write one here. . . . I can't succeed except by getting clear out of the world on top of the mountain at Elmira"; in the second, "I mean to write straight along, without losing a day, all the time we are at Elmira. I must do this, or my book will never be finished."

This was Clemens' mood about a month before he started to write *Huckleberry Finn* in his peaceful study high above the dis-tant city of Elmira.

7

QUARRY FARM, SUMMER, 1876

The double-barreled novel lies torpid. I found I could not go on with it. I . . . gave it up a month ago and began another boy's book—more to be at work than anything else. . . . It is Huck Finn's Autobiography—Clemens, letter to William Dean Howells, Elmira, August 9, 1876.

The Clemenses left for Elmira in mid-June, 1876. On two previous springtime trips the stretch from New York had been a harrowing ordeal for Livy. This year, although the travel was by day, Clemens had had the foresight to charter a sleeping car. Livy relaxed in an easy chair. Rosa, the nursemaid, kept Clara, two, and Susie, four, under control. Since the doors were locked, others passengers were prevented from swarming in the aisle, and the train boy—one of Clemens' huge stock of abominations—could not hawk magazines and candy and raise Clemens' temper to its low boiling point. Though smoke and dust whirled through windows, the heat was stifling, and the journey took ten hours, the party arrived in better than average fettle. "Livy shall always go by special car hereafter," Clemens wrote the Warners, "until we bust." [1]

The family made the usual stopover in the Langdon mansion in Elmira, where Olivia's mother lived with her son Charles, his handsome wife, and their children. But the Clemenses soon left for their summer home, beyond the eastern edge of town, where they would stay until early September.

The house and its trim grounds were owned by Theodore Crane and his wife Sue, Olivia's adopted sister, who lived there all year. At first the farm had been called somewhat coyly "Rest-and-Be-Thankful." Before long an abandoned quarry nearby had suggested the less distressing "Quarry Farm."

Distressing or not, the old name expressed Clemens' sentiments during his stay there, for the Farm afforded marvelous relief from Hartford's harassments. Soon he wrote Dr. John Brown about the delightful solitude and characteristically invited him and his family to hurry over from Scotland and interrupt it: "I wish you were here, to spend the summer. . . . We are perched on a hill-top that overlooks a little world of green valleys, shining rivers, sumptuous forests and billowy uplands veiled in the haze of distance. . . . It is the quietest of all quiet places, and we are hermits that eschew caves and live in the sun." The mood endured into August, when he wrote Moncure Conway: "You never have been here, I believe; therefore you don't know what peace and comfort are; and you never *can* know till you come here . . . and spend a week or so with us." [2] And he told Howells, "The farm is perfectly delightful . . . as quiet and peaceful as a South Sea Island."

For a hermitage the Farm was somewhat overpopulated. In addition to the two Cranes and four Clemenses, there were at least six servants and hired hands, and John Lewis, who ran the farm, had a child. Relatives frequently called, and Clemens' friends often took his hearty invitations seriously and spent a few days. Nevertheless, after the frenetic life in Hartford, Clemens found peace there. Crane worked in Elmira; Sue Crane tended her garden; Olivia rested on the shady porch; the youngsters went away and played. No neighbors marched in to chatter. No clubs had to be entertained. There were no formal dinners. Pilgrims and interviewers came infrequently. A portion of the mail stacked up in Hartford.

And at eight or half past eight almost every morning, Clemens went to his study. Clad in a white summer suit and with paper and pads under his arm, the author (so his daughter recalls) "gave a little caper of delight . . . laughed one of his affectionate laughs," then took off "with a quick, short step" in his undulating walk. "One knew that it was good-bye for the day unless something out of the ordinary were to happen." For the Quarry Farm study, unlike the Hartford billiard room, had been established as off limits for both children and adults.[3]

The dark brown peak-roofed octagon house stood on a pile of stone from the old quarry. The few journalists who came for interviews each summer wrote—more fancifully than objectively —that it looked exactly like a steamboat pilothouse. Wild flowers and morning glories around it and ivy climbing its walls did not enhance the resemblance, nor did the twenty uneven stone steps to its door.

Outlooks were good in every direction, but the view through the door and big windows toward the valley was sensational. Past a grassy sweep lay Elmira, five, six, or seven hundred feet below (Clemens' estimates varied) and two and a half miles away. Beyond, notched blue hills receded into the distance. The interior was less attractive. The furnishings were miscellaneous, and Clemens, like many other authors, was not disturbed by disorder: table, fireplace mantel, and floor were stacked with books, letters, manuscripts, tobacco jars, pipes, and boxes of cigars. Amidst this jumble, he wrote in an atmosphere reeking of smoke. "I allow myself the fullest possible marvel of inspiration," he once said; "consequently, I ordinarily smoke fifteen cigars during my five hours' labors, and if my interest reaches the enthusiastic point, I smoke more. I smoke with all my might, and allow no intervals."[4] But hot days, he opened windows, anchored papers with brickbats, and let the winds—usually strong—sweep in and blow away the smoke.

He worked steadily, without a pause for lunch. Though his average was about five hours a working day, when the mood was right he might put in eight or nine hours. A good day, he wrote 3,000 words, a wonderful day, 5,000. Apparently when the horn blew at five o'clock he initially judged his work on the basis of quantity. Later, with the help of Livy and Howells, he would assay its quality. At five, gathering up manuscript pages and pads, he left the study for the day.

As usual Clemens had brought along a trunkful of unfinished manuscripts, hopeful that the tank had refilled and he might continue them. Inexplicably, he had not brought "Old Times on the Mississippi," though he still had plans to augment it into a plump volume.[5] But he may have brought "Captain Stormfield's Visit to Heaven" (not yet so titled) and "Shem's Diary," both started in Buffalo, the latter never completed.[6] He probably brought "The Mysterious Chamber" started in 1875, a Crusoe-like adventure tale of a man cut off from society for twenty years, not on an island but in subterranean passages beneath an old castle. He probably brought other writings that were under way: the previous November he had told Bliss that he expected to have "a bigger book [than *Tom Sawyer*] ready" by the fall of 1876.[7]

This last may have been "the double-barreled novel" which he tried to continue during the first part of the summer. Or the book may have been *The Prince and the Pauper;* this he did not start until more than a year later, but he was making preliminary studies for it. He was, he says, "reading ancient English books with the purpose of saturating myself with archaic English to a degree which would enable me to do plausible imitations of it in a fairly easy and unlabored way." [8]

The study affected two pieces of writing turned out that summer during pauses in writing *Huck*. The language of an extravagant (and flat) burlesque on collecting, "The Canvasser's Story," was archaic and highfalutin. More notorious and more interesting was the sketch, *1601*, subtitled "Conversation, as It Was by the Social Fireside, in the Time of the Tudors."

In one of these old books [said Clemens] I came across a brief conversation which impressed me . . . with the frank indelicacies of speech permissable among ladies and gentlemen in that ancient time. . . . I was immediately full of a desire to practice my archaics, and contrive one of these stirring conversations out of my own head. I thought I would practice on Twichell. . . . So I contrived that meeting of the illustrious personages in Queen Elizabeth's private parlor, and started a most picturesque and lurid and scandalous conversation between them. . . . I bundled it up and mailed it to Twichell in Hartford. . . . And in the fall [on walks] we used to carry that letter along. . . . We used to laugh ourselves lame and sore over the cupbearer's troubles.

Clemens does not identify the book, but I suspect that two songs in a volume published in London in 1719, D'Urfey's *Wit and Mirth,* or *Pills to Purge Melancholy,* I, 28–36, suggested the first part of the conversation. Early in Twain's sketch, the cupbearer reports: "In ye heat of ye talk . . . one did break wind, yielding an exceeding mightie and distressfull stink, whereat all did laugh full sore. . . ." Queen Elizabeth genially asks several present—Lady Alice Dilberry, Lady Margery Boothy, Jonson, Bacon, and Shakespeare—whether they are guilty, then Sir Walter Raleigh proudly claims the credit. Similarly, in "The FART; Famous for its Satyrical Humour in the Reign of Queen Anne," in D'Urfey's collection, in St. James's,

> When at Noon as in State
> The Queen was at Meat,
> And the Princely Dane sat by Her,
> A Fart there was hear'd,
> That the Company scar'd,
> As a gun at their Ears had been fir'd;
> With a hum, hum, hum, hum.

A conversation follows during which several of the company are accused—fat bishops, the late comptroller, a knight of the garter, duchesses—but all plead not guilty; so eventually a yeoman of the guard is blamed. In the sequel, "The Second Part of the FART; Or the Beef-eaters Appeal to Mr. D'Urfey," the yeoman protests his innocence and accuses a young woman, offering precise and specific documentation.

After his opening paragraphs, Twain draws upon numerous other sources for the rest of the conversation, and members of the company cite a few: Montaigne (rather inaccurately), Shakespeare's *Henry IV* and "Venus and Adonis," cited by Shakespeare himself. The company then engages in gossip which Twain could have drawn from any of a number of histories of England.[9]

This "fireside conversation" offers interesting evidence of some of the author's varied reading in this period—reading which, as I shall show, profoundly influenced *Huckleberry Finn.* Does this unpublished *jeu d'esprit* [10] also, as some biographers believe, represent a fierce rebellion against censorship which had bottled up his instincts and kept him from expressing his true genius in published writings? I doubt it. I suggest that, written as it was for masculine readers, it was not, as some critics have believed, a unique phenomenon.

A magazine published between 1831 and 1856 in New York and circulated throughout the country shows that even in that reticent period writers about similar matters were quite frank when writing for men. This was *The Spirit of the Times,* which young Clemens had known and read. Its subtitle—"A Chronicle of the Turf, Agriculture, Field Sports, Literature and the Stage" —though it lists topics which seem heterogeneous at first glance, actually indicates a homogeneous audience, "the sporting fraternity." This group, like its present-day counterpart, was interested in horse races, sports, and the theater.

For this masculine audience, planters, government officials, race-horse owners, professional men, and army officers wrote tales such as were told over port after the ladies had left the dinner table for coffee in the library; lawyers, yarns spun in taverns on the circuit; hunters and fishers, campfire tales. Several prove that among Victorian men broadly humorous stories dealing with bodily functions and sex were not a novelty. Squire Funk, who had been flirting with Jake's wife, is forced by Jake and his gang to drink a great deal of soda water: "He got such a bustin' hug [from Jake] that everything went—all aft was a wreck, I tell ye! . . . There he lay, explosion behind, a bowie-knife before—certain death, staring him in the face, both sides . . ." Elsewhere in the *Spirit,* rip-roaring backwoods frolics, fornications, and adulterous unions are detailed. Even so, Editor William T. Porter often rejected stories because "details were quite too spicy for our columns"; and once he "claimed that he had on hand fifty or more tales that were unprintable but that were going the rounds, hand to hand, of his friends." There is a strong possibility that, as a recent historian of the *Spirit* suggests, the contributors "had two sets of morals, one for public use and another for private, and that Porter was merely aping these gentry by adopting both sets." [11]

After the Civil War, such respected contemporaries of Mark as James Whitcomb Riley, with his poem, "The Old Back-house," Eugene Field, with "When Little Willie Wet the Bed" and "The French Crisis," and Rudyard Kipling, with "The Bastard King of England," wrote literary travesties as improper as *1601*. None of these had married Olivia Langdon or had had his writings censored by her and by Howells. The sketch was hilariously enjoyed by Twichell, David Gray, Dean Sage, Lord Houghton, Charles Erskine Scott Wood, and "a Jewish Rabbi in Albany, a very learned man and an able critic and lover of old-time literatures."

It is rumored that even today men in bars, in offices, in the forest by campfires, and in some parlors tell "good old questionable stories" (as the Connecticut Yankee would call them) similar to *1601* with no sense of frustration or guilt. College students and professors in ivory towers have heard a few. It is no great shock, therefore, to find Professor DeLancey Ferguson saying: "The skit was done in a spirit of good dirty fun for the edification of a few chosen friends, and as such it served its purpose to admiration. . . . Beyond demonstrating that Mark knew all the short and vulgar words, and had a robust man's pleasure in a tale of bawdry, *1601* is of small importance." [12]

Still, *1601* has a relevance to that part of *Huck* written in 1876 which has been overlooked. No one seems to have paid much attention to Twain's revealing (and unusual) discussion of exactly what he considered particularly funny in his sketch. He says that into the mouths of the august group "I put . . . grossnesses not to be found outside of Rabelais, perhaps. I made their stateliest remarks reek with them, and all this was charming . . . delightful, delicious. . . ." This delight in incongruities between gross terms and stately language gains significance when one recalls that the sketch was written within weeks of the time when Twain launched the first great American novel in the vernacular—which, in its own way, exploits similar incongruities between Huck's vulgar speech and statelier styles.

But the charm of this contrast, said Twain, "was as nothing to that which was afforded me by the outraged cupbearer's comments. . . ." Elsewhere he specifies that both he and Twichell laughed "over the cupbearer's troubles." This cupbearer, says he,

> a dried-up old nobleman, was present to take down the talk—not that he wanted to do it but because it was the Queen's desire and he had to. He loathed all these people because they were of offensively low birth, and because they hadn't a thing to recommend them except their incomparable brains. He dutifully set down everything they said, and commented upon their words and their manners with bitter scorn and indignation.

The chief pleasure is in an effect achieved because of the fictional point of view. Twain shows the recognition of the importance of its choice to the sketch.

Thinking back, one realizes that the selection of the narrator had long been an important concern of Twain and basic to his successes. The "Jumping Frog" derived much of its humor from its telling by the completely humorless Simon Wheeler to an equally humorless auditor; in the best scenes in travel books, Twain assumed the role of a simple-minded humorless fellow unaware that he was being ridiculous—"an innocent abroad," a greenhorn "roughing it." In "Old Times" the narrator represented his cub as naïve and simple-minded. Howells, reviewing *Tom Sawyer*, saw as an important merit that "throughout there is scrupulous regard for *the boy's point of view* in reference to his surroundings and himself, which shows how rapidly Mr. Clemens has grown as an artist." [13] Huck was to join a long procession of figures not only in Twain's writings but in American humor, dating from Franklin's Widow Do-Good, who were lacking in humor and some sorts of perception but who nevertheless communicated important insights of their creators. Although critics over the years have observed astonishingly varied aspects in the novel about Huck, those who praised it have consistently commended the choice of its fictional point of view as well as something closely allied—its style. Thus in 1876 a tradition of popular American humor which Twain knew well, his random experiments as a humorist, and his artistic instinct helped him cope with a problem which Henry James would formulate and solve—more complexly, of course—only after much experimentation and careful thought some years later.

Some months before writing *1601* Mark had first thought of the book which was to be *Huckleberry Finn,* and his early concept was not of a plot but of a fictional point of view. In the spring of 1875, in a conversation and two letters, Howells urged the author to let Tom grow up in the as yet unfinished novel about him. Twain had considered this.[14] But on July 5 he wrote Howells: "I have finished the story and didn't take the chap beyond boyhood. . . . I wish you would read the MS . . . some time, and see if you don't really decide that I am right. . . ." He also said that he believed that to do otherwise "would be fatal . . . in any shape but autobiographically—like Gil Blas. I perhaps made a mistake in not writing it in the first person. . . . By and by I shall take a boy of twelve and run him through life (in the first person) but not Tom Sawyer—he would not be a good character for it." The tentative plans then were: The new novel would run its protagonist "through life"; it therefore had to be written in the first person; *Gil Blas* was the model; and he must find a character better suited than Tom. Subject matter would determine the fictional point of view, and the angle of narration would determine the character of the narrator. Perhaps he saw that more of a picaro than Tom was required.

Howells had read the manuscript of *Tom Sawyer* in November, sitting up until one o'clock because he could not lay it down unfinished. One of his comments was, "I don't seem to think I like that last chapter. I believe I would cut that." [15] By this time, in the course of "a thorough and painstaking revision"—perhaps because of that revision—Mark had apparently discarded a belief, expressed in his letter of June 21, that the book had no plot and therefore might drift anywhere. For now he wrote: "As to that last chapter, I think of just leaving it off and adding nothing in its place. Something told me that the book was done when I got to that point—and so the strong temptation to put Huck's life at the Widow's in detail, instead of generalizing it in a paragraph was resisted." As DeVoto notes, this is puzzling, since the last chapter in the book gives much more than a paragraph to Huck's life at the widow's. There is no problem, though, if the reference was to a different concluding chapter which was discarded. This guess is supported by the fact that "in the amanuensis copy which was sent to England for publication the last page is in Mark's hand-writing. . . ." [16] And the first chapter of *Huck* detailing Huck's life at the widow's probably was a reworking of the chapter removed from *Tom Sawyer.*

Tom Sawyer was much on its author's mind that summer. Chapter proofs followed him to the Farm.[17] In August he acknowledged receipt of copies of the British edition and mentioned at least partially dramatizing the book.[18] Because he had this interest in *Tom,* and because the new book was a sequel, the new book contained the numerous echoes which I have discussed.

"The double-barreled novel" having played out, Twain began *Huck* early in July. A month later he reported, "I have written 400 pages on it—therefore it is half done. . . . I like it only tolerably well, so far as I have got, and may possibly pigeonhole or burn the MS when it is done. He overestimated his accomplishment: he had completed only about a fourth of the published novel. About the same time, he made the sanguine guess that he would "finish it in 6 working weeks." [19] Actually he pigeonholed it for about three years before going back to it again, and he did not finish it until seven years later.

8

HARTFORD, HANNIBAL, AND *HUCK*

The Widow Douglas, she took me for her son, and allowed she would sivilize me, but it was rough living in the house all the time, considering how dismal regular and decent the widow was in all her ways; and so when I couldn't stand it no longer I lit out.—Adventures of Huckleberry Finn, *chapter i.*

The portion of the new novel written during the summer of 1876 [1] starts a little before the point where *Tom Sawyer* ends, with Huck's rebelling against being civilized and Tom's instructing him on robber gang etiquette absorbed from romances. The boys organize their gang and start to play at being robbers. Literal-minded Huck finds this unsatisfactory: "We hadn't robbed nobody, we hadn't killed any people, but only just pretended." He resigns. So far (through chapter iii) rewriting and probably elaborating discarded material from *Tom Sawyer* carried Twain. He enjoyed ridiculing the unlifelike trappings of romance. He also enjoyed letting Huck specify the tortures of being housebroken, which paralleled his own recent tribulations:

She put me in them new clothes again, and I couldn't do nothing but sweat and sweat, and felt all cramped up. . . . The widow rung a bell for supper, and you had to come to time . . . you couldn't go right to eating, but you had to wait for the widow to tuck down her

head and grumble a little over the victuals. . . . Pretty soon I wanted
to smoke, and asked the widow to let me. But she wouldn't. . . . Her
sister, Miss Watson, . . . took a set at me with a spelling-book. . . .
I was fidgety. Miss Watson would say, "Don't put your feet up there,
Huckleberry"; and "don't scrunch up like that, Huckleberry—set up
straight". . . . Then she told me all about the bad place, and I said I
wished I was there. (chapter i)

But the book does not hit its best pace until chapter iv. There,
in accordance with Huck's prediction in *Tom Sawyer*, Pap Finn
shows up and makes trouble. Jim is consulted and, helped by a
magic hairball, makes ambiguous prophecies. The sentimental
judge makes his futile attempt to reform old Finn. When, in
chapter vi, Pap kidnaps Huck and takes him to a hut on the Illinois
shore to live, the boy voices attitudes like those of his creator on
escaping from Hartford to the solitude of Quarry Farm:

It was kind of lazy and jolly, laying off comfortable all day, smoking
and fishing, and no books nor study. . . . I didn't see how I'd ever got
to like it so well at the widow's, where you had to wash, and eat on a
plate, and . . . get up regular, and . . . have old Miss Watson peck-
ing at you all the time. . . . I had stopped cussing, because the widow
didn't like it; but now I took to it again because pap hadn't no objections. It was pretty good times up in the woods there, take it all
around.

The note of contentment is repeated in chapter ix when Huck
has escaped to Jackson's Island and has met Jim, who also has
escaped: " 'Jim, this is nice,' I says. 'I wouldn't want to be nowhere else but here. Pass me along another hunk of fish and some
hot cornbread.' " In chapter xi Huck's talk with shrewd Judith
Loftus warns that pursuers of Jim will soon come to the island,
and the journey downstream begins: "Then we got out the raft
and slipped along down in the shade, past the foot of the island
dead still, never saying a word."

During the journey, days spent on the uninhabited willow
banks are wonderfully peaceful:

We had mountains on the Missouri shore and heavy timber on the
Illinois side, and the channel was down the Missouri shore . . . so we

warn't afraid of anybody running across us. We laid there all day and watched the rafts and up-bound steamboats fight the big river. . . . Mornings, before daylight, I slipped into corn fields and borrowed a watermelon, or a mushmelon, or a punkin. . . . We shot a water-fowl, now and then. . . . Take it all around, we lived pretty high. (chapter xii)

TOM AND HUCK IN *Tom Sawyer,* FINAL CHAPTER

And nights of solitude on the wide river are just as fine:

We catched fish, and talked, and we took a swim now and then to keep off sleepiness. It was kind of solemn, drifting down the big still river, laying on our backs looking up at the stars, and we didn't ever feel like talking loud, and it warn't often that we laughed, only a little kind of low chuckle. We had mighty good weather as a general thing, and nothing ever happened to us at all, that night, nor the next, nor the next. (chapter xii)

Memories of piloting days supplied details in such passages, but the mood, I believe, owed much to the author's situation and feelings in the summer of 1876, when he had fled to the rural solitude and quiet of Quarry Farm.

Huck and Jim plan to go to Cairo, sell the raft, and take a steamboat up the Ohio to the free states. They have no truck with anyone along the river until they begin to wonder when they will reach Cairo. In chapter xvi, Huck swims out, boards a raft, hides there, and eavesdrops on the talk of the raftsmen in hope that they will reveal how near the town is. (This passage was excised later.) When some men looking for runaway slaves come along, Huck lies to them, and they go away—and he asks a man in a skiff about Cairo. For the rest he and Jim are alone during this long stretch. Mark is granting the runaways the solitude he himself is enjoying. A little later, the raft is run down by a steamboat. At this point, apparently, the summer's work ended.

Shaped though it was by the author's situation at the time, like *Tom Sawyer*, this narrative had sources in his memories of his Hannibal boyhood and his piloting days. In his *Autobiography* he says: ". . . 'Huckleberry Finn' was Tom Blankenship . . . exactly as he was . . . ignorant, unwashed, insufficiently fed, but he had as good a heart as ever any boy had. His liberties were totally unrestricted. He was the only really independent person boy or man—in the community, and by consequence he was tranquilly and continually happy. . . ." The sketch is of Huck, only slightly revised from actuality, as he is in *Tom Sawyer* and in the first three chapters of the sequel: his age is unspecified,[2] and he hovers between childhood and adolescence. But at points in these chapters and from chapter iv onward, he ages perceptibly into an adolescent "thirteen or fourteen, or along there." [3] He is a youth who has been educated while shifting for himself in a rough world. He has acquired a knowledge of human frailty and, even more impressive, tolerance toward it. He says (anachronistically) that in *Tom Sawyer* "There were things which [Mr. Mark Twain] stretched, but mainly he told the truth. . . . I never seen anybody but lied one time or another. . . ." The widow prohibits his smoking—"and she took snuff, too; of course that was all right, because she done it herself." His understanding will make possible his getting along in many different situations. Living in a house and attending school, "I liked the old ways best, but I was getting so I liked the new ones, too, a little bit." Staying in an old shack with Pap he decides, "It was pretty good there. . . ."

Huck's experiences have helped him, also, to learn how to handle people. Sometimes he tricks them. Sometimes he lies to them with inventiveness born of long practice and awareness of human foibles. But when his tolerance plays out and lies or trickery no longer work, he does the only thing left for an outcast too weak to fight: he runs away. Twain had indicated the formula when, in the last chapter of *Tom Sawyer*, Huck escaped from the widow and had domiciled in a hogshead near the slaughterhouse. Huck summarizes it in the second paragraph of the new book: "so when I couldn't stand it no longer I lit out." In *Tom*, this had been the pattern of an incident; in *Huck*, it is a repeated sequence which carries the ragamuffin from St. Petersburg deep into the South. This pattern was a sign of Twain's modifying the character of Tom Blankenship, if his description of him in the *Autobiography* is accurate. Huck's liberties are not "totally unrestricted": he runs away because they are intolerably curtailed.

Nor is he "continually happy." One reason is that as the story progresses Mark tends to identify himself with his hero. This starts in chapter i, when Huck describes the nighttime world:

The stars was shining, and the leaves rustled in the woods ever so mournful; and I heard an owl, away off, who-whooing about somebody that was dead, and a dog crying about somebody that was going to die; and the wind was trying to whisper something to me and I couldn't make out what it was, and so it made the cold shivers run over me. Then away out in the woods I heard that kind of a sound that a ghost makes when it wants to tell about something that's on its mind and can't make itself understood, and so can't rest easy in its grave and has to go about that way every night grieving.

The details are similar to those "Mr. Mark Twain" uses in describing night scenes in chapter ix of *Tom Sawyer*, proof sheets of which he was reading in 1876:

By and by, out of the stillness, little, scarcely perceptible noises began to emphasize themselves. The hooting of a distant owl was all the sound that troubled the dead stillness . . . then the howl of a far off dog rose in the night air, and was answered by a fainter howl from a remoter distance. . . . A faint wind moaned through the trees, and Tom feared that it might be the spirits of the dead, complaining at being disturbed.[4]

Huck's passage is in character, since he is a storehouse of superstitious lore; but the parallel passage suggests that he has been endowed with poetic sensitivity pretty certainly borrowed from the man writing about him rather than from his prototype. The change is useful since it enables Huck here and elsewhere to infuse vividness and emotion into his descriptions and since his reactions help make him a sympathetic character for readers who consider sensitivity to nature's beauties admirable.

Such sensitivity, moreover, is associated with a trait—also newly acquired—which Huck manifests in chapter iii. He tells of his feelings after he gets his clothes soiled: "the widow she didn't scold, but only cleaned off the grease and clay, and looked so sorry that I thought I would behave for a while if I could." Again, in chapter xv, Huck tricks Jim and finds that he has hurt Jim's feelings: "It made me feel . . . mean. . . ." In *Tom Sawyer*, Tom had been the one who had agonies of conscience: Huck had had little trouble of this sort. The author, always a sufferer from an overactive conscience himself, endows his new protagonist with this attribute, thus making Huck more like himself, more complex and more sympathetic.

HUCK AS PICTURED
IN *Tom Sawyer*

In contrast with the more mature and complex Huck, Tom has sloughed off maturity and has become a simpler character. In the opening chapters (as he is to be in the closing ones) he is still mischievous, ingenious, and eager for adventures with "style" to them. He is no longer bedeviled, however, by an ulcerated conscience. The one sign of his maturing—if it is a sign—is his enlarged activity as a reader: now his outstanding tendency is to read books and, as before, to imitate them. This, incidentally, is not a trait of any of the boyish models for Tom; so, in endowing him with it, Twain is modifying reality.

Twain also modifies the prototype of Huck's mentor, Widow Douglas. This was Mrs. Richard Holliday, concerning whom he was to make this entry in "Villagers of 1840–3": *"Mrs. Holiday. Was a MacDonald, born Scotch. Wore her father's ivory miniature —a British General in the Revolution. Lived on Holiday's Hill. Well off. Hospitable. Fond of having young people. Old, but anxious to marry. Always consulting fortune-tellers; always managed to make them understand that she had been promised three husbands by the first fraud."* [5] The specific ancestry, the hospitality (mentioned in *Tom Sawyer*), the enthusiasm for fortune-tellers, and the hope for a husband (with its time-hallowed comic potentialities) Twain has omitted. The widow becomes simply a well-to-do pious and goodhearted woman bent on civilizing Huck.

In chapter i Twain gives the widow a sister, Miss Watson, a skinny spinster. Her Hannibal prototype evidently had been Mary Ann Newcomb, a teacher who frequently visited Sam's family. Only a few of many details which he must have remembered about Miss Newcomb are used. She was thin: "you could not tell her breast from her back if she had her head up a stovepipe hole," he said of her elsewhere, and "a Calvinist, devoutly pious." [6] In the novel she shows her Calvinism by stressing the penalties of sin more than the rewards of virtue; she is a harsher oppressor of Huck than the widow is; and she causes Jim to run away by planning to sell him down the river.

In chapter ii, as Huck and Tom sneak away from the widow's for a meeting with Tom's robber gang they see Jim sitting by the

kitchen door asleep and stop to play a trick on him. Jim's prototype was Uncle Dan'l, a slave on the Quarles farm near Florida,
Missouri, which Sam as a boy had visited often. Long after, the
author claimed that in Jim he accurately copied this "faithful and
affectionate good friend, ally, and adviser . . . a middle-aged
slave whose head was the best one in the negro quarter, whose
sympathies were wide and warm, and whose heart was simple
and knew no guile." The claim may be justifiable, but two bits
of information about Uncle Dan'l raise doubts. "His occasional
lockjaw," says Paine, "gave him an unusual distinction"; and
Mark recalled that in his kitchen, "on privileged nights," Uncle
Dan'l told "white and black children grouped on the hearth . . .
the immortal tales which Uncle Remus Harris was to . . . charm
the world with, by and by. . . ." Jim escapes lockjaw and the
dubious distinction accompanying it. And in place of Uncle
Dan'l's acquaintance with folk tales, Jim has been gifted with a
similar knowledge of superstitions. Moreover, Mark invests Jim
with great dignity and courage which, I suspect, went beyond
those that Jim's prototype had a chance to display. But for what
it is worth, we have the author's claim—which cannot be checked
objectively—that Jim was an accurate copy from life.

The prototype of Pap Finn was one Jimmy Finn, who shared
the office of Hannibal's town drunkard with "Gineral" Gaines,
and in time succeeded him. Jimmy died a few weeks before Sam's
tenth birthday, but Twain's memory as of 1877 was, "He was a
monument of rags and dirt; he was the profanest man in town;
he had bleary eyes, and a nose like a mildewed cauliflower; he
slept with the hogs in an abandoned tan-yard." [7] Compare Huck's
description in chapter v:

He was most fifty, and he looked it. His hair was long and tangled
and greasy, and hung down, and you could see his eyes shining through
like he was behind vines. It was all black, no gray; so was his long,
mixed-up whiskers. There warn't no color in his face, where his face
showed; it was white; not like another man's white, but a white
to make a body sick, a white to make a body's flesh crawl—a tree-
toad white, a fish-belly white. As for his clothes—just rags, that
was all.

Gone the bleary eyes, the cauliflower nose: this is a picture in the dead colors, black and white—and the white is made repulsive by comparisons with cold-blooded tree-toads and a dead fish floating belly upward. Pap is made much less likable than his somewhat amusing counterparts were. Soon he is to champion attitudes appropriate for such a loathsome character—self-pity, sentimentality, hatred for learning, and racial prejudices.

Incidents as well as characters in the portion of *Huck* first written come from memories of Hannibal in the 1840's

HANNIBAL'S TOWN DRUNKARD
AS PICTURED
IN *Life on the Mississippi*

PAP FINN AS PICTURED IN *Huckleberry Finn*

and 1850's. In chapters ii and iii Tom, Huck, and other boys meet in a cave and plan careers as robbers. A playmate of Sam's recalls that in an old limestone cave, "we often sat . . . and discussed what we could do were we a gang of thieves with a cave as our headquarters." [8] In chapter iii Huck tells of Miss Watson's claim that if he prays every day,

. . . whatever I asked for, I would get it. But it warn't so. I tried it. Once I got a fish-line, but no hooks. I tried for the hooks three or four

times, but somehow I couldn't make it work. . . . I set down, one
time, back in the woods, and had a long think about it. I says to myself,
if a body can get anything they pray for, why don't Deacon Winn get
back the money he lost on pork? Why can't the widow get back her
snuff-box that was stole? Why can't Miss Watson fatten up? No, says
I to myself, there ain't nothing in it.

Decades ago, in her Hannibal school, Mrs. Horr had expounded
the text, "Ask and ye shall receive." Impressed, young Sam had
tried his luck at praying for some gingerbread which the baker's
daughter had brought:

When I finished my prayer and glanced up, [writes Twain] there it
was in easy reach . . . and I was a convert. . . . I had no end of
wants and they had always remained unsatisfied . . . , but I meant to
supply them and extend them. . . .
But this dream was like almost all . . . other . . . dreams . . . ,
there was nothing in it. I did as much praying during the next two
or three days as any one in that town . . . but nothing came of it.

Again, he tells that his father, as a "spasmodic" reformer, once
tried to reform Jimmy Finn, once, Injun Joe, but failed in both
attempts—this is the basis, as has been noticed, for the passage in
chapter v involving Pap Finn and the sentimental judge.

Much more important, the author was indebted to a memory of
Hannibal for a continuing line of action and some of his most
memorable passages. Tom Blankenship had had an older brother,
Benson, nicknamed Bence, a fisherman. In 1846 Bence had helped
a runaway slave hide on Sny Island across the river from Hannibal, and for several weeks had taken him food. Not only was this
illegal;[9] it was immoral according to Hannibal standards, and it
represented a financial sacrifice since Bence might have collected
a fifty-dollar reward for turning the man in. Out of this incident
grew Huck's promise in chapter viii: "I said I wouldn't [tell],
and I'll stick to it. . . . People would call me a low-down Abolitionist and despise me for keeping mum—but that don't make no
difference." Out of it, too, grew the account of Huck's sharing his
food with Jim and journeying downstream with him, despite
terrific battles with his conscience along the way.

Huck's belief that helping Jim escape is evil was based upon a memory of Hannibal mores. In 1841, when Sam was about six, his father had served on a jury about which R. J. Holcomb tells in his *History of Marion County, Missouri.* On trial were three abolitionists from Quincy, Illinois, who had "tried to induce three negroes to leave and go with them to Illinois and thence to Canada and freedom." The slaves had helped capture their would-be rescuers, and although Negroes were not then allowed to testify against white men, the judge overlooked this little legal technicality. Great crowds attended the trial and at times "threatened to take the prisoners out and hang them." When John Clemens and his fellow jurymen quickly brought in a verdict of guilty, "there was considerable applause," and Judge McBride sentenced each offender to twelve years at hard labor. The good people of Palmyra took up a subscription to reward the slaves—$20.62½. "Kind-hearted and compassionate" though Sam's mother was, he said, he believed that she never questioned the morality of slavery:

She had never heard it assailed in any pulpit, but had heard it defended and sanctified in a thousand; her ears were familiar with Bible texts that approved it, but if there were any that disapproved it they had not been quoted by her pastors; as far as her experience went, the wise and the good and the holy were unanimous in the conviction that slavery was right, righteous, sacred, the peculiar pet of the Deity, and a condition which the slave himself ought to be daily and nightly thankful for.

"Manifestly," Clemens concludes, "training and association can accomplish strange miracles."

9

THE LITERARY FLUX

The reference to Bret Harte reminds me that I often ac-
cuse him of being a deliberate imitator of Dickens; and
this in turn reminds me that I have charged unconscious
plagiarism upon Charley Warner; and this in turn re-
minds me that I have been delighting my soul for two
weeks over a brand new and ingenious way of beginning
a novel—and behold, all at once it flashes upon me that
Charley Warner *originated the idea 3 years ago and told*
me about it! Aha! So much for self-righteousness! . . .
I would not wonder if I am the worst literary thief in
the world, without knowing it.—Clemens to William
Dean Howells, November 23, 1875.

Harriet Beecher Stowe, a next-door neighbor of the Clemenses in
Hartford, in 1859 explained that in her book, *The Minister's Woo-*
ing, she dwelt "in the pleasant valley of childhood because, looking back on it from the extreme end of life [she was forty-eight],
it seems to my weary eyes so fresh and beautiful, the dew of the
morning lies on it; the dew which no coming day will restore."
In 1869 in *Oldtown Folks,* Mrs. Stowe pictured "the loafer and
ne'er-do-well philosopher, Sam Lawson, . . . not only a symbol
of the obdurate handful who refused to accept the community
fetish of unremitting industry, but a delightful gratuity as an individual." [1] In 1871 she featured Sam as a teller of yarns in dialect

in *Sam Lawson's Fireside Stories*—among them one about a ram that upset a meeting and one about seekers (like Tom and Huck) of buried treasure. In 1878 she published *Poganuc People,* an elegaic evocation of her maturing from girlhood in Litchfield, Connecticut. Charles Dudley Warner, another neighbor and an erstwhile collaborator and a close friend of Clemens, in 1878 published *Being A Boy,* simply but poetically recounting how a boy had grown up on a New England farm in the 1830's and 1840's —working and playing out of doors, attending church and school.

Warner's and Mrs. Stowe's recollections of childhood obviously resemble Twain's writings. But though these neighbors knew one another's books, something other than specific influence was involved. These were professional writers whose careers depended upon knowing and satisfying public taste. They studied the market, scanned royalty returns, and wrote for an audience which they hoped would be large. The humorist, on the board of a prosperous publishing firm, knew how its books were doing. He bought current magazines and books, chest-high shelves of his library housed many of these publications, and he read them.

It was not an accident that *Huck Finn* would—like *Innocents, Roughing It,* "Old Times," and *Tom Sawyer*—appeal to a wide public taste. When Twain started his new story which was to carry its chief character deep into the South, local-color fiction about that section, long popular below the Mason-Dixon line, was beginning to attract attention in the North. By the time *Huck* was published, such fiction was more popular nationally, it is probable, than any other brand.

The Civil War had kindled Northern interest in the South. In the 1870's books by Southern humorists who had pictured their section realistically and amusingly before the conflict were republished, and they found audiences—W. T. Thompson's *Major Jones* (1872), Joseph G. Baldwin's *Flush Times in Alabama and Mississippi* (1876), Richard Malcolm Johnston's *Dukesborough Tales* (1871 and 1874). George Washington Harris's *Sut Lovingood,* in which prewar Tennessee tales in mountaineer dialect were collected, was published in 1867 and continued in print beyond the end of the century.

And new Southern writers were appearing. As early as 1867, Sidney Lanier of Georgia published his Southern novel, *Tiger-Lilies;* in 1871 he published Negro dialect poems. Between April, 1874, and April, 1876, George W. Cable of New Orleans published five stories in *Scribner's* and one in *Appleton's Journal* destined to be collected in *Old Creole Days* in 1879. Irwin Russell of Mississippi published the first of his Negro dialect poems in the *Atlantic* for January, 1876. Within the next few years Joel Chandler Harris, Thomas Nelson Page, Mary Noailles Murfree, Grace King, and James Lane Allen, Southerners all, as well as several temporary Southern local colorists such as Constance F. Woolson, all but took over the popular magazines.[2] Southern soil proved well adapted to regional writings: distinctive provincial types flourished there, and troubles in the Reconstruction era made particularly attractive the misty days "befo' the wah." [3]

Bret Harte, once Clemens' associate in the West and still an acquaintance, whose sketches of fractious school children may have been in the humorist's mind when he wrote parts of *Tom Sawyer,* had helped popularize the South even in his tremendously popular Western stories. Many of Harte's favorite characters were Southerners.

Harte, too, had prepared the way for Huckleberry Finn as a leading character. Although he probably took his cue from Charles Dickens, who had been for decades an American favorite, Harte had created a stir from the start by portraying gamblers, thieves, drunkards, and whores sympathetically—and he had made such picturings popular. Twain, eager for acceptance by the literary elite, hardly would have ventured to make Huck the center of a novel if the trail had not been broken by Harte. "Harte shows us the good in the heart of the outcast," as a character observed in a story by Miss Woolson, one of many imitators. Twain's entry in a notebook kept during 1879 shows his awareness of this foible of Harte's characters when he has them meet and say: "We have been the filthiest lot of heartless villains. . . . he hands out (no, not that)—he *manufactures* the one good deed possible to each of us. . . . We owe Harte a deep debt of gratitude—the reverence in which we gamblers, burglars and whores are held in the upper classes today is all due to him, and to him only—for the dime novel circulates only among the lower classes." And a later entry in the notebook, on August 31, 1879, reads, "Harte's saintly wh's and self-sacrificing sons of b's." [4] Growl though he might at such characters, in the new novel Twain was to do a similar thing, though more richly, showing the good in the hearts of a white-trash boy and his lowly companion, an escaped slave.

Mark's choice of Huck as a protagonist marks an interesting progression in the characters of his novels which Harte may have encouraged—the respectable promoter Colonel Sellers in *The Gilded Age*, then the mischievous and amoral but eventually respectable Tom Sawyer, now the river-rat outcast. As the author himself sloughed off reforms, characters in his novels descended the scale of respectability. Yet Livy, who continued to love her husband, apparently would cotton to Huck, too: a few years later, she called him, affectionately, "dear old Huck." [5]

Harte, tracing the development of the short story in America, held that he and his contemporaries in the local-color school broke away from English influences because of the example of American humorists, especially the tellers of anecdotes. In bar-rooms, country stores, political gatherings, he said, anecdotes flourished. At first transmitted orally, the humorous anecdote later was imitated and published by sundry writers:

Crude at first, it received a literary polish in the press, but its dominant quality remained. It was concise and condensed, yet suggestive . . . delightfully extravagant, or a miracle of understatement. It voiced not only the dialect but the habits of thought of a people or locality. . . . it admitted no fine writing or affectation of style. . . . It was burdened by no conscientiousness; it was often irreverent; it was devoid of all moral responsibility.[6]

Though Harte oversimplified, he was right in indicating that the regional humorists of New England (e.g., Shillaber) and of the old Southwest (e.g., Thompson, Baldwin, G. W. Harris) before the Civil War helped the postwar local colorists find ways to picture regional life.

As a youth, Clemens had known such sub-literature better than

Harte did (it will be recalled that he echoes it in *Tom Sawyer*) and while writing *Huck* he remembered much of it in detail. In a passage of 1876 he shows indebtedness to one of the most persistent traditions in the humor of the old Southwest.

Huck, wondering how far he and Jim are from Cairo, swims out to a raft, hides, and listens to the talk of the raftsmen, hoping for a clue. Shortly there is a pattern of action like that in scores of scenes in the older humor. Their anger heated by corn likker (frontiersmen and boatmen had always been pictured as prodigious drinkers), two men make ready for a rough-and-tumble fight. According to ritual of old-time humor, before they fight they engage in wordy preliminaries. Each in turn swaggers around, flapping his arms or leaping into the air, all the while boasting at length about his prowess. Many humorists had used much imagination dreaming up such boasts.[7] In 1842 T. B. Thorpe had had Mike Fink, bully boy of the keelboatmen, shout:

"Well, I walk tall into varmint and Indian, . . . comes as natural as grinning to a hyena. I'm a regular tornado, tough as a hickory withe, long winded as a nor'-wester. I can strike a blow like a falling tree, and every lick makes a gap in the crowd that lets in an acre of sunshine. . . . Whew, boys," shouted Mike, twirling his rifle like a walking stick around his head   "If the Choctaw devils in them ar woods, thar, would give us a brush, just as I feel now, I'd call them gentlemen. I must fight something, or I'll catch the dry rot, burnt brandy won't save me."[8]

Young Sam Clemens had heard Hannibal's leading drunkard, General Gaines, compose similar challenges;[9] he had heard of Mike Fink's celebrated boasts;[10] and he must have encountered many similar flights of fancy in Southwestern humor. Recalling such models the author wrote two wonderfully imaginative boasts, one of which goes, in part:

"Whoo-oop! bow your neck and spread, for the kingdom of sorrow's a-coming! Hold me down to earth, for I feel my powers a-working! whoo-oop! I'm a child of sin, *don't* let me get a start! . . . When I'm playful I use the meridians of longitude and parallels of latitude for a seine, and drag the Atlantic Ocean for whales! I scratch my head with lightning and purr myself to sleep with the thunder! . . . The massacre of isolated communities is the pastime of my idle moments, the destruction of nationalities the serious business of my life! . . ." He jumped up and cracked his heels three times before he lit . . . and as he come down he shouted out: "Whoo-oop! bow your neck and spread, for the Pet Child of Calamity's a-coming!" [11]

SWAGGERING RAFTSMAN IN
Life on the Mississippi

Instead of recounting the fight in gory detail, as his predecessors had, Twain had both his combatants back out, whereupon "a little black-whiskered chap" wallops both of them. But up to that point the episode is completely in a tradition as old as our native humor.

A bit later, the raftsmen tell some tall tales. Like boasts and fights, such tales had long been standard stuff in our humor, especially in the old Southwest. Yarns about the poorness or the fertility of the soil had been told by the hundreds. In his most famous story, "The Big Bear of Arkansas," T. B. Thorpe had Jim Doggett brag about soil on his farm at Shirt-tail Bend on the Mississippi:

I once planted in these diggins a few potatoes and beets; they took a fine start. . . . I went off to old Kentucky on business, and . . . in three months, when I accidentally stumbled on a fellow who had stopped at my place. . . . "How do you like things?" said I. "Pretty well," said he, ". . . but that bottom land ain't worth the first cent. . . . it's full of cedar stumps and Indian mounds . . . and it can't be cleared." "Lord," said I, "them ar 'cedar stumps' is beets, and them ar 'Indian mounds' is tater hills." [12]

There was a similar tradition about the healthfulness of muddy Mississippi water. Dickens in *American Notes* (1842) said, "It is considered wholesome by the natives, and is something more opaque than gruel." Alex MacKay in his book *Western World* (1850) wrote, "The Mississippi water, turgid though it be, is not considered unwholesome, and those long accustomed to it prefer it to any other." [13] Recalling such lore, Twain has a boatman offer proof of the nutritiousness of the river water: "You look at the graveyards, that tells the tale. Trees won't grow worth shucks in a Cincinnati graveyard, but in a Sent Louis graveyard they grow upwards of eight hundred feet high. It's all on account of the water the people drunk before they laid up. A Cincinnati corpse don't richen soil any." Huck finally hears and records another tall tale, a ghost story in an old pattern. The lore which the author had learned in boyhood and the reading he had since engaged in were echoed in *Huck*.

His debts in 1876 to humorists of the prewar period, like his debts to local-color writers, were general. He was also indebted in a number of passages to specific writers.

Tom Sawyer's parade of authorities on robber gang etiquette in chapters ii and iii testifies to both Tom's and Twain's memories of fairly broad reading. Tom starts his band by having members sign solemn oaths after models provided by Carlyle in his *History of the French Revolution,* a favorite book since Clemens had discovered it in 1871.[14] The charming notion that when a boy was a traitor he would have a cross hacked on his breast was suggested by a popular romantic novel of 1837 about the frontier, Robert Montgomery Bird's *Nick of the Woods.*[15] Probably the humorist had both Carlyle's history and Dickens' *Tale of Two Cities* in mind when he had a boy suggest that "it would be good to kill the *families* of boys who told secrets." When Tom sends a boy "to run about town with a blazing stick . . . the sign for the gang to get together," his model is a poem inflicted upon schoolboys

for generations, Scott's *Lady of the Lake*. Shortly after this cere-
mony, Tom discusses genies and magic lamps in *The Arabian
Nights*.

Reading burlesqued in these passages is common enough, but
Tom cites rather more esoteric reading to justify one adventure of
the gang. Told by Tom that his spies have learned that many
Spanish merchants and "A-rabs" will camp in Cave Hollow with
elephants, mules, and camels, all loaded with diamonds, the boys
rush down the hill. To Huck's disgust the victims are nothing but
a Sunday-school class:

I didn't see no di'monds, and I told Tom Sawyer so. He said there was
loads of them . . . A-rabs there, too, and elephants and things. I said,
why couldn't we see them, then? He said if I warn't so ignorant, but
had read a book called "Don Quixote," I would know without asking.
. . . enemies which he called magicians . . . had turned the whole
thing into an infant Sunday school, just out of spite.

Back in 1860 Clemens had read Cervantes' book; he mentioned
reading it in a letter of 1869; he commented upon certain "Quixotic" actions of the pilgrims in *Innocents Abroad;* in *The Gilded
Age* in 1873 he created a character, Colonel Sellers, with traits
patently based upon those of the Don. Moreover, as Professor
Olin Harris Moore has shown, this episode is based upon chapters
xviii and xix of Part II of *Don Quixote of La Mancha.*[16]

Though the incident, like others in chapters ii and iii of *Huck,*
is of interest as an indication of the author's reading and a way
he used the reading when writing, it has another value. The most
important trait of Tom in this novel—his love of books and his
imitation of them—is established. Between 1877 and the beginning of 1879, Twain pictured, in his unfinished novel about Simon
Wheeler (now in the Berg Collection, New York Public Library),
a character who had this trait of Tom, and Twain compared him,
specifically, with Cervantes' hero. This character, said Twain, read
books about his heroes

and accepted them as actual truth. To him these detective heroes were
actualities; and in time their names and their performances came to
be quoted and referred to by him with the facility and the loving faith

with which scholars quote the great names and reveal the great deeds of history. He was another Don Quixote, and his library of shams as honored, as valid, and as faithfully studied and believed as the Don's.[17]

Huck's literal-mindedness and common sense are underlined. The relationship between the boys was suggested by *Don Quixote* (or possibly one of many imitations): in Cervantes' book, Quixote is driven to imitate heroes of romances which he has read despite objections by his unread squire Sancho Panza. As Professor Moore says:

The humor of the romance lies in the contrast between the matter of fact philosophy of Sancho Panza and the romantic spirit of Don Quixote. Usually Sancho Panza tries to dissuade his companion from acts of folly. The hero replies that things must be done according to the books.

For the man Don Quixote Mark Twain substitutes the boy Tom Sawyer. . . . Twain makes of Huck a sort of Sancho Panza, who attempts by commonplace reasoning to put a damper on the fancies of his Quixotic playmate.

Although the formula was useful in only two chapters of the 1876 portion of *Huck*, Twain later would use it in other chapters.

The study of Twain's indebtedness in these two chapters, however, reveals far less about him as a writer than a study of his indebtedness in more lifelike—more realistic—episodes ordinarily does.[18] The reason is that in such episodes his reshaping of the material so that it fits into the novel shows his skill as a writer.

The story of one very important literary influence on *Huck* not heretofore noticed had begun in the spring of 1875. The humorist got to thinking of his old friend William Wright—pen name, Dan De Quille. In 1862 Clemens had taken his first job as a reporter on the Virgina City, Nevada, *Territorial Enterprise* as a replacement for Wright, when the latter had gone East on vacation. On Wright's return, the two became close friends as fellow reporters, rooming together, imbibing together, and taking humorous cracks at one another in the *Enterprise*. After going East, Clemens frequently exchanged letters with Wright.[19]

Clemens' memory of what he called "the oddest thing that ever happened to him" was as follows. On March 2 it occurred to him that his friend ought to write a book, forthwith, about the wonderful Comstock Lode of Nevada and its picturesque history. He penned a letter suggesting the idea and outlining an organization. He put it aside. On March 9 he received a letter addressed in Wright's handwriting. Before opening it he said to a visiting relative, "I will tell you everything this letter contains. . . . It is from a Mr. Wright . . . and is dated the 2d of March. . . . Mr. Wright proposes to make a book about the silver-mines, and the Great Bonanza. . . . He says his subjects are so and so, their order and sequence so and so. . . ." When he opened the letter it justified his prediction. His explanation was that the phenomenon of "mental telegraphy"—one which was to interest him for years—had occurred.[20]

Late that month Clemens sent Wright a letter:

Drop your reporting and come here right away. . . . Here you shall stop at the best hotel, and every morning I will walk down, meet you half way, bring you to my house and we will grind literature all day long in the same room. . . . When it comes to building a book, I can show you a trick or two. . . . Bring along *lots of dry statistics*—it's the very best sauce a humorous book can have. Ingeniously used, they just make a reader smack his chops in gratitude. . . . We shall get up a book that children will cry for. . . .

Now you pack up and come along and go to work. Telegraph me.[21]

By early June, Wright reached Hartford, his trunk crammed with published sketches, manuscripts, notes, and presumably a fine collection of dry statistics, and registered at the Union Hall Hotel. Clemens read and approved the portion of the manuscript already written, discussed the notes with him, and worked with him in a room above the Clemens' stable. During a vacation with the family in Rhode Island and on returning to Hartford, they continued to toil together. When Clemens went to New York, Wright followed him and asked that he read the manuscript, now nearly completed. "After reading a thousand pages, he said it was all right—he did not want to read any more. . . ." [22] That ended the collaboration.

The book, issued by Clemens' publisher at Clemens' suggestion in the autumn, had a long title typical of subscription books— *History of the Big Bonanza, an Authentic Account of the Discovery, History, and Working of the World-Renowned Comstock Lode. . . Etc., Etc., and a Full Exposition of the Production of Pure Silver.* The humorist wrote "Introductory," testifying to Dan De Quille's capability, dated "Hartford, May, 1876."

The likelihood is strong that Clemens read a fair proportion of this book. He read the thousand pages; the book was made up largely of published sketches which he may have seen in Nevada or in the East when the pair conferred. Or he may have overcome his indifference and read the rest of the book in an advance copy before he began *Huck* in July. Chapters i, viii, and xv of the novel —all written in 1876—contain significant parallels to Dan's book.[23]

In one influential passage, Dan shows a mining tycoon, Old Taggart, awaiting death without having experienced religion Deacon Dudley, whom Mrs. Taggart asks to save him, pictures "the wonders and glories of heaven," then asks the sick man if he would not like to go there:

"No"; said old Taggart, "I don't think I should feel at home in the kind of place you tell about." . . . .

"I'm surprised . . . to hear that you don't want to be one of that heavenly band that sit before the throne, playing golden harps, and singing praises forever and forever!"

"Me play on a harp, Deacon?" said Old Taggart. . . .

"Yes; upon the wondrous golden harp!" . . . .

"There," said Old Taggart, doggedly, "I don't want to go to that part of heaven. The Lord will give me a place out in the back settlements. . . ."

"It's wicked to talk as you are doing. . . . You have the worst ideas about heaven of any man I ever saw!"

"Can't help it, Deacon . . . It's all nonsense to talk about me playin' a harp. I tell you plainly, Deacon, that I don't want to go among the musicians up there. It wouldn't suit me!" [24]

Huck's talk with Miss Watson in chapter i is very similar:

Then she told me all about the bad place, and all I wanted was to go somewheres; all I wanted was a change. I said I wished I was there. She got mad then, but I didn't mean no harm. . . . She said it was wicked to say what I said; . . . *she* was going to live so as to go to the good place. Well, I couldn't see no advantage in going where she was going, so I made up my mind I wouldn't try for it. But I never said so, because it would only make trouble. . . . She went on and told me all about the good place. She said all a body would have to do there was to go around all day long with a harp and sing, forever and ever. So I didn't think much of it. But I never said so. I asked her if she reckoned Tom Sawyer would go there, and she said not by a considerable sight. I was glad about that, because I wanted him and me to be together.

Like De Quille, Mark derives comedy from his character's literal-mindedness and unconventional attitudes—important aspects of Huck's makeup. But he so manages his account as to show other qualities of Huck in this opening chapter. Huck does not argue, as Taggart does, when he disagrees; this shows his ability to get along with people. Twain also has Huck indicate his typical reaction to difficulties—escape *from* something, rather than *to* something.

A second anecdote by De Quille, one about a character named Pike and some men on a prospecting trip, is of particular interest. Noticing that Pike is nervous about Indians, his pals stage a fake Indian attack during which several of them pretend they are massacred. Pike scurries in fright to a nearby town, where his friends turn up and convince him that he has dreamed the whole episode. Reminiscences of this anecdote occur in two passages in *Huck,* one quite important.

De Quille shows Pike enlarging upon details in his "dream": "Pike continued to tell his dream for some years, constantly adding new matter, till at last it was a wonderful yarn. He enlarged greatly on the part he took in the fight, and after wearing out the pick on the skulls of the Indians, wound up by thrusting the handle down the throat of a brave, as his last act before beating a retreat." [25] Compare, in chapter ii, Jim's account of his dream during which Tom Sawyer has left him five cents and has hung his hat on a tree:

Afterward Jim said the witches bewitched him and put him in a trance, and rode him all over the State, and then set him under the trees again, and hung his hat on a limb to show who done it. And next time Jim told it he said they rode him down to New Orleans; and, after that, every time he told it he spread it more and more, till by-and-by he said they rode him all over the world. . . . Jim was monstrous proud about it, and he got so he wouldn't hardly notice the other niggers. . . . Jim always kept that five-center piece around his neck with a string, and said it was a charm the devil give to him with his own hands and told him he could . . . fetch witches whenever he wanted to, just by saying something to it. . . . Jim was most ruined, for a servant. . . .

Both characters profit from inventiveness; but the differences between their imaginings and the uses to which they put them show Twain adapting his materials. Pike is convinced that a reality is a dream and, aided by his commonplace imagination, builds up his bravery. Jim, more gifted, invents experiences and comes to believe they are actual. His soaring improvisations prove his mastery of supernatural lore. Huck's comment that Jim "was most ruined" as a servant satirically underlines the conventional view of Jim foisted upon Huck by the community.

Chapter viii contains the next passage reminiscent of *The Big Bonanza*.[26] De Quille details a talk he has with a Piute guide, "Capitan" John:

One evening when we were all seated about our camp-fire, . . . he said, "I was pretty well off once, . . . I had *fifty dollars*." He named the amount with an emphasis which showed that he considered the announcement one of considerable importance.

"Indeed!—Had you so much money?" said I. . . . "And what became of all this wealth?"

"Me burst all to smash!"

"Well, that was bad. In kind of a speculation?"

"Me no understand spectoolation. What you call um spectoolation?"

"Well, it's . . . like you plant wheat. You plant your money in some speculation to get more money."

"Yes; well, me make one bad plant." [27]

Jim in chapter viii tells Huck that hairy arms and a hairy breast show their possessor will be rich. Huck points out that Jim is so adorned, and asks if he is rich. "No," says Jim, "but I ben rich wunst, and gwyne to be rich agin. Wunst I had foteen dollars, but I tuck to specalat'n', en got busted out." Jim then details stories of his "speculations" which show his inability to make money multiply but also show him guided by dreams. These as well as the talk about hairiness as an omen link Jim's naïveté with his superstitious lore.[28]

The anecdote about Pike was influential a second time in a very important passage. Pike at first has trouble believing that he has dreamed the Indian attack because "it don't seem that way at all. . . . I can almost hear the guns crack now." Something that he has not dreamed, he says, "don't seem a bit plainer, nor half as plain. . . . That was the dogonest plainest dream I ever did hev! . . . just the same as bein' awake." And when, later, a fellow prospector tries to tell Pike the truth, Pike is unconvinced. "No," he says, "it was all a dream from fust to last, and the biggest and plainest dream I ever had!" [29]

In chapter xv Huck in the canoe is separated from the raft and Jim in a fog. Huck's attempt to get back fails; exhausted, he lies down and falls asleep. Awakening, "First I didn't know where I was; I thought I was dreaming; and when things begun to come back to me they seemed to come dim out of last week." Eventually Huck gets back to the raft and finds Jim asleep. When Jim awakens, Huck tells him that Huck's disappearance and Jim's worry were things Jim dreamed. Like Pike, Jim needs persuading, and he offers similar arguments: "But Huck, it's all jis' as plain to me as— . . . dog my cats ef it ain't de powerfullest dream I ever see. En I hain't ever had no dream b'fo' dat's tired me like dis one." When Jim is finally persuaded, however, he recounts the dream "just as it happened, only he painted it up considerable. Then he said he must start in and 'terpret' it, because it was sent for a warning":

The whoops was warnings that would come to us every now and then, and if we didn't try hard to make out and understand them they'd just take us into bad luck, 'stead of keeping us out of it. The lot of tow-heads was troubles we was going to get into with quarrelsome people and all kinds of mean folks, but if we minded our business and didn't talk back and aggravate them, we would pull through and get out of the fog and into the big clear river, which was the free States, and wouldn't have no more trouble.

After this interpretation, Huck calls Jim's attention to evidence that the happenings were not, after all, a dream—bits of trash left on the raft by the storm. He asks Jim to interpret these. One of the most poignant passages in the novel follows:

Jim looked at the trash, and then looked at me, and back at the trash again. He had got the dream fixed so strong in his head that he couldn't seem to shake it loose. . . . But when he did get the thing straightened around, he looked at me steady, without ever smiling, and says:

"What do dey stan' for? I's gwyne to tell you. When I got all wore out wid work, en wid de callin' for you, en went to sleep, my heart wuz mos' broke. . . . En when I wake up en fine you back agin all safe en soun', de tears come, en I could a got down on my knees en kiss yo' foot I's so thankful. En all you wuz thinkin' 'bout wuz how you could make a fool uv ole Jim wid a lie. Dat truck dah is *trash;* en trash is what people is dat puts dirt on de head er dey fren's en makes 'em ashamed."

Then he got up slow, and walked to the wigwam, and went in there. . . . It made me feel so mean I could almost kissed *his* foot and get him to take it back.

It was fifteen minutes before I could work myself up to go and humble myself to a nigger—but I done it, and I warn't ever sorry for it afterward, neither. I didn't do him no more mean tricks, and I wouldn't done that one if I'd 'a' knowed it would make him feel that way.

The material is so thoroughly integrated as to seem wholly Twain's own, and his additions are in fact the most important parts. Huck's confusion between dream and reality when he awakens—not paralleled in De Quille—motivates his tricking Jim.

Once he is convinced that he has dreamed, Jim, imaginative as usual, "paints the dream up considerable." Then, believer that he is in portents, he has to interpret the dream as a series of meaning-

Huckleberry Finn, FRONTISPIECE

ful warnings. The dream joins a series of portents which have seemed to the superstitious Huck to be causes of the adventures so far. One ambiguous prophecy, typical of such deciphering, forecasts what is to be an important concern of the book—"troubles . . . with quarrelsome people and all kinds of mean folks." But in suggesting a way to take advantage of the warnings, Jim offers the formula of an enslaved man for getting along—"mind our own business and don't talk back and aggravate them." Then he looks, poetically, beyond the "fog" to the "big clear river," a symbol of freedom which might well have occurred in a spiritual. Later when Jim, unlike Pike, is persuaded that the events actually happened, his dignified rebuke, Huck's realization of his inhumanity, and the boy's apology mark a crucial stage in the relationship between the two outcasts.

Resemblances between passages in *Big Bonanza* and passages in *Huckleberry Finn* which evidently were influenced by them [30] seem striking enough to indicate indebtedness, but, in accordance with the formula of Dumas which Twain endorsed, the differences are great enough to indicate no great indebtedness. It is very unlikely that Twain had the passages by De Quille before him (despite a few parallels in phrasing) or indeed that he had them in mind in any detail. The parallels probably were examples of what Twain called "unconscious plagiarism" when he echoed the Oliver Wendell Holmes dedication: "It lay lost in some dim corner of my memory a year or two, then came forward when I needed a dedication, and was promptly mistaken by me as a child of my own happy fancy." [31] De Quille's anecdotes seem to have lain dimly in Twain's mind until he needed an attitude or an action that characterized Huck or Jim and would motivate actions. Two passages involve the belief of the literal-minded Huck that he would not enjoy heaven as it is conventionally pictured, and the belief of the naïve Jim that a small sum represents riches and that his puny dealings are "speculations." The other two involve Jim's embellishment of a dream for personal glory and his confusion between dream and reality. Such details from De Quille were apropos because they were comic and Twain was writing a humorous book, and because they could be made to reveal not only traits which Huck and Jim shared with De Quille's characters but also characteristics peculiarly their own.

The Big Bonanza was echoed frequently then in realistic scenes in the 1876 portion of *Huck;* an assorted group of other authors (two of whom will be considered in the next chapter) were echoed in others.

Recalling the graveyard scene in *Tom Sawyer* which echoed one concerned with the two Crunchers, junior and senior, in *A Tale of Two Cities*, chapter v of *Huck* included a scene highly reminiscent of one in which Jerry, senior, is featured. Jerry awakens one morning to find his good wife upon her knees and forces her to admit that she is praying. "You're at it again, are you?" he demands:

"Saying your prayers! You're a nice woman! . . . Here! your mother's a nice woman, young Jerry, going a praying agin your father's prosperity. . . . You've got a religious mother, you have, my boy; going and flopping herself down, and praying. . . . B-u-u-ust me! . . . If I ain't, what with piety and one blowed thing and another, being choused this last week into as bad luck as ever a poor devil of a honest tradesman met with! . . . Ah! yes! You're religious, too. . . ."

Mr. Cruncher's temper was not at all improved when he came in to breakfast. He resented Mrs. Cruncher's saying grace with particular animosity.

Cruncher later makes some very similar remarks. The aggrieved attitude and the outrage are incongruous with the admirable activity provoking them—the practice of religion. In a like fashion, Pap Finn is abused and outraged because Huck has gone and put on fine clothes, has got himself educated, and may do something even worse—get religion:

He kept a-looking me all over. By and by he says:

"Starchy clothes—very. You think you're a good deal of a big-bug, *don't* you? . . . educated, too, they say; can read and write. . . . I'll learn people to . . . put on airs over his own father. . . . You lemme catch you fooling around that school again. . . . Say—lemme hear you read."

I took up a book and begun something. . . . When I'd read about half a minute he fetched the book a whack. . . .

"It's so. You can do it. . . . you stop that putting on frills. I won't have it. . . . First you know you'll get religion, too. I never see such a son. . . . *Ain't* you the sweet-scented dandy, though? A bed; and bedclothes; and a look'n glass; and a piece of carpet on the floor—and your own father got to sleep with the hogs in the tanyard. I never see such a son."

The adaptations, like those of De Quille's anecdotes, are functional. Since Huck has no tendency toward religiousness, Twain has Pap emphasize more justifiable complaints and merely guess that getting piety may well be Huck's next downward step. What Pap says characterizes him on his first appearance and motivates his future actions. Huck's cleanliness infuriates a man who shortly will mess up a guest room. Huck's education is an affront to a man whose outrage will mount to a frenzy when he meets an educated Negro. Pap's furious resentment of the inferior station into which bad luck has shoved him will motivate his showing "who is Huck Finn's boss" by taking Huck to a hovel in the woods from which the boy starts his wanderings.

Even more remote than Dickens' novel from the period Twain was portraying in 1876 was a romance by Charles Reade set in fifteenth-century Europe, *The Cloister and the Hearth.* Yet this too seems to have been briefly helpful. In England in 1872 and again in 1873, the American had met Reade and apparently had seen him often; and Reade once had asked him to collaborate on a novel. In chapter lxiii of Reade's novel (popular since its appearance in 1861) the hero Gerard engages in some rather dull debauchery, joins some "libertines" and their girl friends on a boat trip on the Tiber. He brings "a peerless beauty" whom he introduces as Marcia. One of the other girls, suspicious of Gerard's companion, plops some nuts into Marcia's lap. When Marcia brings her knees together, the girl cries: "Aha! you are caught, my lad. . . . 'Tis a man; or a boy. A woman still parteth her knees to catch the nuts the surer in her apron; but a man closeth his for fear them shall fall between his hose." [32]

In chapter xi Huck, disguised as a girl, goes from Jackson's Island to St. Petersburg to learn what is going on. He meets Judith Loftus, a woman newly settled on the edge of town. The chapter is important, since during its course Huck learns that townsmen will soon visit the island to hunt Jim. Twain makes Mrs. Loftus shrewd enough to suspect that Huck is a boy and to confirm her suspicion by tests. For one of these, he uses Reade's device; pretending that a lame shoulder prevents her from heaving a lump of lead at some rats which emerge, Mrs. Loftus asks help. "So," says Huck, "she dropped the lump into my lap . . . and I clapped my legs together on it." Following other tests, Mrs. Loftus, learning that Huck is a boy, forces him to tell a new story, then determines the truth of his spontaneous and unrehearsed invention by additional shrewd questions.

Reade's test is offered as only one of Judith's keen perceptions. "Bless you, child," she says,

when you set out to thread a needle, don't hold the thread still and fetch the needle up to it; hold the needle and poke the thread at it— that's the way a woman most always does. . . . And when you throw at a rat or anything, hitch yourself up a tip-toe and fetch your hand up over your head as awkward as you can, and miss your rat about six or seven foot. Throw stiff-armed from the shoulder, like there was a pivot there for it to turn on—like a girl. . . . And mind you, when a girl tries to catch anything in her lap, she throws her knees apart. . . .

The portrayal of Mrs. Loftus and her piercing of Huck's disguise —for which Reade contributed the idea and one useful instance —inject interest and suspense into what might be a routine incident. During the cross-examination which follows, Huck has to think quickly, and in doing so he shows the glibness that later helps him lie himself out of many tough situations. Therefore he is allowed to hurry back to the island and to shout the words which start the trip downstream: "Get up and hump yourself, Jim! There ain't a minute to lose. They're after us!"

10

"SO NOBLE . . . AND SO BEAUTIFUL A BOOK"

It is so noble a book and so beautiful a book, that I don't want it to have even trivial faults in it.—S. L. Clemens' marginal comment in his copy of W. E. H. Lecky, History of European Morals, *II, 39.*

In addition to portraying scenes, characters, and actions in a better style and more richly, *Huckleberry Finn* surpassed *Tom Sawyer* in commenting on what its author in time would call "the damned human race." Scenes in early chapters embody certain beliefs: the robber gang scenes, a loathing of posturings in romantic fiction; and the account of the judge's attempt to reform Pap, a dislike of sentimentality.

These scenes are isolated; and so are others of 1876 which dramatize ideas and attitudes. Twain had not found a comprehensive theme or ways to develop it at length. Some of his reading and his ponderings about that reading, though, eventually would help him discover a significant theme; and he would learn how to make it permeate much of the book. Some early passages predict these important developments, one stimulated by an old favorite, Carlyle, the rest by a newly discovered author whose concepts would be very influential—W. E. H. Lecky.

The thought of Carlyle which one scene echoes was akin to the thinking of many, the novelist among them, about republican government. Growing political corruption and airings of scandals in the decades following the Civil War shook the faith of many Americans. Even that enthusiast about democracy, Walt Whitman, wrote in *Democratic Vistas,* in 1871: "Genuine belief seems to have left us. . . . the official services of America, national, state, and municipal, in all their branches except the judiciary is tainted." James Russell Lowell, who in periods before the war had been ostentatiously democratic, on July 4, 1875, delivered a Centennial Ode later published in the *Nation.* In it a character tells Columbia what she should display on her centennial:

> Show 'em your Civil Service, and explain
> How all men's loss is everybody's gain. . . .
> Show your State legislatures; show your Rings;
> And challenge Europe to produce such things
> As high officials sitting half in sight
> To share the plunder and to fix things right. . . .

This summarized much of the bitterness of the era.

In 1873, in *The Gilded Age,* Twain and Warner had attacked corruption and Twain had described an American jury: "Low foreheads and heavy faces they all had; some had a look of animal cunning, while the most were only stupid. The entire panel formed that boasted heritage commonly described as the 'bulwark of our liberties.'" On February 15, 1875, before the Monday Evening Club, he read "Universal Suffrage," pointing out the nonsense of allowing everyone to vote and weighing the vote of "a consummate scoundrel" as heavily as that of "a president, a bishop, a college professor, a merchant prince."

Reading, as well as the thought of the period and his own thinking, had fostered distrust of the American government: in 1877 he declared that Carlyle's *History of the French Revolution* had intensified a hatred he long had had for "all shades and forms of republican government." [1] At many points Carlyle attacks democratic processes:

Is it the nature of National Assemblies generally to do, with endless labour and clangour, Nothing? Are Representative Governments mostly at bottom Tyrannies too? Shall we say, the *Tyrants*, the ambitious contentious Persons, from all corners of the country do, in this manner, get gathered in one place; and there, with motion and countermotion, with jargon and hubbub, *cancel* one another, like the fabulous Kilkenny Cats; and produce, for net-result, *zero* . . . ?

The American ignored Carlyle's transcendental explanation of this phenomenon and advanced another—universal suffrage. Republican government with such a system of suffrage, he said, "ought to perish because it is founded in wrong and is weak and bad and tyrannical." [2]

In chapter vi of *Huckleberry Finn*, the weakness of such a system and its cause are attacked in Pap Finn's longest speech as he complains about a Negro's voting:

". . . they said he was a p'fessor in a college, and could talk all kinds of languages, and knowed everything. And that ain't the wust. They said he could *vote*, when he was at home. Well, that let me out. Thinks I, what is the country a-coming to? It was 'lection day, and I was just about to go and vote, myself, if I warn't too drunk to get there; but when they told me there was a State in this country where they'd let that nigger vote, I drawed out. I says I'll never vote ag'in. . . . and the country may rot for all me. . . ."

The mode is hard-hitting satire. Pap, from the start physically, mentally, and morally despicable, voices views completely opposed to those of his creator. For the wrong reason, he attacks a man better qualified to vote than he and, for another wrong reason, disqualifies himself as a voter.

The passage does not suggest Clemens' solution to the problem, but he probably believed it was implied. In the summer of 1875 the humorist sent to the *Atlantic* a sketch, "The Curious Republic of Gondour." This told how exactly this problem had been solved in utopian Gondour. Universal suffrage had been retained by giving "every citizen, however poor or ignorant," one vote,

but if a man possessed a good common-school education and no money, he had two votes; a high school education gave him four; if he had property likewise, to the value of three thousand *sacos*, he wielded one more vote; for every fifty thousand sacos a man added to his property, he was entitled to another vote; a university education entitled a man to nine votes, even if he owned no property. Therefore, learning being more prevalent and more easily acquired than riches, educated men became a wholesome check upon wealthy men, since they could out-vote them. Learning goes usually with uprightness, broad views, and humanity; so the learned voters, possessing the balance of power, be-came the vigilant and efficient protectors of the great lower rank of society.[3]

The belief that either the acquisition of wealth or a B.A. degree certified wisdom and rectitude, though typical in that remote period, seems quaint in the present century when men of wealth in one decade and "eggheads" in the next have automatically and glibly been labeled antisocial. But the author's intent clearly is to grant voting power according to proof of intelligence and virtue. He was still talking along these lines in April, 1876.[4]

Several passages written in 1876 deal with problems of morality: in these was the germ of the chief thought to be developed in the completed novel. Huck's attacks on prayer and his concepts of heaven in chapters i–iii introduce this motif. One should picture Clemens reading these of an evening to the Quarry Farm house-hold, his eyes glancing mischievously from beneath feathery eye-brows at Susan Crane. For Mrs. Crane was a pious woman; fre-quently Clemens invaded her garden to argue about her orthodox beliefs. The ironic nicknames which the pair used were products of their controversies: he called her Sinful Susan, and she called him Holy Samuel. The passages made fun of some of these argu-ments.

Her husband Theodore also would have listened to these chap-ters with interest, for they echo a book which he and Clemens had discovered two summers before and since then had read and discussed while lolling in hammocks on the lawn.[5] It was a fa-vorite of Clemens for years: he called it "noble" and "beautiful," and plentiful underlinings and marginal notations through both volumes attest to his having read the surviving copy (and perhaps another copy which has disappeared) carefully and thoughtfully.[6]

W. E. H. Lecky, an English-Scottish-Irish historian, had leaped to fame at twenty-seven by publishing his *History of Rationalism* in 1865. The book which Clemens and Crane were reading was Lecky's latest, even more popular than his first, *History of European Morals from Augustus to Charlemagne*, a ponderous two-volumer published in 1869.

Lecky's book is in some ways comparable with H. G. Wells' *Outline of History* and the simplification of Arnold Toynbee's simplification of history, best sellers in the twentieth century. Concentrating upon uncomplicated lines of narrative and eschewing minutiae, it covers great spans of time; it provides picturesque details; it is lucid in style. So it was likely to appeal to amateur historians.

Also it dealt with problems about morality such as Clemens had often discussed—favorite problems for theologians—the nature of morality, the extent of moral responsibility. Along the margins of Clemens' copy of Darwin's *The Descent of Man* (New York, 1871)—now in the University of California Library—Clemens earlier had started a discussion which he continued in Lecky's margins. When Darwin, in his chapter on "Moral Sense," discussed theories about the origin of morals, Clemens had made a comment (I, 78) indicating that he thought moral decisions were motivated by "selfishness . . . not charity nor generosity." Lecky, whom Darwin cites, is much concerned with this problem.

At the outset Lecky notices that there are two fundamentally opposed groups of moralists:

One of them is generally described as the stoical, the intuitive, the independent, and the sentimental; the other as the epicurean, the inductive, the utilitarian, or the selfish. The moralists of the former school . . . believe that we have a natural power of perceiving that some qualities such as benevolence, chastity, or veracity, are better than others, and that we ought to cultivate them, and to repress their opposites. . . . They contend, that by the constitution of our nature, the nature of right carries with it an obligation; that to say a course of conduct is our duty, is in itself, and apart from all consequences, an intelligible and sufficient reason for practicing it; and that we derive the first principles of our duty from intuition. The moralist of the opposite school denies that we have any such natural perception. He maintains that we have by nature absolutely no knowledge of merit and demerit, of the comparative excellence of our feelings and actions, and that we derive these notions solely from observation of the course . . . which is conducive to human happiness. That which makes actions good is, that they increase the happiness or diminish the pains of mankind. That which constitutes their demerit is the opposite tendency.

Lecky favored the intuitionists and wrote his history accordingly. In his survey of pagan philosophers he praises the Stoics for believing that "duty, as distinguished from every modification of selfishness, should be the supreme motive of life," and for abstaining from sin "not through fear of punishment" but "from the desire and obligation of what is just and good." Lecky notices that by contrast the populace urged men to be good so as to avoid punishment: "The Greek word for superstition signifies literally 'fear of the gods,' or daemons, and the philosophers sometimes represent the vulgar as shuddering at the thought of death, through dread of certain endless sufferings to which it would lead them." Clemens scored these passages.

Later, in "The Conversion of Rome," Lecky tells of the opposition of philosophers to early Christians because "To agitate the minds of men with religious terrorism, to . . . govern the reason by alarming the imagination, was in the eyes of the Pagan world one of the most heinous of crimes." In the margin Clemens wrote: "It is an odious religion." Then (perhaps thinking of friends in the clergy) he added: "Still I do not think its priests ought to be burned, but only the missionaries."

Recalling the stern tenets of Calvinism according to which he had been reared and his later studies in science, and availing himself of help from De Quille, the humorist has Huck in chapter ii picture counterparts of Lecky's *hoi polloi* of antiquity and his noble Stoics in St. Petersburg. Miss Watson is the selfish philosopher who tries to make Huck behave by talking of "the bad place" and "the good place" and claiming he can get what he prays for. Widow Douglas—a noble Stoic—is one of Lecky's fellow intuitionists: "she said the thing a body could get by praying for it was 'spiritual gifts.' This was too much for me, but she told me what she meant—I must help other people, and do everything I could for other people, and look out for them all the time and never think about myself."

Huck weighs the formulas and like Lecky discovers a dichotomy:

I went out in the woods and turned [the widow's recipe] over in my mind a long time—but I couldn't see no advantage about it—except for the other people—so at last I reckoned I wouldn't worry about it any more, but just let it go. Sometimes the widow would take me one side and talk about Providence in a way to make a body's mouth water; but maybe next day Miss Watson would take hold and knock it all down again. I judged I could see there was two Providences, and a poor chap would stand considerable show with the widow's Providence, but if Miss Watson's got him there warn't no help for him any more. I . . . reckoned I would belong to the widow's if he wanted me, though I couldn't make out how he was agoing to be any better off then than he was before, seeing I was so ignorant, and so kind of low-down and ornery.

Lecky would have considered Huck confused. The boy's natural power of perceiving (to use Lecky's term) makes him sense the superiority of the widow's moral scheme. But he talks like a utilitarian. For since he "can't see no advantages about" the widow's doctrine for himself, he selfishly decides to "let it go." And instead of seeing that he has innate ability to choose virtue, he figures that because he is "ignorant, . . . low-down and ornery" (a matter that would concern only a "selfish" philosopher) he cannot be very good. Early in the book, then, under Lecky's stimulation, the author begins to contrast two moral philosophies which become increasingly important as the book progresses.[7]

Despite his enthusiasm about Lecky, the humorist agreed with Huck that environment determines morality. When Lecky remarked that in different ages men had different ideas as to what was humane but that this fact provided no satisfactory argument against "the reality of innate moral perceptions," Clemens fiercely (and with satirical illogic) disagreed in a marginal comment: "All moral perceptions are acquired by the influences around us; these influences begin in infancy; we never get a chance to find out whether we have any that are innate or not." When Lecky praised Christianity for "quickening greatly our benevolent affections," beginning this influence "with the very earliest stage of human life," Clemens sneered in the margin, "And so nothing of it was innate."

In chapter viii, on agreeing not to report Jim has run away Huck shows how his moral standards are influenced by his upbringing by accepting the fact that "people would call me a lowdown Abolitionist and despise me." This point had been made briefly in chapter xxviii of *Tom Sawyer*, where Huck had agreed with the popular view that he did wrong when he sat and ate with a Negro.[8]

The novelist also agreed with Lecky's opponents that selfish interests govern actions. Lecky paraphrases the philosophical views of Hobbes, Bentham, Mill, Locke, and their group thus: "A desire to obtain happiness and to avoid pain is the only possible motive to action. The reason, and the only reason, why we should perform virtuous actions, or . . . seek the good of others, is that on the whole such a course will bring us the greatest amount of happiness." Clemens underlined this, bracketed the "should," underscored "us," and commented: "Leave the 'should' out—then it is perfect (and true)." Paine's report that he wrote beside this passage "Sound and true"—if accurate—indicates that Clemens read and marked two copies of Lecky's book and twice agreed with Lecky's opponents at this very point.

Paine adds that when Lecky wrote that laws restrain our appetites, "being sustained by rewards and punishments . . . make it the interest of the individual to regard that of the community," Clemens wrote, "Correct! He has proceeded from unreasoned selfishness to reasoned selfishness. All our acts, reasoned and unreasoned, are selfish." Huck illustrates this in chapter xii. He invades farms to "borrow" a melon, corn, or other provisions. Pap had said borrowing things was not wrong "if you was going to pay them back some time but the widow said it warn't anything

but a soft name for stealing, and no decent body would do it."
Taking heed of the widow, Jim and Huck decide "to pick out two
or three things from the list and say we won't borrow them no
more," and award immunity to crabapples and persimmons. "I
was glad the way it come out," says Huck, "because crabapples
ain't ever good, and the p'simmons wouldn't be ripe for two or
three months yet"—a neat instance of selfish interests shaping a
moral decision.

Also illustrated is Lecky's point that when a man's conscience
is active, "If happiness be his object, he must regulate his course
with a view to the actual condition of his being, and there can be
little doubt that his peace will be most promoted by a compromise with vice." [9] In chapter xvi the slave hunters make such a
compromise. Persuaded by Huck that his family is suffering from
smallpox, they refuse to help them but salve their consciences by
giving Huck two twenty-dollar gold pieces.

Chapter xvi repeats other points. As Huck and Jim watch for
Cairo, Huck is worried by Jim's talk of being freed: "it made me
all over trembly and feverish . . . because I begun to get it
through my head that he *was* most free—and who was to blame
for it? Why, *me*." To make the matter clearer, the author, when
preparing readings from a personal copy of the book for a lecture
some years later, made an addition which, like others, helps clar-
ify his meaning. Here he inserted: "O, I had committed a *crime!*
—I knowed it perfectly *well*—I could *see* it, *now*." [10] As he has
indicated in chapter viii, moral standards are made by the community. In chapter xvi Huck, when he lies to help Jim, blames his
own training: "I see it warn't no use for me to try to learn to do
right; a body that don't get *started* right when he's little ain't got
no show." And in the end Huck makes what appears to be a selfish
decision.

It *appears* to be a selfish decision, but, along with a struggle
which preceded it, the decision needs to be carefully examined.
Chapter xvi is particularly interesting because, although in chapters xii and xv [11] Huck has recounted wrestling matches with his
conscience, this chapter contains the most detailed account of
such a battle in the 1876 chapters.

Again, reading Lecky and thinking about Lecky seem to have

been instructive. The intuitive moralist, says Lecky, doubts that a man's conscience alone can make him do right; such a moralist "denies . . . that those pains and pleasures [which conscience affords] are so powerful or so proportioned to our acts as to become an adequate basis for virtue." Also, whether virtue or vice wins, a man's conscience gives him trouble. If it prevents a man's sinning, "the suffering caused by resisting natural tendencies is much greater than will ensue from their moderate gratification." If the man sins, he "possesses a conscience . . . and its sting or approval constitutes a pain or a pleasure so intense, as to redress the balance." "And, indeed, on the whole," Lecky summarizes, "it is more than doubtful whether conscience . . . is not the cause of more pain than pleasure. Its reproaches are more felt than its approval." Anyone, therefore, who believes that "ought or ought not means nothing more than the prospect of acquiring or losing pleasure" should, Lecky suggests, simply get rid of his conscience: "That it would be for the happiness as it would certainly be in the power of a man of a temperament such as I have . . . described, to quench that conscientious feeling which by its painful reproaches prevents him from pursuing the course that would be most conducive to his tranquility, I conceive to be self-evident." [12]

Mark showed clearly that he agreed about the troublesomeness of conscience and the desirability of getting rid of the thing. He read to the Monday Evening Club, January 24, 1876, "The Facts Concerning the Recent Carnival of Crime in Connecticut," published in the *Atlantic Monthly* a month before he started to write *Huck*. In it a deformed dwarf covered with fuzzy green mould, a caricature of the author, visits Mark. This creature, with "a foxlike cunning in the face and the sharp little eyes, and also alertness and malice," reminds his host of past sins and tortures him with remorse:

He reminded me of many dishonest things which I had done; . . . of some which I had planned . . . and been kept from performing by consequences only. . . . With exquisite cruelty he recalled to my mind . . . wrongs and unkindnesses I had inflicted and humiliations I had put upon friends since dead, "who died thinking of those injuries, maybe, and grieving over them," he added, by way of poison to the stab.

The shrunken creature is, he reveals, his own conscience. When he asks why all consciences are "nagging, badgering, fault-finding savages," the dwarf answers, "The *purpose* of it is to improve the man, but *we* are merely disinterested agents. . . . It is my *business*—and my joy—to make you repent of *every*thing you do." Gleefully following Lecky's suggestion, the narrator kills the troublesome dwarf and begins a life of crime:

Nothing in all the world could persuade me to have a conscience again. . . . I killed thirty-eight persons during the first two weeks— all of them on account of ancient grudges. I burned a dwelling that interrupted my view. I swindled a widow and some orphans out of their last cow, which is a very good one, though not a thoroughbred, I believe. I have also committed scores of crimes, . . . and have enjoyed my work exceedingly, whereas it would formerly have broken my heart and turned my hair gray. . . .

This fantasy was particularly exuberant perhaps because an oversensitive conscience long had tortured Clemens himself. Howells says, "Among the half-dozen, or half-hundred personalities that each of us becomes, I should say that Clemens's central and final personality was something exquisite. . . . One could not know him well without realizing him . . . the most conscientious of men." Rudyard Kipling too noticed evidence of great sensitivity—"a mouth as delicate as a woman's." [13] The author's *Autobiography* and his biographies are dotted with instances of his suffering pangs of conscience. His own experiences therefore helped him approve Lecky's thesis that a man's conscience bedevils him whatever he does.

This belief led him, in chapter xvi, to have Huck suffer agonies because he is helping Jim escape. Here is the passage, with additions for the reading bracketed:

. . . conscience up and says, every time, "But you knowed he was running for his freedom, and you could a paddled ashore and told somebody." That was so—[yes it was so—] I couldn't get around that, noway. . . . Conscience says . . . "What had poor Miss Watson done to you, that you could see her nigger go off right under your eyes and never say one single word? What did that poor old woman do to you, that you should treat her so mean? Why, she tried to learn you your book, she tried to learn you your manners, [she tried to learn you to be a Christian],[14] she tried to be good to you. . . ."

I got to feeling so mean and so miserable I most wished I was dead.

And Huck's decision to tell on Jim brings a fine feeling of relief: "[O, it was a blessed thought! I never can *tell* how good it made me feel—cuz I *knowed* I was doing *right*, now.] I felt easy and happy and light as a feather right off. All my troubles was gone." Apparently, such relief follows any decision, wrong or right. After deciding to refrain from borrowing crabapples and persimmons, says Huck, "We warn't feeling just right before that [decision], but it was all comfortable now." Here Twain joins Lecky and other intuitionists in denying that "pains and pleasures" of conscience "are . . . so proportioned to our acts as to become an adequate basis for virtues."

Conscience pulls Huck equally hard the other way. As he paddles toward shore he hears Jim shout, "You's de bes' fren' Jim's ever had; en you's de *only* fren' ole Jim's got now."

I was paddling off, all in a sweat to tell on him; but when he says this, it seemed to kind of take the tuck all out of me. [It kind of all *unsettled* me, and I couldn't seem to *tell* whether I was doing *right* or doing *wrong*.] I went along slow then, and I warn't right down certain whether I was glad I started or whether I warn't. When I was [100 and] fifty yards off, Jim [sings out across the darkness and] says:

"Dah you goes, de ole true Huck; de on'y white genlman dat ever kep' his promise to old Jim."

Well, I just felt sick.

Sick or not, Huck has decided "I *got* to do it," when two slave hunters appear and question him. He tries to tell the truth, "but I warn't man enough—hadn't the spunk of a rabbit." So he lies and saves Jim. Here is the aftermath:

I got aboard the raft, feeling bad and low, because I knowed I had done wrong. . . . Then I thought a minute, and says to myself, hold on; s'pose you'd 'a' done right and give Jim up, would you feel better than what you do now? No, says I, I'd feel bad—I'd feel just the same way I do now. [As fur as I can see, a conscience is put in you just to *object* to whatever you *do* do, don't make no difference what it *is*.]

Well, then, says I, what's the use you learning to do right, when it's troublesome to do right and ain't no trouble to do wrong, and the wages is just the same? I was stuck. So I reckoned I wouldn't bother no more about it, but after this always do whichever come handiest at the time.

Considered in the context of Clemens' argument with Lecky, this is a complex passage. Huck's decision that hereafter he will "do whichever comes handiest at the time" seems to be a decision to do what is expedient. But if he acts as he does on this occasion, the expedient thing, for him, will be the humane thing. Thus he will confound Lecky; for, though acting expediently, he will reach the same sort of decision a noble intuitive philosopher would reach, and for the same reason.

HUCK STRUGGLES WITH HIS CONSCIENCE, FIRST EDITION

But an interpolation in the text and a passage in a notebook which Clemens wrote for his lecture tour in 1895 show that another concept is involved. To Jim's shout about Huck's being his only friend he added, "O bless de good old heart o' you, Huck!" And in his notebook of 1895 he wrote a fascinating interpretation of this very passage. His plan, the notebook makes clear, was to "get up an elaborate and formal lay sermon on morals and the conduct of life, and things of that stately sort" [15] illustrated with readings. The introduction to this passage is quite explicit:

Next, I should exploit the proposition that in a crucial moral emergency a sound heart is a safer guide than an ill-trained conscience. I sh'd support this doctrine with a chapter from a book of mine where a sound heart and a deformed conscience come into collision and conscience suffers defeat. Two persons figure in this chapter: Jim, a middle-aged slave, and Huck Finn, a boy of 14, . . . bosom friends, drawn together by a community of misfortune. . . .

In those old slave-holding days the whole community was agreed as to one thing—the awful sacredness of slave property. To help steal a horse or a cow was a low crime, but to help a hunted slave . . . or hesitate to promptly betray him to a slave-catcher when opportunity offered was a much baser crime, and carried with it a stain, a moral smirch which nothing could wipe away. That this sentiment should exist among slave-holders is comprehensible—there were good commercial reasons for it—but that it should exist and did exist among the paupers . . . and in a passionate and uncompromising form, is not in our remote day realizable. It seemed natural enough to me then; natural enough that Huck and his father the worthless loafer should feel and approve it, though it seems now absurd. It shows that that strange thing, the conscience—that unerring monitor—can be trained to approve any wild thing you *want* it to approve if you begin its education early and stick to it.[16]

If Clemens here interpreted correctly a passage written nineteen years before, he had intended to distinguish between conscience, a person's sense of right and wrong developed by his community, and a sound heart—something innate closely resembling Lecky's "natural power." Huck's virtuous decision results from his heart's triumph over his conscience.

The author's reading, carried on partly for enjoyment, partly to supplement a meager formal education, was beginning to give his fiction new richness. It suggested comic scenes of varying kinds. The robber gang's apings of romances are exuberant burlesque. Huck's discussion of the afterlife and Jim's tale of his dream and his talk about speculation derived from *The Big Bonanza*. Pap's cussing out Huck for getting educated derived from Dickens, and Judith Loftus' shrewd tests suggested by Reade are humor based firmly on character. The passage in which Huck fools Jim and is driven to apologize to him, derived from De Quille, is also that of character, but this is touched with pathos.

More important, Clemens' reading and pondering of intellectual works led him to experiment with fiction as a vehicle for ideas more significant than those with which he had dealt in the past. Pap's diatribe against a Negro voting, inspired by Carlyle, raised questions about democracy and prejudice which still are far from being answered. And Lecky's discussion of moral problems impelled the novelist to find ways to embody in his fiction struggles of permanent significance. Huck's coping with the philosophical systems represented by the widow and her sister, his assumptions about the origins of moral principles, his balancing of attitudes inculcated by society against his innate humanity, brought the book to the verge of greatness. Given vitality as representations of Huck's mind and character in action and recounted with warmth and humor in Huck's vernacular, they give substance and depth such as none of Twain's earlier fiction had had.

Why, then, after such a fine start, did the author "like it only tolerably well, so far as I have got" (p. 400 of the manuscript), consider burning it, and at the summer's end actually shelve it for three or more years? We can only guess at the answer. Apparently his initial enthusiasm often carried him about this far when he started a book: this had happened with *The Gilded Age;* it had happened with *Tom Sawyer;* it may be it had happened with the "double-barreled novel." For *Huck,* as for this recently abandoned book, he perhaps hoped to gain perspective by a vacation; the chapters of the abandoned novel, he had told Howells, "were still too new and familiar." Again, though he had made tremendous discoveries about infusing meaning into fiction, he may have been worried because he had not found a theme which would be more than sporadically developed.

Finally, he had bumped into plot trouble of a very serious sort. Despite his talk about *Gil Blas* as a model he may have been worried about the lack of a plot of the formal sort. Reared in the tradition of novels with three- or four-ply plots such as Dickens and Reade created, he perhaps felt that a self-respecting novel should have several plots. *The Gilded Age* and *Tom Sawyer* seem to us overplotted; but people of their day did not find them so.

At the start of his new book, Twain had provided one plot line which was unusual and was, moreover, an excellent means of characterizing his narrator. In chapter i Huck is warned by portents of dire things to come—"A whippowill and a dog crying about somebody that was going to die," a spider flipped into a

candle. "I didn't need anybody to tell me," he says, "that that
. . . would fetch me some bad luck." In chapter iv he spills a salt-
cellar, a matter easily enough taken care of, but when he tries
to offset the jinx by throwing salt over his shoulder Miss Watson
stops him. Jim's dark prophecies also foretell trouble. In chapters
x and xi the author uses a bit of folklore learned from the Negro
cook Auntie Cord at Quarry Farm: a dead rattlesnake which Huck
hides near Jim's blanket attracts another snake which bites Jim.
Handling a snakeskin, Jim remarks, "is such awful bad luck that
maybe we haven't got to the end of it yet." This proves true. In
chapter xvi the snakeskin causes them to pass Cairo; when the
canoe is lost, "We both knowed well enough," says Huck, "that it
was some more work of that snake-skin." He predicts more bad
results: "Anybody that don't believe yet that it's foolishness to
handle a snake-skin . . . will believe it now if they read on and
see what more it done for us."

The acceptance of such signs characterizes both Huck and the
even more superstitious Jim. Also, the incongruity between humble folk portents and majestic foreshadowings in great tragedies
gives this American odyssey a homely and comic quality. But
Twain either forgot this kind of causation or saw that it would not
do for the long pull, because he dropped it.

Another line of causation had been started—the geographic
movement of Huck and Jim downstream. That the pair get together on Jackson's Island at the start of this line of plotting is
coincidental; but Mark gives their meeting some credibility by
having each arrive as the result of characteristic reactions to circumstances. When Huck first decides to run away, in chapter vi,
he plans to go inland: "I reckoned I would walk off with the gun
and some lines, and take to the woods when I run away. I guessed
I wouldn't stay in one place, but just tramp right across the country, mostly night-times, and hunt and fish to keep alive, and so
get so far away that the old man nor the widow couldn't ever
find me any more." In chapter vii, though, he finds a canoe, and
being adaptable immediately changes his scheme: "I judged I'd
hide the canoe good, and then, 'stead of taking to the woods when
I run off, I'd go down the river about fifty mile and camp in one

place for good. . . ." Then, after he has faked evidence of his murder and knows the townsfolk will soon abandon the search for his corpse, he quickly decides, "I can stop anywhere I want to. Jackson's Island is good enough for me. I know that island pretty well, and nobody ever comes there."

The next night Jim starts for the Illinois shore. He decides not to use a skiff because "dey'd miss dat skift, you see, en dey'd know 'bout whah I'd landed on de yuther side, en whah to pick up my track. So I says, a raff is what I's arter; it doan *make* no track." He boards a raft, figuring that by morning he will be twenty-five miles downriver, where he can swim ashore and take to the Illinois woods. But as the raft comes to the head of Jackson's Island a man starts aft with a lantern; so Jim slides overboard and swims to the island. Jim says, "I went into de woods en jedged I wouldn' fool wid raffs no mo', long as dey move de lantern roun' so." Cunning which an enslaved man has to develop and a fear of bad luck ("I didn' have no luck," he explains) thus bring Jim to the island.

Jim's account disproves a claim often made that Mark shows "a lordly disregard of the fact that Jim . . . could have reached free soil by simply paddling to the Illinois shore." As a matter of fact there are other passages which refer to that shore. In chapter ix, after Huck and Jim explore the house floating downriver, Huck makes Jim lie down in the canoe, paddles to the Illinois shore, then creeps "up the dead water under the bank" so that no one will see him returning to the island. In chapter xi Huck learns from Judith Loftus that Pap has got money from Judge Thatcher "to hunt for [Jim] all over Illinois with." So far as Huck knows, his father is doing just that. Even so, in chapter xii, when Huck and Jim leave the island, they decide that "If a boat was to come along we was going to take the canoe and break for the Illinois shore . . ."

The day after they start, they work on the raft:

Jim took up some of the top planks of the raft and built a snug wigwam to get under in blazing weather and rainy, and to keep things dry. Jim made a floor for the wigwam, and raised it a foot or more above the level of the raft, so now the blankets and all the traps was out of reach of steamboat waves. Right in the middle . . . we made a layer of dirt about five or six inches deep . . . to build a fire on in sloppy weather or chilly; the wigwam would keep it from being seen. We made an extra steering-oar, too, because one of the others might get broke on a snag or something. We fixed up a short forked stick to hang the old lantern on, because we must always light the lantern whenever we see a steamboat coming downstream, to keep from getting run over. . . .

The preparation is for all kinds of weather, for emergencies of all sorts—obviously for a long trip. But Huck says nothing of this, probably to avoid confessing what his fiendish plans are. Not until, after passing St. Louis, they have drifted downstream for five nights does he confess, in chapter xv: "We judged that three nights more would fetch us to Cairo, at the bottom of Illinois, when the Ohio River comes in, and that was what we was after. We would sell the raft and get on a steamboat and go way up the Ohio amongst the free states, and then be out of trouble." But, as Henry Nash Smith has noticed, the author really did not want them to go up the Ohio. Since he himself had not traveled that river, he did not know it. He prized autobiography and authenticity in fiction above almost anything else. In addition he had affection for scenes from the past and a nostalgia which drove him to base this book, like previous writings, upon personal experiences and memories.[17] In chapter xvi he has the pair unwittingly pass Cairo in the fog. In chapter xvi he has them take a long time to discover this. Then he figures out a way to keep them going downstream anyhow. Says Huck: "We talked it all over. It wouldn't do to take to the shore; we couldn't take the raft up the stream, of course. There warn't no way but to wait for dark, and start back in the canoe and take the chances. So we slept all day amongst the cottonwood thicket, so as to be fresh for the work, and when we went back to the raft after dark the canoe was gone!" So, says Huck, "we . . . found there warn't no way but just go along down with the raft till we got a canoe to go back in." And Mark has Huck quickly rule out one way of getting a canoe: "We warn't going to borrow it when there warn't anybody around, . . . for that might set people after us." Careful plotting not only gets the pair together, it also sends them downstream and keeps them going downstream after they have passed Cairo.

Even so, the author must have disliked the idea of their drifting deeper into slave territory while the chances to free Jim became increasingly remote. If they wanted to get a canoe, why, he may well have asked, should they not stop where they were and look for one?

At this point I suspect that the cannon-cracker Clemens' temper exploded and blew the book from the writing table to a pigeonhole.

Many who worked with Clemens testify that when irritated he was angry on a majestic scale. In the *Enterprise* office, he so tickled his associates by rhapsodic cursing when his candle was stolen that hiding his candle and then listening to him became a favorite pastime. His daughter Clara recalls the "regal proportions" of his irritation: "When his [temper] escaped into the open, it was a grand sight. Here was the liberation of the caged animals of the earth. It did one good to see it, a raging flood of waters that tore away puerile dams insulting to freedom. Father's temper shone with the light of his genius." [18] The man's published works never, his acquaintances felt, caught the glory of his rage. One does, however, glimpse its incandescence in a letter he once wrote to the gas company—a model for such correspondence:

DEAR SIRS:

Some day you will move me almost to the verge of irritation by your chuckle-headed Goddamned fashion on shutting your Goddamned gas off without giving any notice to your Goddamned parishioners. Several times you have come within an ace of smothering half of this household in their beds and blowing up the other half in this idiotic, not to say criminal, custom of yours. And it has happened again today. Haven't you any telephone?

YS
S. L. CLEMENS [19]

On August 23, 1876, Clemens wrote Howells a letter which was amiable enough: he liked Howells' recent farce; he was sending "The Canvasser's Tale" for the *Atlantic;* he had good ideas for a series of "blindfold novels"—tellings by sundry authors of the same story; he wanted Howells to see *1601.* On August 30, though, he wrote his sister-in-law a letter which in its original version probably was much less serene. Orion and his wife Mollie had been a perpetual problem. Dreamy Orion had over the years failed in one business effort after another, and Clemens had helped support him and had been forced to talk him out of scores of foolish plans. His and Mollie's latest was to operate a boarding house. Clemens offered arguments against this for five pages: he tore up three and a half of these before he sent the letter. The likelihood is that the discarded pages were so filled with withering blasts that on second thought he removed them.[20]

The next day he wrote the fierce rebuke to his old friend Will Bowen for writing "rot that deals in the 'happy days of yore,'" and prescribed a dose of salts. Will's letter proves that this characterization was inaccurate. Most of it deals with recent business reverses which Bowen has suffered and with the consequent postponement of his wedding. Then in a brief passage Bowen asks a little sympathy:

I feel that a letter from my old time friend would be a sweet morsel and when you have the leisure I hope that you will recall some of the old feeling, that distance and time and their duties have perhaps dimmed a little and write me a word or two. We have both been through the mill before, "Hard up," but we were younger then. Hopes were stronger, and the days brighter. . . . I shall continue the struggle though—bearing along my good name and a brave heart with willing hands. . . . Write me Sam when you have time. I shall be glad to hear from you ever. Tell me something of the new Book and when we will see it.[21]

This was not an unreasonable request, particularly since Clemens had more than once reminisced to Bowen about the past. The answer was six pages of fierce denunciation of Bowen's disgusting sentimentality. Evidence that Clemens realized the injustice of his ferocity is the fact that he rewrote the letter and toned down his scolding.

When a man could get fumingly angry at so many things it is impossible to identify any one cause for a specific outburst. I am inclined, however, to guess that the author's indignation late in August was at least partly fired by his irritation with *Huck*, and that, remembering the way a steamboat tore into a raft now and then, as he had described it in "Old Times," he had one come looming out of the gray thick night in his novel:

She was a big one, and she was coming in a hurry, too, looking like a black cloud with rows of glow-worms around it; but all of a sudden she bulged out, big and scary, with a long row of wide-open furnace doors shining like red-hot teeth, and her monstrous bows and guards hanging right over us. There was a yell at us, and a jingling of bells to stop the engines, a pow-wow of cussing, and whistling of steam— and as Jim went overboard on one side and I on the other, she come smashing straight through the raft.

This is as ferocious a steamboat as ever split a raft into splinters —a dragon-like monster breathing fire through red-hot teeth.

This complete and satisfying smashup marks the point, I believe, where the book halted late in the summer of 1876.

11

MISTAKES AND MISFORTUNES,
1876–1879

All I wanted was to go somewheres; all I wanted was a change, I warn't particular.—Adventures of Huckleberry Finn, *chapter i.*

Perhaps the most absorbing problem concerning *Adventures of Huckleberry Finn* is suggested by a comment which Dixon Wecter makes:

The odyssey of Huck's voyage through the South reveals aspects of life darker than the occasional melodrama of *Tom Sawyer.* We are shown the sloth and sadism of poor whites, backwoods loafers. . . . We remark the cowardice of lynching parties; the chicanery of patent medicine fakers, revivalists, and exploiters of rustic ribaldry; the senseless feudings of the gentry. In the background broods fear: not only a boy's apprehension of ghosts, African superstitions . . . but endless implicated strands of robbery, drowning, and murder.[1]

The statements are true, but note this significant fact: these "darker" aspects looming so large in Wecter's characterization, except as are represented by one character and one only, Pap Finn, all develop in parts of the book written not in 1876 but beginning in 1879 or 1880.

The new chapters start with Huck's splashing ashore from the

smashed raft into the midst of the Grangerford-Shepherdson vendetta—"the senseless feudings of the gentry." Drifting downstream, Huck and Jim meet the "patent medicine fakers, revivalists, and exploiters of rustic ribaldry." Lynchings, robberies,
murders, and the sadistic actions of poor whites come still later.
Thus a memorable feature of parts of the novel written after 1879
is their disillusioned commentary.

What happened in Clemens' life, his thinking, and his writing
to change the nature of the book? Bernard DeVoto says of the
period between the fall of 1876 and that of 1879:

It was, I think, the happiest period of [Clemens'] life. He was rich
and famous, his house in Hartford was the center of a large circle of
friends, and these years are the untroubled ones in his family life.
But there was no development in his literary personality and no direction in his literary activity. He was drifting, writing pleasurably but
aimlessly, making money, enjoying life. . . .[2]

There is evidence for this statement, as for practically every one
which DeVoto makes about Clemens. The humorist still enjoyed
his showy mansion and its luxuries, still savored adulation, large
royalty checks, social splurges, a pleasant family life, gay friendships. Nevertheless that these years were the happiest in his life
is debatable. Furthermore, I believe that this period brought
very important developments—experiences, thinking, and literary
growth—responsible for the new direction *Huckleberry Finn* took.

DeVoto himself notices that Clemens did not have reason to admire much of his literary output in these years: "It was essentially
. . . uncreative"; there were "burlesques which are mostly painful reading now," for instance, "The Loves of Alonzo Fitz-Clarence
and Rosannah Ethelton," "Mrs. McWilliams and the Lightning,"
and the unpublished "Burlesque Etiquette." There was the in-
nocuous travelogue, "Some Rambling Notes of an Idle Excursion,"
which, though Howells disagreed, Clemens suspected was un-
worthy of print.[3] Under way was *A Tramp Abroad*, which was
not going well.

Two plays were sad failures. In the fall of 1876, Bret Harte came to Hartford, dressed as nattily as usual, his handsome features adorned by his formidable moustache, his curly dark hair streaked with silver. He proposed that he and Mark Twain collaborate on a play making use of a Chinese character of Harte's invention and of Scotty Briggs, whom the humorist had pictured in *Roughing It*. Collaboration, hard enough for even-tempered men, was an ordeal for Harte, with his sharp tongue, and Mark Twain, with his volcanic temper. Harte, a clever and self-assured man, impressed his collaborator by the ease with which he mapped out the action of the play. But Harte really had little talent for dramatic construction: his only previous drama had been characterized by a reviewer as "without form and void . . . . like one of Beadle's dime novels struck by lightning." [4] Harte's collaborator was just as weak in this area: he had been able to turn *The Gilded Age* into a successful play chiefly because, by good luck, Gilbert S. Densmore had devised a plot for him with incidents strung together well enough to get by.[5] Nevertheless, somehow *Ah Sin* was finished, rehearsed, and presented—in 1877—in Baltimore and New York, then briefly on the road. But by October 15, 1877, the humorist had to write Howells, " 'Ah Sin' is a most abject and incurable failure! It will leave the stage permanently within a week. . . ." [6]

Not long before this, Twain had hastily concocted another play by himself—*Simon Wheeler, Amateur Detective*. Dion Boucicault, the playwright-producer, paid it the dubious compliment of saying that it was better than *Ah Sin*, but would have none of it. And John Brougham, another producer, let Mark down as gently as possible by saying that, though the drama contained pay dirt, the gold had not been extracted, and it was "altogether too diffuse . . . for dramatic presentation." So, written though both these plays were in a cynical spirit comparable to that of dramatists Howells or Henry James in days when most dramas were as bad as most motion pictures or television plays today, these did not succeed on the stage.

An attempt to salvage *Simon Wheeler* by turning it into a novel also fizzled. By fits and starts the author plodded through page 512, then quit. Anyone reading the manuscript in the Berg Collection of the New York Public Library easily sees why, in 1879, he was driven to give up.[7] By that time he had pumped his well dry not once but several times, and in this instance the best water he had pumped up was muddied.

Such literary failures and false starts were not unusual, but Mark never delighted in them. And having predicted as recently as June, 1876, that he would be played out as a writer within two or three years he may well have worried about his prediction coming true when he failed to produce any successful play or to complete any full-length publishable book between July, 1875, and January, 1880—a much longer period than usual.

Another failure would be hard to take seriously if he and Howells did not testify that it was a matter of deep concern—a speech in Boston, December 17, 1877, at a dinner given by the *Atlantic Monthly to* celebrate John Greenleaf Whittier's seventieth birthday.

According to the thinking of the day, this occasion was an important literary event. Henry James, Walt Whitman, and Herman Melville were not on the guest list, but few then could have foreseen that eight decades later their absence would be marked. William Cullen Bryant was not there either, it may be because at eighty-three he was not up to journeying from New York. James Russell Lowell, whose absence was lamented, was in Madrid. Except for these two, the seating list was a roster of the honored men of letters of America. At the head table alongside Publisher H. O. Houghton and Editor Howells sat a venerable quartet whose presence stirred awe in the breast of everyone present. The guest of honor, Whittier, and Henry Wadsworth Longfellow (also three score and ten) both had gorgeous white beards. Little Oliver Wendell Holmes, aged sixty-eight, had rather skimpy side whiskers but a fine head of white hair. Tall Ralph Waldo Emerson, aged seventy-four, had white muttonchop sideburns, and his natural nobility of countenance was enhanced by unfocused eyes (his mind was wandering) which gave him the look of contemplating Higher Things. Howells does not exaggerate when he speaks of the "extraordinary dignity" of these four and of "the species of religious veneration in which these men were held." [8] A letter of regret from Samuel Bowles, editor of the *Springfield Republican,* read just before Clemens spoke, summed up the feeling of many:

I wonder if these old poets of ours . . . appreciate the benefit they confer upon their fellow citizens by simply consenting to live among them as old men? Do they know how they help to save the American nation from the total wreck and destruction of the sentiment of reverence? . . . The influence which these beloved and venerated poets exercise upon the public mind and character, simply by being lovely and venerable, is, in the highest degree, salutary and salvatory.[9]

Clemens had prepared his speech with as much care as he ordinarily used in working up after-dinner speeches—probably with more. As usual he had written it out and had memorized it—pauses, inflections, and all—well enough to deliver it as if it were extemporaneous. The keynote of the occasion being reverence, the humorist chose to tell an irreverent story.

He told of a visit he had made as a beginning author, "callow and conceited," to a cabin in California in 1862. Hoping to impress, he introduced himself to the miner living there as "Mark Twain." The miner then told in flavorsome speech of a recent visit from three drunken tramps who had also introduced themselves as authors:

Mr. Emerson was a seedy little bit of a chap—red headed. Mr. Holmes was as fat as a balloon—he weighed as much as three hundred, and had double chins all the way down to his stomach. Mr. Longfellow was built like a prize-fighter. His head was cropped and bristly-like as if he had a wig made of hair brushes. His nose lay straight down his face, like a finger, with the end-joint tilted up. They had been drinking. . . .

The miner quoted a number of exchanges with these reprobates. When Mr. Holmes told him, "Build thee more stately mansions, O my Soul!" he replied, "I can't afford it, Mr. Holmes, and moreover I don't want to." When Mr. Longfellow quoted the stately hexameters of "Hiawatha," the miner broke in, "If you'll be so kind as to hold your yawp for about five minutes and let me get this grub ready, you'll do me proud." When Mr. Emerson intoned, "Here once the embattled farmers stood,/And fired the shot heard round the world," his host told him, "O, blackguard the premises as much as you want to—it don't cost you a cent."

The trio "went on drinking, and pretty soon they got out a greasy old deck and went to playing cut-throat euchre at ten cents a corner—on trust," slightly misquoting gems from their poetry. As the evening passed, they cheated at cards, engaged in a little gunplay, and claimed credit for writing Whittier's "Barbara Friet-chie," Lowell's "Bigelow Papers," and Bryant's "Thanatopsis." When they left the next morning Mr. Longfellow wore the miner's boots, preparatory to making "footprints on the sands of time."

Clemens long after remembered how the audience's expressions "turned to a sort of black frost. . . . I went on, but with difficulty . . . . always hoping—but with a gradually perishing hope— that somebody would laugh, or that somebody would at least smile, but nobody did." He struggled to the end "in front of a body of people who seemed turned to stone with horror." Al-though other speeches were listed to follow, this speech, so he recalled, ended the program in a panic. Howells, too, desolately describes a fiasco:

There fell a silence, weighing many tons to the square inch, which deepened from moment to moment, and was broken only by the hysterical and blood-curdling laughter of a single guest. . . . Nobody knew whether to look at the speaker or down at his plate. . . . I chose my plate . . . and so I do not know how Clemens looked, except when I stole a glance at him, and saw him standing solitary amid his ap-palled and appalling listeners, with his joke dead on his hands. . . . Of what happened afterward . . . I have no longer the least remem-brance.

A scene forecast in *1601*—a crowd of stuffy cupbearers disgusted by jesting. A dramatic scene, ready made for historians who want to show concretely the ante-bellum genteel traditionalists con-fronted by post-bellum Western innovators.

Life is not often so funny or so dramatic, though; and it was not on this occasion. Henry Nash Smith, after studying all available evidence, finds that both Clemens (as was his habit) and Howells improved on actuality, grossly exaggerating the shock and the distress. Although some listeners did not laugh, some did. Emerson, bemused, paid little attention; but Whittier, Longfellow, and Holmes managed to laugh. And the festivities did not disintegrate: other speakers made the speeches they had prepared, and the completed program ended at one o'clock in the morning.

Smith suggests that, instead of the banquet, Clemens and Howells remembered the audience's relative lack of hilarity and particularly the newspaper comments. Some journals were rather stern—"in bad taste and entirely out of place" (Boston *Transcript*); "the instincts of a gentleman would have prevented its presentation. . . ." (Cincinnati *Commercial*); and "Nevada delirium tremens" (Springfield *Republican*). Any of these criticisms which Clemens saw would have distressed him. For, reiterating as they did the charge that he was a crude buffoon woefully lacking in refinement, they rubbed salt into an old wound.

However he acquired his impression of the reception of the speech, Clemens' performance did not contribute to his gaiety during the Christmas season. "Poor fellow," Joe Twichell wrote in his diary, "it was a great disappointment to him to have it turn out so. He saw . . . that he had made a fatal blunder." Clemens wrote Howells, on December 23, "My sense of disgrace does not abate. It grows." And two days after Christmas, he wrote Emerson, Longfellow, and Holmes abject apologies for having offended them:

. . . when I perceived what it was that I had done, I felt as real a sorrow and suffered as sharp a mortification as if I had done it with a guilty intent. This continues. That the impulse was innocent, brings no abatement. As to my wife's distress, it is not to be measured; for she is of finer stuff than I; and yours were sacred names to her. We do not talk about the misfortune—it *scorches;* so we only think—and think. . . . I *had* to write you, for the easement . . . , even though the doing of it might be a further offense.

Holmes, Longfellow, and Emerson's daughter wrote reassuring replies; but Clemens was not, at the time, reassured.

In retrospect, none of these literary failures was tragic. Several contributed to the writing of *Huckleberry Finn* and thus acquired significance. But for the moment they played hob with Clemens' felicity.

Failures of a different sort—and a sign of discontent—were Clemens' trip to Europe and his stay there in 1878–1879. While the Whittier birthday debacle may have had something to do with these, Professor Ferguson oversimplifies, I believe, in suggesting that the reception of the speech led to the trip.[10] Less than two months after the affair the ebullient author was writing defiantly, "Nobody has ever convinced me that that speech was not a good one." [11] And he had contemplated the trip long before the speech was delivered.

Going abroad in that period was a habit of American high society in general and Nook Farm in particular. The neighbors of Clemens liked to cross the ocean every two or three years, usually to stay abroad for several months. "I have a friend," Warner had Margaret DeBree remark in his novel, *A Little Journey*, "who says she should be mortified if she reached heaven and there had to confess that she had never seen Europe. It is one of the things that is expected of a person." Like buying a fine house, travel abroad indicated affluence and culture. Foreign sojourns, too, made possible importing more pictures, statuary, and furniture to clutter elegant rooms.

The impulse which often sent the Clemenses to Elmira in the summer also operated. In *A Little Journey*, Warner suggested that fashion's hegiras resulted from "the discovery of the disease called nervous prostration, which demands for its cure constant change of scene." The Clemenses had learned what the disease was and how to cure it. In May, 1877, exhausted after rehearsing *Ah Sin*, Clemens was driven to take what for him was, he said, "a novelty, namely, a trip for pure recreation, the bread-and-butter element left out," [12] to Bermuda with Joe Twichell.

Clemens had thought of paying another visit to Europe at least two years before his departure. In February, 1876, after growling in a letter about burdensome correspondence and the forthcoming loss of his secretary, "I shall go to Europe, then," he predicted, but crossed out the sentence.[13] About a year later, Livy told her mother, "Mr. Clemens grows more and more determined to go to Germany next Summer—I combat it and say the farm next Summer and Germany a year from next Summer if we have money enough—I don't know who will come out ahead but I think I shall." [14] A few weeks later, on March 26, 1877, Clemens addressed the Monday Evening Club, eloquently, one suspects, on "The Advantages of Travel."

Livy won, and the family went to Quarry Farm for the summer, but even in "that bourne from whence," Clemens held, "no traveler returns when sober," [15] he spent a paragraph in a letter envying authors who had had the good luck to be thrust into jail where they could write uninterruptedly:

Only Bunyan, Sir Walter Raleigh, the author of Don Quixote, and a few other people have had the *best* of opportunities for working, in this world. Solitary imprisonment, by compulsion, is the one perfect condition for perfect performance. No letters, no telegrams, no boxes, no responsibilities, no gaddings about, no seductive pleasures beckoning one away and dividing his mind. Then his *work* becomes his pleasure, his recreation, his absorption, his uplifting and all-satisfying enthusiasm. . . . a man so circumstanced. . . . lives in a fairer world than any that is outside, he moves in a goodlier company than any that others know. . . . If it were not for Livy and the cubs, this sun should not set before I would kill somebody in the second degree.[16]

Before leaving the farm that summer, the family had definitely decided to take the trip to Europe.[17]

Reasons Clemens gave then and later boiled down to two. (1) "Badgered" and "harassed" by "business responsibilities and annoyances, and the persecution of kindly letters from well meaning strangers," he went abroad, he said, "to get rid of this inane, brain-softening letter answering" and to find time and opportunity to "complete one of the half dozen books that lie begun, upstairs." (2) "We are in Europe," he wrote back to Mrs. Fairbanks, "to cut down our expenses, and we are doing it the best we can. . . ." [18]

Clemens' plans shifted. In September, 1877, he was going to

"settle down in a German town for 6 months. Then come home." A year later, he was going to take the family "to some little corner of Europe and budge no more" until he had finished a book. In March, 1878, he was going to "find a German village where nobody knows my name or speaks any English, and shut myself up in a closet 2 miles from the hotel, and work every day without interruption" until he had "satisfied his consuming desire" to do uninterrupted writing: his estimate was that this would take two years.[19] Actually, the family was away about seventeen months— from April 11, 1878, to September 3, 1879; they traveled a good deal; and Clemens did not finish any of his books while overseas.

Shortly before leaving he formulated the hoped-for advantages:

We let up on the weight and wear and responsibility of housekeeping —we go and board with somebody, who is suffering it, but it troubles us not. Here we are helping the *nation* keep house—we go abroad and become another nation's guests—we don't have to feel any responsibility. . . . So to go abroad is the true rest—you cease wholly to keep house, then, both national and domestic.

He added words which, as Ferguson guesses, may reflect dissatisfaction with the attitudes of certain critics: "To go abroad has something of the same sense that death brings. . . . I know you will refrain from saying harsh things because they can't hurt me, since I am out of reach and cannot hear them."[20] Two notebooks later, in Europe, he made a similar comment: "When you are in Europe it is such a rest from care. At home every funeral is a personal matter, and you sigh or even cry. Here you look on—are cheerful and even able to say 'I'm glad you're gone!' "[21]

By the time he wrote this, he may have been trying to reassure himself about the advantages of a most disappointing trip. Temporarily at least he and Livy were persuaded that they had reestablished their financial security:

Privately [he wrote Howells from Heidelberg in June, 1878], I have some good news. . . . *we've quit feeling poor!* You know that for two years we have been coming to want, every little while, and have straightway gone to economizing. Yesterday we fell to figuring and discovered that we have more than income enough from investments to live on a generous scale. . . . This thing was so gratifying to me that my first impulse was to run to you with it.[22]

But pleasant aspects were outweighed by unpleasant ones. Aboard ship, Clemens, habitually "disturbed by every noise,"[23] drew a cabin where yelping children, a banging ancient piano, a pounding ship's screw, and rattling crockery rasped his nerves.[24] Two weeks at sea he described with rare restraint as "almost devilish."[25]

Ashore, Clemens, whose mastery of foreign languages was something hoped for rather than something attained, was brash enough on occasion to act as courier for his sizable band. He had to ride herd on a vast collection of miscellaneous baggage and to locate accommodations by instinct. At least once, upon straggling into a dingy-looking suite which Clemens had booked in advance, Olivia Clemens and her friend Clara Spaulding burst into tears, while the two children and Rosa watched uneasily. At other times the party had to perch in railway stations while their courier unsystematically hunted rooms. Often quarters were unseemly and noisy, service bad, food—by Hartford's high standards—unappetizing.

Livy and the children frequently were ill. In August, 1878, Clemens told his mother and sister that "we have had a doctor most of the time since we left home. We have *all* been in the doctor's hands, even Rosa."[26] From Paris, on March 31, 1879, he wrote Mrs. Langdon: "Livy has pains in the back of her neck, and the old ones in her spine. . . . The children have French colds. . . . Rosa has a horrible cold. Clara Spaulding has the twin to it."[27] Two weeks later he said he had been "sick—sick—and sick again—with rheumatism and dysentery. I have spent four-fifths of my six weeks' residence in bed."[28] Since Clemens like many habitually healthy men regarded every illness he had as an imposition, such an experience seemed an outrage.

To add to his woes, the weather, beginning in September, 1878, was often unpleasant. In London, August 10, 1879, he wrote a bitter summary in a notebook: "We still have fires every few days —had one to-night. We have had fires almost all the time, in

Rome, Munich, Paris, Belgium, Condover Hall near Shrewsbury, England, [where the family visited Reginald Cholmondeley for a week], from the 1st of last September (Florence) to the present time—*nearly 12 months.*" [29] Several passages in letters show that

ILLUSTRATION FOR *A Tramp Abroad,* FIRST EDITION

there had been spells of good weather during the period specified. But the writer was correct in remembering that the weather had been atrocious much of the time.

Joining all these troubles was the fading of the dream that in Europe Clemens would be able to write as happily and uninterruptedly as an author in a jail. At several stopping places he rented a room for himself a mile or so from the hotel in which the party was staying. In Heidelberg in June, 1878, his workroom was in a house on a pinnacle seventeen hundred feet above the Rhine Valley. He told Bayard Taylor:

Yes, we live at the Schloss-Hotel, and shall doubtless continue to do so until the neighborhood of August—but I only eat and sleep there; my work-den is in the second story of a little Wirthschaft which stands at the base of the tower on the summit of the Königstuhl. I walk up there every morning at 10, write until 3, talk the most hopeless and unimprovable German with the family until 5, then tramp down to the hotel for the night. It is a sehr schönes Aussicht up there as you may remember. The exercise of climbing up there is invigorating but devilish.[30]

By July 13 he could report a good start on the travel book he planned to produce during the trip, having "written 400 pages of MS.—that is to say 45 to 50,000 words, or one-fourth of a book." "But," he admitted, "it is in disconnected form and cannot be rightly written until we are settled down for the fall and winter in Munich." He would be slowed down, he guessed, by a trip with Joe Twichell, who was coming over to join him, but he hoped to write two hundred additional pages while hiking with his friend.[31]

He was being oversanguine as usual about his progress. He wrote far less than two hundred pages while with Twichell. Furthermore, he decided that he had made a bad start: he would have to tear up most of what he had written and start anew in Munich.[32] He shredded about four hundred pages, wrote some nine hundred more that he thought would do, and figured that he was half done.[33] But again he found that he was living in a fool's paradise, and he had to put in a great burst of effort to approach the halfway mark:

. . . I counted up and found that I had written only 65 to 70 words a page, instead of 100! Consequently, I was only ⅓ done. I had been writing 30 pages a day, and allowing myself Saturdays for holiday. However, I had 8 clear days left before leaving Munich—so I buckled in and wrote 400 pages in those 8 days and so brought my work close up to half-way. . . . During that final 8-day spurt . . . I allowed myself only the Sunday for holiday—and I utilized that Sunday by writing 60 pages of letters.[34]

In rain-drenched Paris the grim weather did not prevent Clemens from showing the same incorrigible tendency to be oversanguine about the date when he would finish his book: the end of July, then—still less realistically—the end of June, then in time for fall publication.[35] But when he went ashore in New York at the conclusion of his wanderings, September 3, 1879, he told reporters he would not finish his travel book for "a few months." [36]

He summarized his feeling about the sojourn in Europe in the inscription in a copy of *A Tramp Abroad* which he gave to Twichell: "We had a mighty good time, Joe, and the six weeks [with you] I would dearly like to repeat *any* time; but the rest of the fourteen months—*never.*"

On occasion while overseas the humorist had consoled himself with the belief that, though he was less than enchanted by shops and galleries, Livy and Clara Spaulding and the children at least were having a fine time. But Livy's letters at intervals suggest that her thoughts often turned fondly to Hartford. From Heidelberg in June, 1878, she wrote her mother a typical comparison: "I'm glad our home is in America. I enjoy it as much as possible here but I should not like to think of living here always, of this being my home—I would rather live just where I do than any place that I know of—and I only hope that we will always have money enough so that we can continue to live there." [37] Her husband joined her in hoping things would go better in the United States. On arriving in New York, he confided to reporters that he had "written more and torn up more manuscript after it was written" than the reporters could imagine, and that he felt "a deep sense of relief in returning to the dearest land in the world." [38]

A few weeks later, though, he was voicing an old complaint. Within two weeks of his return, five strangers scattered over the country had asked him "to read and judge their MS books and 'use my influence' to get publishers for them." Since the manuscripts totaled 11,000 pages, he calculated that if he read them he would have to put in full time for three weeks. Also he was bracing himself to answer about thirty letters:

I have to decline to lecture; and to furnish autograph "sentiments;" and to write articles for periodicals . . . and so on, and so on. This goes on, week in and week out, and is mighty irksome and monotonous. . . . Tiresome? That is the word. It does not anger me, it only makes me low-spirited. These letters are compliments, consequently one cannot disrespect them. But constantly answering the very same questions the very same way is another form of climbing a treadmill. . . .[39]

The family was departing that very day "to that serene hill-top," Quarry Farm.

The farm seemed as delightful as ever. He told Twichell: "You have . . . never seen any place that was so divine as the farm. Why don't you come here and take a foretaste of heaven?" Momentarily, the travel book seemed to be shaping up well. He was still knocking out early chapters, he confided: "Day before yesterday my shovel fetched up three more chapters and laid them, reeking, on the festering shore-pile of their predecessors, and now I think the yarn swims right along, without hitch or halt."

But hitches and halts had not ended. In mid-October when the family got back to Hartford, he had not finished the book, and progress was unsatisfactory. There were interruptions. In November he went to Chicago to speak at a reunion of the army of Tennessee honoring Grant; and at two o'clock in the morning he won a tremendous ovation from listeners whose ears had been battered for hours by oratory. In December he spoke in Boston at a breakfast honoring Oliver Wendell Holmes, and since this speech was more reverent and subdued than the Whittier speech before a similar audience, it received the listeners'—and the newspapers'—approval.

And there were the usual Hartford distractions—visits of traveling literary men, elaborate dinner parties, club affairs. Livy, as usual, was not in the best of health. She had to supervise the installation of a new fresco in the house, the removal of dust covers, and the arranging of furniture and *objets d'art* newly arrived from Europe. She had become pregnant that fall, and her fourth pregnancy was not proving easy for this fragile woman.

On January 8, 1880, Clemens told Howells of another flight from Hartford and, simultaneously, the completion of *A Tramp Abroad:*

Mrs. Clemens and I are starting (without the children!) to stay indefinitely in Elmira. The wear and tear of settling the house broke her down, and she has been growing weaker and weaker for a fortnight. All that time—in fact ever since I saw you—I have been fighting a life-and-death battle with this infernal book and *hoping* to get it done some day. I required 300 pages of MS, and I have written more than 600 since I saw you—and tore it all up except 288. This I was about to tear up yesterday and begin again, when Mrs. Perkins came up to the billiard room and said, "You will never get any woman to do the thing necessary to save her life by mere *persuasion* . . . it is time to use *force;* she must have change; take her and leave the children here. . . ."

So I took the 288 pages to Bliss and told him that was the last line I should ever write on this book. (A book which required 2600 pages of MS, and I have written nearly four thousand, first and last.)

Livy's midwinter departure from Hartford—more remarkable, from the children—unprecedented as it was, shows that Hartford had not proved to be the haven she had pictured while abroad. And Clemens' story of the completion at last of his "infernal" manuscript shows that abroad, in Elmira, and in Hartford he had had a fiendish time writing it.

The literary failures, the "disgrace" of the Whittier birthday speech, the difficulties abroad and at home make it doubtful that the period 1876–1879 can be called the happiest in Clemens' life. The atmosphere in which he worked had something to do with this man of moods writing—in *A Tramp Abroad, The Prince and the Pauper,* and, more important, in *Huckleberry Finn*—passages which did not bubble over with hilarity. Influences which I think were more important than his circumstances and emotions were also at work. A look at his writings, published and unpublished, during these years will indicate what these influences were.

12

"I GENERALIZE WITH INTREPIDITY"

France has neither winter nor summer nor morals—apart from these drawbacks it is a fine country.—1879 entry in Mark Twain's Notebook, *p. 153.*

Except for the fact that it sold well, *A Tramp Abroad* was not worth all the trouble it took to write. Clemens saw that his woes while traveling and while writing might mar his humor. From Munich early in 1879 he wrote Howells: "I wish I *could* give those sharp satires on European life which you mention, but of course a man can't write successful satire except he be in a calm, judicial good-humor; whereas I *hate* travel, and I *hate* hotels, and I *hate* the opera, and I *hate* the old masters. In truth I don't ever seem to be in a good enough humor with *any*thing to satirize it. . . ." [1] This sense of a lack of the necessary detachment and geniality probably had much to do with his tearing up and rewriting a vast number of manuscript pages.

In a labored pursuit of humorous effects he modified facts even more than in his other "autobiographical" books and he invented many details. To provide a less gloomy atmosphere, he omitted mention of the horrible weather which he had bemoaned so often while abroad. He completely left out of his narrative Livy, Clara Spaulding, Rosa, and the children, whose troubles and illnesses had been of such overweening importance to him.[2] In the book only two men make the journey: Mark Twain in his often assumed guise of a humorless simpleton and a character called Harris, who is so vaguely based on Twichell that the writer's testimony barely persuades us that the minister was his prototype.

He invented three completely fictional lines of narrative. The first, which gives the book its title, was based upon an experience which he and Twichell had had in the fall of 1874. Their attempted hike from Hartford to Boston had ended twenty-eight miles out when Clemens had become lame, and they had wired Howells, "Arrive by rail at seven o'clock. The first of a series of grand pedestrian tours . . . to be performed by us *next year.*" The author burlesqued over-hearty accounts of European tours afoot by telling how he and Harris would "*start* on pedestrian tours, but mount the first conveyance that offered . . . endeavoring to seem unconscious that it was not legitimate pedestrianizing." [3] The second line told of his trying "to study art . . . learn to paint." The third recounted how he attempted with an equal lack of success "to learn the German language."

In general the book is an inferior one. Paine, who often manages to praise Twain's writings even when other enthusiasts despair, contrasts it unfavorably with a book using similar materials, *The Innocents Abroad.* The two books are, he says, "as different as was their author at the periods when they were written. . . . In the *Tramp* . . . he has become a cynic. In the *Innocents* he laughs at delusions and fallacies—and enjoys them. In the *Tramp* he laughs at human foibles and affectations—and wants to smash them."

Howells makes similar points in his review of the book, ostensibly contrasting Twain with other popular humorists:

His humor springs from a certain intensity of common sense, a passionate love of justice, and a generous scorn of what is petty and mean; and it is these qualities which his "school" [of humorists] have not been able to convey. They have never been more conspicuous than in this last book of his, to which they may be said to give its sole coherence. . . . At the bottom of his heart he has often the grimness of a reformer; his wit is turned . . . upon matters that are out of joint, that are unfair or unnecessarily ignoble, and cry out to his love of justice and for discipline. . . . His opinions are no longer the opinions of a Western American newly amused and disgusted by European differences, but the Western American's impressions on being a second time confronted with things he has had time to think over. This is the serious undercurrent of the book. . . .[4]

The "wildest extravagance" of the author's humor, Howells says, "is the break and fling from a deep feeling, a wrath with some folly which disquiets him worse than other men, a personal hatred for some humbug or pretension that embitters him beyond anything but laughter." Implied is the fact that what the writer had told Howells he feared, had happened: too much involvement, too much wrath, often sour the humor. Twain is too irritated by cruel Heidelberg student duelists, posturing French duelists, pretentious tourists, incompetent French governors, depraved artists (as he thinks them) to represent them comically.

On occasion he does write with enough detached good humor or enough personal pleasure to charm the reader. The attack on "The Awful German Language" is an instance. A few times, too, as in other books, Twain echoes his own writings: he borrows passages from *Tom Sawyer* and *Huckleberry Finn*. A strong likelihood is that an inner compulsion impels him to repeat descriptions which have a peculiar charm and are coming to have particular meanings for him.

Twice, on visiting the woods—those along the Neckar in chapter ii and the Black Forest in chapter xxii—he finds or imagines and describes spots as secluded and as idyllic as the forest scenes on Jackson's Island and the willow-shadowed shores in his novel:

One cannot describe those noble woods, nor the feeling with which they inspire him. A feature of the feeling, however, is a deep sense of contentment; another feature of it is a buoyant, boyish gladness; and a third . . . is one's sense of the remoteness of the work-day world and his entire emancipation from it and its affairs. . . . A rich cathedral gloom pervades the pillared aisles; so the stray flecks of sunlight that strike a trunk here and a bough yonder are strongly accented, and when they strike the moss they fairly seem to burn. . . . the diffused light of the low afternoon sun . . . pervades the place like a faint, green-tinted mist. . . .[5]

A narrative about a completely fictional voyage down the Neckar on a raft contains a reminiscent description in chapter xv:

The motion of the raft . . . is gentle, and gliding, and smooth and noiseless; it calms down all feverish activities, it soothes to sleep all nervous hurry and impatience; under its restful influence all the troubles and vexations and sorrows that harass the mind vanish away, and existence becomes a dream, a charm, a deep and tranquil ecstasy. How it contrasts with hot and perspiring pedestrianism, and dusty and deafening railroad rush, and tedious jolting . . . over blinding white roads!

We went slipping silently along, between the green and fragrant banks, with a sense of pleasure and contentment that grew, and grew, all the time. Sometimes banks were overhung with thick masses of willows that wholly hid the ground behind; sometimes we had noble hills on the one hand, clothed densely with foliage to their tops, and on the other hand open levels blazing, with poppies . . . ; sometimes we drifted in the shadows of forests. . . .[6]

These repeat the emphases on the remoteness from civilization, the peace, the quiet which occur in similar scenes in *Huck Finn* written in 1876; and they forecast idyllic—and increasingly meaningful—passages in *Huck* still to be written.

Characterization at times creates humor, as in a scene (some-

HARRIS AND MARK TWAIN ABOARD THE RAFT, *A Tramp Abroad*

what reminiscent of Huck's encounter with Judith Loftus) wherein the narrator strings lies together in a talk with a pretty girl, and forgets a name which he has used in one of his false-hoods. Language, too, in phrases, sentences, or paragraphs, frequently succeeds.

The best passage in the book and the one most admired shows Mark using background, characterization, and language so skill-fully that the grimness of the theme has generally been overlooked. This passage derives from a remembered oral anecdote. En route to Europe the author wrote in his notebook, in a series of jottings which he hoped to work up: "Jim Gillis's yarn about the blue jays that tried to fill Carrington's house with acorns—'By George this lays over anything *I* ever struck' says the jay. 'I've put 460 in there.'" [7] He was recalling the visit to Steve Gillis's cabin in Calaveras County, California, in the winter of 1864–65 when, in addition to the Jumping Frog story told by Ben Coon, he had heard several hilarious yarns told by Steve Gillis.

In chapter ii of *A Tramp Abroad,* wandering in the Neckar hills, Twain muses about the "gnomes, and dwarfs, and all sorts of mysterious and uncanny creatures" with whom German legends have peopled the woods:

I presently fell into a train of dreamy thought about animals which talk, and kobolds, and enchanted folk, and the rest of the pleasant legendary stuff; and so, by stimulating my fancy, I finally got to imagining I glimpsed small flitting shapes here and there down the columned aisles of the forest. . . .

When I had stood ten minutes, thinking and imagining, and getting my spirit in tune with the place . . . a raven suddenly uttered a hoarse croak over my head. It made me start.

The raven becomes increasingly insulting as he croaks comments about the tourist. He is joined by a feathered friend:

The two sat side by side on the limb and discussed me as freely and offensively as two great naturalists might discuss a new kind of bug. The thing became more and more embarrassing. They called in another friend. This was too much. I saw that they had the advantage of me, and so I concluded to get out of the scrape by walking out of it . . . when even a raven shouts after you, "What a hat!" "Oh, pull down your vest!" and that sort of thing, it hurts you and humiliates you. . . .

This anticipates the harassed Benchleys and Thurbers of modern humor who picture the characters they pretend to be as victimized and humiliated by inanimate objects, birds, or women in a hostile world. Too, it provides a neat transition from the legendary German creatures to the seemingly human ravens, and then to the bluejays of Jim Gillis's fanciful American tall tale:

Animals talk to each other, of course. There can be no question about that; but I suppose there are very few people who can understand them. I never knew but one man who could. I knew he could, however, because he told me so himself. He was a middle-aged, simple-hearted miner who had lived in a lonely corner of California, among the woods and mountains, a good many years, and had studied the ways of his only neighbors, the beasts and the birds, until he believed he could accurately translate any remark which they made.

Jim tells how, one Sunday morning, sitting before his cabin, "taking the sun, and looking at the blue hills, and listening to the leaves rustling so lonely in the trees, and thinking of the home away yonder in the states, that I hadn't heard from in thirteen years," he sees a bluejay light on the house which his last neighbor left seven years before. Discovering a knothole the jay tries to fill it with acorns. He dumps in acorn after acorn without making any progress, and grows more and more frantic until

he broke loose and cussed himself black in the face. . . . When he got through he walks to the hole and looks in . . . then he says, "Well, you're a long hole, and a deep hole, and a mighty singular hole . . . but I've started in to fill you, and I'm d——d if I *don't* fill you, if it takes a hundred years!"

And with that, away he went . . . and the way he hove acorns into that hole was one of the most exciting and astonishing spectacles I ever struck . . . at last he could hardly flop his wings. . . . He comes a-drooping down . . . sweating like an ice-pitcher . . . he bent down for a look. If you'll believe me, when his head come up again he was just pale with rage. . . . He just had strength enough to crawl up on to the comb and lean his back agin the chimbly, and then he collected his impressions and begun to free his mind. I see in a second that what I had mistook for profanity in the mines was only just the rudiments. . . .

Another jay, attracted by the eloquence, comes along, asks questions, learns that the bird has dumped in "not any less than two tons" of acorns, and calls other jays. Discussing the problem, these offer "as many leather-headed opinions as an average crowd of humans could have done." Finally a jay peers into a door.

"Come here!" he says, "Come here, everybody; hang'd if this fool hasn't been trying to fill up a house with acorns!" They all came a-swooping down like a blue cloud, and as each fellow lit . . . and took a glance . . . he fell over backwards suffocating with laughter, and the next jay took his place and done the same.

Well, sir, they roosted around here on the housetop and the trees for an hour, and guffawed over the thing like human beings. . . . They brought jays here from all over the United States to look down this hole, every summer for three years. Other birds, too. And they could all see the point. . . .

So the story ends with the ambitious bluejay subjected to raucous ridicule similar to that which had sent Mark Twain scurrying from the woods at the beginning of his story.

This interlude has been highly praised—and justly. "Were one asked to choose from all Mark Twain's works," says Ferguson, "the most perfect example of the genuine Western tall story, patiently and skillfully built up from a matter-of-fact prelude to a sustained climax, the choice probably would come down at last to Jim Baker's bluejay yarn."[8] Three ingredients which intermingle in much of the best and most characteristic nineteenth-century American humor are delectably combined: fantasy—here an imaginative "humanization" of animals, elsewhere at its best in Uncle Remus's stories; characterization of a highly individualized, serious-minded, earthy personality; and horse-sense commentary based on wisdom and experience. As DeVoto says:

Its material comes from the Negro's bestiary, interstitial with the life of boyhood in Hannibal; and in this way the humor rises from fantasy, from the imaginative mythmaking of the slaves and the frontier. But also, Jim Baker, the narrator, exists; he is a creation from the world of reality. He lives, and no fantasy has gone into his creation, but only the sharp perception of an individual. His patient, explanatory mind actually works before our eyes and no one can doubt him. His speech has been caught so cunningly that its rhythms produce complete conviction. Fantasy is thus an instrument of realism and the humor of Mark Twain merges into the fiction that is his highest reach.[9]

The nature of Baker's fantasy and of his philosophy derives from his character and his situation. It is natural for this recluse, alone so long, to give "his only neighbors, the beasts and the birds," human qualities: he has been "touched" just enough to attribute to them the speech, the foibles, the experiences of humans. He is pathetic; but pathos escapes sentimentality because of his unsentimental way of thinking and talking about men and their bluejay prototypes.

For he is a misanthropist (a fact which may explain his living in solitude) who thus proves that jays, actually, are human:

You may call a jay a bird. Well, so he is, in a measure—because he's got feathers on him, and don't belong to no church, perhaps; but otherwise he is just as much a human as you be. And I'll tell you for why. A jay's gifts, and instincts, and feelings, and interests, cover the whole ground. A jay hasn't got any more principle than a Congressman. A jay will lie, a jay will steal, a jay will deceive, a jay will betray; and four times out of five, a jay will go back on his solemnest promise. The sacredness of an obligation is a thing which you can't cram into no bluejay's head. Now, on top of all this, there's another thing; a jay can outswear any gentleman in the mines. . . . Yes, sir, a jay is everything that a man is. A jay can cry, a jay can laugh, a jay can feel shame, a jay can reason and plan and discuss, a jay likes gossip and scandal, a jay has got a sense of humor, a jay knows when he is an ass just as well as you do—maybe better. If a jay ain't human, he better take in his sign, that's all.

The tale he tells is comical because, although it exaggerates human foolishness, frailty, and futility, it does so in the comic language and the fantastic terms of a simple-minded and harmlessly demented recluse.

But it is also cynical because, though obliquely, it defines human beings in devastating terms. The best piece of writing in *A Tramp Abroad* differs from less successful parts not so much in matter as in manner. This effective humorous passage, like less effective ones, has a grim quality.

Here as elsewhere the author's biography evidently was influential: his personal situation helped him develop this wry story with feeling. He himself recently had known what it was to dump money, or the manuscript pages for a book, into holes which seemed too huge ever to fill.

The direction of Clemens' thinking at this time, shaped by much reading and study, also was important. Notebooks, letters, and other portions of his travel book—both published and unpublished—show his thought moving toward the severe representation of humanity which was to become a memorable feature of *Huckleberry Finn.*

The trend of this thinking had started as far back as the summer of 1876, when Pap's speech on suffrage satirically set forth Clemens' disillusionment about a fairly large group of people— the American electorate. In a letter written in the fall of the same year Clemens summarized the belief documented by Pap's remarks —that "the average Southerner . . . Northerners, too, of a certain grade," were ignorant, intolerant, egotistical, self-assertive, and stupid.[10] And a later passage discarded from *A Tramp Abroad* reiterated the point that "the mass of Ignorance and Incapacity" rules the United States.[11]

Clemens' travel abroad in 1879, bolstered by reading, led him to condemn a vast group of Europeans even more harshly than he had Americans and thereby to enlarge the portion of mankind about which he was disillusioned. Although he attacked ferociously the scarred Heidelberg dueling corps, he made relatively few attacks on the German people. But after reaching Paris in February, 1879, he filled pages of notebooks with savage comments on the French. Then, too, or somewhat later he wrote for *A Tramp Abroad* several chapters of immoderate attacks on the French. Perhaps because their ferocity made them inappropriate for a humorous book he left them out. With few exceptions his criticisms have heretofore been unpublished. Nevertheless they indicate an important intellectual development.

One thinks of several reasons for these savage attacks. Livy may have been partly responsible. Even before the stay in Paris she mentioned her growing dislike for the French in a letter to her mother: "I believe the old puritan education [in America] brings better men and women than any of these looser methods. . . ." [12] The illnesses of the Clemens party and the horrid weather did not foster a genial outlook; and illogical or not, Clemens—like tourists before and since—let personal experiences influence his attitudes. Unhappy encounters with individual Frenchmen may have helped him make hasty generalizations. Enough of a wry critic of himself to recognize this, he commented in a notebook, "You perceive I generalize with intrepidity from single instances. It is the tourist's custom. When I see a man jump from the Vendome column, I say 'They like to do that in France.' "

A very important additional reason for Clemens' distress was the French point of view which still fascinates and astonishes American tourists—the un-American attitude of France toward sex. One notebook entry combines this distress about French immorality with exasperation about the weather: "France has neither winter nor summer nor morals—apart from these drawbacks it is a fine country." [13] Other entries equate French immorality with sexual laxity: " 'Tis a wise Frenchman that knows his own father." "A Frenchman's home is where another man's wife is." "They probably have an idea of decency, but it is not easy to imagine what it can be. It is about what a scavenger's idea of cleanliness is." "To be witty in France is very simple—one merely needs to be dirty." [14] Chapters and notes written for the book but not included discuss French impurity, marriage customs, and art. Clemens' puritanical attitudes surely stimulated his criticisms.

Also, the author's great sensitivity was at work. Twichell, who joined him for a few weeks of travel, remarked this quality in letters home. "I never knew," he wrote, "a person so regardful of the feelings of others. . . . He hates to pass another person walking, and will practice some subterfuge to take off what he feels is the discourtesy of it. . . ." This oversensitive man was engaged while in Paris in a fairly macabre project which must have harrowed his feelings. The Clemens family, says Paine, "read histories and other books relating to France. . . . The Reign of Terror interested him. He read Carlyle's *Revolution,* a book he was never long without reading, and they all read *A Tale of Two Cities.* When the weather permitted they visited the scenes of that grim period." These gruesome little excursions made even more vivid the impressions he had recently acquired from a remarkable amount of reading about the bloodiest and most savage period in French history. Varied though the causes of Clemens' anti-French feelings were, French history, especially of the Revolution, made a living part of Clemens' thought as a result of such absorption, loomed large among them. When he wrote of his disillusionments about the race, he interrelated them by means of his personal version of French history.

This was based upon a course of reading which had begun before the visit to Paris. On June 27, 1877, Clemens had written Twichell from Elmira thanking him for a copy of *In Exitu Israel,* "a very able novel by Baring-Gould, the purpose of which is to show the effect of some of the most odious of the privileges of the French nobles under *l'ancien regème,* and of the dischurching of the Catholic Church . . . in '92." "Thanks, Joe," he told Twichell. "Been reading a lot of French rot here and am glad to get this." [15]

Either the prospective trip or Dickens' and Carlyle's books about the French Revolution apparently had directed his interest in history—always strong—toward histories, biographies, legendary lore, and fiction dealing with the Revolution and the decades in France immediately following it. The "French rot" of 1877 included Charles D. Yonge's two-volume *Life of Marie Antoinette,* "a small history of France in French," an unidentified story of Mme. de Genlis, Taine's *Ancient Regime,* Dumas' *The Taking of the Bastille,* an unspecified book about "the march of the rioters on Versailles," and several other books.[16] In Paris, while visiting historic scenes, he studied still other sources.

The chief evidence of this interest in *A Tramp Abroad* occurs in chapter xxvi, where, in a discussion of the Lion of Lucerne, he comments on the martyrdom of Louis XVI and evaluates his character:

Martyrdom . . . makes him out to be a person with a meek and modest spirit, the heart of a female saint, and a wrong head. None of these qualities are kingly but the last. . . . With the best intentions to do the right thing, he always managed to do the wrong one. Moreover, nothing could get the female saint out of him. He knew, well enough, that in national emergencies he must not consider how he ought to act, as a man, but how he ought to act as a king; so he honestly tried to sink the man and be the king,—but he only succeeded in being the female saint. . . . the most pitiable spectacle in [his royal career] was his sentimental treachery to his Swiss guard on that memorable 10th of August, when he allowed these heroes to be massacred in his cause, and forbade them to shed the "sacred French blood" purporting to be flowing in the veins of the red-capped mob of miscreants who were raging around the palace.

Mark is equally stern with martyrdom for "making a saint of the trivial and foolish Marie Antoinette"—she who had "the instinct to root out and get rid of an honest, able, and loyal official, where-ever she found him." "The hideous but beneficial French Revolution," he continues, to which "the world owes a great deal," was actually promoted by "Louis the Poor in Spirit and his queen."

The majority of histories and novels about the French Revolution which Clemens had been reading—and certainly his favorite, Carlyle's history—paint royalty in black hues. Clemens, how-ever, went beyond Carlyle in his attitude. When he first read Carlyle, he told Howells, he was a moderate revolutionist, "a Girondin"; but after several readings, "changed, little by little, by life and environment (and Taine and St. Simon) . . . I am a Sansculotte! And not a pale, characterless Sansculotte, but a Marat. Carlyle teaches no such gospel; so the change is in me—in my vision of the evidence." Though he does not define his terms, his remarks then and later suggest that for him a Sansculotte is one who fiercely and recklessly battles to destroy not only royalty but also nobility. With the exception of Yonge's biography of Marie Antoinette, most of the books Clemens read about the French Revolution were of a sort to incline him toward this at-titude. Baring-Gould's *In Exitu Israel*, as his description of it shows, attacked the nobility. The chapters in Taine which he most admired emphasize the maltreatment of the peasants by nobles and royalty; so do Dickens, Dumas, and Michelet.

But Clemens' study of the French Revolutionary period led him to condemn not only kings and nobles but commoners as well. A notebook entry comments:

The Reign of Terror showed that without distinction of rank the people were savages—marquises, dukes, lawyers, blacksmiths, they each figure there in due proportion to their crafts' numbers—fewer marquises than blacksmiths because there were fewer marquises than blacksmiths. There was no difference between the city exquisites and the country clods—in savagery they were equal and it was the equality of perfection.[17]

Eventually Clemens applied this statement to the French of all classes not merely during the Revolution but at all times. Another note reads:

For 1000 years this savage nation has indulged itself in massacre; every now and then there is a big massacre or a little one. The spirit is peculiar to France—I mean in Christendom—no other state has had it. In this France has always . . . kept her end up with her brethren, the Turks and the Burmese. Their chief traits—love of glory and massacre.

He made use of this note and others in a chapter written for *A Tramp Abroad* which offers a long comparison between the French and the Comanche Indians, pretty much to the disadvantage of the French. Of particular interest in this chapter is a Twainian history of France. The continuum which he finds in this history is "cruelty, savagery, the spirit of massacre" which shows itself "from time immemorial" in massacres wherein members of the race "burn and slaughter . . . each other." The French Revolution is an instance among many. It was preceded, he notices, by a long period of unequaled docility. During this period the French were "insulted and trodden under foot for a thousand years" without resisting—for, unlike other European countries, France had no "William Tells and Wat Tylers." Foolish King Louis XVI, however, did not "do the needful thing at the needful time."

Then the nation cast its rabbit skin and put on its other national garment, the tiger-skin: being closely pressed by Europe in arms, it went a step further and asserted its manhood, and was doubtless surprised to find how much it had of it. Napoleon, the great foreigner, brought the people's soldiership up to the summit of perfection; and when he got ready he dressed the nation in their rabbit skins again and put his foot on their necks, and they glorified him for it. Napoleon III accommodated them in the same way, to their vast satisfaction. . . . The Frenchman is made up of the littlest littlenesses conceivable, and the greatest greatnesses. . . . The tiger that is in him . . . fits him to become, through repression and careful training, the mightiest of soldiers. . . . The rabbit docility which has been bred in him by ages of meek putting up with wrongs . . . is the thing which will enable him to endure this repression and training without murmur. His gigantic vanity will move him to attempt miracles in art, mechanics, statesmanship and literature which would appall another, and his fervid and frantic imagination and his restless energy will enable him to carry them to a successful conclusion.[18]

This is a strange performance—this account wherein Twain, in the brash spirit only an amateur has, blandly and dubiously generalizes about French character through the centuries. It is significant that both the misdeeds and the most admired achievements of the nation are attributed to the bad qualities—the sadism, the docility, and the vanity—not of French leaders alone but of the entire French nation.

This may seem remote from a novel about Huck and Jim in the America of the 1830's or 1840's. But such was the impact of the author's research that when he returned to *Huck* within a few months and again in 1883 he worked into it an extraordinary amount of material about European royalty and nobility. A detailed discussion of such material will be appropriate for a later chapter; but one instance may be cited here to show that on occasion he incorporated minute facts.

In chapter xix of the novel written in 1880–1883 two rapscallions introduce themselves, the first as a duke, the second as "the pore disappeared Dauphin, Looy the Seventeen, son of Looy the Sixteen and Marry Antonette." Both impostors know enough history to notice that if, as Huck testifies, the dauphin's age is "about seventy or upwards," he is too old; for at the time of the novel the dauphin, had he lived, would have been between fifty and sixty.

"You! At your age! No!" says the duke. The dauphin feels called upon to explain that "trouble . . . has brung these gray hairs and premature balditude." He gives no evidence of knowing other details about his alleged past, but the duke shows that he has learned from some source, Carlyle or Dumas it may be, that after his removal from the throne Louis XVI was given a title indicating his lowered estate, "Citizen Louis Capet"; twice he uses an even more derogatory term, calling him merely "Capet." This is a subtle attack for one not familiar with French history, and the dauphin fails to object; but the dauphin is partly repaid for calling him not Bridgewater as he has asked, but Bilgewater instead.

Even more important to future chapters of *Huck* was the thinking of Clemens which carried him beyond the condemnation of kings and nobles to broader condemnations. The novel would stress vices and frailties of folk on every level—the aristocracy, the middle classes, the poor whites, the flotsam and jetsam of the river.

The author's strictures apply to growing segments of mankind: American politicians, then the whole American electorate, then French royalty and nobility, then the rest of the French populace, but at first only in the Revolutionary period, then in all periods. "A man who is a pessimist before forty-eight knows too much"; Clemens wrote in 1902, "if he is an optimist after it, he knows too little." [19] If he was modestly prescribing for men in general a course of development which he himself followed, Clemens had four years to go before embracing pessimism.

But he was making progress. Already, now and then, like Jim Baker of his bluejay yarn, he was making statements derogatory not simply of a nation but of humanity in general. A notebook entry of 1879 supplies a predicate for a sentence attributing folly to most of mankind: " 'Es gibt Leute' as the Baroness used to say —'There are people'—finish the sentence as you please—*she* never finished it. It might usually be finished thus—'who are fool enough to do anything.' " [20]

Even before writing this, he had in 1878 written a chapter for *A Tramp Abroad* which proves the truth of this generalization. This chapter, "The Great Revolution in Pitcairn," destined to be published in the *Atlantic Monthly* and not to be restored to the book, is a fable. Inspired by favorite summertime reading of Clemens and Crane about the *Bounty* mutineers, it purports to tell the recent history of the descendants of the mutineers who had settled on Pitcairn's Island. The natives of this South Sea community have been living "in a deep Sabbath tranquillity, far from the world and its ambitions and vexations, and neither knowing nor caring what was going on in the mighty empires that lay beyond their limitless ocean solitudes."

To this paradise with its ninety inhabitants comes Butterworth Stavely, an American hungering for personal power. Cunningly he ingratiates himself with the inhabitants, assumes a pose of piety, and starts to exploit the discontents of various groups. On a trumped-up charge, he brings about the impeachment of the chief magistrate. He then gets himself elected magistrate and institutes reforms which make him a public idol. Thereafter, using arguments which though specious are good enough to cozen his stupid subjects, he gets them to proclaim the island independent and to make him Emperor Butterworth I.

He begins at once to institute Imperial reforms. Orders of nobility are established. Ministers of the navy and of war, a first lord of the treasury, generals and admirals are appointed. Jealous and hostile factions form and struggle for honors and power. Taxes become a burden, the people complain, some rebel and are punished. By now a Social Democrat has "been developed." One day as the emperor "stepped into the gilded imperial wheelbarrow . . . the social democrat stabbed at him fifteen or sixteen times with a harpoon, but fortunately with such a peculiar social democratic imprecision of aim as to do no damage."

Driven too far at last, that very night the populace seizes the deposed emperor, punishes him and the social democrat, and runs up a flag which signals its return to the older regime. They reduce "the nobility to the condition of commoners" and return to "the old useful industries and the old healing and solacing pieties," and presumably live happily until another Butterworth Stavely comes along.

Twain, I think, meant this little tale to be a history of civilization in miniature. Stavely, as the institutor of civilization, comes to an island which, like the tranquil Hannibal of "Old Times on the Mississippi," the St. Petersburg of *Tom Sawyer*, the raft of Huck or of Twain and Harris on a carefree river, is untroubled by the woes of the civilized world. Stavely plays upon selfish desires, he uses arguments calculated to sway dull-minded people; but since here as everywhere those who have mean motives and who are stupid are the great majority he achieves his aims. When society has its royalty, its nobles, its bureaucracy, its classes, everyone begins greedily to struggle for position and power. Mankind as represented in miniature on this island is anything but an admirable spectacle. It has many vices and weaknesses and its sole redeeming quality is that, like the French in Twain's history of that people, when pushed too far it rebels.

Gladys Bellamy has noticed, with typical insight, that "The Great Revolution in Pitcairn" foreshadows the stories which Twain was to tell much later: *A Connecticut Yankee in King Arthur's Court* (1889) and "The Man that Corrupted Hadleyburg" (1899).[21] To some extent it rehearses an even sterner narrative, *The Mysterious Stranger*. These three were written after Clemens had reached the proper age—according to his schedule —to acquire a pessimistic attitude. It is significant that a story written when he was forty-three or forty-four was in some degree a rehearsal for these later narratives.

Formidable as are the indictments which this story presents, they were repeated and augmented, incredibly enough, in a book for children published in 1881—*The Prince and the Pauper*. Since this book was completed during the months when Twain wrote some of the later portions of *Huckleberry Finn*, and since it embodies concepts of humanity held by its author at this time, its story contributes important details to an account of *Huck's* development.

13

STRONG MILK FOR BABES

He [Tom Canty] enjoyed his splendid clothes, and ordered more; he found his four hundred servants too few for his proper grandeur, and trebled them. The adulation of salaaming courtiers came to be sweet music to his ears. He remained kind and gentle, and a sturdy and determined champion of all that were oppressed, and he made tireless war upon unjust laws; yet upon occasion, being offended, he could turn upon an earl, or even a duke, and give him a look that would make him tremble.—Mark Twain, The Prince and the Pauper, *chapter xxx.*

Just as Clemens' visit to France in 1879 and his reading of French history led to his disillusionment about the French people, his visit to England the same year and his reading of English history led to his disillusionment with the English people. Though his condemnation of the British was less sweeping, it augmented the increasing portion of the human race which he ranked among the damned.

Clemens had first gone to England in 1872, planning to write a book in the mode of *Innocents Abroad* satirizing that country. But he was so favorably impressed on this trip and others during 1873–1874 that he abandoned the book. Comparing the American political system with the British system, he decided that the latter had many advantages. In a burst of Anglophilia, he told Mrs. Fields in 1876 that he "wished he were not an American," and that he "thought seriously of going to England to live for a while." A year later when in Bermuda with Twichell, he decided that British supervision there meant "efficient government and good order" which strongly contrasted with American government.[1]

But when he began research for *The Prince and the Pauper* he started a course of reading that lowered his esteem for the English. The sketch *1601* was inspired by the discovery that fireside talk in Elizabeth's day was sprinkled with improprieties. His frequent reading of Pepys could not have persuaded him that purity was rife during the Restoration period, and entries in notebooks suggest that the eighteenth-century frankness of Fielding and Smollett made an unfavorable impression. Possibly his discovery that the British, like the French, had not always conformed to Hartford's sexual code initiated doubts about their soundness.

Exactly when he formulated the plot of *The Prince and the Pauper* is not certain, but probably he determined its general nature by the summer of 1877. He wrote the title in a notebook in the spring of that year, and that summer he took to Quarry Farm volumes of Hume's *History of England* covering the period of the story. He started to write in the fall of 1877 or the winter of 1878.[2] His interest slowed to a stop more rapidly than usual—after about 200 pages. Though he wrote none of the book while abroad, in London in 1879, as he had done in Paris, he bought historical books and visited scenes they described.[3]

He returned to the novel in the winter of 1880, "ground away . . . with an interest that almost amounted to intemperance," and was somewhat beyond page 400 when he went to Quarry Farm in June. There, on September 14, he believed that he had finished the book. Characteristically, he rejoiced too soon, but did complete it after some revisions and deletions in January or February, 1881.[4]

Clemens outlined the plot for Howells in March, 1880:

It begins at 9 a.m., Jan. 27, 1547, seventeen and a half hours before Henry VIII's death, by the swapping of clothes *and places*, between the prince of Wales and a pauper boy of the same age and countenance (and half as much learning and still more genius and imagination) and after that, the rightful small King has a rough time among tramps and ruffians in the country parts of Kent, while the small bogus King has a gilded and worshipped and dreary and restrained and cussed time of it on the throne—and this all goes on for three weeks—till the midst of the coronation grandeurs in Westminster Abbey, Feb. 20, when the ragged true King forces his way in but cannot prove his genuineness—until the bogus King, by a remembered incident of the first day is able to prove it *for* him—whereupon clothes are changed and the coronation proceeds under the new and rightful conditions.

Since this line of action required that the little king go forth and witness the cruelty and suffering of his people, the author made numerous notes recording these:

Religious burnings. Anabaptists burnt. People burnt for denying the royal authority in religious matters. 60,000 in prison for debt and crime . . . 72,000 executed in Henry's reign, for *theft* and *robbery*. Whipping, degradation and expulsion for pronouncing Greek in the Protestant fashion. Drunken habits of James I and his court. Killing of Jack Straw. Orlean's imprisonment. . . . Murder of Overbury. Used to gouge prisoners. . . . Petitioning the King against a judge for injustice, ears cut off &c. Man who wrote imprudent tract against maypoles, festivals, &c.—he is proceeding to have the *remains* of his ears cut off. Pressing to death. Women's punishments for counterfeiting, irreligion, &c., to be burnt alive. Poisoners boiled to death. 2d larceny of 13 pence, *death*. He sees a *witch* and daughter 9 years burnt.[5]

It was obviously an exploration of cruelty and suffering which, like the study of the French Revolutionary period, emphasized the more ferocious aspects of a national history.

The reading rather than the visit to England must have inspired one critical passage, for it was written while Clemens was still in Paris:

The English ought not to patronize the Zulus, the Livingstone River Cannibals and say piously we are better than thou, for it is very plain that they haven't been better more than a hundred years. They are a very fine and pure and elevated people now, but what they were between the Roman invasion and a time within the memory of a centenarian was but a small improvement upon the Shoshone Indians.—I select the Shoshones because they have certain peculiar vices and certain conspicuous virtues.[6]

The English here, like the French, fare badly when compared with a tribe of Indians. They come out better than the French only because Clemens believes that they have managed to reform during the last century.

Reading, and the visit to England—and perhaps the bad weather in England—prompted Clemens on the voyage home to make a comparison between the English nation and the United States that was very different from the sort he had made after previous visits:

> For some years a custom has been growing up in our literature to praise everything English and do it affectionately. This is not met half-way and so it will cease. English individuals like and respect American individuals, but the English nation despises America and the Americans. But this does not sting us as it did when we were smaller. We shall presently be indifferent to being looked down upon by a nation no bigger and no better than our own. We made the telegraph a practical thing; we invented the fast press, the sewing machine, the sleeping and parlor car, the telephone, the iron-clad, we have done our share for the century, we have introduced foretelling of the weather. Nobody writes a finer and purer English than Motley, Howells, Hawthorne and Holmes.[7]

Although we may regret the list of inventions, which sounds rather Soviet Russian, and be surprised at the authors listed, we cannot avoid concluding that Clemens left England in 1879 with a lowered opinion of the country.

Because of this, and because his novel dealt with cruelty and injustice in a period much more than a century earlier, the likelihood would seem to be strong that *The Prince and the Pauper* would offer a grim picture of England. One aspect of the book, however, made the representations of torture and bloodshed about as appropriate as pictures of dismembered corpses would be on the walls of a nursery.

The title page describes the book as "A Tale for Young People of All Ages." The dedication reads: "To those good-natured and agreeable children Susie and Clara Clemens. . . ." The first edition has nearly two hundred pretty illustrations which show even beggars in picturesque costumes and poses, and make its boy heroes look "like delicate little girls in ballet costumes." [8] This book was intended to appeal to children. Such are its manner and matter that it no longer has much appeal for American adults. On hearing that it was in preparation, Joe Goodman, who had been Clemens' hardbitten boss out in Nevada on the *Enterprise,* wrote to ask him, in effect, what in hell he thought he was up to.[9] In some ways the book was a lavish waste of time and talent. Nevertheless, this novel, with its prettinesses, its prithee-mayhap-enow dialogue, embodies significant attitudes and ideas of its author at the time it was written. And it was written shortly after *Tom Sawyer* and, in part, contemporaneously with *The Tramp Abroad* and *Huckleberry Finn.* Its repetitions of matter in these books and its forecasting of portions of *Huck* are interesting and important.

Just as *Tom* and *Huck,* set in mid-America of the 1830's or 1840's, recall Clemens' situation in the 1870's so does this novel set in sixteenth-century England. In chapter xx Tom Canty, distressed to hear that the king's expenses outrun his income, says, "We be going to the dogs, 'tis plain. 'Tis meet and necessary that we take a smaller house and set the servants at large. . . ." This sounds like a paraphrase of a letter from Clemens to Mrs. Fairbanks. A bit later Tom Canty is depressed by business and like Clemens longs to get away from it all, preferably in the out-of-door world of Tom Sawyer's childhood: "The dull work went tediously on. Petitions were read, and proclamations, patents, and all manner of wordy, repetitious, and wearisome papers relating to public business; and at last Tom sighed pathetically and murmured to himself, 'In what have I offended, that the good God should take me away from the fields and free air and sunshine, to shut me up here . . . and afflict me so.' " Again, chapter xxx describes Tom Canty, his love of splendor and his passion for justice, in words that his creator might well apply to himself. (The passage is quoted at the beginning of this chapter.) In chapter xvii a sixteenth-century robber pays tribute to the eloquence of a woman whose profanity Clemens would have been proud to have uttered: "Cursing them, said I?—cursing them! Why an' thou shouldst live a thousand years thoud'st never hear so masterful a cursing. Alack, her art died with her. There be base and weakling imitators left, but no true blasphemy." Such rhapsodic praise of eloquent profanity is rarely found even today in children's books.

The book by echoing several passages in the two novels about nineteenth-century Missouri boys shows the kinds of scenes its writer enjoyed recording. In chapter vii, just as Huck has suffered from a nose that itches at an awkward time, Tom Canty suffers. In chapter xiii a sixteenth-century roisterer sings a song which the raftsmen have chanted in *Huck,* cleansed a bit, at Howells' suggestion, for juvenile readers.[10] In chapter xvii a description is highly reminiscent of picturings of Huck and Jim alone on the river at night:

All his sensations and experiences, as he moved through . . . the empty vastness of the night, were new and strange. . . . At intervals he heard voices approach, pass by, and fade into silence; and he saw nothing more of the bodies they belonged to than a sort of formless drifting blur. . . . Occasionally he caught a twinkle of light—always far away. . . . All sounds were remote; they made the little king feel . . . that he stood solitary, companionless, in the center of a measureless solitude.

In chapter xix a woman tries, as Judith Loftus had, to identify a boyish visitor by asking shrewd questions; in chapter xx a demented hermit who believes himself an archangel tries to knife a boy, much as Pap, believing that Huck was the Angel of Death, had tried to kill his son.

There are more important resemblances. Tom Canty, as the synopsis of the plot shows, is in the same fix as Huck Finn and Huck's creator: he is suffering from the restraints of "civilization," though—since the stuffy restraints of kingship are imposed upon him—his tortures are even worse.

Tom Canty is an amalgam of the characteristics of Huck Finn and Tom Sawyer. Like the former he is an unlearned child of poverty abused by a sadistic drunken father. Like the latter he is obsessed with imitating what he reads, and his gang join in acting out his reading: "Daily the mock prince," says chapter ii, "was received with elaborate ceremonials borrowed . . . from his romantic readings . . . and daily his mimic highness issued decrees to his imaginary armies, navies, and vice-royalties." Like Tom Sawyer, Tom Canty enjoys sensational adventures and applause. The prince, though somewhat sketchily drawn, is blinded to reality in a Sawyerish way: Tom Canty unrealistically dreams of ceremonials; the prince unrealistically dreams of the free and easy life of the poor. As Tom Sawyer envies restraint-free Huck, the prince envies restraint-free Tom Canty.

TOM CANTY AND PRINCE EDWARD, *The Prince and the Pauper*

Both boys have the innate goodness of heart that Tom and Huck have, and both, like Huck, oppose contemporaneous attitudes which they respect. Both demonstrate the truths which Clemens advocated in response to Lecky. David Hume's account of Edward, a historical source, quite possibly made Edward attractive to the author precisely because it indicated that he had this sort of internal conflict. Roger Blaine Salomon has noticed that Hume saw Edward as combining "mildness of disposition . . . and an attachment to equity and justice" with tendencies toward "bigotry and persecution" which he "seems only to have contracted from his education, and from the age in which he lived." [11] At the outset of the story, in chapter iii, Edward shows his innate benevolence by sympathizing with Tom Canty; at the conclusion, having learned at first hand about unjust laws, he shows it by ruling benevolently. In chapter xv Tom Canty as the bogus king, on hearing that a man, a woman, and a young girl have been condemned to death for crimes against the realm, has these thoughts:

Death—and violent death—for those poor unfortunates! The thought wrung Tom's heartstrings. The spirit of compassion took control of him, to the exclusion of all other considerations; he never thought of the offended laws, or of the grief or loss which these three criminals had inflicted upon their victims; he would think of nothing but . . . the grisly fate hanging over the heads of the condemned.

Here is a sixteenth-century parallel for Huck's helping Jim escape from slavery despite his having been taught that such an act is sinful. The kindness of heart, Salomon notices, is in each instance an attribute of childhood.[12] The idea is reiterated in chapter xix, when Edward, sleeping in rags in a barn, awakens to find two children "staring with innocent eyes" at him. When he tells them that he is the king, unlike adults they instinctively believe him. Similarly, in chapter xxv, when all appearances are against the truth of a claim made by the king's traveling companion, Miles Hendon, " 'I do not doubt thee,' says the king, with a childlike simplicity and faith." Miles, an adult, by contrast does doubt Edward's legal claims. "Children and fools," Clemens remarked in a notebook about the time he set down this incident, "*always* speak truth." [13]

These encounters occur while Edward is journeying across country. During much of the journey he is accompanied by Miles, who, although he does not believe that the ragged youngster is the king, humors him by waiting on him and by pretending to believe that honors the boy bestows upon him are real—"a most odd and strange position, truly," he muses in chapter xii, "for one so matter-of-fact as I." As this remark suggests, Hendon is to the king what Huck has been to Tom—Sancho Panza to Don Quixote, and the journey is a sixteenth-century counterpart of the nineteenth-century journey of Huck and Jim.

Not only does Mark Twain repeat in this fiction his beliefs about instinctive goodness; he also repeats his ideas—and Lecky's

—about a bedeviling conscience. In chapter xxx Tom Canty suffers severe pangs because he remembers his injustice to Edward.[14] In chapter xxxi he suffers similarly when he has denied recognizing his mother. Twain also shows characters deriving selfish pleasure from virtuous actions. In chapter xix, after a peasant woman and Edward have exchanged kindnesses: "This good woman was made happy all day by the applauses she got of herself for her magnanimous condescension to a tramp; and the king was just as self-complacent over his gracious humility toward a humble peasant woman." For childish readers who derive a moral from their reading, the author affixes one: "It does us all good to unbend some times." All the points except that made in the moralizing sentence—an ironic one—are reiterations of observations already made in *Huck*.[15]

Gladys Bellamy, in her study of Mark Twain's thought, calls attention to a final point made in this novel that repeats a concept already developed in *Huck* and to be developed there again. She sees *The Prince and the Pauper* as

Mark Twain's first full-length study of the power of determining environment and circumstance. The transformation of beggar into prince and vice versa was effected by a mere change of clothes. The significance of clothes . . . rests upon some such explanation as this: since the world judges by outward appearance, the clothes one wears become a part of the exterior determining circumstances which decide what everyone will be. . . . Mark Twain gave . . . his attention to the pressure of environment upon the moral fiber . . . of Tom Canty. . . . Tom lapses from a sturdy rebellion . . . into slothful enjoyment of the splendors that surround him. Finally he sinks into a corrupt resignation. . . .[16]

Though I have, perhaps rather impolitely, omitted a few commentaries of Miss Bellamy's with which I do not agree,[17] and though I believe that Tom—since he is endowed with a good heart—never becomes as corrupt as she indicates, I am convinced that in general Miss Bellamy's analysis is sound. Here as elsewhere Twain is conducting the discussion with Lecky which he had begun in *Huckleberry Finn* and which he resumed in later parts of that novel.

When, however, we make a distinction between the journey of Huck and Jim recounted in chapters of *Huck* written in 1876 and that recounted in the portions written later, we see that *The Prince and the Pauper* foreshadows important developments.

The little king during his wanderings meets criminals and confidence men; he is taken to be a vagrant who is pretending to be of royal blood. The king and the duke in *Huck* are vagrant confidence men who pretend that they are of noble and royal descent.[18] Despite the fact that they disbelieve Edward's claims, the boys at Christ hospital, the Canty family, Miles Hendon, and the band of beggars and robbers all humor Edward by addressing him as royalty and bowing to him. Hendon calls him "my liege," serves him, and helps him dress. In chapter xix of *Huck* the duke "said we ought to bow when we spoke to him, and say 'Your Grace,' or 'Your Lordship' . . . and one of us ought to wait on him. . . ." The bogus dauphin "said it made him feel easier and better for a while if people treated him according to his rights and got down on one knee to speak to him, and always called him 'Your Majesty,' and waited on him first. . . ." Huck comments: "It didn't take me long to make up my mind that these liars warn't no kings nor dukes at all, but just low-down humbugs and frauds. But I . . . kept it to myself; it's the best way; then you don't have no quarrels, and don't get in no trouble. If they wanted us to call them kings and dukes, I hadn't no objections, 'long as it would keep peace. . . ." The characters in *The Prince and the Pauper* defer to what they consider a whim for purposes of mockery or because of kindness; Huck defers because of his habit of generating as little friction as possible. Yet the essentially similar situations seemed to Twain to be good literary material.

These are foreshadowings of situations to be embodied in *Huck* when Mark returned to it. Far above these in importance are foreshadowings of a whole line of action and important related themes.

In his letter to Howells outlining the plot of *The Prince and the Pauper* the author said: "My idea is to afford a realizing sense of the exceeding severity of the laws of that day by inflicting some of the penalties upon the King himself and allowing him a chance to see the rest of them applied to others—all of which is to account for certain mildnesses which distinguish Edward VI's reign from those that preceded and followed it." Considered with the author's outline of his plot, this suggests an interrelationship between happenings and a theme: Edward "has a rough time amongst tramps and ruffians"; some penalties of the day are inflicted upon him and he sees others applied to his people. Because he thus acquires "a realizing sense" of the harsh laws, when he returns to his throne he becomes a mild ruler. The novel is so patterned. After seeing and personally experiencing sundry injustices, Edward, restored to his throne, rights injustices in a crammed final chapter. "The world is made wrong," he moralizes; "kings should go to school to their own laws at times and so learn mercy."

The Prince and the Pauper has relationships with Mark's previous stories of educational journeyings in which each character loses his romantic conception of a sort of life, and each learns the actualities of that sort of life—Tom Canty, the life of the court; Edward, the life of his subjects.

It is Edward's encounters on his journeyings which enlarge his understanding. These are with people of many sorts—outcasts who have no excuse for their lawlessness but who prey upon others; well-intentioned folk who have been driven to lawbreaking because they have suffered unjustly; victims of injustice. In chapter xxvii, when Edward sees two Baptist women burned at the stake for their faith while their horrified children watch, his comments show how deeply he is shaken: "The king glanced from the frantic girls to the stake, then turned his ashen face to the wall, and looked no more. He said: 'That which I have seen, in that one little moment, will never go out from my memory, but will abide there; and I shall see it all the days, and dream of it all the nights, till I die. Would God I had been blind!'"

In chapters of *Huckleberry Finn* written about this time or soon after, the nineteenth-century ragamuffin, like the sixteenth-century king in rags, on a journey encounters many sorts of men and women. He, too, has harrowing encounters with human depravity and cruelty. He, too, watches a manifestation of human brutality (chapter xviii) so horrible that it sears his memory: "It made me so sick I almost fell out of the tree. I ain't a-going to tell *all* that happened—it would make me sick again if I was to do that. I wished I hadn't ever come ashore that night to see those things. I ain't ever going to get shut of them—lots of times I dream about them." The differences in language do not conceal the essential identity in content of the two passages.

In both instances, although the boys are horrified by the violence of the crowd, something other than mob violence is involved. But noteworthy in *The Prince and the Pauper* is the picturing of many mobs in action—often violent action. In chapter iii a mob at the gate to Westminster jeers at Tom, grovels when the prince rebukes them, then maltreats Edward when he reappears in Tom's rags. In chapter x a priest who comes to Tom's defense when another mob bedevils him is struck down and: "The mob pressed on, their enjoyment nothing disturbed." In chapter xi, when a mob sees Edward attempting to enter the Guildhall, they "taunt and mock him." When Hendon comes to his aid "a score of voices shouted 'Kill the dog! kill him! kill him!'" [19] and he barely misses being destroyed. In chapter xiv a sadistic mob eagerly surges forward to watch an execution. In chapter xxviii a mob is impressed into silence by Hendon's bravery, and in chapter xxxii a mob demonstrates its fickleness by siding alternately with Tom and with Edward.

There are similar representations of mobs as fickle, cruel, and cowardly in the new chapters of *Huck*. There, too, the mobs shift rapidly, backing one force and then another; they gloat as they watch human suffering; they overwhelm and torture their victims; they slink away when faced by a brave man. As I shall indicate, details about these Mississippi River mobs, like those about mobs in the historical romance, where inspired largely by reading about mobs active during the French Revolution. And the depiction of these frantic groups was to enable Mark Twain, in *Huck,* to say important things about man's nature.

The author, I suggest, hit upon the scheme of most of the rest of *Huckleberry Finn* in part as a result of his working with similar lines of action in his historical novel.

The essential meanings of the novels are, to be sure, different in important respects. The injustices which the king discovers are injustices in the England of his day, and the implication is that a just king will remedy them. Huck observes, specifically, the injustice, the cruelty, the hypocrisy, of the ante-bellum Southwest; but the author's condemnation is broadened to include not simply Southerners but all humanity; and the implication is that the tendencies are innate and beyond eradication. Nevertheless, I suggest that Mark Twain learned a great deal about ways to develop this theme as he wrote his novel for children.

14

THE GRANGERFORDS

I liked all that family, dead ones and all, and warn't going to let anything come between us.—Adventures of Huckleberry Finn, *chapter xvii.*

___

If, as I have suggested, the pigeonholed manuscript of *Huckleberry Finn* ended with the splintering of the raft by a steamboat,[1] Mark Twain, on returning to the novel, told how Huck saved himself and went ashore. Like the cub pilot in "Old Times on the Mississippi," the boy dives under the steamboat paddle wheel:

I dived—and I aimed to find the bottom, too, for a thirty-foot wheel had got to go over me, and I wanted to have plenty of room. I could always stay under water a minute; this time I reckon I staid under water a minute and a half. Then I bounced for the top in a hurry, for I was nearly busting. . . . of course that boat started her engines again ten seconds after she stopped them, for they never cared much for raftsmen. . . .

I sung out for Jim about a dozen times, but I didn't get any answer; so I grabbed a plank that touched me while I was "treading water," and struck out for shore. . . .

It was one of those long, slanting, two-mile crossings; so I was a good long time in getting over. I made a safe landing, and clum up the bank.

Huck goes "over rough ground for a quarter of a mile or more" and comes to a house. The Grangerford family cautiously admits him. After he reassures them that he is not a Shepherdson and tells them one of his lugubrious (and inaccurate) autobiographies, he becomes a guest. Since he stays with them for some time, he is able to give a detailed account of the family and of the way they live. This leisurely survey runs through chapter xvii and several pages of chapter xviii before the ancient Grangerford-Shepherdson feud flares up, and at the end of chapter xviii Huck flees from its horrible consequences.

Before considering chapters xvii and xviii in more detail I must discuss a very relevant matter—exactly when they were written.

In 1942 Bernard DeVoto published a careful study of the writing of *Huckleberry Finn* which held that the novel was written in the summer of 1876 and the summer of 1883 in Elmira.[2] Persuaded by his convincing arguments, until recently scholars have accepted his findings. I believe, however, that a recent study of mine proves that Mark Twain wrote chapters xvii and xviii between mid-October, 1879, and mid-June, 1880, in Hartford; that he wrote chapters xix–xxi between mid-June, 1880, and mid-June, 1883, and that he wrote the rest of the novel at Quarry Farm in the summer of 1883. Since I have set down elsewhere at some length the reasons for this belief,[3] I shall outline here only three pieces of evidence for it. There are other proofs; but I hope and believe that these will be convincing.

The first piece of evidence consists of a group of remarks about the writing of *Huck* which the author made, indicating that he worked on it during more than two periods. In 1882 he removed the raftsman passage written in 1876 from *Huck* to chapter iii of *Life on the Mississippi*. He introduced it as "a chapter from a book which I have worked at, by fits and starts, during the past five or six years." He had, indeed, started the book six years before; and this close to the writing he says not that he put the book aside for several years but that he worked on it at intervals. On July 20, 1883, writing to Howells, he called *Huck* "a big one that I half-finished two or three years ago." That would mean that he half-finished it not in 1876 but in 1880 or 1881. Finally, on July

21, 1883, in a letter to his mother, Orion, and Orion's wife, he spoke of *Huck* as "a book which I have been fooling over for 7 years." If "fooling over" implies anything, surely it is that he worked on the book between 1876 and 1883.[4]

The second piece of evidence, though more complicated, is equally convincing. It is offered by assorted pages, each with Twain's handwriting on it, which DeVoto found among Mark Twain's Papers. Some contain ideas for episodes in *Huck;* others are reminders concerning characters and actions occurring in the portion of *Huck* written in 1876; some are suggestions for handling dialect.[5]

DeVoto saw that if these working notes could be ordered properly they would provide a clue to the way in which the book was written. Examining paper, writing materials, and contents, he decided that they fell into three groups which he labeled A, B, and C, according to the order in which he believed they had been written. The ink used in Group A was, he thought, a clue—violet ink which the author used "frequently during the 1870's, less often during the 1880's, and not at all thereafter."

Suspecting that Twain's use of the violet ink and of the paper of the notes might be dated more precisely, I examined all his notebooks, manuscripts, and letters housed in nine important public and private collections scattered between California and New York. I had a memorable experience—spending hours, not reading Twain's words, but noticing the kind of writing material used and holding up pages to the light so that I might discover watermarks in thousands of pages. Even worse, I imposed upon scholars and librarians in American cities which I could not visit—and on one scholar studying in the British Museum in London—asking them to make similar studies of Mark Twain's holographs and to send records. Eventually I had information about the nature of the working notes, more than four hundred letters, twenty-six manuscripts, and all notebook entries written between 1876 and 1884 inclusive.

If all this work had proved useless, it is possible that I would have been somewhat irritated. For a time this seemed the likely outcome, because it soon became clear that Twain had been versatile and very unsystematic. During this period he used about thirty kinds of paper. He wrote with pencil, with a typewriter, and used at least five kinds of ink. Often his lack of system was awe-inspiring: he might use two kinds of paper in two letters during the same day—or even in one letter. And if he wrote a fairly long manuscript he was almost sure to use six different kinds of paper. This was discouraging. Fortunately, though, after all the data were set down in charts, some revealing patterns emerged.

One had to do with Twain's use of that violet ink. Although he wrote in pencil at random, when he wrote with ink he used violet ink consistently between these dates: late November, 1876, and mid-June, 1877; late September, 1877, and late March, 1878; mid-November, 1879, and mid-June, 1880. He used it sporadically in Europe during the winter of 1878–79. Therefore, except when abroad, he used such ink only in Hartford. Every time he went to Quarry Farm he switched to black, bluish-gray, or brown ink or to pencil; then, soon after returning to Hartford, he began to use violet ink again.

Another significant fact is that when he returned to Hartford in the fall of 1880, he did not as usual resume the use of violet ink. No scrap of writing in letters, datable manuscripts, or note-books written between June 15, 1880, and the end of December, 1884, when *Huck* was off the press, is in violet ink. And on envelopes of letters which he received—many preserved in the Mark Twain Papers—he immediately wrote brief notations summarizing the contents. Dates of these notations can therefore be determined. The ink used for these conforms exactly to the pattern indicated. The violet ink therefore shows that Group A of the notes was written in Hartford (or just possibly in Europe) before the summer of 1880.

The paper used in Group A helps narrow down their period somewhat more. One page is embossed with a design containing the letters "P & P": the author did not use such paper in any writing datable after June 15, 1880. Each of the other ten pages in the group is fairly heavy paper, white, unlined, torn or cut across the left side, and measuring four and a half by seven inches. This was used in no letters or manuscripts datable before his return from Europe in September, 1879. The last letter I have seen in which he used it is dated June 4, 1881; the last manuscript using it was written in the spring of 1881. Therefore the testimony of the ink and the paper is that Group A of the notes was written between mid-November, 1879, and mid-June, 1880, in Hartford.

Similar evidence indicates that one of the two pages of Group B of the notes was written during the same period. This is B-1, which is Crystal Lake Mills paper; Twain did not use such paper after mid-June, 1880.

The third argument for a spell of writing in 1879–1880 is particularly important in dating the chapters which deal with the Grangerfords and their feud. Note A-7 (the crossed-out letters and number are italicized here and the columns are spaced as in the original) reads:

George Jackson (Huck)		
Shepherdsons		
Bob & Tom Grangerford	28 & 30	*abt 30*
Old man (Saul) Col. ”		60
Betsy (negro) ”		
Old lady (Rachel)		
Buck ”		12–14
Emmeline (dead)		
Charlotte (proud & grand) ”		25
Sophia (sweet & gentle) ”		20
Harvney Shepherdson		

This page is written with a finer pen than other notes in Group A, and therefore at a different time. It is the only page in the group which does not contain a suggestion for a happening but which lists characters. Among all the working notes, the one most similar to it is C-1, which lists characters in the order of their appearance through the first nineteen or twenty chapters of the novel. De-

Voto soundly deduced that C-1 was made when Twain was studying his manuscript closely in order to recall characters and what he had written about each. For instance, "Miss Watson (goggles) sister to Wd Douglas" names the spinster at the point of her first appearance, then records what has been said about her. (The word "goggles" is inserted. "Her sister, Miss Watson, a tolerable slim old maid with goggles on," Huck says.) Note A-7 similarly lists characters in the order of their appearance, and records, usually in the sequence of the narrative, what Huck has said about each.

Put the note alongside the text and you see at once what is happening. As the episode begins, Huck tells his hosts that he is George Jackson: Mark reminds himself of this. The Shepherdsons are mentioned: a note is made of this. Bob and Tom are mentioned and described as "thirty or more": Mark writes their names and "abt 30," then lists other characters and, in the column under "abt 30," their ages. When, later in his reading, he comes to "Bob was the oldest and Tom was next," he crosses out "abt 30," and puts in a new column—out of line with other notations—"28 & 30." Introducing Grangerford, Huck has mentioned "the oldest . . . about sixty"; soon this character is called "Saul"; still later, "Col." The entry follows a similar order: "Old man (Saul) Col. Grangerford . . . 60." Mrs. Grangerford had been described as an "old gray-headed lady," and later she had been called "Rachel": Mark's note follows this order. Her age is not given in the narrative or the note. And so on. The page refers back to chapter xvii and the first pages of chapter xviii (where Harney Shepherdson, misremembered as "Harvey," first appears—the italicized "v" is crossed out). Since this was written on the paper and in the ink of 1879–1880, it shows that by mid-June, 1880, Mark Twain had written this part of his novel. And A-10, which will be discussed later, similarly looks back to a later point in chapter xviii.

Shortly after the Grangerfords have been introduced in the pages summarized in Note A-7, Huck talks with Buck Grangerford, who "looked about as old as me—thirteen or fourteen or along there, though he was a little bigger than me":

. . . he asked me what my name was, but before I could tell him, he started to tell me about a blue jay and a young rabbit he had catched in the woods day before yesterday. . . .

"Say, how long you going to stay here? You got to stay always. We can just have booming times—they don't have no school now. Do you own a dog? I've got a dog—and he'll go in the river and bring out chips that you throw in. Do you like to comb up Sundays, and all kind of foolishness? You bet I don't, but ma she makes me. Confound these ole britches! I reckon I'd better put 'em on, but I'd ruther not, it's so warm. Are you all ready? All right. Come along, old hoss."

Back in 1870, in *Boy's Manuscript*, Mark had written Billy Rogers' account of his talk with Amy when they first met:

"What's your name?—Eddie, or Joe?"
I said, "It ain't neither—it's Billy."
"Billy what?"
"Billy Rogers."
"Has your sister got a doll?"
"I ain't got any sister."
"It ain't a pretty name I don't think—much."
"Which?"
"Why Billy Rogers. . . . Did you ever see two cats fighting?—I have."
"Well I reckon I have. I've *made* 'em fight. . . . Your name's Amy, ain't it? . . . I've had the scarlet fever and the mumps, and the hoop'n cough, and ever so many things. . . ."

In chapter vii of *The Gilded Age*, in 1873, the Sellers twins chant remarks at the newly arrived Washington Hawkins: " 'Great-grandmother died before hardly any of us was born—she was an Old-school Baptist and had warts. . . . She had an uncle that was baldheaded and had fits. . . . We used to have a calf that et apples and just chawed up dishrags like nothing, and if you stay here you'll see lots of funerals. . . . Did you ever see a house afire? *I* have!' " In chapters vi and vii of *Tom Sawyer*, in 1876, Becky and Tom have similar conversations.

The emphasis on childish interests, including a fascination with names, an interest in animals, a pride in personal experiences, marks the passages. Staccato rhythms and quick shifts in topics occur in the rehearsals as well as in *Huck*. In each animated exchange, Mark conveys the liveliness, the irresponsibility, the innocence, the comic illogic of children, and thereby wins liking for them. So Buck, whose death late in chapter xviii is one of the most moving passages in the novel, is introduced as a highly sympathetic character.

Next, Huck describes the Grangerford house. The passage deals chiefly with the parlor, which is told of in great detail. Mark had been working toward such a description for some years. In chapter vii of *The Gilded Age* he had remarked on the one glory of the dingy Sellers parlor, "a clock which never came within fifteen strokes of striking the right time":

"Remarkable clock!" said Sellers, and got up and wound it. "I've been offered—well, I wouldn't expect you to believe what I've been offered. . . . But my goodness I'd as soon sell my wife. As I was saying to— silence in the court, now, she's begun to strike! You can't talk against her—just be patient and hold up till she's said her say. Ah. . . . she's beginning again! Nineteen, twenty, twenty-one, twenty-two, twen—ah, that's all. Yes, as I was saying to old Judge—go it, old girl, don't mind me. Now how is that? Isn't that a good, spirited tone? She can wake the dead! . . . Why you might as well try to sleep in a thunder-factory. . . . She'll strike a hundred and fifty, now, without stopping. . . ."

Into a rather flat story, "The Loves of Alonzo Fitz-Clarence and Rosannah Ethelton," written in 1877, he had heaved an inordinate number of details to establish the fact that his heroine was sitting in what was "manifestly the private parlor of a refined and sensitive lady, if signs and symbols may go for anything"—describing chairs, a workstand, a rug, a "luxurious sofa," a number of books, the piano, the pictures, "the quaint and pretty gimcracks, and rare and costly specimens of peculiarly devilish china." The passage had practically no function in the story, since the parlor had been furnished not by the heroine but by a minor character whom she was visiting.

In 1878–1879 in Europe, Twain had written a similarly detailed description of the family parlor in Cassel. Also in a notebook he had headed a long description, "St. James parlor," which in some details anticipated the description of the Grangerford parlor: the "faded and shabby" dust-covered artificial flowers, the ugly chairs and sofa, "a sham Persian carpet, full of strong splotches of red, green and pale blue—and how these colors do swear at the scarlet chairs and sofa"—"the aged lawn shades and heavy dark red curtains—walls and ceilings formerly white stucco work—elaborate birds, cupids, wreaths, etc.—yellow and very dirty, now. Discolored shabby clock . . . the very hatefulest room I have seen in Europe." Evidently there had been a companion description, now lost, for after this one he wrote, "Here insert parlor of Normandy Hotel." [6]

Huck's description of the Grangerford parlor, more detailed than any of these, is a culmination:

There was a big fireplace that was bricked on the bottom, and the bricks was kept clean and red by pouring water on them and scrubbing them with another brick. . . . There was a clock on the middle of the mantel-piece, with a picture of a town painted on the bottom half of the glass front, and a round place in the middle of it for the sun, and you could see the pendulum swinging behind it. It was beautiful to hear that clock tick; and sometimes when one of these peddlers had been along and scoured her up and got her in good shape, she would start in and strike a hundred and fifty before she got tuckered out. They wouldn't took any money for her.

Well, there was a big outlandish parrot on each side of the clock, made out of something like chalk, and painted up gaudy. By one . . . was a cat made of crockery, and a crockery dog by the other; and when you pressed down on them they squeaked, but didn't open their mouths nor look different nor interested. They squeaked through underneath. . . . On the table in the middle of the room was a . . . lovely crockery basket that had apples and oranges and peaches and grapes piled up in it which was much redder and yellower and prettier than real ones is, but they warn't real because you could see where pieces had got chipped off. . . .

This table had a cover made of beautiful oil-cloth, with a red and blue spread-eagle painted on it, and a painted border. . . . There was some books too, piled up perfectly exact, on each corner of the table . . . a big family Bible, . . . Henry Clay's Speeches . . . Dr. Gunn's Family Medicine . . . a Hymn Book, and a lot of other books. . . .

They had pictures hung on the walls—mainly Washingtons and Lafayettes, and battles, and Highland Marys. . . . There was some that they called crayons . . . different from any pictures I ever see before, blacker, mostly, than is common.

Seen through Huck's unsophisticated eyes, the parlor neverthe-less shows forth in all its ugliness. Yet because Huck admires it

SPIDERY WOMAN, *Huckleberry Finn*, FIRST EDITION

consistently for the wrong reasons, he describes it with uncon-scious humor; and his description acquires a warmth which makes the reader feel kindly toward the family who have committed the interior desecration. Mark Twain's nostalgic fondling of evoca-tive details gives the room an attractiveness which accrues to the Grangerfords.

The uncommonly black crayons, Huck mentions, "one of the daughters which was dead made her own self when she was only fifteen":

One was a woman in a slim black dress . . . leaning pensive on a tombstone on her right elbow, under a weeping willow . . . underneath the picture it said "Shall I Never See Thee More Alas." Another one was a young lady . . . crying into a handkerchief and had a dead bird laying on its back in her other hand with its heels up, and underneath the picture it said "I Shall Never Hear Thy Sweet Chirrup More Alas." . . . She was at work on what they said was her greatest picture when she took sick . . . of a young woman in a long white gown, standing on the rail of a bridge all ready to jump off, with her hair all down her back, and looking up at the moon, with the tears running down her face, and she had two arms folded across her breast, and two arms stretched out in front, and two more reaching up towards the moon—and the idea was, to see which would look best, and then scratch out all the other arms; but . . . she died before she got her mind made up . . . The young woman in the picture had a kind of a nice sweet face, but there were so many arms it made her look too spidery. . . .

Again, Huck's naïve admiration and Twain's amused recollection of details favorably affect the attitude of the reader.

Huck offers biographical details about the artist. She had kept a scrapbook in which she had pasted "obituaries and accidents and cases of patient suffering out of the *Presbyterian Observer*," and had written "very good poetry" "after them": "Every time a man died, or a woman died, or a child died, she would be on hand with her 'tribute' before he was cold." Huck quotes a sample. This splendidly constructed "Ode to Stephen Dowling Bots, Dec'd" starts by telling how its hero did *not* die—not from sickness (stanzas 1–3), not from blighted love or stomach trouble (stanza 4). It then turns to the actual cause (stanza 5): "By falling down a well." Stanza 6 demands quotation:

> They got him out and emptied him;
>   Alas it was too late;
> His spirit had gone for to sport aloft
>   In the realms of the good and great.

A lesser artist might have ambled on for a stanza or two, but Emmeline concludes with this climax of heartbreaking pathos.

In the Clemens library in Hartford the humorist was wont to entertain his daughters as they sat on the arms of his chair by telling stories about the pictures and ornaments strung along the wall and across the mantelpiece. The rules required that each romance start with a cat pictured in an oil painting, that it proceed—in exact order—through pictures and bric-a-brac, ending with "a head of a beautiful girl, life size. . . . an impressionistic water-color" purchased in Europe. The girl, says Clemens, was "called Emmeline, because she looked just about like that." [7] If a picture of the fireplace published in 1885 includes this impressionistic painting—and I believe it does—the girl was frail, pensive, smallish of chin, with lace at her throat, an ornament in her hair, and long locks falling over her shoulders.

Emmeline's Christian name probably came from the picture; but Emmeline as a character had a long ancestry. Between 1877 and 1879, in his play *Simon Wheeler, Amateur Detective,* and in the unfinished novel based upon it, Twain had pictured Hugh Burnside, "clearly a prototype," as Franklin R. Rogers has noted, "of Emmeline Grangerford." [8] Hugh "was giddy and thoughtless," says he, "when he was not sappy and sentimental . . . and he was more than likely to shut himself up in his room and write some stuff about 'bruised hearts' or 'the despised and friendless.'" Hugh is capable of deciding that "he will mysteriously disappear from the haunts and the eyes of men" because "there is nothing in literature more romantic." And rejected in love, the morbid youth writes a poem comparable for sentimentality with Emmeline's tribute—"The Crushed Heart's Farewell." Moreover, in a conversation with his sister, Hugh outlines the climax for the "Ode": "Why once when Hank Miller got the cramp in the river . . . they pumped and pumped about a barrel of water out of him. . . ." [9]

Long before picturing Hugh, though, Twain had been fascinated and delighted with the comic possibilities of lugubrious poems about death. Burlesque obituary poems had been produced by many American humorists—Mrs. Whitcher and John Phoenix in 1856, Max Adeler in 1874, and Eugene Field in 1880, to name only a few. Twain, with his affection for the macabre, was destined to work this vein. In a recent article,[10] Robert J. Lowenherz has traced the author's jokes about such outpourings to 1853, when at seventeen he wrote a parody, "The Burial of Sir Abner Gilstrap," for the Hannibal *Daily Journal*. Lowenherz mentions a letter of May 7, 1869, to Olivia during the courtship period; an article, "Post-Mortem Poetry" of 1870; the "nursed and petted melancholy" of chapter xxi of *Tom Sawyer* in 1876; and an article written in the spring of 1880 and later published anonymously.

Lowenherz does not happen to mention the obituary poet whom the humorist most admired and who, I believe, most influenced the characterization and also the poetry of Emmeline Grangerford. This was Julia A. Moore. Born Julia Davis in Plainfield, Michigan, in 1847, this singer had taken over the duties of managing the Davis family from an invalid mother. She had attended school, nevertheless, long enough to learn to write songs which she proudly described as "sentimental." These were inspired by her memories, her reading in books and newspapers (usually about calamities), and—like those of the Grangerford girl—by the deaths of neighbors. In 1876 she was living as a farmer's wife near Edgerton, and was famed locally as "The Sweet Singer of Michigan."

That year was not only the hundredth anniversary of American independence but also the year of Mrs. Moore's first volume, *The Sentimental Song Book*. Prefaced with a portrait of the poetess which looked like a patent medicine illustration (the one labeled "Before Taking"), it was published by J. F. Ryder of Cleveland, Ohio. He promised in a letter accompanying review copies, "If a sufficient success should attend the sale of this work, it would be our purpose to complete the Washington monument."

The success was not, as it happened, sufficient, but it was noteworthy. Critics commented extravagantly: "Shakespeare, could he read it, would be glad that he was dead. . . . If Julia A. Moore would kindly deign to shed some of her poetry on our humble grave, we should be but too glad to go out and shoot ourselves tomorrow" (Rochester *Democrat*). "To meet such steady and unremitting demands on the lachrymal ducts, one must be provided, as Sam Weller suspected Job Trotter was, 'with a main, as is allus on'" (Hartford *Daily Times*). "The poet is one who reaches for the sympathy of humanity as a Rhode Islander reaches for a quahaug, clutches the soul as a garden rake clutches a hop vine, and hauls the reader into a closer sympathy than that which exists between a man and his undershirt" (Worcester *Daily Press*).

The Sentimental Song Book (1876), FRONTISPIECE

When, in 1878, Mrs. Moore published her second book, *A Few Choice Words to the Public, With New and Original Poems,* she included seventy-four pages of reviews, most of them as ecstatic as those quoted. Her first volume went through three editions, and every few decades since, some lover of poetry had made her songs available in new printings.[11] She has been quoted and praised by Robert Frost, and Ogden Nash acknowledged in the preface to his first book his debt to her—for help, one suspects, in developing an airy attitude toward meters and a mastery of recalcitrant rhymes.

Clemens acquired Mrs. Moore's book the year it was published; and in chapter xxxvi of *Following the Equator* he wrote:

Monday . . . I have been reading the poems . . . again, and I find in them the same grace and melody that attracted me when they were first published, twenty years ago, and have held me in happy bonds ever since. *The Sentimental Song Book* has long been out of print, and has been forgotten by the world in general, but not by me. I carry it with me always. . . . Indeed it has the same deep charm for me that the *Vicar of Wakefield* has, and I find in it the same subtle touch—the touch that makes an intentionally humorous episode pathetic and an intentionally pathetic one funny.

Ten years later he thanked a correspondent for an "enchanting" book which he felt "belongs with 'the Sweet Singer of Michigan,' Queen and Empress of the Hogwash Guild until now." [12]

Emmeline Grangerford's poetry was inspired and composed after the pattern of Mrs. Moore's. As the "Sweet Singer" announces in her preface: "This little book is composed of truthful pieces. All those which speak of being killed, died or drowned, are truthful songs; others are 'more truth than poetry.' They are all composed by the author." In 1896 Clemens liked best Mrs. Moore's "William Upson," perhaps because of its famous couplet, "Come all good people, far and near, Oh, come and see what you can hear." But I suspect that in 1879–1880 the Bots elegy was chiefly influenced by two other poems. "Little Charlie Hades" begins, as the "Ode" ends, by picturing its protagonist happy in heaven:

> Little Charlie Hades has gone
> To dwell with God above,
> Where live the angel throng
> In perfect peace and love.

And the climactic verse of "Little Libbie" pictures its heroine dying in a fashion which Mrs. Moore must have had as tough a time transmuting into poetry as Emmeline had poetizing Bots' undignified exit:

> While eating dinner, this dear little child
> Was choked on a piece of beef.

> Doctors came, tried their skill awhile
> But none could give relief.

It seems unlikely that Clemens could read verse as touching as this without feeling an urge to emulate it.[13]

The opening paragraphs of chapter xviii enlarge the account of the Grangerfords. Colonel Grangerford, Huck says, "was a gentleman all over; and so was his family." Huck tells about the politeness of these folk toward one another. When the colonel and his wife descend for breakfast, the rest of the family stand until the pair is seated. Then Tom, Bob, Buck, and Huck toast them. (Mark has them sip his favorite drink—Old-Fashioneds.) Huck also tells of the Grangerford affluence. The colonel has many farms and more than a hundred slaves. Each member of the household, including Huck, has a personal servant. Often people from fifteen miles around come for six-day visits—"dances and picnics in the woods daytimes, and balls at the house nights."

Excepting Mrs. Grangerford, earlier called "the sweetest old gray-haired lady," each member of the family is further characterized. Bob and Tom are "tall, beautiful men with very broad shoulders and brown faces, and long black hair and black eyes . . . dressed in white linen from head to foot." Miss Charlotte

> was twenty-five, and tall and proud and grand, but good as she could be when she warn't stirred up; but when she was she had a look that would make you wilt in your tracks. . . . She was beautiful.
>
> So was her sister, Miss Sophia, but it was a different kind. She was gentle and sweet like a dove, and she was only twenty.

Readers of nineteenth-century American novels will recognize here a pair of "females"—often sisters—who appear again and again. But characterized at greater length than any of these is the head of the clan:

> Col. Grangerford was very tall and very slim, and had a darkish-paly complexion, not a sign of red in it anywheres; he was clean-shaved every morning, all over his thin face, and he had the thinnest kind of lips, and the thinnest kind of nostrils, and a high nose, and heavy eyebrows, and the blackest kind of eyes, sunk so deep back that they

seemed like they was looking out of caverns at you, as you may say. His forehead was high, and his hair was black and straight and hung to his shoulders. His hands was long and thin, and every day of his life he put on a clean shirt and a full suit from head to foot made out of linen so white it hurt your eyes to look at it; and on Sundays he wore a blue tail-coat with brass buttons on it. He carried a mahogany cane with a silver head to it. There warn't no frivolishness about him, not a bit, and he warn't ever loud. He was as kind as he could be—you could feel that, you know, and so you had confidence. Sometimes he smiled, and it was good to see; but when he straightened himself up like a liberty-pole, and the lightning begun to flicker out from under his eyebrows you wanted to climb a tree first, and find out what the matter was afterwards. He didn't have to tell anybody to mind their manners—everybody was always good-mannered where he was. . . . When he turned into a cloud-bank it was awful dark for half a minute, and that was enough; there wouldn't nothing go wrong again for a week.

In writing this, Mark apparently dug out his unfinished novel about Simon Wheeler, looked up his description of Judge Griswold, and rewrote it. The earlier passage reads:

He was sixty years old, very tall, very spare, with a long, thin, smooth-shaven, intellectual face, and long black hair that lay close to his head, was kept in the rear by his ears. . . . He had an eagle's beak and eagle's eyes. He was a Kentuckian by birth and rearing; he came of the oldest and best Kentucky Griswolds and they came from the oldest and proudest Griswolds of Virginia. Judge Griswold's manner and carriage were of the courtly old-fashioned sort; he had never worked; he was a gentleman.[14]

Twain's levying upon the pigeonholed manuscript probably led to his outfitting Grangerford with hair which, like Griswold's, is black in chapter xviii, having undergone an otherwise inexplicable change since Huck has noticed in chapter xvii that it is gray. (Years later, some proofreader noticed the discrepancy and substituted "gray" for "black.")

In describing both Griswold and Grangerford, Twain drew upon his memory. The author's family, without resisting strongly, had managed to persuade themselves that their ancestry traced back to Gregory Clement of England, who had had the honor of being beheaded for voting for the execution of King Charles. The author recalled that his father, John Marshall Clemens, a Virginian by birth who had moved to Kentucky, took great pride in his descent. Like the colonel, John Clemens often wore a blue swallow-tail coat with brass buttons. He was "very tall, very spare, with a long, thin smooth-shaven face"; he had "an eagle's beak and an eagle's eyes." Although he had a volatile temper, he seldom blew up, since he could stare his family into obedience: "a look was enough, and more than enough." Like Grangerford, he had elaborate manners: every night before retiring he shook hands with the rest of the family.

But Mark gave Grangerford a quality which he did not believe his father had. In his reminiscences the author mentions only one occasion when John Clemens was "soft-hearted"; elsewhere he pictures him as "stern," "unsmiling," "ungentle of manner toward his children." Grangerford by contrast radiates geniality. "Everybody," Huck says, "loved to have him around . . . he was sunshine most always—I mean he made it seem like good weather." This modification fits in with the representation of the rest of the Grangerfords, since it tends to make him sympathetic. Huck indicates what Twain must have wanted readers to feel after reading chapter xvii when he says, "I liked all that family, dead ones and all."

Something more than memory and the wish to create a genial atmosphere was involved, though, in this characterization of the colonel. Compare with that of Grangerford the description of the planter Champ Effingham, Esquire, in John Esten Cooke's novel of 1854, *The Virginia Comedians:* "the whole face plainly giving indication of fiery passion, and no less of tender softness." The same paradox is involved. Yet such a picturing is far from being confined to these two books. Portrayals like it and like those of others in the Grangerford family occur in many books, following a tradition which had been established over a long period.

The tradition began early in the nineteenth century when Americans made a discovery that astonished and fascinated them— that their compatriots differed—New Englanders from Virginians or Carolinians, Westerners from both. Travel-book writers from abroad had helped greatly with the discovery. "Generalizing with intrepidity from single instances," as Clemens was to do later, they had noticed that Yankees were sharp and parsimonious, Westerners—like the raftsmen in *Huck*—rough and tough, and that Southerners (all, most travelers seemed to believe, opulent planters) had definite unique qualities. Scores of British travelers found Southern gentlefolk paradoxical. On the one hand they were "high-spirited, fiery, and impetuous, with great difficulty restraining their passions." On the other hand, in family circles or among friends, they were gentle and genteel. Their dress was splendid, their manners impeccable, their hospitality prodigal and in fine taste.[15] At least one commentator was able to reconcile the ferocity and the geniality in sketching "the hot and peremptory Virginian, full of generous blood, which he is ready to pour out, like his generous wine, *for* anybody or *with* anybody." [16]

Interested as usual in type characterizations, jokesters and journalists began to use "Southerners" in aphorisms and anecdotes many of which circulated widely. Soon fiction writers took up the type. As early as 1809 Washington Irving maliciously described Virginians and Marylanders as "a gigantic, gunpowder race . . . expert at warfare," who so enjoyed the social amenities that they were "much given to revel on hoe-cake and bacon, mint-julep and apple-toddy." [17] And a few years later critic W. H. Gardner saw the type so clearly defined that he could urge other fiction writers to portray "the highminded, vainglorious Virginian, living on his plantation baronial estate, an aristocrat among his slaves, a nobleman among his peers." [18]

In 1832 John Pendleton Kennedy thus portrayed the planter class in a book long to be admired, *Swallow Barn; or a Sojourn in the Old Dominion*. Chapter i describes "a time-honored mansion" quaintly called Swallow Barn and the vast acreage around it. Chapter ii introduces Frank Meriwether, "the master," with his "fine intellectual brow," his "coat of blue broadcloth, astonishingly glossy." "His home," says Kennedy, "is open to everybody, as freely almost, as an inn," and the author notices that Meriwether

is admired for "his kind and considerate bearing towards his servants and dependents." Then Kennedy gives the planter some less
genial aspects of the typical Virginian: he arrogantly believes
himself "as infallible as the Pope; . . . [and] is apt to be impatient of contradiction, and is always very touchy on a point of
honor." Chapters iii and iv introduce other members of the family: Mrs. Meriwether, famous for the superlative table she sets;
two lovely daughters, the younger sweet and delicate and the
other high-spirited; and a thirteen-year-old son, full of mischief.

Huck's awed description of the Grangerford mansion, followed
by discussion of its kindly but fiery-tempered master, the great
hospitality of the family, the glorious food, the haughty and hot-
tempered Miss Charlotte and her younger sister the dovelike Miss
Sophia, and the mischievous thirteen-or-fourteen-year-old Buck is
almost a comic paraphrase. One might see specific literary indebtedness here if it were not for the fact that approximately the
same ground had been traversed in scores of novels before *Huck*.
So many authors had followed in the footsteps of Kennedy and
Cooke that critics had perceived "a plantation tradition" in American fiction.

Francis Pendleton Gaines, in *The Southern Plantation*, chronicles the development of this tradition. And he notices an important change which, significantly, took place between 1870 and
1879. In that decade, portrayals of plantation life greatly increased
and "the scale of life steadily enlarged. . . . Estates swelled in
size. . . . Gentlemen were perfected in courtly grace, gay girls
in loveliness. . . . Parties were more and more elaborate. . . .
Swords flashed more gleamingly the arbitraments of honor."
Gaines suspects that "the wide-spread hunt for local color" caused
writers to produce these romantic portrayals and that a sense of
guilt led Northerners to read them avidly. Van Wyck Brooks and
Paul H. Buck add other explanations: Brooks holds that the pro-
vincialism and the traditionalism of the South encouraged such
treatments. Buck believes that writers were vindicating the ante-
bellum South. "A culture," he says, "which in its life was anathema
to the North, could in its death be honored. This was the richest

legacy the Southern writers inherited. Without offense to any living interest they could at last tell what they deemed to be the truth about the land they loved." [19]

Whatever the reason, a very popular theme for fictionists between 1870 and 1880 and beyond was the splendid life of Southern aristocrats. In the feud chapters of *Huck*, Mark Twain, sensitive as usual to new interests of the public, was developing his own peculiar version of this popular theme.

Exactly which of the host of writers about Southern aristocrats were influential we cannot be sure. But I have encountered two who might well have been.

One of them, Bret Harte, created a memorable character, majestic Colonel Culpepper Starbottle, before leaving California. He used him in numerous stories, in the novel *Gabriel Conway* (1875), serialized in *Scribner's* and issued in book form by Mark Twain's publishers, and in the play *Two Men of Sandy Bar*, staged just before Harte and Twain wrote *Ah Sin*. Starbottle was based upon an "extreme type of Southerner" whom Harte had encountered in Sacramento.[20] His bearing is noble; his brow is high; his nose is aquiline; he wears a blue frock coat, brass buttons, blue or white trousers; he carries a cane—so he looks like Grangerford. He is similar in other ways: he savors his liquor; his manners and his style of speaking are elaborate; he has a hot temper; he sternly adheres to the code of the Southern gentleman. He therefore could have stepped into *Huck Finn* and have assumed the role of Grangerford perfectly.

The other author is J. W. DeForest. His novel which might have been influential is *Kate Beaumont*, serialized in the *Atlantic Monthly* beginning in January, 1871, and published as a book by Clemens' friend James R. Osgood the next year. Howells, whose taste Clemens greatly respected, reviewed the book in the *Atlantic* for March, 1872. He noticed that in it "the high-tone Southern society . . . before the war . . . with slavery and chivalry, with hard drinking and easy shooting appears *again*," but called the novel "the first full and perfect picture" of prewar Southern aristocratic living.[21] Two years later Howells went so far as to call DeForest "really the only great American novelist." [22] On July 31,

1874, DeForest wrote Clemens a letter proposing that the two publish a book of their short stories, and on the envelope Clemens wrote, "J. W. DeForest, Novelist." [23] These facts suggest that the humorist may have read the book.

The novel is about two aristocratic plantation families in South Carolina. Peyton Beaumont, the master of one plantation, is, in Howells' words, "a quivering mass of affection for his own flesh and blood, an impersonation of the highest and stupidest family pride, his hot blood afire with constant cocktails and his life always in his hand for the resentment of an insult, an impatient parent and an impenitent homicide." [24] Judge McAlister, head of the other family, is likewise paradoxical. "He a fighter of duels, a champion of a family feud . . . !" writes DeForest. "Why, bless you, he is obviously one solid chunk of goodness; his philanthropy shines out. . . ." The Beaumont daughters are the typical pair, the older high-mettled and haughty, the younger delicate and docile.

The families are engaged in a feud dating from the all but forgotten past which has mowed down member after member of each family. The plot centers about a love affair between the demure younger sister, Kate Beaumont, and Frank McAlister which is frequently compared to the union of a Capulet and a Montague.

In chapter xviii of *Huck* a similar union between the gentle and sweet Sophia Grangerford starts a conflict between the families during which a Shepherdson is wounded and seven or eight members of the feuding families are killed. Once the humorous introduction of the Grangerfords is completed, Huck was to recount this conflict—one so devastating that he would wish he "hadn't come ashore that night" to witness such horror.

15

THE FEUD

"Well," says Buck, "a feud is this way. A man has a quarrel with another man, and kills him; then that other man's brother kills him; then the other brothers, on both sides, goes for one another; then the cousins *chip in—and by-and-by everybody's killed off, and there ain't no more feud. But it's kind of slow, and takes a long time."—Ad*ventures of Huckleberry Finn, *chapter xviii.*

Novelists of the 1870's and 1880's would have testified that Huck's account of the way things went in the Grangerford household mirrored life in the ante-bellum South. Clemens must have considered even Emmeline as more than a comic figure—as a representative of an attitude widely prevalent in her day. Some years after *Huck* was published, he stated that in the 1840's, "Songs tended to regrets for bygone days and vanished joys. . . . *Negro Melodies* the same trend. . . . All that sentimentality . . . was soft, sappy, melancholy." [1]

Two working notes of 1879–1880 suggest that the novel incorporate scenes of violence, "Duel with rifles" and "A lynching scene." The author did not treat the duel in his novel. Though he did write about five lynchings (four abortive) later on, at this time he pictured a feud. When the Grangerford chapters were written, this and other forms of violence were considered by many typically "Southern." "It is imagined in the North," Clemens wrote in 1882 or 1883, "that the South is one vast and gory murder-field, and that every man goes armed, and has at one time or another taken a neighbor's life." [2]

A reason for this belief is suggested in a notebook entry: "There is not a single celebrated Southern name in any of the departments of human industry except those of war, murder [crossed out: assassination, lynching], the duel, repudiation, and massacre." [3] This statement is intemperate even for the explosive Clemens, but a look at what was happening in America in the 1870's and early 1880's suggests that it was less intemperate than it sounds. For in those years "murder," "lynching," "assassination," and "repudiation" were words recklessly juggled by political orators, roughly the equivalent, say, of such epithets in our less vituperative days as "Fifth Amendment communist," "fascist," "America Firster," and "traitor."

Both parties in that distant period skittered away like frightened things from discussions of vital issues. Republican and Democratic leaders were as drab a lot as any in our history. Therefore both parties resorted to oratory and an allied art, melodrama. The numerical difference between the two parties was less than 11,000; so the oratory that preceded a national election was unusually fervent and the melodrama preposterous and lurid.

The favorite Republican strategy, successful ever since the war, was "waving the bloody shirt." The Democratic party was held to be made up of the Solid South plus its Northern dupes. In 1879–1880 Republicans were making the incredible claim that if the election was close but Republicans won, the South would rise and seize the government, but if the Democrats won they would at once exterminate Southern Republicans and haul the country back to ante-bellum conditions. *The Republican Campaign Text Book for 1880* by a congressional committee described "the grand object of all the conspiracies":

. . . to recapture the control of the Southern States—to seize upon their political organization by the violent suppression of the Republican vote, and thus, through the "solid South," aided by the Northern Democracy, to subjugate the North and the West—to tax its wealth and industries as a means of indemnifying the Confederate populations for losses in the rebellion, and to degrade their intelligent majorities into "hewers of wood and drawers of water" for the service of the rebel Brigadiers.[4]

Clemens had been converted to the Republican faith years before. In November, 1879, he took part in a jamboree which was a political rally disguised as an army reunion. In October he had written Howells of his dream of "a descent upon Chicago . . . to witness the reunion of the Grant Commanders of the Western Army Corps":

> My sluggish soul needs a fierce upstirring, and if it would not get it when Grant enters the meeting place I must doubtless "lay" for the final resurrection. . . . I would give a heap to be there. I mean to heave some holiness into the Hartford primaries when I go back; and if there was a solitary office in the land which majestic ignorance and incapacity, coupled with purity of heart, could fill, I would run for it.

His statement casts doubt upon Paine's claim: "A Presidential year was coming up, but if there was anything political in the project there were no surface indications." Clemens was going to the gathering to get the gospel; indeed, unless the gospel was to be preached the gathering had little justification. True, Grant had circled the world; but this hardly called for a celebration. Appomattox was fourteen years back; and it is not usual to celebrate a fourteenth anniversary so strenuously. The really important facts were that Grant was being backed for a third term and that the meeting would help his candidacy and publicize Republican beliefs.

A newspaper which Clemens sent Livy telling about one of the meetings he attended gives the secret away (if there was any secret). The meeting was held under the auspices of the Veteran Club of Chicago on November 13. Early in the session one Colonel Brownell, introduced as "the first man to draw rebel blood," now an officeholder, remarked that he hardly knew what to say, since a member of the club had recently spoken in St. Louis:

> They said [he plaintively complained] that he was waving the bloody shirt; that he was a soldier politician.

A Voice—"He needn't be afraid of that here." [Laughter.]

Now, it has been stated I know in the different meetings that have been held that they are non-sectarian. I have a slight intimation that the Veteran Chicago club is something of a political organization. Am I right? [Laughter.] . . . the men in the army ought to vote as they fought. [Loud applause.] . . . I never heard of a man who was at Andersonville, or Belle Isle, or Saulsbury, or any other rebel prison that did not vote the way he fought. [Loud applause.] . . . Many people claim that we soldiers should take no part in politics. I think that this is wrong. . . . If any people should interest themselves in politics it is the soldiers. [Cheers.] [5]

Other speakers, both at this meeting and at the climactic banquet where Mark Twain scored a triumph with one of his funniest speeches, followed similar patterns. Generals and lesser officers who were veterans, and a number of politicians who were not, hung the bloody shirt on the party line and let it wave.

Robert G. Ingersoll, the chief orator, in his peroration contrasted the angelic North and the wicked South:

The soldiers of the Republic . . . blotted from the statute-books laws that had been passed by hypocrites at the instigation of robbers . . . battled for the rights of others, for the nobility of labor, fought that mothers might own their babes, that arrogant idleness might not scar the back of patient toil. . . . Will all the wounds of war be healed? I answer, Yes. The Southern people must submit, not to the dictation of the North, but to the North's will and to the verdict of mankind. They were wrong, and the time will come when they will say that they are victors who have been vanquished by the right. Freedom conquered them, and freedom will cultivate their fields, educate their children, weave for them the robes of wealth, execute their laws, and fill their land with happy homes.

This was what everyone else at the celebration was saying, though in more highfalutin language. Clemens went into ecstasies over Ingersoll's oratory.

If Clemens read Republican propaganda after he returned to Hartford he encountered other pictures of the South as a violent section. "Of seventy campaign documents published by the Republican Congressional Committee in a campaign," says a historian, "twenty-six dealt with some phase of the Southern question." [6] From 1865 to 1876, the party claimed, "twenty thousand persons—mostly colored—were killed, maimed, or cruelly beaten" in the South. From 1876 to 1880, it held, "assassination and intimidation," "outrages," "lynchings," "warfare," and "bloody murders" continued.[7]

Assassinations or murders committed during feuds were publicized. Beginning in 1878 (an election year) several feuds had become picturesque enough to be reported widely. These had been in Kentucky, the Grangerfords' state, though in a different part—Breathitt County. The Little-Burnett vendetta, the first to attract national attention, had become so violent in 1878 that the governor had sent troops to keep order during circuit court sittings.[8] Historian Virgil Carrington Jones finds that after this many Kentucky feuds "flared up in quick succession, and every short while throughout the 80's, the names of new factions appeared in the headlines." [9] Northern newspapers, predominantly Republican, somehow found these newsworthy.

It seems almost incredible that a man reared in the South—even if he had not revisited it since 1868—could have accepted without question the pictures of Southern fiends created by propaganda. Yet coupled with his growing misanthropy and his political zeal, campaign documents, fervent oratory, and heated editorials must have caused the author to emphasize rougher aspects of Southern life which lay in his memory.

In the best fiction about the old South, too, writers were telling about hot-headed Southerners who pumped lead into long-time enemies of their families. These may have had an influence. Clemens' reading in less respectable fiction may also have been influential. Diverted by Allan Pinkerton's recent series of lurid novels about the exploits of his detective agency, in his play and his novel about Simon Wheeler the writer had parodied wrongheaded deductions recounted by the detective turned author. In Munich in 1879 he had written a chapter (later excised) for *A Tramp Abroad* in which he "extravagantly burlesqued the detective business—if it *is* possible to burlesque that business extravagantly." Pinkerton's *Mississippi Outlaws and Detectives* (1879) contains a scene wherein at night a detective enters a firelit room of suspicious Southerners, which just possibly suggested Huck's entrance into the Grangerford house. Its setting is in the vicinity of the Grangerfords, as F. R. Rogers has noticed—"the Kentucky border region, and [the book] features Island Number 10 and Reelfoot Lake, places mentioned by Twain in Group A of the working notes." [10] Pinkerton shows the folk of the region to be rough and courageous, constantly armed and—like Grangerfords and Shepherdsons—not deterred by any sporting code from taking shots at one another from ambush.

Pinkerton's Mississippi detective story, however, contains no hint of the *Romeo and Juliet* motif, and there is evidence that Twain had hit upon this before reading the book. For in the plot of the uncompleted novel about Simon Wheeler in 1877–1878, marriages between feuding families are important. This, I suspect, he borrowed (if not from Shakespeare) from DeForest or some other writer about the South, possibly even from one of many novels about the Civil War in which the very similar theme of North-South love was the theme "the most frequently used." [11]

Though reading probably suggested the feud, the love affair, and some details about the fighting, the author drew upon his memory for important incidents. In time, Reginald Cholmondeley, an Englishman whose castle the Clemenses had visited, read the feud chapters and asked, "Is it possible that blood feuds really existed in Arkansas within fifty years?" Clemens, foregoing the chance to correct the location of the episode, answered: "Yes, indeed, feuds existed in Kentucky, Tennessee and Arkansas, of the nature described, within my time and memory. I came very near being an eye-witness to the general engagement detailed in the book. The details are historical and correct." [12]

He referred to an experience during his piloting days. When preparing for his trip on the Mississippi in 1882, he reminded himself: "Stop at Cairo, Hickman or New Madrid (1 hour) and ask about old feuds"; and he questioned his memory about a locale connected with these: "Compromise?" he asked himself. [13] On the trip he had a talk with a pilot which his secretary recorded. The

pilot contributes the names of the feudists—Darnell and Watson
—and incidents in the feud. Then the stenographer specifies that
several paragraphs are "By Mr. Clemens." These say that one
family "lived on the Kentucky side the other on the Missouri side
near New Madrid." The Grangerfords live on what Huck, going
downstream, calls "the left-hand shore"—Kentucky; the Shepherdsons "on t'other side of the river"—Missouri. One of Clemens'
dictated reminiscences was: "Once a boy 12 years old connected
with the Kentucky family was riding thro the woods on the Mo.
side. He was overtaken by a full grown man and he shot that boy
dead." [14] Elsewhere, in a note for some unidentifiable story, the
author repeats this haunting detail: "Refugee from a wornout
feud in Kentucky or Tenn. Told his story. Afraid he might be
hunted down. Fictitious name. Saw his boy of 12 riddled but he
and his ambushed an open wagon of the enemy driving home
from church. . . ." [15] And chapter xxvi of *Life on the Mississippi*
repeats this striking incident. In the novel, Baldy Shepherdson
shoots Buck's cousin in the same way.

The author's dictation continues, "They used to attend church
on the line (part of the church in Tenn. part in Ky.). Both Darnell
and Watson went to that church armed with shotguns." Chapter
xxvi of *Life on the Mississippi* repeats this statement and adds
that "the church was at a landing called Compromise." Huck records this phenomenon, though only in part: "Next Sunday we
all went to church. . . . The men took their guns along, so did
Buck, and kept them between their knees or stood them handy
against the wall. The Shepherdsons done the same."

Nowhere does Twain show dependence upon memory more
clearly than in accounts of three skirmishes. The first involves
Baldy Shepherdson and three Grangerfords: "They was all a-
horseback; [Baldy] lit off his horse and got behind a little woodpile, and kep' his horse before him to stop the bullets; but the
Grangerfords stayed on their horses and capered around the old
man and he peppered away at them." In the second skirmish Buck
and a kinsman crouch "behind the wood-rank alongside the steamboat landing" and shoot at "four or five men cavorting around on
their horses in the open place before the log-store." In the third,

when a Shepherdson is wounded his companions bear him to the store and the boys dash to another woodpile. The Shepherdsons "rip around awhile," shooting, ride away, then return afoot to shoot again. In all three engagements, enemies circle around one or two feudists behind a woodpile exchanging shots.

A reason for such singular repetitiousness is suggested by Clemens' dictation of his memories: "I was on a Memphis packet and at a landing on the Kentucky side there was a row. Don't remember as there was anybody hurt then; but shortly afterwards there was another row at that place and a youth of 19 belonging to the Mo. tribe had wandered over there. Half a dozen of that Ky. tribe got after him. He dodged along the wood pile and answered their shots." The setting and the action, which the author used three times (on one occasion switching them from one side of the river to the other and changing characters), he himself had seen and heard about.

Back in 1868 Clemens had written, "I don't care anything about being humorous, or poetical, or eloquent, or anything of that kind—the end and aim of my ambition is to be authentic—to be considered authentic." And in 1895 he was to say, "Almost the whole capital of the novelist is the slow accumulation of unconscious observation—absorption." [16] The desire to be "authentic," to use unconsciously acquired materials, in this instance must have been greater than a desire for variety.

The working note "Describe aunt Patsy's house . . ." specifies another remembered setting, the Quarles place visited during boyhood vacations—"a double log affair," says Wecter, "with an open but roofed-over hallway nine feet high, where the dinner table was spread in summer." Compare the Grangerford house in *Huck:* "a big-old-fashioned double log house . . . the big open space between them was roofed and floored, and sometimes the table was set there . . . and it was a cool, comfortable place." The Quarles sitting room, like the Grangerford parlor, had a fireplace bricked on the bottom, brass andirons, a memorable clock, split-bottom chairs. The author also recalled that at the Quarles house he had gorged on prodigious meals. Huck says, "And warn't the cooking good, and just bushels of it too!"

In the 1879–1880 chapters as elsewhere, though, Mark was far from slavish in copying actuality. Cholmondeley, although uninformed in a typical British (and American) way about American geography, was not entirely to blame for mislocating the feud. Huck never mentions Kentucky or Missouri or the way the feudists' church straddles a state line. A good reason is that such details would unduly complicate the narrative. A better reason is that Huck characteristically is sparing in his use of place names. During Sam's pilot years his notebook " 'fairly bristled,' " as Paine says, "with the names of towns, points, bars, islands, bends, and reaches," and he memorized many of these. But with artistic restraint in this episode and the rest of the novel the author has Huck mention only the few place names an uneducated boy might learn during a sporadic journey.

Also Twain manipulates remembered details to make them do more than tell a story—comment upon the Grangerfords. In this lengthy episode he develops a theme, not sporadically in anecdotes or conversations as in the 1876 chapters, but in settings, dialogues, and happenings throughout.

Writing Huck's longest description, Twain refurnishes the middle-class Quarles "common sitting room" to make it the more elegant "parlor" of the aristocratic Grangerfords. The Quarles room, he testifies, had "no carpeting anywhere"; in the Grangerford house "most" rooms "have carpets on the floors." The Quarles room had " 'split'-bottomed chairs here and there"—condition unspecified; the parlor, "nice split-bottomed chairs, and perfectly sound, too—not bagged down in the middle and busted." The Quarles room housed a spinning wheel and "a dining table with leaves"; these are not in the Grangerford parlor, presumably because such mundane objects are kept elsewhere. The Quarles room contained "a bed, with a white counterpane" and a cradle; but at the Grangerfords' "There warn't no bed in the parlor, nor a sign of a bed; but heaps of parlors in town has beds in them."

In addition to thus refurnishing the "parlor" the author has Huck mention details which more subtly suggest a significant fact about the Grangerfords. Fireplace bricks they keep redder than ordinary fire-darkened bricks "by pouring water on them and scrubbing them with another brick; sometimes they wash them over with red water-paint they call Spanish brown." "When in good shape" the clock fills the family with pride by performing more spectacularly than ordinary clocks, striking a hundred and fifty times. An "outlandish parrot" on each side of the clock is "painted up gaudy." The fruits in the basket on the table are "much redder and yellower and prettier than real ones is."

But the bricks are only discolored bricks painted over. The showy clock keeps poor time, and "a picture on the bottom half of the glass front" has "a round place in the middle of it" which reveals "the pendulum swinging behind it." The gaudy parrots are "made out of something like chalk." The cat and dog ornaments are crockery, and "when you press down on them, they squeak, but don't open their mouths nor look different nor interested. They squeak through underneath." Huck knows that the fruit "in a lovely crockery basket" is not real "because you can see where pieces have got chipped off and show the white chalk, or whatever it is, underneath." If this parlor—as rooms in fiction often do—embodies the qualities of those who furnished it, the Grangerfords are folk who try to look finer than they are.

The books on the table help create this impression. "Piled up perfectly exact, on each corner of the table," they are less for use than for ostentation. One, Henry Clay's speeches, is standard equipment in that period for a house in Kentucky, whose adored spokesman Clay was. The others are equally characteristic. But of the many books which Twain could recall (compare *Life on the Mississippi,* chapter xxviii) only those are mentioned which —if we consider their disuse—ironically enforce the evidence of fraudulent pretense. *Friendship's Offering* is one of the flashy annuals which in that era flaunted affectations of sentiment and cultivation on tables everywhere; and "the beautiful stuff and poetry" Huck finds in it are unlikely to make friendship burgeon in this house of hatred. Religious books—"a big family Bible," *Pilgrim's Progress,* and a hymnbook—are unlikely to persuade the bellicose family to follow the Christian injunction to love one's neighbors. *Family Medicine,* which "tells you what to do if a body is sick or dead," will not be removed from its neat pile and used if the ailing or the defunct is a Shepherdson. The author's name underlines the incongruity of even an unused book on healing in this house of killers: it is Dr. Gunn. Huck says that there are "a lot of other books," but names only those which say something important about the Grangerfords.

Huck turns next to the pictures, especially to those by Emmeline, then to the ghoulish young lady herself. Humorless and objective though it is, his report shows that like the rest of the family she is something of a fraud. Huck's remark that her crayons are "different from any pictures that I see before—blacker, mostly, than is common," suggests that, like chalk animals or fruit more colorful "than real ones is," her pictures attempt to surpass reality —pretend to compassion finer than ordinary sorrow. But Huck sees nothing worth remarking about the expressions of the females they portray except that one is, of all things, "sweet"; and he chiefly reports the absurd fashionable costumes and the hackneyed though graceful poses, picturing both in far from sorrowful terms. "Bulges like a cabbage in the middle of the sleeves," "a large scoop-shovel bonnet," and "wee black slippers, like a chisel" are typical details in describing their dress; and a typical pose is that of a lady "leaning pensive on a tombstone on her right elbow, under a weeping willow." The absence of punctuation from picture titles such as "Shall I Never See Thee More Alas" and "Thou Art Gone Yes Thou Art Gone Alas" suggests that, desolate though their sentiments are, these have been given readings—and significations—more mechanical than heartfelt. Huck's sensible and logical comment puts pictures and their creator in perspective: "These was all nice pictures, I reckon, but I didn't somehow seem to take to them, because if ever I was down a little they always give me the fan-tods. Everybody was sorry she died, because she had laid out a lot more of these pictures to do, and a body could see by what she had done what they had lost. But I reckoned, that with her disposition, she was having a better time in the graveyard."

Emmeline's poetry, likewise, is grossly inappropriate for expressions of woe with any real substance. Buck's story of the way she wrote suggests that more than ineptitude is responsible:

"Buck said she could rattle off poetry like nothing. She didn't ever have to stop and think. He said she would slap down a line, and if she didn't find anything to rhyme with it she would just scratch it out and slap down another, and go ahead. She warn't particular; she could write about anything . . . just so it was sadful." The incongruous concern with facile rhyming in elegies purportedly voicing frantic grief repeats the implication of pretense. Also the manner of Emmeline's dying shows vainglory rather than sympathy as her chief impetus: "The neighbors said it was the doctor first, then Emmeline, then the undertaker—the undertaker never got in ahead of Emmeline but once, and then she hung fire on a rhyme for the dead person's name, which was Whistler. She warn't ever the same after that; she never complained, but she kind of pined away and did not live long." Huck's experience when he has a go at versifying provides a contrast which again offers perspective, for, unlike his glib model, honest Huck bogs down: "Poor Emmeline made poetry about all the dead people . . . and it didn't seem right that there warn't nobody to make some about her . . . so I tried to sweat out a verse or two myself, but I couldn't make it go, somehow."

Emmeline is not the only sentimentalizing Grangerford. Evenings, accompanied by "the little old piano, with tin pans in it" (a typical piece of Grangerford furniture), Miss Charlotte and Miss Sophia chant for appreciative listeners a lugubrious ditty with a title like those of the dead girl's pictures, "The Last Link Is Broken." The family keeps Emmeline's bedroom exactly as it was when she died. Mrs. Grangerford cares for it herself, "sews there a good deal and reads her Bible there mostly." The family hangs the girl's unfinished crayon of the spidery woman, covered with a curtain, above her bed. On her birthday they ceremoniously open the curtain and drape flowers over the picture. Like that in Emmeline's art and poetry, the ostentatious and exaggerated mourning arouses suspicions that it is not wholly sincere.

The family's dress and manners also are ostentatious. The colonel's costume bedazzles—"so white it hurt your eyes." Bob and Tom also "dressed in white linen from head to foot . . . and wore broad Panama hats." Sunday, even more resplendent, Grangerford dons "a bluetail coat with brass buttons" and "carries a cane with a silver head." Breakfast is a ritual, with standings, formal greetings, drink-mixing ceremonies, and toasts: "Then they bowed and said, 'Our duty to you, sir, and madam'; and *they* bowed the least

COLONEL GRANGERFORD IN *Huckleberry Finn,* FIRST EDITION

bit in the world and said thank you, and so they drank, all three, and Bob and Tom poured a spoonful of water and a mite of whisky or apple-brandy in the bottom of their tumblers, and give it to me and Buck, and we drank to the old people too." Even for quality in a part of the country where ceremonial drinking was traditional, this is a formidable rite.

Mark must have been of two minds about such foibles. Though he found jokes about undertakers and inept obituaries hilarious, he liked above all poems "The Burial of Moses" and Negro spirituals, and he attempted to write serious poetry only (I believe) in the form of elegies. As a wearer of white suits, he shared the Grangerford liking for the stir they caused. As the product of a section where manners were florid, as a man who, like Tom Sawyer, admired "style," and had been instructed in the importance of etiquette by Mother Fairbanks and Livy, he was not entirely unsympathetic to elaborate manners. But as one who had suffered because of his unconventional dress and decorum, as the affectionate creator of uncouth Huck and Tom Canty and as a scoffer at French punctilio, he was irritated and amused by excesses. Before long he was to show this at length in an unfinished burlesque etiquette book. Here as elsewhere his ambivalence helped him combine admiration with scorn and genially satirize the Grangerfords' pretentiousness and meticulousness.

Huck's picture of the feudists at worship brings out a related incongruity:

Next Sunday we all went to church. . . . The men took their guns along, so did Buck, and kept them between their knees or stood them handy against the wall. The Shepherdsons done the same. It was pretty ornery preaching—all about brotherly love, and such-like tiresomeness; but everybody said it was a good sermon, and they all talked it over going home, and had such a powerful lot to say about faith, and good works, and free grace, and preforeordestination, and I don't know what all. . . .

The image is of folk who praise God and listen to preachments on brotherly love with loaded guns in easy reach, then praise the sermon but show indifference to its substance by discussing niceties of abstract doctrines. Telling about returning to the church after services, Huck favorably contrasts the church-going motives of hogs: ". . . there warn't anybody at the church, except maybe a hog or two, for there warn't any lock on the door, and hogs likes a puncheon floor in summer-time because it's cool. If you notice, most folks go to church only when they've got to; but a hog is different."

The Grangerfords' pretense of piety, like the parlor décor, shows of culture, mawkish pictures and poems, bedazzling clothes, elaborate etiquette, does not quite hide something less creditable underlying it. Beneath displays of civilization is a savagery which erupts above the surface when the feud breaks out.

Just before the church service, Huck has learned about this vendetta. In the woods one day Buck shoots from ambush at Harney Shepherdson. This vicious little prank prompts Huck to ask questions and Buck gives him a lecture on feuding. One exchange echoes a passage in the aborted Simon Wheeler novel which follows the judge's boasting to his wife that his family feuded with the Morgans for three generations. Says she:

"Yes, I know. What was it about?"

"I do not remember—that is, I never knew. I think it never occurred to me to ask. But no matter: it was not likely that any of my generation could have told me. Besides, the feud itself was the only thing of consequence; how it originated was a circumstance of no interest. I was only taught that when I should meet a Morgan there was a thing to be done; it was very simple—kill him." [17]

Buck is similarly uninformed about the start, now thirty years in the past, of the Grangerford-Shepherdson feud. He vaguely recalls that there was a lawsuit and a shooting; other details have been forgotten.

"What was the trouble about, Buck?—land?"

"I reckon maybe—I don't know."

"Well, who done the shooting?—was it a Grangerford or a Shepherdson?"

"Laws, how do I know? it was so long ago."

"Don't anybody know?"

"Oh, yes, pa knows, I reckon, and some of the other old people; but they don't know, now, what the row was about in the first place."

Stressed here as in the Simon Wheeler passage—a point stressed, incidentally, at several points in *Kate Beaumont*—is unreasoning acceptance of the rightness of the feud regardless of the cause.

Buck tells about a recent shooting: "My cousin Bud, fourteen year old . . . riding through the woods on t'other side of the river, and didn't have no weapon . . . he . . . sees old Baldy Shepherdson a-linkin' after him . . . and the old man he rode up and shot him down." Since, in remembering the actual incident from which this derives, Twain three times states specifically that the boy's age was twelve, clearly that age was fixed in his memory. Why did he deliberately add two years to the boy's age?

I believe that a passage in chapter vi of *A Tramp Abroad* bears on the answer. Writing about the Heidelberg duelists, Twain tells about youths stoically enduring the pain caused by gashings inflicted by sword blades—without a wince, a moan, even "any fleeting expression." "Such endurance," he says, "is to be expected in savages and prize fighters, for they are born and educated to it; but to find it in such perfection in these gently-bred and kindly-natured young fellows is matter for surprise." Huck says of Baldy Shepherdson, "I reckon that old man was a coward." Buck replies, "Not by a blame' sight. There ain't a coward amongst them Shepherdsons—not a one. And there ain't no cowards among the Grangerfords either." In both instances the habitual perceiver of incongruity sees noble bravery displayed in an ignoble cause. The attitudes have something in common which this opponent of Lecky must have pondered: they are inculcated, even as attitudes of savages and prize fighters are, by tradition and training. And all the Grangerford attitudes have such origins: taste, sentimentality, manners, religion, bravery, savagery. In representing them, Mark brings out their incongruities, and the incongruities embody his comment.

The most noteworthy incongruity in chapters xvii and xviii, though, results from the use of a device which remains to be considered. Twain used the procedure as far back as *Innocents Abroad*, in which a solemn ass, William C. Prime, tells about his tear-spattered wanderings through the Holy Land; this passage is placed a few pages before a parallel but exaggerated account of the author's own achievements in the way of dribbling plentiful tears. Similarly, in *Roughing It* the writer juxtaposed the tender-foot's book-nourished picture of Western life and the old-timer's realization of life in the West; in "Old Times on the Mississippi," the boy's gaudy dreams of a riverman's life and the pilot's disillusioned realization of it. But he first described the procedure in discussing two passages in *A Tramp Abroad*. A burlesque account of a French duel, ridiculing the *code duello* by detailing elaborate preparations, pretentious posturings, and pronouncements is followed by a pitifully harmless conflict. Concerning this chapter he wrote Mrs. Fairbanks: "It will follow a perfectly serious description of 5 very bloody student duels which I witnessed in Heidelberg one day—a description which simply *describes* the terrific spectacle, with no jests interlarded and no comments added. The contrast between that chapter and the next one (The Gambetta duel) will be silent but eloquent comment." [18] He saw that placing cheek by jowl these passages, similar in subject matter but contrasting in tone, implied a comment.

The device, which has been used by many contemporary fictionists, is described by a character in Aldous Huxley's novel *Point Counter Point* (chapter xxii), which itself embodied the process in 1928:

The musicalization of fiction . . . on a large scale, in the construction. Meditate on Beethoven. The changes of moods, the abrupt transitions. (Majesty alternating with a joke, for example, in the first movement of the B flat major Quartet. Comedy suddenly hinting at prodigious and tragic solemnities in the C sharp minor Quartet.) . . . Get this into a novel. How? The abrupt transitions are easy enough. All you need is a sufficiency of characters and parallel, contrapuntal plots. . . . A novelist modulates by reduplicating situations and characters. He shows several people falling in love, or dying, or praying in different ways—dissimilars solving the same problem. Or, *vice versa,* similar people confronted with dissimilar problems. In this way you can modulate through all the aspects of your theme, you can write variations in any number of different moods.

The extensive use of this device in *The Prince and the Pauper* (the plots of which almost inevitably suggested its use) may well have helped the writer formulate the procedure and find

ways to use it in *Huck*. In many passages in this novel he juxtaposed real obsequiousness in the court and the mocking obsequiousness of folk who jeer at the ragged king, thus providing
"silent but eloquent comment." [19] The device is used in half
a dozen other duplications of situations and characters.

The Grangerford-Shepherdson episode has an over-all pattern
which makes use of such a violent modulation—achieving a contrast which has important implications. The contrast is between
Emmeline Grangerford's sentimentalized pictures and rhymes
about death and Huck's remarkably restrained story of the skirmish in which Buck is killed—"the terrific spectacle, with no
jests interlarded and no comments added." The order of the
passages is the reverse of that in *A Tramp Abroad*, for in *Huck*
the comic one precedes its serious counterpart. Nevertheless the
principle is the same as that which led Mark to juxtapose the
two dueling scenes in the travel book.

These chapters in this pioneer novel in the vernacular clearly
show how the author varies the medium to adapt it to his
purposes. Early in the episode the descriptions of Emmeline's
monstrosities in crayon and the burlesque obituary poem quoted
in full show mawkish feeling reduced to an absurdity. A passage
about one of the pictures not previously quoted goes: "There
was one where a young lady was at a window looking up at the
moon, and tears running down her cheeks; and she had an open
letter in one hand with black sealing-wax showing on one edge
of it, and she was mashing a locket with a chain to it against
her mouth, and underneath the picture it said 'And Art Thou
Gone Yes Thou Art Gone Alas.' " Properly punctuated according to the romantic literary usage of the 1840's, the title of this
picture would read, "And Art Thou Gone? Yes! Thou Art Gone!
Alas!" Even when the title is not so punctuated, it has a rhetorical
form that contrasts comically with Huck's informally constructed
jack-built sentence. And his talking about "a young lady" instead of "a maiden," "a window" instead of "a casement," "looking up" instead of "pensively gazing," "tears running down her
cheeks" instead of "tears bedewing her pallid cheeks," and "mashing a locket against her mouth" instead of "pressing a locket to

her trembling lips" further emphasizes the artificiality of Emmeline's style.

Contrast with this Huck's account of the fight during which Buck is killed. "I don't want to talk much about the next day," he begins. "I reckon I'll cut it pretty short." As Clemens remembered the incident upon which this episode was based, a nineteen-year-old of the Missouri clan was on the Kentucky side when six men in the enemy clan came upon him. From behind the woodpile he exchanged shots. "Presently he jumped into the river and they followed on after and he had to make for the shore. By that time he was about dead—did shortly die."[20] In the novel the nineteen-year-old is transferred to the Grangerford clan, and Buck joins him. While Huck, hidden in a tree above, watches, the two crouch behind the woodpile, shoot at the Shepherdsons, and drive them away. Then:

All of a sudden, bang! bang! bang! goes three or four guns—the men had slipped around through the woods and come in from behind with their horses! The boys jumped for the river—both of them hurt— and as they swum down the current the men run along the bank shooting at them and singing out, "Kill them, kill them!" It made me so sick I most fell out of the tree. I ain't agoing to tell *all* that happened—it would make me sick again if I was to do that. I wished I hadn't ever come ashore that night, to see such things. I ain't ever going to get shut of them—lots of times I dream about them.

I staid in the trees till it begun to get dark, afraid to come down. Sometimes I heard guns away off in the woods; and twice I seen little gangs of men gallop past the log store with guns; so I reckoned the trouble was still agoing on. I was mighty down-hearted; so I made up my mind I wouldn't ever go anear that house again. . . .

When I got down out of the tree, I crept along down the river bank a piece, and found the two bodies laying on the edge of the water, and tugged at them till I got them ashore; then I covered up their faces, and got away as quick as I could. I cried a little when I was covering up Buck's face, for he was mighty good to me.

Ernest Hemingway once said, "I know the ten-dollar words. There are older and better words which if you arrange them in the proper combination you make it stick."[21] The passage just quoted recalls the remark because the simplicity of the language is amazing. Of about two hundred and sixty words, less than forty are of more than one syllable, and the only words with as many as three syllables are "agoing" and "covering." The words are "arranged in the proper combination" to sound like talk and to present well-chosen details. Simple though they are, the words make the action vivid and move with a staccato rhythm which suggests its rapidity. Huck's statements about his emotions are flat understatements: "It made me . . . sick," "I was mighty down-hearted," and "I cried a little." The emotion is conveyed rather than stated, and even Huck's omission of details about the most horrible happening—Buck's death—helps convey it. The indirection and the understatement are particularly poignant here because they contrast with the insincere overstatements of Emmeline Grangerford about which Huck has told a few pages back.

16

"THE CHIEF (LOW-COMEDY) HUMORISTS"

The aim of the author was to supply a chasm in history which has always been overlooked—the manners, customs, amusements, wit, dialect, as they appear in all grades of society to an ear and eye witness to them—Augustus Baldwin Longstreet, Georgia Scenes (1835).

A project which engaged a part of Clemens' darting attention between 1879 and the completion of *Huckleberry Finn* had a great deal of influence upon the portions of the novel written after 1879. This project involved the remembering and rereading of a number of writings which were peculiarly American. But its effects are evident, I believe, in *A Tramp Abroad*, though it concerns travels in Europe, and in *The Prince and the Pauper*, though it concerns England during the sixteenth century.

A day after he had a comic adventure in a Munich hotel during the family's stay there in 1879 Clemens wrote Twichell, back in Hartford, a letter about it. Dressing in the dark and taking great pains to be quiet so he would not awaken Livy, he finished except for one sock. Refraining with an effort from shouting profane imprecations, for half an hour he crawled about the room before finding the missing article.

He expanded the account to ten long paragraphs in chapter

xiii of A Tramp Abroad and added several details. There during his search he encounters four umbrellas, "all alike," standing around the room. "I found a chair," he continues, "then the wall; then another chair; then a sofa; then an alpenstock, then another sofa; this confounded me, for I had thought there was only one sofa. I hunted up the table again and took a fresh start; found some more chairs." After waking the whole household, in the lighted room he looked around: "There was only one sofa; it was against the wall; there was only one chair where a body could get at it,—and I had been revolving around it like a planet, and colliding with it like a comet half the night."

Long before, William Tappan Thompson, a Georgia journalist, had published "A Coon Hunt in a Fency Country," which had been copied by many newspapers. A famous anthology of humor, Polly Peablossom's Wedding, in 1851 had included it. More recently Thompson had published it in his Major Jones's Courtship . . . [and] Thirteen Humorous Sketches in New York in 1872. Clemens had been strongly influenced by Thompson as far back as 1856–1857, when he had tried his apprentice hand at writing for a Keokuk newspaper humorous letters by a rustic who signed his name "Thomas Jefferson Snodgrass."

In "A Coon Hunt in a Fency Country" two old coon hunters likker up before starting for a hunt on old Starlin Jones's new ground and continue to wet their whistles at intervals. Jones's place proves harder to reach than they expect. They hike all night, interrupted time after time by fences which became harder to climb as the night progresses and by branches which become increasingly wet and uncomfortable each time they splash into them. "If this ain't a fency country, dad fetch my buttons," says Bill. "Yes, and a branchy one, too!" says Tom. The story ends:

The bottle broke, and they come monstrous nigh havin a fight about the catastrofy. But it was a very good thing the likker was spilt, fer after crossin three or four more branches and climbin as many more fences, it got to be daylight, when to their great astonishment they found out that they had been climbin the same fence and wadin the same branch all night, not more'n a hundred yards from the place whar they first come to 'em.

Bill Sweeney ses he can't account for it no other way but that the likker sort o' turned their heads. . . .[1]

An old-time Southwestern humorous yarn set in Georgia thus contributed details to Twain's highly fictionized account of an incident which happened in Munich.

Bernard DeVoto has noticed that "the fragrant account of the Limburger cheese and the coffin box full of guns," written for *A Tramp Abroad* but excised and published separately, was based upon a sketch by another ante-bellum Southwestern humorist, J. M. Field: "A Resurrectionist and His Freight" had been published in a St. Louis newspaper and in *The Spirit of the Times* in 1846 as well as in books of 1847 and 1858.[2]

For *The Prince and the Pauper* Mark wrote "a story of a boy, a bull, and some bees" told to Tom Canty by the whipping boy. On a hot summer day, it goes, the boy's father holds a religious meeting to "pray a most notorious and pestilent devil out of the carcass of Gammer Hooker, an evil-minded beldame that had been long and grievously oppressed by that devil's presence, and in truth a legion more." At home the boy dons a handsome costume of his father's and goes out to enjoy its splendors in sunlight. He meets a bull and, following a wild impulse, leaps astride the animal. Carrying him across country, the bull kicks a beehive; the bees pursue the animal and his rider; bull, boy, and bees go larruping into the midst of the father's prayerful congregation, and the meeting adjourns in bee stings and confusion.[3]

The humorist may have come upon what is essentially this story in a number of places. Thompson of the "Coon Hunt" yarn had written a version published under one of two titles, "Into a Hornets' Nest" and "The Unclad Horseman" in 1843, 1849 (magazines and newspapers), 1851 (a collection by various humorists), and in the 1872 edition of *Major Jones's Courtship*. The earliest telling of it I have found is in Henry Junius Nott, *Novellettes of a Traveler* (New York, 1834). Signed "Scroggins" and featuring the legendary keelboatman of its subtitle, another telling, "Deacon Smith's Bull, or Mike Fink in a Tight Place," was published in 1851 in the Milton (Pa.) *Miltonian*, in *The*

Spirit of the Times, and—significantly—in the Hannibal *Missouri Courier* when Sam, fifteen, lived in Hannibal. It was retold in essence as "Sicily Burns's Wedding" by Sut Lovingood, one of the roughest and most refreshing old-time Southwestern characters, the creation of George Washington Harris of Tennessee. Sut's version appeared in journals in 1858 and in the book, *Sut Lovingood's Yarns* in 1867. Clemens had reviewed the book when it appeared, remarking that it "contains all of [Harris'] early sketches, that used to be so popular in the West . . . together with new ones." "It will sell in the West," he had predicted, "but the Eastern people will call it coarse and possibly taboo it."[4] Finally, the story was told by "Shepard Tom" Hazard about Timothy Crumb of Rhode Island in 1880, probably too late for Clemens to have seen it before he wrote his version.

On Howells' advice Clemens removed the yarn from his historical novel but published it in the Hartford *Bazar Budget*, June 4, 1880. Years later he sneaked it into *Personal Recollections of Joan of Arc.* The introduction in the *Bazar Budget* mentions that it is told by "a . . . gentle, smileless creature, void of all sense of humor, and given over to melancholy," obviously a narrator of the Huck stamp.

The project on which the writer was working probably recalled early tellings of these anecdotes or led him to read them. In a notebook entry of 1879 made in Paris he told himself, "See scrap book for Am and British humor."[5] This was the start of thinking and reading which culminated in the compilation of *Mark Twain's Library of Humor*. Although the book was not published until 1888, work on it engaged his attention for several years. Since Howells, Osgood, and a Hartford newspaperman, Charles Clark, helped with the collection, biographers have believed that Clemens had relatively little to do with it. But letters show clearly that he was quite active—that he made the initial selections, that by March, 1882, he had accumulated selections totaling more than 93,000 words, and that he planned to continue his reading of humorous works during the summer of 1882.[6]

Between 1879 and 1882 he was listing in notebooks the names of humorists who might provide material. In addition to contemporaries, he recalled an impressive number of comic writers who had been active during his boyhood: Eastern humorists such as Seba Smith (Jack Downing), Mortimer Thompson (Doesticks), Frances M. Whitcher (Widow Bedott),[7] Thomas Chandler Haliburton (Sam Slick), and several ante-bellum Southwestern humorists such as Augustus Baldwin Longstreet, Joseph G. Baldwin, Johnson Jones Hooper, William Tappan Thompson, and George Washington Harris. "Doesticks," Smith, and the last three Southwesterners were represented in the anthology, Harris by his bull story. Clemens also mentioned two anonymous sketches which had been very popular in the ante-bellum Southwest—"The Harp of a Thousand Strings" and "Cousin Sally Dilliard."[8]

A few years later he indicated his great appreciation for regional humor by proposing as a subject for discussion, "Why the West and South have produced the chief (low-comedy) humorists,"[9] a tantalizing suggestion which evidently he never followed.

In his working notes for *Huck* he suggests typical events for inclusion in his panorama of life before the Civil War: "A house-raising. . . . Fire in village—buckets and 'Big Mo.' engine and swell village fire co. . . . The country cotillion. The horse-trade. Country quilting. Candy-pulling. Country funeral. . . . Dinner manners at tavern with a crowd. . . . A wake." Clemens had personal memories of the lot of these, but old-time Southwestern humorists may well have made him think of some or all of them. Longstreet had described a country cotillion and a horse trade; George Washington Harris, five of the other happenings. "The Circus," wrote Clemens, and he summarized an anecdote which Thompson had told and he himself later used in his novel.

These old-time Southwestern humorists whose names Clemens jotted down and whose works he reread had limned the rougher aspects of the life of their era and section. Here is part of Longstreet's description in 1835 of two rough-and-tumble fighters in Georgia:

I looked, and saw that Bob had entirely lost his left ear and a large piece from his left cheek. His right eye was a little discolored, and the blood flowed profusely from his wounds.

Bill presented a hideous spectacle. About a third of his nose, at the lower extremity, was bit off, and his face so swelled and bruised that it was difficult to discover in it anything of the human visage, much more the fine features which he had carried into the ring.

Baldwin, in *Flush Times in Alabama and Mississippi* (1835), claims that "the pursuits of industry neglected, riot and debauchery filled up the vacant hours. . . . The groceries—*vulgice* —doggeries, were in full blast in those days, no village having less than a half-dozen all busy at the same time: gambling and horse-racing were polite and well patronized amusements. . . . Occasionally the scene was diversified by a murder or two. . . ." Johnson J. Hooper of Alabama in the 1840's created Simon Suggs, a watery-eyed, hawk-nosed dupester who made his way around the frontier living up to his motto, "It is good to be shifty in a new country." He started as a boy cheating his ministerial father at cards (the story is in Mark's anthology of humor); as a man, he collected money from an overanxious claim filer, passed himself off as a rich uncle, and fooled folk at a camp meeting by pretending that he had been saved. He succeeded in his knavish schemes by taking advantage of human frailties. And Harris's Sut Lovingood of the Knobs of Tennessee loved above all things telling tall tales, gorging on good food, swagging "cork screw kill-devil whiskey," rumpling pretty girls and worldly-wise widows, and playing brutal pranks.

Here, as in political writings of the 1870's, the emphasis was on Southern roughness and lawlessness. A summary of life on this ante-bellum frontier as the humorists showed it went into a paragraph in *The Spirit of the Times* in 1851:

"Out West" is certainly a great country . . . there is one little town . . . which . . . is "all sorts of a stirring place." In one day, they recently had two street fights, hung a man, rode three men out of town on a rail, got up a quarter race, a turkey shooting, a gander pulling, a match dog fight, had preaching by a circus rider, who afterwards ran a footrace for applejack all round, and, as if this was not enough, the judge of the court, after losing his year's salary at single-handed poker, and licking a person who said he didn't understand the game, went out and helped lynch his grandfather for hog stealing.[10]

During this period of partisan propaganda with its emphasis upon violence in the South, had Clemens' recollections of such humorists and their pictures of Southwestern life and his reread-ing of the humor influenced his thinking about the ante-bellum South, somewhat as his reading of French and English history had influenced his thinking about those countries? Years ago, reading through the notebooks, I came to this conclusion. Much more recently, on the basis of similar reading, Roger Blaine Salomon independently arrived at the same belief.[11] I believe, also, that the recollections and the rereading played a part in suggesting much matter in new portions of *Huckleberry Finn.*

The passage just quoted mentions a disreputable layman preaching in a frontier town: in chapter xx of *Huck* that old reprobate, the dauphin, preaches at a camp meeting. It tells of a dog fight: Mark's working notes for *Huck* include the injunc-tion, "Dog fight—describe in detail," [12] and in chapter xxi Huck writes about the no-account loafers of Bricksville who enjoy sicking a dog on a sow and her litter:

And pretty soon you'd hear a loafer sing out, "Hi! *so* boy! sick him, Tige!" and away the sow would go, squealing most horrible, with a dog or two swinging to each ear, and three or four dozen more a-coming; and then you would see all the loafers get up and watch the thing out of sight, and laugh at the fun and look grateful for the noise. Then they'd settle back again till there was a dog-fight. There couldn't any-thing wake them up all over, and make them happy all over, like a dog-fight—unless it might be putting turpentine on a stray dog and setting fire to him, or tying a tin pan to his tail and see him run himself to death.

The passage in *The Spirit of the Times* mentions a street fight: in chapter xxi Huck tells about Colonel Sherburn shooting down Boggs in the sunlit street of Bricksville. It reports a lynching: in chapters xxi–xxii the Bricksville mob attempts to lynch Sher-

burn. It speaks of a hard-drinking circus (quite possibly a mis-
print for "circuit") rider: a working note for the novel reads,
"Drunken man rides in circus," and chapter xxii describes the
incident. It states that the Western villagers "rode three men out
of town on a rail," and in chapter xxxiii the king and the duke are
accorded this honor. The "turkey shooting" and the "quarter race"
of the passage are not paralleled in the novel, but one working
note reads "*Beef-shooting*" and another "Scrub race"; so Mark
thought of including such incidents.

Though the humorist may have read the paragraph about the
lively Western town as a youth when it appeared in various
journals, or in the books of humor he was scanning between
1879 and 1882, I have no evidence that he did. It would be
rash, therefore, to claim that this particular paragraph suggested
the scenes in *Huckleberry Finn* which I have cited. But these
facts seem to me to be significant: the paragraph shows the life
in a Western village as it was represented in typical ante-bellum
humor; Clemens was recalling and reading such humor during
tho years when he completed his novel; and these typical details
got into the novel.

The old-time humor of the South and the West may well have
been influential in another way. Augustus Baldwin Longstreet,
pioneer humorist, held that his aim in *Georgia Scenes* in 1835
was to show "the manners, customs, amusements, wit, dialect, as
they appear in all grades of society." [13] When William T. Porter,
the ebullient editor of *The Spirit of the Times*, made an anthology
of his favorite humorous stories—*The Big Bear of Arkansas*—in
1845, he used the subtitle, "Illustrative of Characters and Incidents in the Southwest." Baldwin in his preface to *Flush Times
in Alabama and Mississippi* in 1853 said that his object was "to
illustrate the periods, the characters, and the phases of society."
These objectives are typical. A great achievement of this group
of humorists was to display a panorama of the life of a certain
place and period.

The working notes of 1879–1880, Bernard DeVoto holds, show
that Mark Twain had "found the true purpose" of *Huck:* he had

reached the decision that "he was going to exhibit the rich variety of life in the central valley." [14] Granting that this was at least one of Twain's purposes, revisiting the ante-bellum humorous writings after not having revisited the South itself for seventeen or eighteen years may well have helped him find it.

17

BACK ON THE RIVER

I never felt easy till the raft was two mile below there and out in the middle of the Missisippi. Then we hung up our signal lanterns, and judged that we was free and safe once more. . . . I was powerful glad to get away from the feuds, and so was Jim to get away from the swamp. We said there warn't no home like a raft, after all. Other places do seem so cramped up and smothery, but a raft don't. You feel mighty free and easy and comfortable on a raft.—Adventures of Huckleberry Finn, chapter xviii.

If in 1879–1880 he decided to offer a panorama of ante-bellum Southern life, Mark Twain was faced with the problem of discovering a pattern of events that would allow Huck to view this cross section. By wrecking the raft and having Huck swim ashore for adventures at the Grangerfords he had halted the improbable flight of a runaway slave and his companion ever deeper into slave territory. But he had done so only temporarily. After the feud chapters, what was he to do with his characters?

One possibility which, as Franklin R. Rogers plausibly argues, he may have contemplated was the use of a plot with which he had played for some years. In 1877 his and Harte's *Ah Sin* had "included a supposed murder, a false accusation, and a general clearing up of the mystery." So had both Twain's play and his unfinished novel about Simon Wheeler. Early chapters of *Huck* had told of Pap Finn's real murder and Huck's simulated murder. Rogers points out that in three working notes of 1879–1880 the novelist reminds himself of references in the novel to Pap's murder. He remarks that another reads, "boys give bill of sale for Jim"—which may indicate a plan to reunite Huck and Tom, and that still another may refer to a trial. So he suggests that

in its early stages *Huckleberry Finn* was to be a burlesque detective story. Apparently its denouement was to feature Jim's trial for Huck's murder, a crime never committed; Pap's murder as well as the mock murder were to be connected with the Grangerford-Shepherdson feud in a plot-complex similar to that in *Simon Wheeler*. . . . Tom . . . was to play a role similar to that of Simon Wheeler, . . . exonerating Jim.[1]

If this was Mark's plan, he abandoned it while still writing the notes and the chapters of 1879–1880. It would not provide for Huck's experiencing and recording the aspects of life he wanted to show.

Briefly at least he probably considered having his hero see some of the details while staying with the Grangerfords. A note outlining an episode which might have been developed in such a setting reads: "Village school—they haze Huck the first day—describe Dawsons or Miss N[ewcomb]'s school"; another, "Fire in the village." Developing either of these and similar scenes Twain would have exploited Hannibal memories of pastimes and rituals—dances, parades, wakes, and the like—shifted downstream to Kentucky. Perhaps he thought of sending Huck out across country for a time. One note shows him contemplating a rather implausible means of transportation. When Huck goes to a circus, "Can't he," Mark asks himself, "escape from somewhere on an elephant?" Luckily he decided that he could not.

But if he had Huck stay with the Grangerfords or go across country, Mark had a problem. If he brought Jim ashore from the wrecked raft—and by now Jim had become so important that he should—what was he to do with him? One note suggests, "Jim has fever and is in concealment while Huck makes these observations." Though this would do for a short time, obviously it would

OLE BURNS, THE BULL AND THE BEES, *Mark Twain's*
Library of Humor

not do for a period long enough to allow Huck to have many
adventures.

Eventually Mark hit on a better expedient. Since 1865 he had
cherished in his memory an anecdote which he had heard dur-

The Country cotillion.

The horse-trade.

Country quilting.

Candy-pulling.

Country funeral.

Describe aunt Patsy's house.

& Uncle Dan, aunt Hanner, & the 90-year blind negroes.

(Jim has fever & is in conceal-ment while Huck makes these observations.) (Keep 'em along,) &c. The two printers deliver temp. lectures, teach dancing elocution, feel heads, distribute tracts, preach, fiddle, doctor (quack)

WORKING NOTE FOR *Huckleberry Finn*

ing his visit to Gillis's cabin in Jackass Gulch, California. "The Burning Shame" told how a wandering tragedian hoaxed some small-towners by giving a wild performance in the local play-house. In 1877, writing a novel (destined like others never to be finished) based on his brother Orion's eccentric character and career, [2] he had thought of using this tidbit as the basis for an episode, and had conceived of a character who might play the trick—a tramp printer. Character and episode turned up in this working note: "Listens to printer tramp and is charmed. Goes on a month's expedition with him, delivering temperance lectures and spreeing on proceeds. Burning Shame." [3]

He had the happy inspiration to use the episode in *Huck*. "The Burning Shame at Napoleon, Ark.," he scribbled on one page of working notes, and on another, "Rich[ard] III—15¢—B[urning] S[hame] 50¢." Later he recalled his tramp printer and evidently decided to multiply him by two and wrote, "The two printers deliver temp[erance] lectures, teach dancing, elocution, feel heads, distribute tracts, fiddle, doctor (quack)."

The idea was a lifesaver for a reason which he indicated when he wrote, just before the latter entry, "Keep 'em along." The wandering typos enabled him to do exactly that. In chapter xix, rescued by Huck from irate townsfolk whom they have been hoodwinking, they board the raft, list as theirs the cozening talents mentioned in the note, and take command. Without a permanent loss of probability, this motivated Huck's and Jim's continuing downstream. The rogues use the owners of the raft as roustabouts and servants, halt at river towns, gull the yokels, then escape on the raft. Huck can show facets of riverside life by reporting what he sees during stops.

Twain had reached a point somewhat beyond the middle of the chapter about the feud when he hit upon this expedient. He wrote himself a note: "Back a little, CHANGE—raft only crippled by steamer." So, after Huck has been led to Jim (who is hiding in the swamp) by a servant, the author inserted a conversation which put the raft together again:

"Why didn't you tell my Jack to fetch me here sooner, Jim?"
"Well, 'twarn't no use to 'sturb you, Huck, tell we could do sumfn—but we's all right now. I ben a-buyin' pots en pans en vittles . . . en a patchin' up de raf', nights, when—"

"*What* raft, Jim?"

"Our ole raf'."

"You mean to say our old raft warn't smashed all to flinders?"

"No, she warn't. She was tore up a good deal—one en' of her was; but dey warn't no great harm done. . . ."

Mark had discovered a way to keep his story going beyond the feud chapters. In addition, as the 1879–1880 working notes show, he had thought of episodes which he would be using down into chapter xxiii of the novel. The likelihood is that sometime between the spring of 1880 and the summer of 1883 he wrote at least chapters xix, xx, and xxi.

Evidence does not show exactly when he did this. If he kept grinding out literature, good, bad, and indifferent, at the rate which he tried to maintain, he had time to write some or all of them during the winter or summer of 1880, the year 1881, and between mid-January and mid-June, 1883. Paine says unequivocally that during the summer of 1880 Twain "varied his work . . . writing alternately on *The Prince and the Pauper* and the story about Huck. . . ." Paine does not cite his authority, but the author himself may have told his official biographer this when Paine was hovering about, listening to dictations for the *Autobiography,* and questioning his subject between spells. Paine remarks on an interesting phenomenon—that, although Clemens often remembered events inaccurately, his recollections about "the genesis of his books" were usually quite accurate. Also, in December, 1880, Clemens spoke to his sister of a book which may well have been *Huck*—"two or three months' work on it yet," he airily guessed—and indicated that he planned to work on it presently. And there was a time in 1883, when he had both the time and the inclination to write; it was then, I believe, that he wrote chapter xxi.

A few indications support the guess that Mark returned to the manuscript later rather than earlier in the 1880–1883 span. Introducing the chapter from *Huck* which he stole from the manuscript to insert in *Life on the Mississippi* in 1882, he guessed that he might finish the novel "in five or six more years," and it seems likely that he would not have so overestimated the time required if he had made much additional progress between 1880 and 1882. The synopsis of the novel given in the same introductory passage contains some inaccuracies which he might have avoided if he had studied his manuscript recently.[4] Finally, in Group C of the working notes made in the summer of 1883 he reminded himself of facts about the opening part of his novel which he might have remembered if he had not been away from it for some time.

But unless new evidence turns up, all we can know for certain is that, between 1880 and 1883, attitudes and subject matter which were fresh in the author's mind may have influenced the novel. At the end of chapter xviii and the start of chapter xix Huck writes his finest lyrical passage about the beauty of the river and the joys of life on the raft; and in chapter xx he writes an ecstatic description of a storm on the river. Mark, glad to have his story on the move again and, like Huck, "feeling mighty free and comfortable on a raft," may have been moved in 1880 to write these paeans of praise. But if, as I believe, the author was inclined to write such passages when problems concerning the big mansion in Hartford and all it stood for loomed large or when hosts of correspondents irked him, he might have written the passages at almost any time during these years.

In the fall of 1881, writing to Charles Warren Stoddard, for old, old reasons he was longing for a holocaust:

If the house would burn down we would pack up the cubs and fly to the isles of the blest, and shut ourselves up in the healing solitudes of the crater of Haleakala and get a good rest; for the mails do not intrude there, nor the telephones and the telegraph. And after resting we would come down the mountain a piece and board with a godly, breach-clouted native, and eat poi and dirt and give thanks to whom all thanks belong for these privileges, and never house-keep any more.

In January, 1882, he wrote Howells in similar vein, "A life of don't-care-a-damn in a boarding house is what I have asked for in many a secret prayer." In a letter to his sister Pamela in October of the same year he was fuming about autograph seekers as "a more infernal distress to me than any other grievance" and wailing that he had "been persecuted to the verge of lunacy by strangers." [5]

At times, instead of a South Sea Island or a boardinghouse he naturally thought of a river and a raft as havens. In March, 1880, he received a letter from a twelve-year-old Texas boy, Wattie Bowser. Wattie's class had been asked to write compositions titled, "With Whom I Would Change Places"; the favorites "were yourself, Mr. Edison, Mr. Tennyson, O. W. Holmes, Longfellow &c," and Wattie had favored Mark Twain. The boy's composition, which he enclosed, gave reasons which probably show what the image of the humorist was not only in Dallas but elsewhere:

I do not care to be Prince of Wales, who was "born with a silver spoon in his mouth," as the saying is. Rather would I be an American who has climbed step by step up the ladder of fame, until he stands at the top; the admiration and envy of the world. Now there are many such, and among them *all*, I have chosen Mark Twain. . . . First, because he is so Jolly; I imagine him to be a funny man . . . who always keeps every body laughing and who is happy as the Man in the Moon looks. Second—Because he makes so much money . . . he is worth millions. . . . Third—Because he has a beautiful wife and children. Fourth—Because I have been an agent for his book, ("A Tramp Abroad") and because he has everything a man could have.

Would the writer in turn, Wattie asked, like to change places with his young admirer? [6]

Despite his frequent distaste for correspondence, Clemens promptly answered that under certain conditions he would like to be a boy again:

The main condition would be that I should emerge from boyhood as a "cub pilot" on a Mississippi boat, and that I should by and by become a pilot and remain one.

The minor conditions would be these: Summer always; the magnolias at Rifle Point always in bloom so that the dreary twilight should have the added charm of their perfume; the oleanders on the "coast" always in bloom, likewise the sugar cane always green, never any "bagasse" burnings, the river always bank-full, so we could run all the chutes— how heavenly that would be!

Then in the foot of [Island] 63 [near Napoleon, Ark.] and in a thousand other places, we should see the thick banks of young willows dripping their leaves into the currentless water, and we could thrash right along against them without any danger . . . and I would require a new "cut-off" to experiment on every season. . . . I should require that there be a dog-watch in the evening but none in the morning. . . .

I would rule out the middle-watch in the night, except on moon-, light nights . . . the middle watch in summer moonlight night[s] is a gracious time, especially if the boat steers like a duck, and friends have staid up to keep one company, and sing, and smoke, and blow the whistle when other boats are met. . . .

And I would have the trips long, the stays in port short, and my boat should be a big dignified freight boat, with a stately contempt for passenger hails and a tranquil willingness to lay-up for fog—being never in a hurry, and her crew would never change; one such crew I have in mind, and can call their names and see their faces, now; but two decades have done their work on them and half are dead, and the rest scattered, and the boat's bones are rotting five fathom deep in Madrid bend.[7]

The evocative details and the bittersweet nostalgic mood here are very similar to those of Huck's descriptive passages.

Slightly less than three years later, in answer to a complaint by William Dean Howells concerning interruptions of work in Europe, Clemens suggested a similar means of escape:

I learned something last night, and maybe it will reconcile me to going to Europe again sometime. I attended one of the astonishingly popular lectures of an idiot by the name of Stoddard . . . he described how retired tradesmen and farmers in Holland load a lazy scow with the family and the household effects, and then loaf along the waterways of the Low Countries all the summer long, paying no visits, receiving none, and just lazying a heavenly life out in their own private un-pestered society, and doing their literary work, if they have any, wholly uninterrupted. If you had hired such a boat and sent for us we should have a couple of satisfactory books ready for the press now with no marks of interruption, vexatious weariness, and other hellish-nesses visible upon them anywhere. We shall have to do this another time.[8]

On many occasions between 1880 and 1883, Mark, in a similar mood, might have written Huck's rhapsody about the pleasures of returning to the raft and drifting downstream at night or laying up the raft under the branches of young cottonwoods and willows and resting in the daytime. Huck and Jim would watch the sunrise and "the lonesomeness of the river, and lazy along, and by and by would lazy off to sleep"; after darkness fell, they would shove the raft into midstream, "let her alone, and let her drift wherever the current wanted her to." On the wooded shore or on the river, they are delightfully free from pressures to do anything. Their escape from civilization is indicated by their remoteness from all human activities and by their casting off clothes which signify restrictions—"always naked, day and night, whenever the mosquitos let us—the new clothes Buck's folks made for me was too good to be comfortable, and besides I didn't go much for clothes, nohow." One of the most memorable paragraphs in the book perfectly suggests the circumstances and the mood:

Sometimes we'd have the whole river all to ourselves for the longest time. Yonder was the banks and the islands, across the water; and maybe a spark—which was a candle in a cabin window—and sometimes on the water you could see a spark or two . . . and maybe you could hear a fiddle or a song coming over from one of them crafts. It's lovely to live on a raft. We had the sky, up there, all speckled with stars, and we used to lay on our backs and look up at them, and discuss whether they was made, or only just happened—Jim he allowed they was made, but I allowed they happened; I judged it would have took too long to *make* so many. Jim said the moon could a *laid* them; well, that looked kind of reasonable, so I didn't say nothing against it, because I've seen a frog lay most as many, so of course it could be done. We used to watch the stars that fell, too, and see them streak down. Jim allowed they'd got spoiled and was hove out of the nest.

Distant sparks, strains of far-off music, are the only signs that there are others in the world than this pair lazying away a life of contentment and companionship in an imagined world far from the hectic Hartford of the 1880's.

Characteristically there is a sudden shift of mood. The arrival of the two confidence men who live by victimizing the folk on the shore breaks the spell. This pair too, in a different way, were products of the life which their creator was living when he wrote of them. The author's picturing of them was shaped by experiences in the world of business which increasingly absorbed his attention and his energies.

18

FRENZIED FINANCE

*"I ain' gwyne to len' no mo' money 'dout I see de security.
Boun' to git yo' money back a hund'd times, de preacher
says! Ef I could git de ten cents back, I'd call it squah, en
be glad er de chanst."*—Jim in Adventures of Huckleberry
Finn, *chapter viii.*

Kate Leary, still in her teens, went to Hartford in 1880 to begin
three decades of serving the Clemens family. Forty-four years
later, she dictated her memories to Mary Lawton. Rearranged
and padded, with some inaccuracies resulting, these were published as *A Lifetime with Mark Twain.* The account of what this
young woman from the country saw with her wide dark eyes
makes vivid the life of the Clemenses during her first years with
them.

Kate, Mrs. Clemens' personal maid, had as duties combing her
mistress's hair every morning, noon, and night, sewing (she had
been a seamstress in Elmira), doing household chores, and helping George serve formal dinners. Naturally her first impressions
were of Mrs. Clemens. Telling about their first interview in the
Langdon parlor in Elmira, Kate found a word which she constantly used to describe her—wonderful: "This wonderful, wonderful woman appeared, and startled me with all her beauty . . .
her face and manner were wonderful." In the great Hartford man-

sion, Mrs. Clemens, "a very busy woman, a wonderful house-keeper, wonderful with the children," took charge of Kate at once and began to guide her gently but firmly down righteous pathways.

But Kate before long saw that even this overpowering woman exercised little control over her husband. Mistakenly she believed that it had always been that way:

He'd say hard, severe things about religion, and Mrs. Clemens . . . said she'd made up her mind when they first married that her husband was going to be *free* to *say* anything and everything that he wanted to . . . say and do what he wanted. It struck me as kind of wonderful. . . . It showed how much she loved him and what a lot of common sense she had and how she never believed in interfering with other people's rights—even if they was her husband's.

Willy-nilly, the master, she saw, would have his way. She thought him rather like his own Colonel Grangerford: "He had nice manners" and "was lovely and kind," full of affection for his wife and daughters. Each morning he sat quietly while Kate massaged his gray head ("he used to think it helped his hair stay in"). But like Grangerford he had a hot temper, though unlike the colonel he did not control its explosion.

For instance, "if he found a shirt in his drawer without a button on, he'd take every single shirt out of that drawer and throw them out the window, . . . and I'd have to go and bring them back in." Each morning Kate looked out to see whether the lawn was whitened with shirts. Or the bedroom floor might be whitened, for if Clemens was in a vile mood when a shirt displeased him, cursing, he tore it to shreds and threw them on the floor. ("He swore like an angel," Kate said, admiringly.) The biggest rows were about manuscripts which the author suspected Kate enjoyed misplacing or burning: "of course we had a good many tough fights." Once she asked her mistress what color Mr. Clemens' eyes were:

And she says, "Why Katy, don't you know?"
"No, I don't," I says, "because sometimes when Mr. Clemens is very jolly and happy his eyes are *blue* to me; but when he gets angry

or upset at anything, like losing his wonderful manuscript, his eyes are very fierce and *black*."

And Mrs. Clemens laughed and laughed, and said: "Yes, I guess that's true, Katy; but his eyes are really blue."

But I couldn't tell actually, because he had two kinds of eyes to me.

Kate pictures the mercurial master rushing around as wildly as he had on first occupying the mansion. If anything, he was presiding over more dinners, entertaining more visitors and neighbors. If anything, he was attending more club meetings, giving more readings, staging more amateur theatricals, having more friends in for billiards.

Others than Kate were awed by his energy and activity. His daughter Clara recalls that "he never seemed physically tired"— that "after a day filled with business problems, literary work, fatiguing visits, he arrived at the dinner table as full of life and vigor as though he had just started the day." [1] And Howells wryly tells how, during a visit, he and Clemens were carried away by the author's energy and enthusiasm. After agreeing "that the years had tamed us, and we no longer had any literary ambition," "before we went to bed we had planned a play, a lecturing tour, a book of travel, and a library of humor." [2]

Actually such literary planning, compared with other projects, was admirable. There were many other projects. The irony in one of the most ironic passages Clemens ever wrote was unintentional. Orion's latest project was an autobiography which the author had suggested he write. But Orion pestered his famous brother with installments, and the work interfered with Orion's attempt to earn a living—for the nonce as a journalist. Clemens sent a postcard May 12, 1880: "My Dear Bro—Drop that book and give your entire mind to the newspaper. The bane of Americans is over work —and the ruin of *any* work is divided interest. Concentrate—concentrate. One thing at a time." [3] If ever a man needed such advice, Clemens himself did. For, as if his exhausting social, literary, and political activities were not enough, he was becoming involved in a growing number of frenzied business affairs.

The worry about finances which had been an important cause of Clemens' going to Europe had pretty well disappeared by the time he returned. Soon, carefree as a bird, he was moulting money with the old abandon. Although exact statistics for 1879 and 1880 are not available, they are for 1881—and they are startling. His disbursements for that year totaled "considerably more than $100,000." Of this sum, earnings from books and dividends paid only for household expenses and princely entertaining; the rest came from principal. That year Clemens had some extraordinary expenses. But over the next decade his expenses continued to be extraordinary.

He paid in excess of $30,000 for a one-hundred-foot strip of adjacent land to prevent a neighbor from building there, and for the extensive remodeling of a house only seven years old. He had the kitchen rebuilt to double its size, the reception hall torn out to add its space to that of the main hall, and all the walls and ceilings on the first floor redecorated—some by Tiffany's. He had the grounds lowered, as he explained, "to bring the house into view," and the driveway completely rerouted.[4]

He made investments totaling $46,000. Of this amount, Paine says, "less than $5,000 would cover legitimate purposes; the rest had gone in the 'ventures' from whose bourne no dollar would ever return." Exactly which wild investments shared the wealth that year we cannot be sure, but probably one or more of three inventions into which Entrepreneur Clemens sank $25,000 or $30,000 about this time got a share: a patent steam generator, a steam pulley, and a device for marine telegraphy.[5]

But $30,000 was chicken feed. Two ventures which appealed particularly to an ex-printer, as time would show, were really expensive. One day a Hartford jeweler, Dwight Buell, somehow persuaded George to let him corner Clemens in the billiard room. Buell was peddling stock in a typesetting machine being "perfected" by its inventor, James W. Paige, a worker in the Colt factory. Sight unseen, Clemens bought $2,000 worth of stock in this machine. Clemens eventually dumped bushels of dollars into the thing and when in 1894 he went bankrupt this speculation was a chief cause.

More important immediately was his investment in a new chalk-plate engraving process, Kaolatype. A crony from the *Quaker City* voyage, Dan Slote, manufacturer of the Mark Twain Scrap Book, had acquired the patent. Clemens bought a four-fifths interest and predicted the invention would "utterly annihilate and sweep out of existence . . . an industry which has existed for 300 years." To enhance this great potential he dreamed up a modification that would "increase its value a hundred-fold." [6] This was his first of several brilliant refinements of the process. Soon he was supervising experiments with brass, copper, chalk, and sand which he believed would further "perfect" Kaolatype. He kept shoveling out money.

At the same time he had a running battle with the American Publishing Company, the publisher of his books since *Innocents Abroad*. Arguments which had started as far back as 1871 became hotter and more frequent.[7] Though he deviled the company into boosting his royalty percentage to 5, then 7½, then 10 per cent, he was increasingly dissatisfied. In 1875 his attempt to arrange for publication of a book by another firm was frustrated when the company produced a forgotten contract prohibiting this.[8] In 1879 in Europe he arranged with Frank Bliss, son of the Elisha Bliss who headed the American Publishing Company, to publish *A Tramp Abroad* independently.[9] When Clemens and young Bliss grudgingly allowed themselves to be persuaded to let the firm have the book, the author dictated terms: he would get what the elder Bliss long had held Clemens' percentage royalty amounted to—half the profits. Elisha died in the fall of 1880, just in time to escape a thunderbolt of invective which the writer would have hurled at him when the first statement on the book was issued. For this statement convinced Clemens that he would "within the twelve month get $40,000 out of the 'Tramp' instead of $20,000" which he would have received under the old arrangement. And looking back he calculated that Elisha's misrepresentations over the years had gulled him out of $60,000.

Meanwhile he had taken a step which was to have tremendous significance in his business affairs, his life, and even his writings: he had acquired a business manager.

During the fall of 1879 on returning from Europe, the Clemens family ran over to Fredonia, New York, for a visit with Jane Clemens and other relatives. These included Clemens' sister Pamela, a widow for some years; her daughter Annie; and Annie's husband, Charles L. Webster. Webster, a bewhiskered young man of twenty-eight, had been trained as a civil engineer but now was a real estate salesman with prospects in local politics. When the author left Fredonia he told Pamela he had "achieved a higher opinion than ever of Charley and his energy, capacity and industry." [10]

In the spring of 1881 the Howard Brothers of Fredonia were looking for purchasers of stock in their Independent Watch Factory. They persuaded Webster to go to Hartford and to urge his uncle to buy some stock or to let them honor him by christening one of their watch movements "the Mark Twain movement." [11] Although Clemens did not grant the right to use his name, he let himself be persuaded to buy $5,000 worth of stock. During the negotiations he found Webster so impressive that he kept him in Hartford three weeks to go over his business affairs, then made an offer. For some time the author had been dubious about Slote's management of the Scrap Book and Kaolatype. [12] Despite the brilliant improvements in the process, the latter company still was not prospering. Clemens now proposed that Webster take charge of it, alternating stays of two or three weeks in New York and Fredonia throughout the summer. [13]

Soon the new superintendent of the engraving company was very busy. In May, Pamela wrote her son Samuel, out in California:

Annie hears from C[harles] only once a week. He says he is working very hard, trying to get order out of chaos; that the business has been miserably managed &c &c. He has made a definite arrangement with Sam, and has it in writing; I think he is wise in that. Sam is to pay him $1800 a year, until the business begins to pay, if it ever does, and after that he is to pay him at least as much, and give him an interest in the business besides. [14]

By June, Webster was convinced that, hard though the work was, the brightness of his prospects justified it. [15] Developments shortly supported his belief. On July 18 Clemens put him in control of "interests connected with the American Publishing Company," [16] and eight days later Pamela wrote her son that "your Uncle Sam is putting all his business in [Webster's] hands." [17] Sixteen months later, Clemens informed his nephew that "about Christmas" he would go "get all documents and everything connected with my business" from Charles E. Perkins, the lawyer who was handling Clemens' legal affairs, "so that Perkins' salary can stop with the year." Clemens showed in words as well as deeds that he was well satisfied with Webster's work. In November, 1881, he wrote his manager, "You have wrought admirably, from the beginning, in everything you have undertaken. . . . And although I *do* lose my temper 30 times a day, on an average, you will observe that it is not my habit to let it out on you." [18] Webster's income grew apace.

Webster had two abilities which helped him win success. The first was that of working unceasingly to perform the multitudinous errands which Clemens was imaginative enough to devise. A breathless letter the harassed agent wrote his wife shows some typically varied chores he performed during the first few days of August, 1881:

I have enough news to keep a dozen men busy. 1st I have to go to see a plumber and get prices so as to scrutinize a bill sent in to Uncle Sam. Next I have got to haul Sheldon & Co. former publishers of the Galaxy for not accounting to Uncle Sam in the matter of the Royalty of a book. Next I have got to see the N. Y. Herald about an old bill of his. Next I have got to hunt up a brass engraving and have those Providence plates finished up. Next I have got to see a N. Y. theatre man for him on business. Next I have got to overhaul John T. Raymond on the 'Col. Sellers' contract. Next I have got to make a contract with a Frenchman to play the play in France. Next I have got to make a new contract with Bliss on the publication of Tramp Abroad. Next I have got to overhaul the man who is building the addition to Uncle Sam's house. Next I have got to overhaul Dan Slote's Scrap Book account. Next I have got to see Maurice Joyce of Washington in regard to his Kaolatype stock. Next I have got to make a contract with the New Orleans Democrat for Kaolatype for the states of Texas, Lou., Ark. and Ala. Next I have got to see that Kaolatype runs all right and have also got a proposition to consider from a man in Chicago for Kaolatype there.

What do you think of that and that is not all there are lots of other little things.[19]

Exhausting though this summary is merely to read, it was far from exhaustive. As time passed, Clemens' fertile mind proliferated chores. Within the next few years he called upon Webster to find a repairman for an imported music box, buy and sell stocks, check credit ratings, handle lawsuits in which his employer was involved, charter railway cars, make hotel reservations, buy opera and theater tickets, locate books, purchase gifts for members of the family, patent inventions and try to market them, peddle unsalable plays, sign lecture and publishing contracts, frighten publishers who took the name of Mark Twain in vain, watch for newspaper publicity, secure copyrights, canvass for books, write advertising copy, arrange for the manufacture and sale of inventions, and, as Pamela Moffett so eloquently put it, "&c &c."

It is debatable whether Clemens, superintending all these activities and thinking up others and fussing all the while, devoted more or less time to business than he would have spent without an agent. Regardless, his time for writing and his productivity were curtailed.

Webster's second ability—one which influenced *Huckleberry Finn*—was skill in discovering hanky-panky among his employer's business associates. When it came to ferreting out swindlers, Webster compared favorably with Clemens' favorite detective, Pinkerton.

Soon after beginning his new business association, Webster discovered that one Sneider, who claimed he had invented the new engraving process, had made an unjustifiable claim. A bit later he informed his uncle that Slote also had committed "fraudful misrepresentations," was fleecing him on the engraving business, and paying him only a third of the Scrap Book royalties due him.[20] Within a few weeks Webster was in Hartford checking contracts for the remodeling of the house. He wrote his uncle in Elmira: "Seems to me Garvies [the plumber's] estimate is enormous"—and he proffered statistical proof. Garvie and Ahern, another contractor, he continued, "propose to swindle you in a genteel way."[21]

In another few weeks he had secured a contract which he estimated would save his employer $1,500.[22] While he was in Hartford he dropped in on the American Publishing Company, and came out with a report that young Bliss was being suspiciously indefinite—and therefore probably fraudulent—in reporting production costs on *A Tramp Abroad.*[23]

So Webster flushed coveys of cheats from every bush he poked his nose into. The year 1882 saw him exposing the Independent Watch Company for which he had peddled stock; "these Ogilvie bastards" (as Uncle Sam affectionately called them), who had falsely attributed to Mark Twain a "witless" book they had published; Sheldon and Company, which had not paid royalties on the agreed basis; and Raymond, the actor-manager.[24]

On one occasion Clemens found Webster's revelations disappointing. "Look here, have the Am. Pub. Co. swindled me out of only $2,000? I thought it was *five.*"[25] But usually he found the business manager's exposés satisfactory. He believed Webster's claim, "There is one thing . . . that you can depend upon. You are not being cheated and stolen from while I am here watching."[26]

At this distance I find it impossible to discover what percentage of the shenanigans that Webster reported to his employer were fraudulent. There is no doubt that he sincerely believed his uncle was being gypped left and right. Pamela summarized for her son the man's reports to his wife: "Charley . . . writes that he has just saved Sam five hundred dollars on a plumber's bill by making a new contract. He says it makes him sick to see how S. lets money slip through his hands. Says he will be a poor man yet, if he keeps this up—though he makes more money now than he knows what to do with."[27] Webster saw himself, therefore, as a shrewd businessman who helped save a guileless dupe from exploitation.

But whether this was a rationalization it is hard to say. Clemens for some reason was a very suspicious person. Perhaps his growing distrust of humanity or his disastrous investments in recent years had made him wary. Whatever the cause, he was capable on his own of discovering real or nonexistent "swindles." "As nearly as I can make it out," he wrote Webster on May 19, 1881, "my

London publisher has succeeded (by conniving with my London agent) in gouging me out of $19,000 on a recent book." [28] He could work up suspicion with little evidence. Hearing, in 1882, that Whitelaw Reid of the New York *Tribune* was "flinging sneers and brutalities at me with . . . persistent frequency," he planned a counterattack. He collected instances of Reid's villainy and started a scathing satire. At this point, Livy mildly suggested that before going further he might investigate the claim that Reid was attacking him. So to Webster's assignments he added scanning the *Tribune* for two months. He told Howells the result: "Oh, what a pitiable wreck of high hopes! . . . Can you conceive of a man's getting himself into a sweat over so vague a provocation?" Webster had found four puny items which could be swollen into attacks only with the aid of a powerful magnifying glass.[29]

Such a man hired Webster to safeguard his interests and egged on his search for swindlers. "Scan that mason's bill *sharply*," he urged in a typical letter, "for that mason is an infernal thief, I'm afraid." He offered what was, after all, rather convincing evidence: "He is a prominent politician." [30] Like a reader of scandal magazines, he was avid for increasingly lurid revelations. He rewarded Webster for making them. Whether this led Webster to discover crooks even when they did not exist, it is impossible to say.

There is, however, an interesting relationship between these exposures and *Huckleberry Finn*. Before, during, or shortly after all these unmaskings of brazen cheats, diddlers, and confidence men, the author wrote chapters xix–xxiii of the novel. Whether Nature imitated Art or vice versa it is impossible to be sure: probably the influence operated in both directions. At any rate, these were the chapters in which, accompanied by the perceptive Huck, two arrant scoundrels brazenly cheated folk in a series of towns along the Mississippi River.

19

THE DUKE AND THE DAUPHIN

*I don't believe an author . . . ever lived, who created
a character. It was always drawn from his recollection of
some one he had known. Sometimes, like a composite
photograph, an author's presentation of a character may
possibly be from the blending of two or more real characters in his recollection. But even when he is making no
attempt to draw his character from life . . . , he is yet
unconsciously drawing from memory. . . .*

*In attempting to represent some characters which he
cannot recall, which he draws from what he thinks is his
imagination, an author may often fall into the error of
copying in part a character already drawn by another, a
character which impressed itself upon his memory from
some book. . . . We mortals can't create, we can only
copy.—Mark Twain in an interview, Portland Oregonian,
August 11, 1895.*

Characters who behave in *Huck* as Clemens believed many men
did in business deals appear early in chapter xix. One morning
Huck finds a canoe and paddles up a creek in search of berries.
Two fugitives come "tearing up the path," dogs and men on their
trail. Huck takes them aboard and paddles them to the raft. The
escapees explain their hasty exit from the town, reveal their pasts,

real and fanciful, list their skills as confidence men, and join forces. They figure importantly in chapters xix–xxiii and disappear as late as chapter xxxiii.

Two of the most delightful rascals in literature, they give the novel a quality of picaresque fiction—the fiction of wandering rogues' adventures—which it has not had before, and augment its memorable portraits. Because they can be used for humor and satire, they help Mark comment upon humanity.

Like other characters, these were based upon their portrayer's acquaintances and upon his reading. The unscrupulous sharpers resemble not only men whom Webster exposed but also identifiable figures of the past or the immediate period.

The younger says he is "a jour printer by trade." An itinerant printer at eighteen, Sam Clemens had seen enough of the species to learn to generalize in a speech, "The Old-Fashioned Printer," about "the tramping 'jour' . . . with his wallet stuffed with one shirt and a hatfull of handbills, for if he couldn't get any type to set he could do a . . . lecture . . . all he wanted was plate and bed and money enough to get drunk on. . . ."[1] Paine says (no doubt on the author's authority) that the character in *Huck* "was patterned after a journeyman-printer Clemens had known in Virginia City." Perhaps; but the generalized printer of the speech has most of the qualities of the character in his role as a printer. This one carries handbills advertising a lecture on phrenology, the discovery of gold or water by divining rod, and similar specialties. He uses his trade in Pokeville when he invades a deserted print shop, collects payments from farmers for jobs and for newspaper subscriptions, and prepares a sheet concerning a runaway slave to be shown as an advertisement for Jim to anyone stopping the raft. In payment for the use of the press he considerately leaves set up a poem of the Emmeline Grangerford sort he has composed, "Yes, crush, cold world, this breaking heart." (Hugh Burnside, the poet in the unfinished novel about Simon Wheeler, had poetized about the same touching topic.)

Not long after, the printer in *Huck* adds a detail to his biography that is unusual for a wandering type or anyone else: he is "the rightful Duke of Bridgewater . . . torn from his high estate."

Fantastic though this claim is, the author based it upon claims made by men whom he had encountered in real life.

In England in 1873 Clemens had been so fascinated by the Tichborne trial, a fight by an illiterate pretender to establish himself as heir to a great estate, that he had a secretary fill six scrapbooks with day-by-day clippings of court reports. The trial led him to recall a claimant to another title about whom he had heard from boyhood. His mother boasted that her ancestors included the Lamptons and that their descendants claimed the earlship of Durham. James Lampton, the original of Colonel Sellers, often told listeners

the whole disastrous history of how the Lambton heir came to this country a hundred and fifty years or so ago, disgusted with that foolish fraud, hereditary aristocracy, and married, and shut himself away from the world in the remoteness of the wilderness, and went to breeding ancestors of future American claimants, while at home in England he was given up as dead and his titles and estates turned over to his younger brother, usurper and personally responsible for the perverse and unseatable usurpers of our day.[2]

The duke's tale in *Huck* is similar:

"My great-grandfather, eldest son of the Duke of Bridgewater, fled to this country about the end of the last century, to breathe the pure air of freedom; married here, and died, leaving a son, his own father dying about the same time. The second son of the late duke seized the title and estates—the infant real duke was ignored. I am the lineal descendant of that infant—I am the rightful Duke of Bridgewater. . . ."

The fancy cliché-dotted style sharply sets this off from Mark's account. Mark's heir "came" to America; the duke's "fled." Mark's heir was "disgusted with . . . hereditary aristocracy"; the duke's wanted "to breathe the pure air of freedom." The duke's way of talking resembles the style in which the current "rightful Earl of Durham," Jesse Leathers, a distant cousin, wrote to Clemens. Excerpt from a letter of November 25, 1879: "I met a Lady about a year ago at Dr. Miller's 'Turkish Bath' place (Hotel) who spoke to me in the highest terms of your Wife declaring her to be the finest Lady she had ever known. So that I can felicitate you on more than one score." From an answer to an invitation, four days later: "I shall be on hand and shall be only too happy if I can bring my own little sunbeam to mingle with the pure light which cheers your humble hearth and home."[3]

Clemens, who found the old charlatan delightful, once urged Howells to work this "perfectly stunning literary bonanza," and suggested to Osgood that he try out Leathers as a writer: "I think he'll write a gassy, extravagant, idiotic book that will be delicious reading, for I've read some of his rot; and it is just the sort of windy stuff which a Kentucky tramp who has been choused out of an English earldom would write. By George I believe this ass will write a serious book which will make a cast-iron dog laugh."[4] Often in *Huck* the duke's talk accords with the humorist's characterization of Leathers' style:

Misfortune has broken my once haughty spirit; I yield, I submit, 'tis my fate. . . . Let the cold world do its worst; one thing I know— there's a grave somewhere for me . . . some day I'll lie down in it and forget it all, and my poor broken heart will be at rest. . . . To the bitter death! . . . the secret of your being: speak! . . . But the histrionic muse is the darling. Have you ever trod the boards . . . ? . . . we must preserve the unities, as we say on the boards. . . . Hamlet's soliloquy . . . the most celebrated thing in Shakespeare. Ah, it's sublime, sublime! Always fetches the house.

These remarks, so in keeping with the character, seem to echo the fustian periods of Jesse Leathers. These in turn echo the dialogue of nineteenth-century melodrama and fiction.

Because this shabby fraud (who foreshadows the character played by the late W. C. Fields) claims the dukeship of Bridgewater, his companion can deform his title to "Bilgewater," and constantly does. In a notebook of 1865, perhaps recalling some unfortunate whom he had met, Mark had twice written a variant as a comic possibility: "W. Bilgewater, says she, Good God what a name," and "W. Bilgewater. Jesus Maria (Luce Marieau)."[5] In his "Fireside Conversation" he had introduced "ye Duchess of Bilgewater," who, Walter Raleigh remarked, had the distinction of being "roger'd by four lords before she had a husband." Recalling this name, probably enchanted with what (without the best justification) he considered its hilarious possibilities, Mark named his character Bridgewater and used this jape. Possibly, too, he liked the designation "Bilgewater" because it aptly described the duke's style.

The other rascal, the older of the pair, explains his flight:

"Well, I'd ben a-runnin' a little temperance revival thar, 'bout a week, and was the pet of the women-folks, big and little, for I was makin' it mighty warm for the rummies . . . when somehow or another a little report got around . . . that I had a way of puttin' in my time with a private jug, on the sly . . . this mornin' . . . the people was getherin' on the quiet, with their dogs and horses. . . . I didn't wait for no breakfast—I warn't hungry."

THE DAUPHIN AND THE DUKE,
Huckleberry Finn, FIRST EDITION

Since Twain's generic jour printer gave temperance lectures between sprees and a working note refers to both cheats as "printers," their common ancestry is obvious. But when Twain wrote this passage, or soon after, I believe that in real life he had hit upon a very different model for his second rogue—Charles C. Duncan, who had captained the *Quaker City* during the Holy Land excursion.

In the first edition of *Innocents Abroad* a portrait of Duncan which the humorist called "*very* good" [6] shows a thoroughly bald, gray-whiskered oldster in a coat which (if it resembles those of other ship's officers pictured) is long-tailed, probably navy blue and brass buttoned. The con man in *Huck,* "seventy, or upwards," has "a bald head and very gray whiskers" and wears "an old long-tailed blue coat with slick brass buttons."

More important, the author attributed to Duncan qualities like those of his old sharper. In 1877, Duncan, lecturing on the Holy Land expedition, claimed that when Clemens booked passage he "filled [the captain's] office with the fumes of bad whiskey" and represented himself as "a Baptist minister cruising after health." Clemens sent several steaming letters to the New York *World* denying these charges and assailing Duncan's character. He set forth that, like the rascal in *Huck,* Duncan while "posing" as "a

PORTRAIT OF CAPTAIN DUNCAN, *Innocents Abroad*

total-abstinence gladiator" had hypocritically denied that he drank every day "the cheap wines" of Italy. He also deposed:

I have known and observed Mr. Duncan for ten years, and I think I have reason for believing him to be wholly without principle, without moral sense, without honor of any kind. I think I am justified in believing that he is cruel enough and heartless enough to rob any sailor or sailor's widow or orphan he can get his clutches upon; and I know him to be coward enough. I know him to be a canting hypocrite, full to the chin with sham godliness, and forever oozing and dripping false piety and pharasaical prayers.

The charges of the letters were repeated in an unpublished article in which the author added that Duncan was an "over-pious hypocrite" and "a glittering and majestic embezzler." He filed the article and clippings of the newspaper letters. In 1883 or before, he possibly refreshed his memory by rereading some of them, for in an interview in the New York *Times* he reused a number of phrases—"cruel," "heartless," "without principle," and "canting hypocrite." [7]

These exactly fit the graybearded chiseler of the novel. His outline of his talents shows this: " 'Layin' on o' hands is my best holt —for cancer, and paralysis, and sich things; and I k'n tell a fortune pretty good, when I've got somebody along to find out the facts for me. Preachin's my line, too; and workin' camp-meetin's; and missionaryin' around.' " He works religion. His reference to "layin' on o' hands" to cure these diseases, since Livy had been cured of paralysis by a charlatan of this ilk, was a test of her sense of humor which she must have passed when she read this. Before long the rascal demonstrates his skill as a pseudo-preacher. In two episodes he oozes and drips "false piety and pharasaical prayers." In chapter xx, at a camp meeting, "busting into tears," he confesses his sins and promises reform so eloquently that a collection is taken for him. And in chapters xxiv–xxx, looking "that grand and pious that you'd say he walked right out of the ark," "sobbing and swabbing," he "slobbers" "soul-butter and hogwash" sermons and at intervals kneels in prayer. The performance has as its purpose robbing three orphan girls of their inheritance.

His talk (often reminiscent of hypocritical Senator Dilworthy in *The Gilded Age*) is studded with religious bromides:

the blessedest thing . . . a changed man . . . the true path. . . . I'm one o' the Lord's poor servants . . . we've all got to go, one time or another. So what we want is to be prepared . . . a trial that's sweetened and sanctified to us by this dear sympathy and these holy tears. . . . Thish yere comes of trust'n to Providence . . . the vale of sorrers . . . poor little lambs.

The hackneyed style, like the trite phrasing of the duke, suggests hypocrisy. So does the fact that between these protestations, in shows for the Bricksville yokelry, his naked old carcass painted with stripes, the rascal lewdly cavorts before guffawing audiences.

I suggest that Mark Twain wrote about this character with gusto and malice partly because he had in mind that antique hypocrite, Captain Duncan.

The portraits of the rogues also were influenced by their creator's reading. The duke has precipitously left the river town because "I'd been selling an article to take the tartar off the teeth—and it does take it off, too, and generly the enamel off with it"—an after-effect resented by his customers. Joseph Jones has found mention of a counterpart in a *New York Weekly* editorial of August 24, 1871. This rejoices because the peddler of such a dentifrice in Boston recently "obtained his deserts by being sentenced to a year's imprisonment." [8] Clemens well may have happened upon this item and dredged it from his memory to introduce the duke.

Though this is a guess, it seems pretty clear that the claim of the other rascal, that he is "the pore disappeared Dauphin, Looy the Seventeen," was based upon something Clemens had read or heard about. Much of the French history, biography, and fiction which he read dealt with the lost dauphin. Legends current in Clemens' region from his boyhood, as DeVoto has pointed out, concerned this character:

The ambiguity surrounding the death of Louis XVII . . . gave mythology a superb legend, which at once accommodated American belief. Up the river from New Orleans, one of the most pious repositories of all allegiance, stories of the dethroned Bourbon gratified believers during three generations. The legend must have entertained Mark's boyhood.[9]

At least twenty-seven claimants to the crown, most of them scoundrels, presented cases which have been debated in a long shelf of books.

Two claimants who spent time in the United States were famous. "The Duke of Normandy" visited New York and traveled in the South and along the Amazon. He claimed in his memoirs (1831; revised 1843, 1848): "I travelled through these uninhabited wilds, nourishing myself with fruits and turtle eggs, which I found everywhere along the banks of the river; sleeping at night upon [sic] the trees. . . ." Another claimant gained international notice in 1853, when John H. Hanson published in New York *The Lost Prince: Facts Tending to Prove the Identity of Louis the Seventeenth, of France, and the Rev. Eleazer Williams, Missionary among the Indians of North America.* Eleazer, the book said, was an imbecile until, jumping from a high rock, he hit Lake George with considerable force. He not only recovered his senses but also had memories of past scenes which tallied with scenes in the lost dauphin's life. In 1841 M. le Prince de Joinville, upon meeting him, immediately recognized him as the dauphin. Although study later proved that this man of God was a Mohawk half-breed who for years defrauded his people, in 1853 he won many champions.

In July, 1870, in an article for the Buffalo *Express*, Mark pictured a Wild Man named "Sensation" who tells of "creating fraudulent history" and "perpetrating all sorts of humbugs." An instance shows his creator had heard about Eleazer: "I poked around your Northern forests, among your vagabond Indians, a solemn French idiot, personating the ghost of a dead Dauphin, that the gaping world might wonder if we had 'a Bourbon among us' . . ." [10] Although Twain's dauphin gives his biography in very general terms, the likelihood is that Twain had Williams' wild claims in mind as he wrote about him.

The humorist once distinguished three sorts of fictional characters: one the author draws "from his recollection of someone he has known"; one he blends from "two or more real characters in his recollection"; one he copies from "a character which impressed itself upon [the author's] memory from some book." The dauphin seems to be a fourth type in which the author blends a real character with a character about whom he has read or heard. The images coalesce because the fictional and the real model both are frauds who pretend to be pious men of God.

Mark Twain possibly gave his other rascal, the duke, a speech suggested by Eleazer Williams. One of Williams' most memorable plaints is an entry purportedly written in his journal after the prince has told him his true identity:

Is it true, that I am among the number, who are destined to . . .
degradation—from a mighty power to a helpless prisoner of the state
—from a palace to a prison and dungeon—to be exiled from one of
the finest empires in Europe, and to be a wanderer in the wilds of
America—from the society of the most polite and accomplished courtiers, to be associated with ignorant and degraded Indians?

Compare the duke's complaint:

"To think that I should have lived to be leading such a life, and to be
degraded down into such company. . . . I don't blame anybody. I deserve it all . . . here am I, forlorn, torn from my high estate, hunted
of men, despised by the cold world, ragged, worn, heart-broken, and
degraded to the companionship of felons on a raft!"

The duke's prose is more bejeweled; but only the likelihood that
sundry other deposed nobles made similar speeches in Victorian
novels prevents one from assuming a direct indebtedness here.

In the chapters about the king and the duke then, the novelist's
reading of history and biography seems to have been echoed. Also,
his reading in American humor was influential. A long procession
of wandering sharpers wended through this humor. From the beginning it had shown Yankee peddlers playing "cute tricks." And
Southwestern humor repeatedly celebrated horse swappers, land
speculators, cardsharps, and cheats: writers for *The Spirit of the
Times* supplied it with "plentiful humor of sharp practices and
shady dealing." [11] Itinerant actors who staged plays almost as inept
as those of Huck's rogues had been pictured in numerous anecdotes and books by Sol. Smith (1845, 1854) and Joseph M. Field
(1847)—and Mark had found a source for his Limburger cheese
story in Field's book. Tricky jour printers wended their shady
ways through humorous autobiographies such as "Odds and Ends
from the Knapsack of Thomas Singularity" (1834) and "The
Western Wanderings of a Typo" (1846), both of which the author
probably had encountered as a youth or while compiling his *Library of Humor*.[12] Like the boastful rivermen and like the Grangerfords, the king and the duke were typical figures in American
humor.

In one scene in chapter xx, as DeVoto has noticed, Mark

duplicated the exploit of a famous rogue in Southwestern humor, Simon Suggs. Evidence that he recalled Simon in 1880 is his jotting from memory, among suggestions for his humorous library, "Simon Suggs" and, somewhat later, "The man who 'went in on nary a pair' (at camp meeting)." [13] Johnson J. Hooper's tales about shifty Captain Simon Suggs were in newspapers and magazines when Sam Clemens was a youngster and were in books in 1845, 1846, 1848, and 1881. In "The Captain Attends a Camp-Meeting," Simon pretends to be converted, harangues the crowd, takes a collection to found a church in his neighborhood, and runs away. In a speech he applies poker players' terms to religion: "No matter what sort of a hand you've got . . . take stock! Here am *I*, the wickedest and blindest of sinners . . . has now come in on *narry pair* and won a *pile!*" It may be relevant that Scotty Briggs in *Roughing It* similarly mingles poker and religion. It certainly is relevant that the author could repeat so brief a passage by rote in 1880.

In chapter xx of *Huck*, landing at Pokeville and finding the townsfolk are at a camp meeting two miles away, the king, with Huck, visits the gathering. He pretends to be converted, takes a collection to help his "missionary work," then lights out. The indebtedness is clear.

But a comparison between the passages shows differences:

Mark Twain [DeVoto claims] falls below his predecessor. . . . Hooper lacks the Olympian detachment of Mark Twain and his sketch therefore exists on a lower level, but its realism is sharper, its intelligence quite as great, and its conviction considerably greater. Simon Suggs repents his life of sin and deception quite naturally. His conviction and conversion are set in the experiences of his audience and his swindling is therefore credible. A high moment in *Huckleberry Finn* would be better if Mark Twain had adhered to the scene that unquestionably produced it. The instance is memorable as the only one in which the literature to which he belonged surpassed him in a subject of his choice.[14]

I believe that even in this instance the superiority of the model is dubious. There are several points in Twain's favor. Twain's episode makes every comment on camp meetings that Hooper's

chapter does, and in a fifth of the space. Whereas Hooper represents far more figures—preachers, individuals, groups (several far
removed from Suggs)—Twain centers attention on the king and
the spot where he stands. Hooper devotes two paragraphs to
"a sensual seeming man, of a stout mould and florid countenance,
who was exhorting among a bevy of young women, upon whom
he was lavishing caresses." The man's relationship with Suggs is
slight: that gentleman notices him and ruminates on the fact that
"preachers never hugs up the old, ugly women." Twain also brings
out lascivious aspects of the meeting, but illustrates them by the
actions of his chief character: as the king takes the collection, "the
prettiest kind of girls, with tears running down their cheeks,
would up and ask him would he let them kiss him . . . and he
always done it; and some . . . he hugged and kissed as many as
five or six times. . . ."

Which passage is more convincing is a matter of opinion. It
seems worth remarking, though, that the king's past as temperance
lecturer, preacher, and missionary and his habitual use of religious
phrases make believable his speaking so eloquently, whereas the
effect of Simon's harangue is less probable because of his lack of
oratorical experience and the mundane quality of his style. Again,
the king works up the crowd's emotions and then immediately
passes the hat. His success seems more plausible than Suggs' taking up a large collection not at the height of the crowd's fervor
but the next morning. A difference in the situations also is relevant: Simon is known by his victims and must make his speech
accord with their knowledge; the king is a stranger and therefore
can concoct a more imaginative lie and expect belief.

DeVoto is particularly distressed by the extravagance of the
dauphin's placing "his evil-doing among the pirates of the Indian
Ocean and his exhortation for funds with which to convert them."
But the implausibility of the speech is related to an idea which
Twain has been developing sporadically in his earlier chapters—
one which now becomes a very important concern.

The king's tale is by no means the first false autobiography in
the book: Huck has concocted several untrue life histories. Smith

has noticed that "the thumbnail autobiographies [Huck] invents, usually as a means for getting himself out of a tight place, . . . are uniformly sombre." [15] In chapter xi Huck is an orphan who has been apprenticed to a mean farmer; in chapter xvi his father, mother, and sister are prostrated with smallpox on a raft; in chapter xvii his sister and his brothers have left him and his parents have died bequeathing him nothing. In chapter xx he tells a harrowing tale to the duke and the dauphin:

"My folks was living in Pike County, in Missouri . . . and they all died off but me and pa and my brother Ike. Pa, he 'lowed he'd break up and go down and live with Uncle Ben . . . below New Orleans. Pa was pretty poor. . . . Well, when the river rose, pa had a streak of luck one day; he ketched this piece of raft; so we reckoned we'd go down to Orleans on it. Pa's luck didn't hold out; a steamboat run over the forrard corner of the raft, one night, and we all went overboard and dove under the wheel; Jim and me come up, all right, but pa was drunk, and Ike was only four years old, so they never come up no more."

True, as Smith notices, this and Huck's other "autobiographies" do two things: underline humorlessness characteristic of the narrator of an American humorous story, and show that as a result of a hard life Huck "has the imagination of disaster." But like Huck's other calculated actions they have practical value: he expects them to play upon his hearers' sensibilities in a sentimental era when melancholy stories can be expected, as Huck's lies usually do, to touch the heart.

The duke claims noble ancestry and the dauphin royal ancestry for similar practical reasons—to arouse the pity of Huck and Jim so that they may exploit them. Just so the dauphin's lurid confession at the camp meeting plays upon the susceptibilities of pious folk.

If his lie is outrageous, so much the better to help Twain make a point. The more ridiculous and brazen the impostures practiced by these cheats, the sillier the sentimentality and the greater the gullibility of their victims. Twain's reading of history and his experiences with cheats whom he had trusted had led him to damn not only the victimizers but also the victims, thus approaching the universal condemnation he soon would voice.

Having the pair pose as a king and a duke served another purpose: it allowed him to attack hereditary rank. A copy of *The Memoirs of the Duke of Saint-Simon,* inscribed "S. L. Clemens, Hartford, Nov. 1881," shows that after that date he still was fuming at French aristocracy. Typical marginalia:

The Court is a family of cats and dogs who are always quarreling over scraps of offal. (I, 86) Why did Christ come into the world to save men when it would have been so much more respectable to come into the world to save lice? (I, 120) Louis the Louse, King of the Lice. (I, 125) In the memoires of this period the Duchesse of St. Claire makes this striking remark: "sometimes one could tell a gentleman from a son of a bitch, but it was only by his manner of using his fork." (II, 334) [16]

Huck comments that Jim "was the most down on Solomon" of any Negro "he ever see." Clemens had a similar overweening prejudice against aristocrats.

The feud chapters expressed this prejudice. Huck insisted that "Col. Grangerford was a gentleman all over; and so was his family"; that kinsfolk over a fifteen-mile radius were "a handsome lot of quality"; and that the Shepherdsons were "another clan of aristocracy . . . as high-toned and well born and rich and grand." Yet the locale was not an aristocratic one: it was the country of the "shakes" where Davy Crockett, anything but an aristocrat, hunted not long before Huck's visit. It was on the northern fringe of the cotton and tobacco belts in which most aristocrats lived. As a former pilot, the author knew that the great body of aristocratic planters lived far South. What is said about the real-life prototypes of the Shepherdsons and the Grangerfords in the Secretarial Notebook indicates that they were not planters but small farmers: they state that Darnell employed a white "hired man" and even more significantly his wife.[17] And the fashion of feuding was more in the manner of Kentucky mountaineers than of the quality.[18] I believe that Mark deliberately elevated the Grangerfords and

Shepherdsons to a social position above that of their prototypes in order to level certain criticisms at the aristocratic Southerners.

Now, having introduced a pseudo-king and a pseudo-duke, he can have worldly-wise Huck—on the basis of reading he had done since his adventures began—remark that "kings is kings" and "take them all around, they're a mighty ornery lot," and when the duke is drunk "there ain't no near-sighted man could tell him from a king." He can have the guileless Jim express relief when Huck guesses that no more kings will join the party: "I doan' mine one er two kings, but dat's enough. Dis one's powerful drunk, en de duke ain' much better." Or he can have Huck compare real aristocrats with the fakes on the raft to the advantage of the latter:

"Look at Henry the Eight; this'n's a Sunday-School Superintendent to *him*. And look at Charles Second, and Louis Fourteen, and Louis Fifteen, and James Second, and Edward Second, and Richard Third, and forty more; besides all them Saxon heptarchies that used to rip around so in old times and raise Cain. My, you ought to see old Henry the Eight when he was in bloom. He *was* a blossom. He used to marry a new wife every day, and chop off her head next morning. . . . just as indifferent as if he was ordering up eggs. . . . I don't say that ourn is lambs . . . but they ain't nothing to *that* old ram. . . ."

By the time Huck makes these observations, in chapter xxiii, he has seen evidence that not only aristocracy but also folk on lower levels—like the people of France and England who had bowed to disreputable rulers—have grievous faults. The gullible worshipers at the camp meeting provide only one instance; chapters xxi–xxxii furnish others. But probably before writing these chapters, Clemens revitalized his memories of life along the river and his feelings about it by revisiting the Mississippi.

20

LIFE ON THE MISSISSIPPI (PART II)

I remember the annual processions of mighty rafts that used to glide by Hannibal when I was a boy—an acre or so of white, sweet-smelling boards in each raft, a crew of two dozen men or more . . . and I remember the rude ways and tremendous talk of their big crews . . . for we used to swim out . . . and get on these rafts and have a ride. (chapter iii)

. . . we met massed acres of lumber rafts . . . the small crews were quiet, orderly men, of a sedate business aspect, with not a suggestion of romance about them anywhere. (chapter lviii)—Mark Twain, Life on the Mississippi.

In 1882 Clemens made a long-deferred trip. Part way through "Old Times on the Mississippi" in 1875, determining to expand the series into a book, he decided that revisiting the river would be helpful. Although he and Howells had often talked wistfully about making the journey together, they never had managed it. In 1882 Howells again was not available, but Osgood, publisher of *The Prince and the Pauper,* who gave promise of being a good traveling companion, agreed to go. Young Roswell Phelps of Hartford signed as a stenographer.

In mid-April the trio went by train to St. Louis. From there they went downstream by boat, making frequent stops as Huck and Jim had done, then continued to New Orleans. They halted there a few days, plunged into "a whirlpool of hospitality—breakfasts, dinners, luncheons, cock-fights, Sunday-schools, mule-races, lake excursions, social gatherings," [1] and Clemens enjoyed several meetings with little George Washington Cable and one with shy Joel Chandler Harris, both of whose writings he praised in recounting his experiences.[2] The party then went upstream to St. Louis on a boat captained by Horace Bixby, who had taught young Clemens piloting.

Reports of two interviews in St. Louis which biographers seem to have missed give revealing glimpses of the humorist: one was by an anonymous reporter; the other by John Henton Carter (pseudonym Commodore Rollingpin), conductor of a river column and humorist in his own right.[3]

Both journalists found the visitor's aspect impressive enough to move them to describe it in detail: "middle-sized," his hair "slightly gray," his memorable head "well-formed . . . massive . . . well-poised," "nose slightly aquiline, thin and pointed at the extreme," the "rakish" gray moustache giving "a slightly devil-may-care appearance," the chin "firm-set." Both mention "his remarkably drawling way of speaking," his wide-legged stance, and his "reckless rolling gait which," guesses the reporter, "he probably caught when, as a cub pilot, he swaggered on the upper deck."

They stressed important facts about Clemens' current situation. The reporter spoke of newspapers representing him "as being fabulously wealthy, and living in great splendor in Hartford," and told how Clemens more than hinted that his writings were bringing large returns. To Carter, Clemens revealed his interest in manufacturing by describing an invention in progress, a suspender of a revolutionary sort which when perfected "would . . . come into general use by every sensible man in the world." Carter told how Clemens and he discussed an ancient grievance—the handicap a man suffers by starting as a humorist. They mentioned two examples, Holmes and Lowell, but it was clear that they had another victim in mind, for Carter commented:

And Mark Twain cannot hope to be made an exception to the general rule. He recognizes the inevitable, and bows to it with the resignation of the true philosopher. With all his vast store of common sense and practical capability, he is expected ever to appear in his cap and bells and do the risible. . . . But Mark Twain is a man of parts, and much that he has done will live. He is endowed with strong, common sense, steadiness of purpose, judgment and an insight into human nature. . . . No one can read him for an hour without being convinced that while he is a humorist of the first order, he is something more.

Going on upriver the party made its next lengthy stop at Hannibal, where Clemens spent three days peering at scenes and talking with acquaintances remembered from boyhood. His letters to Livy—and subsequently the chapters of his book—dwell on changes. The Garths, former schoolmates with whom he stayed, had a nineteen- or twenty-year-old daughter. Since they last met, A. W. Lamb had married a woman the author had known as a girl; he talked with the couple's "grown-up sons and daughters." "Lieutenant Hickman, the handsomely-uniformed volunteer of 1846, called on me—a grisly elephantine patriarch of 65 now, his grace all vanished."

"That world I knew in its blossoming youth," he told Livy, "is old and bowed and melancholy, now; its soft cheeks are leathery and wrinkled, the fire is gone out of its eyes, and the spring from its step. It will be dust and ashes when I come again. I have been clasping hands with the moribund—and usually they said, 'It is for the last time.'" "Alas! everything was changed in Hannibal," he said in a notebook entry, and in another, "The romance of boating is gone now. In Hannibal the steamboatman is no longer a god. The youth don't talk river slang any more." [4]

The party continued upstream to St. Paul. They had been on Mark Twain's and Huckleberry Finn's river, or one at least which bore the same name, about a month before starting the return trip by rail. Back in Hartford the author began to augment "Old Times on the Mississippi" to book size.

An initial plan was to resume in the new chapters the narrative about piloting days and possibly to carry the story through the expanded book. Says a notebook entry written before the trip: "Tell, now, in full, the nights preceding and following the Pennsylvania's explosion: the fight with Brown; the boat steaming down the Bend of 103 with nobody at the wheel—the white-aproned servants and passengers on deck applauding the fight—the prophetic talk on the levee between Henry and me that night in N.O. before Pa. sailed on her fatal voyage." One entry is in the form of a question: "Begin with a chapter of my experiences as a *pilot?*" [5] And if the St. Louis reporter is accurate, an exchange during the interview shows that while on the trip the writer still believed that he would devote the whole book to his piloting period:

"I have been writing a series of articles in the Atlantic Monthly on subjects connected with the Mississippi, and I found that I had got my distances a little mixed. I took this trip for the purpose of making observations on this subject. I was getting a little rusty about it."
"The new book will treat of your early life on the river?"
"Yes; altogether of that subject."
"When will it be finished?"
"In about nine months."

(Inexplicably, this time Clemens did not greatly underestimate the period he would need to finish his book. Not long after, though, he reverted to normal by revising his estimate downward.)

Chapters xviii–xx do carry along the older narrative in accounts of the hassle with Brown and of Henry Clemens' death. At that point, though, the writer abandoned this line of development, briefly summarized in chapter xxi his experiences between his leaving the river and 1882, and then (with the usual digressions) told of his trip in chapters xxii–lx. To preface the "Old Times" chapters (iv–xvii) he prepared three chapters on "the Mississippi's physical history—so to speak"; then he dumped some material into appendices, and the manuscript was completed. As he finished portions he had them typed—an unusual procedure at the time. (He himself had experimented with the newfangled typewriter a few years before and had abandoned it with upbraidings and curses.)

Just why he changed his plans he did not, so far as I know, ever reveal. However, for a second time he rejected the idea of writing explicitly and at length about what some psychoanalytical biographers have decided was his happiest period, his days as a pilot. Moreover, the notebooks show that from the start he had the travel narrative in mind as a possible alternative.

Making slower progress, as usual, than he had expected, he suffered the customary agonies. "The spur and burden of the contract are intolerable to me," he wrote Howells, October 30, 1882. "I can endure the irritation of it no longer." Five days later—"I never had such a fight over a book in my life before. . . ." He probably finished it late in December, since on January 3 he fiercely told Webster, "I will not interest myself in *any*thing connected with this wretched God-damned book." [6]

There are signs of his difficulty in stretching the manuscript to a satisfactory length. One is his insertion of two unusually irrelevant and inferior passages evidently salvaged from leftovers from *A Tramp Abroad*.[7] A second is his borrowing or adapting passages from *Huckleberry Finn*. Most of chapter iii is the raftsmen's chapter lifted bodily. Chapter xxvi contains a retelling of the Grangerford-Shepherdson-Watson-Darnell feud story augmented with new information. Chapter xxxviii describes the Grangerford parlor as "The House Beautiful." (A comparison between this description written by the wry and critical humorist and that of the admiring Huck throws brilliant light upon the comic values of Huck's angle of narration.)

A third sign of Mark's struggle is the amount of matter quoted from early travel books and the lengthy comments on them. In the letter of October 30 he told Howells: "I went to work at nine o'clock yesterday morning, and went to bed an hour after midnight. Result of the day, (mainly stolen from books, tho' credit given,) 9500 words, so I reduced my burden by nearly one third in one day . . . five days work in one. I have nothing more to borrow or steal; the rest must all be written." Regardless of his reason for working them in, he utilized these borrowings and commentaries and indeed the purloinings from the novel in developing ideas and attitudes which were tremendously important

to him and to the new chapters. The new chapters reveal con-
flicting emotions which constantly tugged at the writer during
the trip and the period of his recounting it. When he returned
to the novel these emotions were important forces shaping it.[8]

Inevitably this man with such deep feelings about the town and
the river of his youth was moved by the changes he saw in well-
remembered scenes. "Mr. Clemens," said the *Atlantic* reviewer,
"is never tired of noting the extraordinary changes which take
place in the Mississippi and the conformation of the banks. . . .
The general reader stands in some peril of finding these observations wearisome." [9] To a man who had carefully memorized the
river mile after mile for the purpose of protecting steamboats and
their passengers from possible destruction, they could not have
been wearisome in the least; they must have been shattering. The
changes at Hannibal, a town which had long remained serene
and unchanged in his memories as a place far more idyllic than
the real Hannibal ever had been, must have been even more disturbing. He wrote feelingly and at length about them, and told
how the visit set him to recalling in detail traumatic boyhood experiences when his conscience had tortured him after a man's
death he feared he might have caused, and the drownings of two
playmates. Too, this man for whom the river had been a way of
life found tremendously interesting changes in the lives of those
who worked on the river and those who dwelt on the shores. And
toward both the past as he recalled it and the present which he
now pondered he had mixed feelings.

The builder of the magnificent Hartford mansion and the recent
student of interior decoration in chapter xxi admires "the fine
new houses" in St. Louis—"noble and beautiful and modern,"
standing "by themselves . . . with green lawns around them."
They are infinitely better in taste than the old neighboring homes
and the old Southern mansion of chapter xxxviii.

The man of business compliments Southern towns for their
booming industry. In chapter xxix he remarks that Memphis "has
a great wholesale jobbing trade; foundries, machine shops, man-
ufactories of wagons, carriages, and cotton-seed oil; and is shortly

to have cotton-mills and elevators." "Out from her healthy commercial heart," he continues, "issue five trunk lines of railways; and a sixth is being added." By chapter lviii, having reached the upper river, he is even more ecstatic as he hails "this amazing region, bristling with great towns, projected day before yesterday . . . all comely, all well built, clean, orderly. . . . [All have] factories, newspapers, and institutions of learning, telephones, telegrams, an electric alarm, an admirable paid fire department, churches," and of course railways.

The ex-pilot vigorously cheers improvements in handling river traffic: the more efficient neat uniformed steamboatmen, the superior mapping and marking of safe courses, the deepened channels.

He compliments the new architecture, and in chapter xxxviii ridicules the ante-bellum bad taste of "The House Beautiful." (He borrowed the ironic name from Clarence Chatham Cook's *The House Beautiful: Essays on Beds and Tables, Stools and Candlesticks,* serialized in *Scribner's Magazine,* and published as a book in 1878.) But his tone in passages about modern buildings is cool and detached; in the chapter deriding the old mansion, even as he heaps up horrible details, he is indulgent and affectionate. He realizes that the old-time steamer with which he compares the mansion is in equally bad taste, but he caresses its gay and gaudy details. And he ends the passage with a sad look at the same boat in 1882 "caked over with a layer of obdurate dirt."

As a businessman who has learned (or believes he has) how others cheat and exploit their fellows, he looks with cynical eyes at commercial men along the river. Chapter xxxix quotes two drummers—"the dollar their god, how to get it their religion"— gloating about passing off oleomargarine for butter and cottonseed oil for imported olive oil: the passage is devastating. Even fiercer is the undertaker's monologue in chapter xliii on exploiting bereaved folk by overcharging on coffins, funeral equipage, and embalming: "It's human nature . . . in grief. . . . All you've got to do is jest be ca'm and stack it up. . . ."

The ex-pilot's admiration for modern rivermen is tempered by his feeling that they are a drab lot compared with their predecessors. Again and again he bemoans the change noticed in chapter xxii: "A glory that once was has dissolved and vanished. . . ." The steamboatman "is no more . . . he is absorbed into the common herd. . . ." Fondly he recalls the glory as he introduces the raftsmen kidnaped from *Huck*—"rude, uneducated, brave, . . . reckless . . . elephantinely jolly . . . yet, in the main, honest, trustworthy, faithful to promises and duty, and often picturesquely magnanimous." One of the few characterizations he develops sympathetically and at length is Uncle Mumford, "a mate of the blessed old-time kind," "a man of practical sense and a level head" whom he honors by assigning to him some of his own ideas and favorite curses. In chapter lviii he explicitly draws a contrast in favor of the older rivermen when he tells of the men on lumber rafts "not floating leisurely along, in the old-fashioned way, manned with joyous and reckless crews of fiddling, song-singing, whisky-drinking, breakdown-dancing rapscallions," but "shoved swiftly along . . . modern-fashion . . . the small crews . . . quiet, orderly men, of a sedate business aspect, with not a suggestion of romance about them anywhere."

Despite the fact that he shows greater affection for the old than for the new in these passages, in others he is sharply critical of the ante-bellum South. In chapter xxvi he condemns the senseless and brutal feuding "in old times" of the Watsons and the Darnells. In chapter xlvi he ferociously assails the old South for letting Sir Walter Scott make it fall in love "with decayed and swinish forms of religion; with decayed and degraded systems of government; with the silliness and emptiness, sham grandeurs, sham gauds, and sham chivalries of a brainless and long-vanished society." "The Sir Walter Scott disease," he says, "blocked progress" and "created rank and caste"; and "something of a plausible argument might, perhaps, be made in support of [the] wild proposition" that "we never should have had any war but for Sir Walter." Mark Twain is unusually tentative as he makes this qualified suggestion, and of course it is easy to attack him.[10] Yet he overstates a conviction that he had already implied in his picture of the Grangerfords.

Such is the context of many passages borrowed from travel

books and the commentaries they suggest. The hardest-hitting criticisms of the old South are in portions of the manuscript chiefly inspired by travel books—passages which, at Osgood's suggestion,[11] Mark Twain did not publish. Chapter xxix ends with two brief quotations from one of the score or so of such books cited at intervals [12]—Mrs. Trollope's *Domestic Manners of the Americans* (1832). To contrast the new Memphis with the old, Mark quotes Mrs. Trollope's description of the folk at a Memphis hotel noisily gobbling their food. Then to show her using a favorite word when dealing with Americans, "spitting," he quotes another description of a similarly boorish tableful of diners, quality folk this time, on board a steamboat.

A chapter written to follow this, but which on Osgood's advice he omitted,[13] continues a treatise on Mrs. Trollope and other writing tourists. Cursed and reviled though that lady was, he believed she was "painting a state of things which . . . lasted well along in my youth, and I remember it." The same accuracy, Mark claims, characterized most such commentators. But he holds that Mrs. Trollope was the best, since she lived three years "in this civilization of ours; in the body of it—not on the surface," and "She did not gild us; neither did she whitewash us." "She found here," he specifies, "a tissue-cuticled semi-barbarism which set itself up as a lofty civilization; and she skinned this thing and showed the world (and it) just what it was." [14] Two other deleted chapters intended to follow chapter xl return to prewar comments by visitors. The first offers added glimpses of "the strange world that these touring foreigners . . . take us into"—strange in part because of its primitive ways of living, in part because of its religious and racial intolerance, chauvinism, intemperance, and injustice. It was, the chapter concludes, "good rotten material for burial." [15]

But just as in the published portions, in the unpublished portions Mark refused to stop with a comparison between the old and the new that was entirely advantageous to the new. Starting the second of these omitted chapters, "The noticeable features of that departed America," he remarks, "are not *all* gone from us." He holds that many attacks against the old America are still valid:

against "bribery, robbery and general corruption . . . in Washington"; Congress, "a den of thieves and a sort of asylum"; an apathetic public; "a nation of patient, put-upon, outraged, insolence-swallowing, good-natured, all-enduring moral cowards" and fools who—at least in the South—engage in that "cruel and brutal custom," the duel.[16]

Another excised chapter, which in the manuscript followed chapter xlvii, severely scolds the modern South because violence flourishes there. He gives instances.[17] These were evidently so important to him that he was impelled in mid-January, 1883, to rescue them from his discarded sheets and insert them as "some Southern assassinations" in an overgrown footnote to a boast quoted in chapter xl that the Southern was "the highest type of civilization this continent has ever seen." [18]

Twain is irritated with one of his prewar travelers because "nearly every time he says a harsh thing of us he hastens to salve the hurt by saying a still harsher thing, in the same connection, about England." [19] The author himself, however, vacillates in a similar fashion when contrasting the past with the present and when discussing each period. His reasons, I believe, are different, the chief being the emotional impact of his return to remembered but changed scenes of his youth.

"In *Life on the Mississippi*," writes Edward Wagenknecht, "we see—we taste, we handle—the stuff of which *Huckleberry Finn* was made; here is the raw material of a great literary masterpiece." [20] My revised dating of chapters xvii–xx of the novel shows that some influences once thought to have been exerted on the fiction by the trip and the writing of the travel chapters operated in a reverse direction. Nevertheless, the return to the river, the research in the old travel books, and the writing of the new manuscript shaped parts of *Huck* written in 1883.

Chapter xxi, the first of these parts, starts on the raft with the duke teaching the king his version of Hamlet's soliloquy. Huck and the two rascals land in Bricksville, hire a hall, put up posters and investigate the town; this gives Huck an opportunity to describe the town and its shiftless inhabitants. Old Boggs appears, shouting abuse of Sherburn. When Boggs fails to heed Sherburn's demand that he stop, Sherburn shoots him. In chapter xxii the mob marches to Sherburn's house bent on a lynching. Sherburn appears with a shotgun, reviles the mob, and sends them away. Huck's visit to a circus, the Shakespearean performance, and the advertisement of "The Royal Nonesuch" performance end the chapter.

Recently, before the claim had been advanced that chapters xxi and xxii marked a new stage in the writing, Robert Hunting wrote an interesting commentary on them. He holds that "in point of view and tone they stand apart from the rest of the novel": "Presumably, the details . . . are reported to us by Huck Finn, Mark Twain's persona. . . . I say presumably because I think that the mask slips and that the reporter . . . looks suspiciously like Mark Twain himself. . . . What is lacking is, I believe, compassion. . . . I do not believe that the compassionate Huck is the only reporter in these chapters. . . ."[21] This is a perceptive and to some extent a valid insight, but in my opinion it needs to be qualified: the objective or even condemnatory reporting that occurs in these chapters is not entirely new, as a study of Huck's earlier accounts of Pap's first appearance and of skirmishes in the feud will show. Huck, I believe, manifests explicitly as much distress when Boggs dies in chapter xxi as he does in telling about Buck Grangerford's death. Chapter xxi begins and—as Hunting notices—chapter xxii ends with broadly humorous passages; and between these the loafers, Boggs, and a villager who reënacts the murder are comically portrayed. True, the humor is satirical, not compassionate, but it requires tolerance, even sympathy, and these are akin to compassion. On the other hand, the details presented do condemn the villagers, then Sherburn; and in Sherburn's speech blasting the folk of Bricksville and beyond Bricksville the mask of the narrator definitely slips.

So there are clashes between the humor and the pathos or tragedy in these chapters. It seems to me that not only here but elsewhere in *Huckleberry Finn* there is a combination of nostalgia and nausea, of affection and anger, similar to that in the new part of *Life on the Mississippi*. Indeed, I would argue that such tensions are basic causes of both the objectivity and the humor of Huck's reporting.

But even if these two chapters do not initiate the direct attack on ante-bellum "civilization"—the feud chapters have done this —they consolidate and emphasize it. Part of Twain's suppressed discussion of Mrs. Trollope's merits may suggest at least one reason:

Dame Trollope . . . found a "civilization" here which you, reader, could not have endured; and which you would not have regarded as a civilization at all. Mrs. Trollope spoke of this civilization in plain terms—plain and unsugared, but honest and without malice, and without hate. Her voice rose to indignation, sometimes, but the object justifies the attitude—being rowdyism, "chivalrous" assassinations, sham godliness, and several other devilishnesses which would be as hateful to you, now, as they were to her then. She was holily hated for her "prejudices"; but they seem to have been simply the prejudices of a humane spirit against inhumanities; of an honest nature against humbug; of a clean breeding against grossness; of a right heart against unright speech and deed.[22]

If, as all-too-human authors have a way of doing, Mark here is praising another writer for having merits that he hopes he himself possesses, he indicates that when he wrote this he had a clear concept of what he wanted to do in his novel. And if he achieved a clearer formulation of his purpose, the older travel-book writers, Mrs. Trollope in particular,[23] assisted him in doing so.

In addition to the stance Mark took in the 1883 portions of *Huck*, details concerning the river trip and published and unpublished chapters of *Life on the Mississippi* (Part II) foreshadow specific scenes. As fictional counterparts of the drummers and the undertaker, the king and the duke continue their careers as cheats. Their first victims are the folk of Bricksville. The theatrical performance for which they are preparing as chapter xxi starts includes the recitation from *Hamlet*, the balcony scene from *Romeo and Juliet*, and the sword fight from *Richard III*. (The latter two items are mentioned in a passage in chapter xx which I believe Twain went back and inserted.[24]) On May 1, 1882, at the home of Cable's friend James B. Guthrie in New Orleans, Clemens had been impressed when his host's "little boy (aged 6) and little girl (aged 4), performed the balcony scene in Romeo and Juliet in the quaintest and most captivating way." [25] Although he found this performance very moving, the incongruity of the young actors in mature roles may have suggested the greater incongruity understated by the king when he describes himself acting Juliet's part: "If Juliet's such a young gal, duke, my peeled head and my white whiskers is goin' to look uncommon odd on her, maybe." In Group A of his working notes in 1879–1880 Mark had conceived of using a scene from *Richard III,* but more recently, in chapter li of his travel account, he recalled that during his boyhood "a couple of Englishmen came to our town and sojourned for a while, and one day did the Richard III. sword-fight with maniac energy and prodigious powwow. . . ." In a deleted passage Mark writes at length about an English troupe's burlesque performance of *Hamlet* as a travel book described it; in another he notes that "the stage was almost exclusively occupied by the English—very few native actors would 'draw' "—a state of affairs historically justifying the duke's advertising himself and the king as British actors.[26]

Huck's description of Bricksville and its loafers had, to be sure, been rehearsed in *The Gilded Age* and "Old Times." Still, during the trip the writer had revisited very similar towns. Arkansas City, for instance, was styled by an inhabitant as "a hell of a place" with its "several rows and clusters of shabby frame houses, and a supply of mud sufficient to insure the town against a famine in that article for a hundred years" (*Life on the Mississippi,* chapter xxx). "The stores and houses was mostly all old, shackly, dried up frame concerns," says Huck, "that hadn't ever been painted. . . . All the streets and lanes . . . warn't nothing else *but* mud . . ." On the trip, too, Clemens had noticed Pilcher's Point (chapter xxiii), where houses were constantly shifted away from caving riverbanks. "Such a town . . . [as Bricksville]," Huck says, "has to be always moving back, and back, because the river's always gnawing at them."

Describing the Bricksville loafer, Huck notices that "he almost always had his hands in his britches pockets": in chapter xxii of

Life on the Mississippi Twain quotes a note made when traveling westward: "At all the railway-stations the loafers carry *both* hands in their breeches pockets. . . . This is an important fact in geography." A few lines later: "By and by we entered the tobacco-chewing region. Fifty years ago the tobacco-chewing region covered the Union. It is greatly restricted now." He hardly could have missed this phenomenon in the old travel books. Says Jane Louise Mesick in her study of them: "The constant use of tobacco was, to the Englishman, undoubtedly the most objectionable of all the American idiosyncrasies. Certainly more is said about it, and the attendant spitting, than about any other habit, and many authors agreed that it was what detracted most from the refinement of American manners." [27] Mark's observation that Mrs. Trollope often used the word "spitting" shows that he recalled her frequent distressed comments on tobacco chewing. A poem back in 1832 had noticed this obsession, beginning,

> Mrs. Trollope is commendably bitter
> Against the filthy American spitter. . . .[28]

Huck writes nine paragraphs about the tobacco-chewing proclivities of the Bricksville trash.

The shooting of Boggs duplicates in some of its aspects the footnote on "Southern assassinations" that Mark added to proofs of his own travel account, purportedly "Extracts from the Public Journals." One—Thomas O'Connor's shooting of Joseph T. Mabry on the street in Knoxville—resembles the fictional shooting to a great degree and two others in lesser degree. Political propaganda, as I have shown, offered generalizations about such violence. More immediately, travel books had, and they possibly encouraged the author to include the shooting in his novel.

The travel books could have encouraged, too, his telling about the attempted lynching of Sherburn at the start of chapter xxii. Mrs. Trollope had not learned about American lynchings during her stay here, but in the 1839 edition of her *Domestic Manners* she included a footnote saying that she had since learned of them and they were "now well known throughout Europe." Numerous travel books which came after hers made them known. One book which Mark Twain read and quoted, Alexander Mackay's *Western World, or Travels in the United States in 1846–47*, treated the subject at length.[29]

These echoes occur through chapter xxi and the opening pages of chapter xxii of the novel. Thereafter echoes are more general and sporadic. But the picture of the undertaker in *Life on the Mississippi* foreshadows the Wilks episode of chapters xxiv–xxx where the king and the duke brazenly exploit the grief of a bereaved family. Mark's tales of wrestlings with his conscience recalled by the visit to Hannibal are preparatory for Huck's similar torture in chapter xxxi. The ridicule of Walter Scott's romanticism is paralleled at length in Tom Sawyer's apings of other types of romanticism during the liberation of Jim in the final chapters of *Huck*. There, like the book-muddled carpenter of chapter lv who "had his poor head turned" by reading *Nick of the Woods*, Tom tries to rearrange actuality to conform with fiction.

The river trip, the reading of travel books, and the writing of the new portions of *Life on the Mississippi*, then, though they did not shape *Huck* beginning at as early a point or to the extent scholars have believed, had definite and important influences upon the novel.

21

LIVELY TIMES IN BRICKSVILLE

We struck it mighty lucky; there was going to be a circus there that afternoon, and the country people was already beginning to come in. . . . There was considerable whiskey drinking going on, and I seen three fights.—Adventures of Huckleberry Finn, *chapter xxi.*

For a month or two after he finished *Life on the Mississippi* in early January, 1883, Clemens, as he told Howells March 1, was "an utterly free person." "Of course," he continued, "the highest pleasure to be got out of freedom, and having nothing to do, is labor. Therefore I labor. But I take my time . . . work an hour or four as happens to suit my mind."

Only weeks before, the author had been uncertain about ever finishing *Huck.* Actually, he concluded it in the following summer. I believe that some of the work he mentioned to Howells was on the novel—through chapter xxi and possibly a bit beyond. I have mentioned one reason: chapter xxi and the opening part of chapter xxii contain much matter closely related to the river trip or the writing of chapters about it, but thereafter echoes are less frequent. And there is additional evidence.[1]

Exactly how far he got that spring it is impossible to be sure.[2] But either then or soon after the family went to Quarry Farm on June 15 he wrote chapters xxi–xxiii, which recount events happening in or near Bricksville. These end with the "Royal None-such" performances, the escape to the raft, and two chats between Huck and Jim.

In addition to the 1882–1883 influences I have mentioned, other biographical and literary influences alternately (or simultaneously) shape this sequence. A study of how these contribute to each episode shows Mark Twain working in a typical fashion.

The soliloquy allegedly from *Hamlet* which the duke teaches the king at the beginning of chapter xxi may have been suggested (as DeVoto mentions) by any of several ante-bellum humorists. Sol. Smith, for instance, writing his reminiscences in 1854, offers a rendition of Jaques' "seven ages" soliloquy with incongruous interpolations.[3] In the same decade Dan Rice mingled Shakespearean quotations with japes of a painted circus clown; and young Clemens in the last newspaper item he wrote in Hannibal hailed Rice as "the unrivaled comic gester [*sic*]" and urged townsfolk to give his performance "a warm welcome." [4]

A recent literary project also was relevant. In London in 1873 during a backstage chat with Booth after a presentation of *Hamlet,* the humorist had proposed refurbishing the play by adding the role of a nineteenth-century humorous commentator. Booth, it was said, "laughed immoderately"—perhaps one suspects hysterically. Soon Twain tried such a revision, disliked it, and burned it. But he had not been cured. In 1881, abetted by Joe Goodman and incredibly enough encouraged by Howells, he tried again.[5] Act I and two scenes of Act II, the result, perpetrated in three days, are preserved in the Mark Twain Papers. In them a book agent wanders into Elsinore commenting in vernacular on events and speeches. Writing this atrocity helped familiarize Mark with the text and probably helped with the writing of the burlesque soliloquy—more accurately the pastiche.

A page which I came upon among the Mark Twain Papers tells a story of the writing of the speech. On Monday, March 19, 1883, the author and Livy began a four-day stay in New York.[6] They received a note of that date from Webster: "Dear Aunt Livy: Annie and I will be at the Brunswick [Hotel] about 7:30 P.M. I have secured three box seats the last good ones left that were together." The indication is that Webster and his wife took his aunt to the opera that night while Webster's employer enjoyed staying away from entertainment of a sort he detested. That evening (I believe, since he wrote "Mch 19/–" in a corner of the page) or possibly later, he wrote on the portion of the sheet not used by his nephew the following draft of the soliloquy:

> To be or not to be, that is the bare bodkin
> Makes calamity of so long life;
> For who would fardels bear, till Birnam wood
>   do come to Dunsinane,
> But that the fear of *something after death*
>   Murders the innocent sleep,
>   Great Nature's second course,
> And makes us rather sling the arrows of
>   outrageous fortune
> Than fly to others that we know not of.
>
> ———
>
> *There* lies the deep damnation of our
>   taking off—
> Wake Duncan with thy knocking.
>   I would thou couldst—
> For who would bear the whips and scorns of time, the oppressor's
>   wrong, the proud man's contumely, the insolence of office
>   and the pangs which he himself might take
>
> ———
>
> In the dead waste and middle of the night
> When churchyards yawn
> In customary suits of solemn black
> But that the undiscovered country
> From whose bourn no traveller returns
> Breathes forth contagion on the world—
> And all the clouds &c
>   And thus the native hue of resolution
>   (Like the poor cat 'i' the adage,)
> With this regard their currents turn away,
>   and lose the NAME of action.
>
> ———
>
> Tis a consummation devoutly to be
>   wished—sh—sh—

But soft you, the fair Ophelia!
Ope not thy ponderous and marble jaws
But get thee to a nunnery—go.[7]

The lines unnaturally joined together come from scattered
scenes in *Macbeth* and *Hamlet,* most of those in the latter play
from the soliloquy of Act III, scene ii, which the dauphin believes
he is reciting. Most are lines often quoted by school children, but
the likelihood is small that the author learned them during his
short schooling. More probably he learned them by attending
plays, by hearing George Ealer intone them in the pilothouse
during his river days, and by reading.[8] However he learned them,
he wrote them out—from memory it appears—pretty accurately.
Revising them for his novel he made few changes: he supplied
words in place of "&c," deleted a line and "sh—sh," added a line,
moved one, changed some spelling and punctuation, rearranged
some line divisions, changed some capitals to lower case, and
lower-case letters to capitals. (A notebook reference to the pastiche seems to indicate that it was written as an insert for chapter
xxi and that therefore by March 19 he had written beyond this
point.[9])

Like Emmeline Grangerford's burlesques on somber paintings
and obituary poetry, this mutilation of a great romantic soliloquy
on death initiates a series of happenings which terminate in murder and violence. When the duke, the king, and Huck go ashore
the duke nails up playbills which are broadly comic. In addition
to travel-book accounts of foreign actors, Joseph M. Fields, the
originator of the coffin and limburger cheese anecdote, may have
provided ideas for these advertisements. In the title story of *The
Drama in Pokerville* (1847) Fields had produced a similar play-
bill to announce performances in a sleazy Southern town by "the
Great Small Affair Company." Fields' Mr. T. Fitzgerald, like the
duke, is "from the Drury Lane Theatre, London." Mrs. Oscar Dust
"of the principal eastern houses" is appearing for "the last engagement which she will perform prior to her *departure for
Europe!*" Just so the duke's poster warns that the Bricksville engagement is "For One Night Only, On account of imperative European engagements!" And the tribulations of Fields' strolling play-

ers in the town with a name close to that of Huck's Pokeville resemble those of the king and the duke.

The bedraggled town, Bricksville, and the poor white inhabitants described by Huck are in a tradition as hoary as any in American literature. While notations on improvised shacks, thick black mud, and disreputable loafers occur often in travel books, similar descriptions occur even more often in our humor. Back in 1728 William Byrd had described uncouth Southern loafers in his journals; by the time his picturings were published in 1841 many an author had portrayed shiftless trash in pathetic towns— celebrators of the plantation who mentioned them briefly; historical novelists such as Tucker, Caruthers, Kennedy, and Simms; Northern abolitionists and scores of humorists. In general the humorists had written by far the most detailed passages.[10]

So frequent, in fact, are comic picturings of worthless whites in Southwestern humor that one is hard put to argue any individual source here. There is a bit, though, by that old favorite of Twain's, William Tappan Thompson, which is close enough to invite comparison. In drab Pineville, Georgia, "the most interesting group," Thompson says, "was that which assembled around the piazza of the village hotel, to pick their teeth in company, whittle the backs of split-bottomed chairs, and discuss the topics of the day."

Billy Wilder asked if anybody had any good tobacco; upon which Bob Echols pulled out a piece about the size of his hand . . . and passed it to Billy, after which it passed through divers other hands until the greater part found its way into the mouths of the bystanders, and not even the slightest moiety would ever have reached its owner again, had not some one at the outskirts of the crowd—who probably had a hole in his pocket—called out "who's tobacco's this?" Bob owned the remnant, remarking that he *"bought* it at Harley's," and conversation and expectoration became brisk and general.[11]

Compare Huck's loafers roosting on dry-goods boxes, "whittling them with their Barlow knives; and chawing tobacco":

They get all their chawing by borrowing—they say to a fellow, "I wisht you'd len' me a chaw, Jack, I jist this minute give Ben Thompson the last chaw I had"—which is a lie, pretty much every time; it don't fool nobody but a stranger; but Jack ain't no stranger, so he says—

"*You* give him a chaw, did you? so did your sister's cat's grand-mother. You pay me back the chaws you've awready borry'd off'n me, Lafe Buckner, then I'll loan you one or two ton of it, and won't charge you no back intrust, nuther."

"Well, I *did* pay you back some of it wunst."

"Yes, you did—'bout six chaws. You borry'd store tobacker and paid back nigger-head."

Store tobacco is flat black plug, but these fellows mostly chaws the natural leaf twisted . . . sometimes the one that owns the tobacco looks mournful at it when it's handed back, and says, sarcastic—

"Here, gimme the *chaw*, and you take the *plug*."

The complex ritual, the information about store tobacco, and the rapidly diminishing plug are not in both passages, I suspect, co-incidentally. Mark's superiority results in part from his use of Huck's style and his fine rendition of dialogue, in part from his elaboration of the trivial incident which builds up the inactivity of the loafers to comic proportions. And, as in *The Gilded Age*, "Old Times," *Tom Sawyer*, and earlier chapters of *Huck*, the jux-taposition of the picture of the drowsy town with one of Bricks-ville activated by the Boggs-Sherburn episode which follows em-bodies one of the humorist's favorite contrasts.

In working note A-1 in 1879–1880 Mark had specified that one Bricksville episode was to occur at Napoleon, Arkansas,[12] and probably this was the locale he had in mind. In chapter xxxii of *Life on the Mississippi* he recalls associations with Napoleon—his knowing a very pretty and accomplished girl there, and his re-ceiving there the news of the *Pennsylvania's* explosion: he also remembers it as "town of innumerable fights—an inquest every day." Arkansas had long been famed for its toughness. William T. Porter prefaced his famous *Big Bear of Arkansas* anthology in 1845 by characterizing its folk "as fond of whiskey as of hunting, . . . desperate and utterly reckless"; and in 1854 Jonathan F. Kelly spoke of "the never ending Arkansaw stories . . . vivid, thrilling or ludicrous" and usually about violent deeds.[13] Such stories, "a grotesque mixture of fun and terror," "more or less exaggerated" accounts of "the sanguinary propensities of some classes of the inhabitants," were still discouraging visitors, Edward S. King reported, when he visited the South in 1873–1874.

Napoleon [says King] did not have a good reputation in past days. Various anecdotes, not entirely devoid of grim humor, were told of it, illustrating the manners of the town. It was at Napoleon that the man showed a casual passerby . . . a pocket full of ears, and, with a grin, announced that he was among the boys while they were having a frolic last night. Murder, daily, was the rule, and not the exception. Brawls always ended in burials.[14]

Arkansas and Bricksville, alias Napoleon, thus are locales which by repute are appropriate for the violent events Huck witnesses there.

I have noticed that the shooting of Boggs by Sherburn, the first of these, closely resembles the footnote in chapter xl of *Life on the Mississippi* about General Mabry's shooting of Thomas O'Connor in Knoxville. This affair, though, is so much like a shooting in Hannibal during the author's boyhood that I suspect Mark of having based it upon memory rather than upon the "Associated Press Telegram" which he credits. And the author himself testified that the shooting in *Huck* derived from the shooting near the Clemens doorstep in Hannibal of Sam Smarr by William Owsley.[15]

Concerning this murder we have unusually good information: John Marshall Clemens, J.P., who earned a $1.81 fee for administering oaths to twenty-nine witnesses and a $13.50 fee for writing out depositions totaling 13,500 words, left a full account in his own hand. These tell this story:

Early in January, 1845, Smarr traveled from his farm to nearby Hannibal for one of his occasional sprees. Shortly, as was his habit when turbulent with drink, he began cursing wealthy merchant Owsley before audiences of townsfolk. None who knew Smarr well worried much: he was doing this in a neighborly spirit, since he believed the damned pickpocket and son of a bitch (as he called Owsley) had cheated not him but two friends. Smarr had done this before without any aftermath, and acquaintances agreed that he was not dangerous. When the early winter twilight fell he was reeling along the street, firing his pistol, shouting, "O yes, here's Bill Owsley, has got a stock of goods here, and stole two thousand dollars from Thompson in Palmyra!"

From his store Owsley, a haughty dandified migrant from Kentucky, heard the accusation. "He had a kind of twitching," a customer testified, "and said it was insufferable." But the merchant did nothing that night and Smarr returned home.

Two or three weeks later, Smarr was again in Hannibal on the corner of Hill and Main. Owsley came up behind him. At four paces he shouted, "You, Sam Smarr!" The farmer whirled, saw Owsley draw a pistol, and begged him not to shoot. Owsley fired. As Smarr stumbled backward, Owsley without lowering his arm fired again. Bystanders lifted the wounded man and carried him to Dr. Grant's drugstore a few steps away. There Grant and another doctor opened the victim's clothes but left him alone when he showed signs of fainting. About half an hour later he died.

The remarkable accuracy with which Mark Twain duplicated this incident in *Huck* suggests that it made a deep impression upon him as a nine-year-old, a likelihood supported by his recounting it on at least four other occasions [16] and by his stating in his *Autobiography* that it haunted his dreams. Yet a study of invented details which he added is revealing. Some make Boggs, Smarr's fictional counterpart, more sympathetic. The townsfolk, Huck reports, welcome him because they are "used to having fun out of Boggs." Huck's description shows a comic red-faced drunk "a-tearing along on his horse, whooping and yelling like an Injun, . . . singing out . . . weaving about in his saddle." He shouts, "Cler the track, thar. I'm on the waw-path, and the price uv coffins is a gwyne to raise." His exchanges with the loafers are good-natured: "Everybody yelled at him, and laughed at him, and sassed him, and he sassed back, and said he'd attend to them and lay them out in their regular turns, but he couldn't wait now, because he'd come to town to kill old Colonel Sherburn, and his motto was 'meat first, and spoon vittles to top off on.'" Like the extravagant boasts in the traditional comic pattern in the raftsmen chapter, this good-natured banter and four specific statements by townspeople that Boggs is harmless underline the nonseriousness of his threats.

One detail, though, makes Boggs slightly less sympathetic than Smarr: he is angry because he believes the merchant has swindled not friends but Boggs himself. And some invented details make Sherburn more sympathetic than Owsley. As Boggs abuses this "proud-looking man," not a handful of customers but "the whole street packed with people" is shown "listening and laughing and going on." More important, Sherburn, unlike his counterpart, specifically warns his torturer that he will endure his abuse until one o'clock, thus giving him a chance to escape. (The author based this detail upon another violent scene of his Hannibal youth— Widow Wier's warning that she would shoot a man bent on invading her home and raping her if he did not leave before she counted to ten.[17])

But all the invented details which follow this warning build sympathy for Boggs at Sherburn's expense. Boggs is shown trying desperately to escape, "a-reeling . . . , bare-headed, with a friend on both sides of him aholt of his arms and hurrying him along. He was quiet, and looked uneasy; and he warn't hanging back any, but was doing some of the hurrying himself." Sherburn is completely unmoved by this pitiful spectacle and by Boggs' pleadings —"standing perfectly still," his pistol uplifted, then bringing the gun down "slow and steady to a level—both barrels cocked," shooting twice so efficiently that both shots take effect. Then "Colonel Sherburn he tossed his pistol onto the ground, and turned around on his heels and walked off."

None of the many 1845 witnesses mentions a daughter of the murdered man who is sent for by worried townsfolk and who arrives just as her father is shot; so the likelihood is that she is an imagined character. She too serves to avert sympathy from Sherburn: "That young girl screamed out, and comes rushing, and down she throws herself on her father, crying, and saying, 'Oh, he's killed him, he's killed him!'" After Boggs' death the crowd pulls her away from him "screaming and crying." Huck ends the account with other pathetic details: "She was about sixteen, and very sweet and gentle-looking, but awful pale and scared."

22

THE BRICKSVILLE MOB AND THE ORNERINESS OF KINGS

. . . a mighty ornery lot.—Adventures of Huckleberry Finn, *chapters xxi and xxiii.*

As chapter xxi ends, the focus shifts from individual Bricksvillites to the townspeople as a group. They prove to be sorry specimens. Mark Twain has prepared for this near the start of the chapter when describing the village loafers. Besides being as dirty and as lazy as the villagers he described in previous books, these he shows to be cruel. When the scavengering sow which customarily invades his descriptions of small towns stretches in the muddy street of Bricksville to nurse her piglets, the group engages in a favorite pastime—sicking dogs on her and watching with delight while she runs squealing with the dogs clinging to her ears. Like the loafers described earlier, these men love a dog fight, but these differ in relishing even more "putting turpentine on a stray dog and setting fire to him, or tying a tin pan to his tail and seeing him run himself to death."

Such is their premeditated cruelty. In picturing Boggs' death the author, recalling a detail about Smarr's death which has haunted him for years, tells of it in such a way as to emphasize the Bricksvillites' unconscious cruelty—committed in the name of religion: "They laid him on the floor, and put one large Bible under his head, and opened another one and spread it on his breast. . . . He made about a dozen long gasps, his breast lifting the Bible up when he drawed in his breath, and letting it down again when he breathed it out—and after that he laid still; he was dead."

After Boggs' death the Bricksvillites coalesce into a mob. Their actions support my claim that Twain's portrayals of mobs in action in *The Prince and the Pauper*, themselves quite damning, anticipated even more condemnatory ones in *Huck*.

A common source of the picturings in both books must have been the author's extensive reading about the French Revolution. In books of all sorts dealing with that era, representations of mobs in action are endlessly reiterated. As he told a friend, he had learned, from the books he had read, that "men in a crowd do not act as they would as individuals . . . they don't think for themselves, but become impregnated by the mass sentiment uppermost in the minds which happen to be en masse." [1] Compare S. Baring-Gould in a book which Clemens admired, *In Exitu Israel:* ". . . the mob swayed and roared, like one living body, not as an assemblage of individuals, each with a will and thoughts of its own." Many other writers remark or represent the same phenomenon.

This mass sentiment might be morbid fascination of the sort Carlyle in his *French Revolution* emphasizes as he tells about the execution of Robespierre: "Never before were the streets of Paris so crowded . . . one dense stirring mass; all windows crammed; the very roofs and ridge-tiles budding forth Curiosity, in strange gladness. . . . All eyes are on Robespierre's tumbril. . . . The Gendarmes point their swords at him, to show the people which is he. . . . Samson's work [with the guillotine] done, there bursts forth shout on shout of applause." When Boggs is carried to the drugstore to die, the Bricksville mob manifests "strange gladness": "Well, pretty soon the whole town was there, squirming and scrouging and pushing and shoving to get at the window and have a look, but people that had the places wouldn't give them up, and folks behind them was saying all the time. 'Say, now, you've looked enough, you fellows; 'taint right and 'taint fair, for you to stay thar all the time, and never give nobody a chance; other folks has their rights as well as you.' " The same quality appears in both mobs, but it is enlightening to contrast Twain's way with Carlyle's way of showing that quality. The impression of a surging, packed crowd which Carlyle achieves by describing the crowded streets, the crammed windows, and the stirring mass, Twain conveys by a series of participles, "squirming and scrouging and pushing and shoving." [2] "Scrouging," since it is a word in the vernacular, introduces a comic note absent from Carlyle. The representation of the insatiable curiosity, the refusal to budge, of those at the window initiates satire. This becomes cutting in the pleas of those behind who, ironically, demand in the names of "fairness" and innate human "rights" that they be allowed to sate their inhuman curiosity.

The next paragraph distills the same commentary into a specific incident:

The streets was full, and everybody was excited. Everybody that seen the shooting was telling how it happened, and there was a big crowd packed around each. . . . One long lanky man, with long hair and a big white fur stove-pipe hat on the back of his head, and a crooked-handled cane, marked out the places on the ground where Boggs stood, and where Sherburn stood, and the people following him around from one place to t'other and watching . . . and then he stood up straight and stiff where Sherburn had stood, frowning . . . , and sung out, "Boggs!" and then fetched his cane down slow to a level, and says "Bang!" staggered backwards, says "Bang!" again, and fell down flat on his back. The people that had seen the thing said he done it perfect; said it was exactly the way it all happened. Then as much as a dozen people got out their bottles and treated him.

This river-town Bottom who grabs both roles in his chronicle play and his gloating audience memorably embody the "strange gladness" derived from a gory scene as they wallow in morbid memories. The uptilted bottles at the end climax a bodying forth of human insensibility. And the commentary gains force because the incident is so patently a repetition in burlesque form of the horrors just described objectively.

Dickens, also, in *A Tale of Two Cities* shows a character smacking his lips over his memories of violent deaths—the little wood sawyer. But I believe that Twain, instead of having this scene specifically in mind, recalled an incident which he claimed had happened when he and Twichell had been wandering through Germany a few years back. In chapter xxiii of *A Tramp Abroad,* a boy has fallen down a steep hillside and a crowd gathers: "All who had seen the catastrophe were describing it at once, and each trying to talk louder than his neighbors; and one youth of a superior genius ran a little way up the hill, called attention, tripped, fell, rolled down among us, and thus triumphantly showed exactly how the thing had been done." In *Huck,* Mark turns this matter into a condemnation by enlarging the reënactment of the incident and adding details about the delighted admiration of the onlookers.

The Bricksville crowd next shows the "mob-lawlessness" which their portrayer equated with "lynch law"—a phenomenon which he had found exemplified in *Le Moniteur,* Carlyle, and Dickens. Dickens' picture of a mob following a funeral shows a mercurial group acting in an unreasoning fashion as one man. When the cry, "Spies!" starts, everyone joins in. "Pull 'em out, there!" yells someone:

The idea was so acceptable in the prevalent absence of any idea, that the crowd caught it up with eagerness, and loudly repeating the suggestion . . . mobbed the two vehicles. . . . The dead man disposed of, and the crowd being under the necessity of providing some other entertainment for itself, another bright genius (or perhaps the same) conceived the humour of impeaching casual passersby, as Old Bailey spies, and wreaking vengeance on them. Chase was given to some scores of inoffensive persons. . . . At last . . . a rumour got about that the Guards were coming. Before this rumour, the crowd gradually melted away . . . and this was the usual progress of a mob.

Compare the Bricksville mob: "Well, by and by somebody said Sherburn ought to be lynched. In about a minute everybody was saying it; so away they went, mad and yelling, and snatching down every clothes-line they come to to do the hanging with."

What follows resembles many spectacular scenes in Twain's reading. A forceful figure appears before a raging mob, speaks, and sways or even quells it. In Carlyle, the speakers are Mirabeau, Marat, Robespierre, and Danton. Dickens, who acknowledges Carlyle as a source, has several such scenes; so does Baring-Gould. Only Carlyle, however, steps into his book to ask, "Is it not miraculous how one man moves hundreds of thousands. . . . Military mobs are mobs with muskets in their hands. . . . To the soldier himself, revolt is frightful and oftenest perhaps pitiable."

In *Huck,* Sherburn appears on his porch and with a quelling look reminiscent of those of Colonel Grangerford and John Marshall Clemens—as well as many French Revolutionary leaders— stares the crowd to silence. Then he makes a contemptuous speech which runs in part:

> "The idea of *you* lynching anybody! . . . Your mistake is, that you didn't bring a man with you. . . . You brought *part* of a man—Buck Harkness, there—and if you hadn't had him to start you, you'd a taken it out in blowing. . . . The pitifulest thing out is a mob; that's what an army is—a mob; they don't fight with courage that's born in them, but with courage that's borrowed from their mass, and from their officers. But a mob without any *man* at the head of it, is *beneath* pitifulness. . . . Now *leave*—and take your half-a-man with you."

The reaction of the crowd is craven: "The crowd washed back sudden,[3] and then broke all apart and went tearing off. . . ."

This ending of the Sherburn episode differs completely from that involving Owsley as the author recalled it. "Acquitted," wrote Mark Twain. "His party brought him huzzaing in from Palmyra at midnight. But there was a cloud upon him—a social chill—and he presently moved away." [4] Sherburn suffers no such fate. This omission and details in the account of the quelling of the mob make Sherburn, so unsympathetic in the previous chapter, admirable in this one. Two results are that Sherburn's remarks against lynching gain weight and the mob continues to be pictured unsympathetically.

The author's indebtedness to accounts of the French Revolution and to old travel books for details about attempted lynchings should not obscure the fact that when he wrote this attack on lynching—as indeed when he wrote others dating back to 1869 [5]

SHERBURN FACES THE MOB, *Huckleberry Finn*, FIRST EDITION

—he was hitting at a contemporary evil. During the Reconstruction period, lynchings had increased and they still were frequent. In 1882, public journals told of 114 lynchings, 68 of whites, 46 of Negroes; by the end of 1883, 134 lynchings had occurred, 77 of whites and 45 of Negroes, the majority for alleged murders.[6] The mob on a murderous rampage was a very present danger when Twain wrote about the march on Sherburn's house.

The next episode in busy Bricksville is "a real bully circus" that Huck attends. Like the description of the Grangerford parlor, the account of this performance glows with humor created by Huck's naïve delight—in the horseback-riding gentlemen and ladies "dressed in clothes that cost millions of dollars, and just littered with diamonds"; [7] the clown who, so Huck believes, ad libs "the funniest things a body ever said . . . so sudden and pat"; the drunk who insists on riding a circus horse and who upon shucking off his clothes astonishes the boy by standing revealed as a member of the troupe.

The drunk's strip tease about which Mark had told himself to write in an 1879–1880 working note had previously been attractive enough to challenge the talents of at least four humorists whose writings he knew: George Washington Harris, Dan De Quille, William Tappan Thompson, and Richard Malcolm Johnston. The versions of the first two, published in 1867 and 1868, he probably did not see; [8] but he probably saw Thompson's "The Great Attraction" in a book of 1843, 1845, and subsequent years; and he did see Johnston's "The Expensive Treat of Col. Moses Grice" as a magazine story in 1881 or in a book issued in January, 1883. [9] The date of the working note and its reference to details peculiar to Thompson's version argue that this was a source; but since these details are not in Huck's account while some peculiar to Johnston's are, I tend to believe that both authors were influential. [10]

But they were not very influential. Huck's version is so different that it is fairly accurate to say that little save the pattern of events has been utilized. The context is different: the fact that the Bricksvillites go to the circus immediately after witnessing a murder and attempting a lynching shows that they have not found these horrible experiences very disturbing. Too, the parallelism between the fatal ride of the drunken Boggs and the comic ride, so soon after, of the pseudo-drunken clown is of a sort that Mark Twain found appealing and believed commented implicitly on both incidents.

Moreover, the reactions of Huck's circus audience are significantly different: Thompson has one character look forward fearfully to the drunk's being injured and the ladies in his audience scream with terror. Johnston plays up general worriment: "An anxious time it was. Kind-hearted people were sorry they had come." And he has the audience learn with vast relief that the man is a showman. Huck's audience is more savage. When the drunk fusses with the ringmaster and the painted clown, it shouts and laughs and gibes at him. The drunk's show of resentment stirs the watchers further and "a lot of men begin to pile down off the benches and swarm towards the ring, saying, 'Knock him down! throw him out!' and one or two women begin to scream." When the drunk, mounting the horse, appears to be in danger, Huck tells of "the whole crowd . . . standing up shouting and laughing till the tears rolled down . . . just crazy. It warn't funny to me, though; I was all of a tremble to see his danger." The description of the mob's behavior in its context continues the attack on the cruel Bricksvillites.

It is a fact, though, that in the episode there is a change of pace. Huck's boyish admiration of the gaudy spectacle, his pleasure in the equestrian act, the masterful ringmaster, the witty clown, and the drunk's performance imbue the passage with gaiety.

The great charm of the scene derives from the fact that this is one of the rare occasions in the whole novel when the ordinarily humorless Huck is amused. The cream of the jest is that he completely misunderstands what is going on. He is tickled by the clown's memorized jests because "how he ever *could* think of so many of them, and so sudden and pat . . . I couldn't no way understand." And he mistakenly believes that not the crowd but the ringmaster is the chief victim of the pseudo-drunken clown's trickery. The final comic fillup is Huck's announcement that this is the bulliest circus he ever saw and his generous promise that "whenever I run across it, it can have all of *my* custom"—a less reassuring promise than it might be since he has avoided buying a ticket by diving under the tent.

The rest of the Bricksville stopover is featured by more entertainments. First there is the "Shakespeare Revival," sparsely attended and greeted with laughter. Deciding that "these Arkansaw lunkheads couldn't come up to Shakespeare; what they want is low comedy and maybe something ruther worse," the duke advertises a three-night run of "The King's Camelopard or The Royal None-such!!! Admission 50 cents," then adds at the bottom of the hand-bills, in "the biggest line of all," "LADIES AND CHILDREN NOT ADMITTED." "There," he says, "if that line don't fetch them, I don't know Arkansaw!"

The title of this spectacle in the manuscript is "The Burning Shame"; so the new title was substituted in the typescript or the proofs. Long before, as I have shown, Mark had thought of hav-ing "a printer-tramp" perform this, and in an 1879–1880 working note he had considered using it in *Huck.* In a 1907 chapter of his *Autobiography* recalling his 1865 visit to Jim Gillis in Jackass Gulch he wrote:

In one of my books—*Huckleberry Finn,* I think—I have used one of Jim's impromptu tales, which he called "The Tragedy of the Burning Shame." I had to modify it considerably to make it proper for print, and this was a great damage. As Jim told it, inventing it as he went along, I think it was one of the most outrageously funny things I have ever listened to. How mild it is in the book, and how pale; how extravagant and how gorgeous in its unprintable form!

The attribution is doubtful: the author in a letter of January 26, 1870, to Gillis speaks of the "great specialty" of Jim's partner Dick Stoker, "his wonderful rendition of 'Rinalds' in the 'Burning Shame!'" Whoever the raconteur was in his notebook of 1865, Mark set down the title and the injunction "No Women Ad-mitted." [11]

In Huck's version the performance consists of the king onstage "a-prancing out on all fours, naked; and . . . painted all over ring-streaked-and-striped, all sorts of colors, as splendid as a rainbow. And—but never mind the rest of his outfit, it was just wild. . . ." For the second time that day Huck appreciates humor, for he finds the king's prancings "awful funny." The audience too is en-tranced, but when it learns that these gyrations twice encored make up the whole performance it grows angry. A leader, as the duke has foreseen, persuades the crowd to keep quiet about the hoax so that others will be similarly cheated. So the next night another packed house is diddled. The third night parts of both audiences come bringing rotten eggs, decayed vegetables, and dead cats, intending to pelt the performers. But after collecting their money the duke and Huck rush away, join the king who is waiting on the raft, and shove off.

The review of *Huck* in *Life*, February 26, 1885, identifies the king's cavorting as "a polite version of the 'Giascutus' story," [12] thereby relating it to a bit of ancient comic American lore. For the tale of the Gyascutus hoax had wandered through newspapers and books for decades. One version had appeared in the *Whig*, published in nearby Palmyra, on October 9, 1845, when Sam Clemens was a ten-year-old in Hannibal; [13] but the humorist may have heard or seen it or variants in any of a hundred places.[14]

In the *Whig* version two Yankee clock peddlers, finding themselves broke in the South, advertise a showing of a "ferocious and terrible beast," the Gyascutus. A crowd gathers, pays admissions, and sees beneath a curtain stretched across a corner of the hall "four horrible feet, which to less excited fancies would have borne a wonderful resemblance to the feet and hands of a live Yankee, with strips of coonskin sewed round his wrists and ankles." The Yankee barker lectures on the beast's ferocity and stirs the creature by poking it with a stick. Roars behind the curtain become increasingly savage until the showman manifests great terror and cries, "Ladies and gentlemen—*save yourselves —the Gyascutus is loose!*" "Pell-mell, hurly-burly, screaming, leaping, crowding, the terrified spectators roll out" while the two Yankees escape through a rear exit.

Of course this is a long way from Huck's account: it has in common only two rascally cheats, a strange animal played by one of them, a showman played by the other, and the hoaxing of the crowd. The Jackass Gulch raconteur or Mark Twain (one cannot know which) provides a more complicated and more amusing stratagem for which I have found as a prototype only a vaguely similar piece of trickery in a yarn by William Tappan Thompson.[15]

Huck's description of the king's gyrations is less specific than one might wish. The manuscript says that he was "stark naked" and later the "stark" was deleted, but the change made little difference; nor did the deletion of Huck's original description of the costume as "outrageous" [16] (changed to "wild"). Huck probably is hinting at some obscene touch, and since B. J. Whiting, an expert on folklore, believes "the king's performance was, no doubt, a burlesque phallic dance," [17] one deduces that it is a phallus. This detail would account for both the boy's reticence and his amusement.

The changing of the name of the performance raises interesting questions. Since, so far as I know, "The Burning Shame" has no indecent connotations, why replace it? And why the particular new title and subtitle? Both "The King's Camelopard" and "The Royal Nonesuch" stress royalty—and Mark had been having at kings. Was he continuing the attack? Support for this guess is offered when one examines a possible literary source.

This is a tale by Edgar Allan Poe included in his *Tales of the Grotesque and Arabesque* in 1845 and often reprinted—"Four Beasts in One; or The Homocameleopard." It concerns the Seleucid king Antiochus Epiphanes and his subjects, bestial worshipers of a baboon deity. Courtiers wander the streets "half naked, with their faces painted" to "shout and gesticulate to the rabble . . . executing . . . some laudable comicality of the king." A ragged urchin bawls that the king, having just killed with his own hand a thousand chained Jews, "is coming in triumph . . . dressed in state." Then the king appears "ensconced in the hide of a beast," "doing his best to play the part of a cameleopard." "With how superior a dignity," mocks Poe, "the monarch perambulates on all fours! His tail . . . is held aloft by his two chief concubines. . . ." His fawning subjects try to kiss his feet. At this point "Nature asserts her violated dominion": wild animals domesticated to serve the citizens become a mob and mutiny. The king shows great agility in escaping. At the end, amidst uproarious cheers, the populace, "satisfied of the faith, valor, wisdom and dignity of their king," proudly "invest his brows . . . with the wreath of victory in the foot-race."

The half-naked courtiers with striped faces, the king prancing on all fours as a cameleopard,[18] the mob—one of animals but still an enraged mob—and the escape: all these strikingly parallel the Bricksville episode. But in giving his pseudo-king's prancings some of their aspects and a new title, did Mark Twain draw upon Poe's story? [19] The answer awaits the discovery of a prototype of the episode more like it than any version of the Gyascutus story which has been found.

It is hard to believe that the author expected so obscure an allusion to have meaning for his readers, and it was not his habit to engage in private symbolism. Yet consideration of the aim of Poe's fable suggests interesting questions. That aim, as Edward H. Davidson states, "is to reduce man from his assumed humanity to his bestial counterpart and, as in the fables of LaFontaine, Rabelais, Voltaire and Swift, to reveal the disgusting side of man's existence . . . man is the destructive beast, whereas the animals are humane." [20] Did Twain know and have in mind this preachment? And does his use of a title referring to the tale obliquely refer to a personal belief?

It is impossible to be sure. Notice, though, that Huck, on first encountering the inhabitants of Bricksville, calls them "a mighty ornery lot," and many a detail about them justifies the epithet— their torturing of sows and dogs, their behavior when Sherburn shoots Boggs and afterward—at the drug store, in front of Sherburn's house, at the circus, at the king's and duke's performances.

Poe's tale gibes not only at the commoners of his ancient city but also at the king. As his monarch scuds away from the pursuing beasts, the narrator hails him with resounding titles: "Antiochus the Illustrious! . . . Glory of the East, Delight of the Universe and [anticlimactically] most Remarkable of Cameleopards!" And the king's garb symbolizes his beastliness.

After the king and the duke, back on the raft, have gloated over their triumph, counted their proceeds ($465), and fallen asleep, Jim asks Huck whether he is not surprised by "de way dem kings carries on." "No," says Huck, . . . "all kings is mostly rapscallions. . . . You read about them once—you'll see." Then from his creator's reading in French and English history he cites Henry VIII, Charles II, Louis XV, James II, Edward II, Richard III, "and forty more"—along with sundry more or less accurate facts—to back his claim. In reply to Jim's questions he extends his condemnation to nobles.

And one of Huck's phrases near the end of chapter xxiii interestingly echoes his comment near the start of chapter xxi: "All I say is, kings is kings, and you've got to make allowances. Take them all around, they're a mighty ornery lot." His use of the identical phrase he has applied to Bricksville trash to characterize monarchs emphasizes the broad scope of his creator's condemnation of humanity in this series of chapters. The chapters to follow would continue the indictment.

23

THE WILKS FUNERAL ORGIES

*They pawed the yaller-boys, and sifted them through
their fingers and let them jingle down on the floor; and
the king says:*
*"It ain't no use talkin'; bein' brothers to a rich dead
man, and representatives of furrin heirs that's got left, is
the line for you and me, Bilge."*—Adventures of Huckleberry Finn, *chapter xxv.*

Echoes of old-time humorists in the Bricksville chapters show that
Mark Twain's recent reading of them shaped specific scenes. The
sweep from loafers to royalty supports my guess that Mark followed the humorists in another way, attempting, in Longstreet's
words, to portray "manners, customs, amusements . . . in all
grades of society." [1] (Not long after finishing *Huck* he indicated
that it presented such a panorama.[2]) The 1879–1880 working
notes show plans to portray Southern "diversions"—dance, parade,
circus, country funeral, wake, even lynching. Also they single
out classes—"poor white family," "keelboatman," "printers."
   One note lists Quarles farm slaves: "Uncle Dan [Jim's proto-
type], aunt Hanner, and the 90-year blind negress." Two notations in Group A and one in B concern "Negro Sermons"; two
quote Negro dialect punch lines—"See dat sinner how he run"
and "po' $22 nigger will set in Heaven wid de $1500 niggers." [3]

Mark planned then to include Negroes in his cross section. He had briefly characterized Jack, the Negro servant assigned Huck by the Grangerfords, by showing how he led the boy to Jim's hiding place, but cannily avoided an overt admission that he was doing so. Also, he had made Jim a leading character. But so far the qualities assigned Jim showed him as little more than a type —the ignorant, superstitious Negro of ante-bellum humorists— though with affection for Huck and dependent on him like the faithful servitors emphasized by writers in the plantation tradition.

Two scenes had gone somewhat beyond conventional picturings. After fooling Jim in chapter xv, Huck discovers the man's sensitivity and essential dignity, and resolves never to "make him feel that way" again. In a brief paragraph in chapter xvi Jim shows affection for his family by resolving to scrimp and save to buy their freedom.

Reading his typescript in 1883 the author noted the latter scene on page 90 and suggested a sequel, "Jim cries, to think of wife and 2 ch^n." [4] Chapter xxiii ends not with Huck's condemnation of royalty but with a picturing of Jim filled with pathos. This (partly because it closely follows Huck's farcical account of Henry VIII's rather inconsiderate family relationships) greatly augments Jim's stature.

The scene represented Clemens' personal convictions. Having overcome childhood prejudices, he now fervently advocated Negro rights. He had met and admired Frederick Douglass, ex-slave and abolitionist whom the Langdons entertained in Elmira. (Possibly he had him in mind when he had Pap viciously condemn an educated Negro.) In 1881 when just before Garfield's nomination rumors had spread that Douglass would lose an appointive post, he broke a rule about exercising political influence and wrote Garfield "because I so honor this man's high and blemishless character, and so admire his brave, long crusade." He was tender toward the race and its members and made many efforts to aid them. In the years of writing *Huck* he was financing college educations for two Negroes "as part of the reparation due from every white to every black man." During the period when proofs for the novel were coming he showed such partiality that Livy suggested a motto, "Consider every man colored till he is proved white."

If literary influences suggested including the scene about Jim, two authors quite possibly exerted them: Joel Chandler Harris and George Washington Cable. Clemens so liked the former's Uncle Remus tales, which he bought late in 1880, that he wrote a complimentary letter. When Harris protested that he was merely recording folk tales the humorist disagreed. The stories, he said in a letter of August 10, 1881, were nothing compared with the characterization: "Uncle Remus is most deftly drawn, and is a lovable and delightful creation; he, and the little boy, and their relations with each other, are high and fine literature, and worthy to live, for their own sakes." On the Mississippi River trip, as has been indicated, he had met Harris and in the book about this trip had praised his writings.

Clemens had so admired Cable that in June, 1881, he interrupted a vacation in Branford, Connecticut, to travel to Hartford and meet him. After the 1882 river trip he saw much of Cable, and in the following fall and the spring of 1883 they had frequent visits in Hartford. By June 4, 1883, they had exchanged twenty-two letters. As Guy Cardwell says, "In his short stories and early novels [Cable] tried to portray Negroes as having naturally the complement of virtues and vices normal to all men; and he was shrewd enough to show, also, how they differed from other men by reason of environmental pressures." Also, Cardwell argues, Cable may have influenced Clemens' views during discussions of "civil rights in the New South" and Cable "expounded . . . views on the need for justice in human relations" that he later elaborated in *The Silent South* (1885) and *The Negro Question* (1888).[5]

But Jim's experience came not from literature but from life. Working note A-11 reads: "L.A. punished her child several days for refusing to answer ? and inattention (5 yr old) then while punishing discovered it was deaf and dumb! (from scarlet fever). It showed no reproachfulness for the whippings—kissed the punisher and showed non-comprehension of what it was all about." [6]

I have not identified "L.A." It is noteworthy that instead of sympathizing with her the note stresses the child's lack of resentment. In his 1882 notebook Mark contemplated narrating the incident in "some rhymes" which would be "about the little child." [7]

Using the incident to portray Jim sympathetically, though, he makes the central matter not the child's forgiveness (which is not even mentioned) but Jim's remorse. As preparation he has Huck recall in retrospect other instances of Jim's humanity:

> I went to sleep, and Jim didn't call me when it was my turn. He often done that. When I waked up, just at day-break, he was setting there with his head down betwixt his knees, moaning and mourning to himself. I didn't take notice, nor let on. I knowed what it was about. He was thinking of his wife and his children, away up yonder, and he was low and homesick; because he hadn't ever been away from home before in his life; and I do believe that he cared just as much for his people as white folks does for their'n. It don't seem natural, but I reckon it's so. He was often moaning and mourning that way, nights, when he judged I was asleep. . . . He was a mighty good nigger, Jim was.

Jim says he is recalling how he punished Elizabeth for inattention, then discovered why she was inattentive. He is full of regret and self-reproach:

> "My breff mos' hop outer me; en I feel so—so—I doan' know *how* I feel. . . . Oh, Huck, I bust out a-cryin' en grab her up in my arms, en say, 'Oh, de po' little thing! de Lord God Almighty fogive po' ole Jim, kaze he never gwyne to fogive hisself as long's he live!' Oh she was plumb deef en dumb, Huck, plumb deef en dumb—en I'd been a treat'n her so!"

The author's frequent suffering of agonies of remorse helped him write poignantly. His eagerness to make Jim's language strong is attested by a marginal note—presumably to Livy—opposite "de Lord God Almighty fogive po' ole Jim" which is underlined: "This expression shall not be changed." Strong language was needed for emphasis here, since in this passage Jim joins Huck in being superior to the folk previously encountered and still to be encountered on the shore. And the sincerity of his grief contrasts with the insincere expressions of mourning in the Wilks episode to follow.

Working notes of 1883 still show interest in historical Southern diversions: "Sunday School," "HOUSE-RAISING," "*Beef-shooting*," "Debating Society," "cadets temperance—masons—oddfellows —militia." [8] Twain considers other violent scenes—the lynching of a free Negro, desperadoes shooting up a village. None of these was pictured; instead, the funeral and the wake of the 1879–1880 notes were. The violent scenes mentioned were not developed, but four abortive lynchings and an accomplished one were.

Having represented the quality (Widow Douglas and the feudists), the mercantile class (Sherburn), Pokeville camp-meeting folk, Bricksville poor whites, Negroes, and the rascally king and duke, he thought of adding middle-class folk and a neglected aspect: "Talk among Ark [ansas] family and visitors.—using snuff with a stick. . . . He must hear some Arkansas women, over their pipes and knitting (spitting from between their teeth), swap reminiscences of Sister this and Brother that, and 'what became of so and so?—what was his first wife's name?' Very religious people." One fascinating bit is a prose poem in the elegaic mood of *Life on the Mississippi:* "Quilting. The world of gossip 75 years ago, that lies silent, stitched into quilt by hands that long ago lost their taper and silkiness and eyes and faces their beauty, and all gone down to dust and silence; and to indifference to all gossip." This statement of a mood rather than a suggestion (like other notes) for matter to be set forth by a naïve narrator recalled a Southern custom and a domestic group. Such a group is represented when Huck visits—as he has the Grangerfords—the Wilks girls, daughters of a carpenter and nieces of a well-to-do tanner, then the Phelpses, owners of a sawmill and a "little one horse plantation."

Chapters xxiv–xxix tell how the king and the duke, posing as brothers of the late Peter Wilks and passing Huck off as a servant, try to defraud Peter's three nieces of their inheritance. Simon Suggs, Hooper's old cheat, similarly had posed as a missing relative in a typical adventure, and I shall notice one detail in the sketch which Mark perhaps found useful. It appears, though, that another source provided an outline for the episode in *Huck*.

Howells mentions his friend's liking for "vital books" which had "the root of human matter" in them and "gave him life at first hand": "a volume of great trials" was typical.[9] Many such books were in the author's library when he died: *Early Trials . . . in Great Britain and Ireland in Capital Cases, viz: Heresy, Treason, Felony, Incest, Poisoning, Adultery, Rapes, Sodomy, Witchcraft, Pyracy, Murder, Robbery, etc.* (London, 1715); *Causes Célèbres de Tous les Peuples* (n.p., n.d., with a table of contents in the author's hand); C. Theodore Wilkinson, *The Newgate Calendar Improved* (London, n.d.), in six volumes.[10]

In the same category was Horace W. Fuller, *Impostors and Adventurers: Noted French Trials* (Boston, 1882), on the flyleaf of which he wrote "S. L. Clemens, June, 1882." [11] A long chapter which surely interested him and possibly influenced his depiction of the king, "The Seven False Dauphins," discusses among others "Eleazer [Williams] the Iroquois." Fuller often mentions qualities of these impostors and their victims which Mark and Huck comment on—the rogues' brazen audacity and the childlike trust (the "imperturbable" credulity, Fuller puts it) of their gulls.

One of Fuller's "dauphins," Mathurin Bruneau, rehearses for his big role by impersonating sundry nobles and gentlemen. When a Saumur peasant sees his resemblance to a widow's missing son, "Bruneau caught the ball on the bound; hastily acquired information in regard to the family, and at once presented himself to the widow as her returned son. Received with joy . . . he sustained for some time this deception, and then disappeared." On the river one day "a nice innocent-looking young country jake" (on his way as young Clemens once had been to New Orleans and thence to South America) mistakes the king for a missing Wilks brother. The king pumps him about the family, moves in with the duke and Huck, and dupes the Wilkses and their townsfolk.

Then comes a twist: rival claimants arrive, offer proofs of their identity, and urge a test involving the disinterment of Peter's body. There is a somewhat similar incident in the story of a pseudo-dauphin, "The Duke of Normandy." It seems likely, though, that the first narrative in Fuller's book, "The False Martin Guerre"—one of four about impostors posing as relatives—was germinal. Guerre posing as a lost spouse has, like Huck's rogues, disposed of most of the opposition when his trial is interrupted: ". . . when . . . the judges . . . were about to give the accused the benefit of the doubt, there arrived . . . a new Martin Guerre . . . he recognized the house where he was born, his neighbors, his relatives, his friends, as the other had done before him. . . . The new-comer arrived just at the right time to drag the judges back into uncertainty. . . ."

As usual Twain's manipulations of his material are more interesting than his borrowings. So that the king and the duke may work together and the king may have a confidant, the author equips the dead man with two brothers. William, impersonated by the duke, he makes deaf and dumb—partly, I suspect, to achieve a contrast by having the rascal pretend to be so afflicted just after Jim tells his tragic tale about his deaf-and-dumb daughter, partly to get comic effects by showing the rogue ineptly enacting his role. And to add interest and to continue his satirizing of human foibles he created characters—Wilks girls and neighbors—and concretely represented actions in ways appropriate for a novel as contrasted with Fuller's baldly factual account.

Beginning with the rogues' arrival in chapter xxv in the unnamed town of the Wilkses, the townspeople display qualities like those of the Bricksvillites: "The news was all over town in two minutes, and you could see the people tearing down on the run, from every which way, some of them putting on their coats as they come. Pretty soon we was in the middle of a crowd, and the noise of the tramping was like a soldier-march. . . . When we got to the house, the street in front . . . was packed." "Like a soldier-march." Recalling Sherburn's (and Carlyle's) comparison of a mob and an army, we see that here is another unreasoning mob. As Henry Nash Smith says in an acute analysis of the opening of this chapter, Huck's details and his diction condemn the crowd—"their greed for sensation"—"any event that breaks the monotony." But at the start this mob's excess is not anger but the opposite, and the satire hits "their sentimentality, their tendency to luxuriate in emotion for its own sake." [12]

Hooper had perhaps suggested a way to use the comedy of a pseudo-relative's weepy reunion with purported kinsfolk to attack what Huck once calls "sentimentering." "Jeems," says Simon after establishing his relationship, "hug your old uncle!" Hooper reports:

Young Mr. James Peyton and Captain Simon Suggs then embraced. Several of the bystanders laughed, but a large majority sympathized with the Captain. A few wept at the affecting sight, and one person expressed the opinion that nothing so soul-stirring had ever before taken place in the city. . . . As for Simon, the tears rolled down his face, as naturally as if they had been called forth by real emotion, instead of being pumped up mechanically. . . .

Hooper anticipates the welling up and the summoning up of tears in an emotional binge. But Mark Twain's scenes of guzzled sentimentality are more condemnatory because nobody laughs and practically everybody weeps. Also Huck's incongruous manner of describing them underlines their excesses. Hearing that Peter is dead, the king "fell up against the man, and put his chin on his shoulder, and cried down his back"; the duke "bust out a crying" and "both of them took on . . . like they'd lost the twelve disciples." The picture of the king dribbling tears down a man's back and the simile which shows the rascals wailing as if instead of an obscure tanner the apostles of Christianity have been struck down both make the display ridiculous. At the house, "[Mary Jane's] face and her eyes was all lit up like glory, she was so glad her uncles was come. . . . The king he spread his arms, and . . . she jumped for them, and [Joanna] jumped for the duke, and there they *had* it! Everybody most, leastwise women, cried for joy to see them meet again at last and have such good times." The "jumping" girls are funnier than they are pathetic; nevertheless everybody weeps for reasons which Huck implies in his blithe phrase "good times." The king and the duke standing by the coffin "leak" tears "for three minutes, or maybe four," and again they have plenty of company: "Everybody was doing the same, and the place was that damp . . . it worked the crowd . . . every woman, nearly, went up to the girls . . . and kissed them . . . then busted out and went off sobbing and swabbing. . . ."

Not merely the kind of details and the diction but the sheer profusion of details contribute to the excoriating effect. And still Mark has not finished. For he has the king "work himself up" and trot out his threadbare pulpit oratory: "[He] slobbers out a speech, all full of tears and flapdoodle about its being a sore trial . . . but it's a trial that's sweetened and sanctified to us by this dear sympathy and these holy tears, and so he thanks them out of his heart and out of his brother's heart, because out of their mouths they can't, words being too weak and cold. . . ." And this is only the first of several such performances.

While having the king deliver one of his tearful talks, his creator bethought himself of a comic device dating at least from the eighteenth-century *Vicar of Wakefield* and I suspect recalled its use in that book. For in 1860 Pilot Clemens had read and admired Goldsmith; a decade later he had parodied him; and some years later he would confess that he perversely treasured "Goldsmith's deathless story" and "carried it with him always" because it constantly "makes an intentionally humorous episode pathetic and an intentionally pathetic one funny." [13] In chapter xiv and again in chapter xxv of the *Vicar*, Goldsmith has his sharper Ephraim Jenkinson bolster claims to learning by tracing purported etymologies. The earlier passage illustrates: "The latter has these words, *Anarchon ara kai atelutaion to pan,* which imply that all things have neither beginning nor end. Manetho also, who lived about the time of Nebuchadon-Asser—Asser being a Syriac word, usually applied as a surname to kings of that country . . . formed a conjecture equally absurd; for as we usually say, *ek to biblion kubermetes,* which implies that books will never teach the world. . . ." When the king several times mentions the Wilks "funeral orgies" and the duke nervously writes a note, "obsequies, you old fool," the king brazens it out: "I say orgies, *not* because it's the common term, because it ain't—obsequies bein' the common term —but because orgies is the right term . . . a word that's made up out'n the Greek *orgo,* outside, open, abroad; and the Hebrew *jeesum,* to plant, cover up; hence *inter.* So, you see, funeral orgies is an open er public funeral." The incident stresses how assured the king is that he can "work" his trustful audience. And "orgies" is an inspired malapropism, wonderfully apt for the emotional excesses attending the last rites.[14]

In recounting the funeral in chapter xxvii the author recalled a couple of incidents. A notebook entry aboard the *Quaker City* before the 1867 trip read: "Tableau—in the midst of sermon Capt. Duncan rushed madly out with one of those damned dogs, but didn't throw him overboard." [15] Since Duncan was the king's prototype, associating this tableau with the king was understandable. A similar incident, one of several undertaker yarns which Twain had thought of working into *A Tramp Abroad,* or a desire to make his friend Twichell the hero of an anecdote, led the author to write in his 1882 notebook, "Twichell's Deco. Day prayer — —[G—— d——that dog!]"; and then a bit later, "He had a rat!" [16]

The Wilks funeral sermon is interrupted by a racket which the dog is perpetrating in the cellar. An undertaker whom Huck has introduced as "the softest, glidingest, stealthiest man I ever see" takes charge:

Then he stooped down and begun to glide along the wall, just his shoulders showing over the people's heads . . . the pow-wow and the racket getting worse all the time . . . when he had gone around two sides of the room, he disappears. . . . Then in about two seconds we heard a whack, and the dog he finished up with a most amazing howl or two, and then everything was dead still, and the parson begun his solemn talk where he left off. In a minute or two here comes this undertaker's back and shoulders . . . ; and so he glided . . . around three sides of the room, and then rose up, and shaded his mouth with his hands, and stretched his neck out towards the preacher . . . and says, in a kind of hoarse whisper, *"He had a rat!"* Then he dropped down and glided along the wall again to his place. You could see it was a great satisfaction to the people, because naturally they wanted to know. A little thing like that don't cost nothing, and it's just the little things that makes a man to be looked up to and liked. There warn't no more popular man in that town than what that undertaker was.

Though more genially portrayed than the undertaker in *Life on the Mississippi,* this efficient commercialized glider is a blood relative. His show of concern parodies the real grief of the Wilks girls; and the force of the curiosity of the audience about a howling dog suggests that although they have wept over the corpse they are not devastated by sorrow.

While Huck conveys his creator's attitude chiefly by his unwitting use of details and words which imply it in these chapters, he also voices disgust. The weeping of the king and the duke in chapter xxv he calls "enough to make a body ashamed of the human race"; the keening over the coffin in chapter xxvi prompts his comment, "I never see anything so disgusting"; and when the king's platitudes are ended by the singing of "the doxologer" he notices that "it warmed you up and made you feel . . . good. . . ." "Music," he explains, "*is* a good thing; and after all that soul-butter and hogwash, I never see it . . . sound so honest and bully." He expresses irritation with the townspeople when they shake hands with the duke "a-smiling and bobbing their heads like a passel of sapheads."

Nonparticipant in the feud and in the events in Bricksville, Huck has become a participant in the Wilks chapters and later in the Phelps chapters—a sign of his growing concern about others. Disgusted with his associates and moved to compassion by the suffering and then the kindness of the three girls, he decides he must help them: "I felt so ornery and low down and mean, that I says to myself, My mind's made up; I'll hive that money for them. . . ."[17] Not only does he hive the money: against his principles he "ups and tells the truth" to Mary Jane and arranges for her to have the two frauds jailed. The plan is balked by the appearance of the rival claimants, the trip to the cemetery, and the escape of Huck and the two rogues.[18] Nevertheless his condemnations and his making a moral decision and then acting upon it show growing involvement and responsibility.

Final happenings in the episode (chapters xxviii and xxix) turn attention again to the townspeople and their "mob qualities"—their pathetic delight in excitement when the real brothers appear; their sheeplike attitudes; their fickleness as they side with one pair of claimants then the other; their cruelty—for they mean "to lynch the whole gang" of disputants if their stories prove untrue.

Eventually even the most rational men in the mob—those holding the king, the duke, and Huck captive—are victims of what Carlyle calls "Curiosity, in strange gladness." Peter Wilks' gold is discovered in the disinterred coffin where Huck has hidden it. Hines, Huck's captor, "let out a whoop, like everybody else, and dropped my wrist and give a big surge to bust his way in and get a good look"; and Dr. Robinson and Lawyer Bell, in charge of the rogues, also "let go all holts" and rushed to look.[19]

The mere sight of the gold stirs greed in the breasts of people such as are pictured here. When the king sees it his eyes shine; he and the duke caressingly trickle it between their fingers and delightedly listen to its jingle. When it is stacked on the Wilks table, "Everybody looked hungry at it, and licked their chops." Greed in the end foils the cheats: chapter xxviii in recent editions is titled, "Overreaching Don't Pay." Paradoxically and significantly it also saves them from lynching by distracting their equally money-hungry captors: chapter xxx is titled "The Gold Saves the Thieves." Aboard the raft the ugliest scene involving the cheats—a violent clash during which the duke chokes the old king until he gurgles—results from a disagreement about which stole the gold from the other. Thus the Wilks episode, while repeating several indictments against the people whom Huck has encountered, emphasizes a new one—that they lust for gold.

24

"THE END. YOURS TRULY, HUCK FINN."

I've done two seasons' work in one, and haven't anything left to do, now, but revise. I've written eight or nine hundred MS pages in such a brief space of time that I mustn't name the number of days. . . . I've wrought from breakfast to 5.15 p.m. six days a week; and once or twice I smouched a Sunday when the boss wasn't looking. Nothing is half so good as literature hooked on Sunday, on the sly.—Mark Twain to William Dean Howells, August 22, 1883.

Twain thought of having Huck's revelation of his associates' perfidy bring about their selling Jim. But, deciding to end the Wilks episode with the ironic twist, he developed another line of causation.[1] In chapter xxxi the two cheats (with their unwilling companions) drift downstream. At a safe distance they try "mesmerizering, and doctoring, and telling fortunes" and other frauds with small success. After devious planning they turn Jim in as a runaway for a forty-dollar reward.

Learning that Jim is imprisoned at Phelps' plantation, Huck ponders writing Miss Watson so she can get him back. In a scene readers have found the most memorable in the book, Huck struggles with his conscience. The debate embodies a meaningful contrast.

334

One aspect of the contrast has been developed in another memorable scene, Sherburn's speech. Twain, as I have shown, stresses the merchant's remarks by making Sherburn sympathetic and his listeners unsympathetic. Drama also augments the emphasis. The mob has come "a-whooping and raging." Screaming women and wailing children run from its fury. The quiet Sherburn appears. His speech causes this mob bent on hanging him to disperse.

The sympathetic attitude and the impact of Sherburn's words suggest that Sherburn is a *raisonneur*. Comparison between his denunciation and a suppressed chapter of *Life on the Mississippi* verifies this. In the chapter, writing seriously in the first person, Mark says, as his character does, that although most Southerners dislike injustice and violence they endure them because they hate trouble and danger; but in the South a man can lead a masked mob at night into violent action.[2]

As significant as these resemblances between chapter and speech are the differences between the two. The chapter's concern is Southern politics. Since slavery has vanished, says Twain, half the South is free: "But the white half is as far from emancipation as ever." His proof is that the South, "solid" for one party, has a unity impossible in a truly free region. He blames hotheads. These, he holds, are impotent in the North because citizens there support law and defy intimidation. They are powerful in the South because a hothead leading masked lynchers can frighten communities into conformity. Sherburn's thesis by contrast is that the Bricksville mob is impotent because it is being led by only *"part of a man"* in the daytime, and "if any real lynching's going to be done, it'll be done in the dark, Southern fashion; and . . . they'll bring their masks, and fetch a *man* along."

The dramatic situation makes necessary this difference in emphasis. But it does not make necessary Sherburn's learning in the way he has the truths he states:

"I know you clear through. I was born and raised in the South, and I've lived in the North; so I know the average all around. The average man's a coward. In the North he lets anybody walk over him . . . and prays for a humble spirit. . . . In the South one man, all by himself, has stopped a stage full of men, in the day-time, and robbed the lot . . . you're . . . no braver [than any other people]."

hearts. I was born ~~& raised~~
in the ~~South~~, & I've lived in the
north; ~~so~~ I know the average
man of ~~the~~ country, & the
average man of the world.
The average man of the
world is a coward. In the
north he lets anybody ~~who~~
walk over him that wants
to, & goes home & prays for
a humble spirit to bear the
insult. In the ~~south~~ one man,
all alone, has ~~stopped~~ a stage
full of men, in broad daylight
& robbed the lot. Your newspapers call you a ~~brave~~

MANUSCRIPT OF *Huckleberry Finn,* PAGE 165

Fictional probability requires that Sherburn know only Bricksville. But having given him exactly the same magnificent chance to observe Americans that his creator has had, Mark has him condemn them all. Moreover, Sherburn's knowing "the average all around" suggests an even broader generalization which the original manuscript had explicitly stated: "I know the . . . average man *of the world*. The average man *of the world* is a coward." [3] The author may have revised this because so sweeping a claim seemed out of character for a Bricksvillite.[4] Regardless, the revised phrasing still implies universal condemnation. Thus, where more clearly than anywhere else in the novel a character's voice becomes that of his creator, it announces that man is as cowardly, sheeplike, and cruel as he dares be.

The indictment is one which Twain himself had formulated shortly after writing his travel chapter. In the river trip notebook, as Dixon Wecter has seen, he prepared for it by composing a fictional argument between two Negro deckhands about moral responsibility.[5] The wiser holds that not man but an outside force which he calls "de Lawd" is responsible for man's sins.[6] On June 21, 1882, after his trip, the author made two entries: "Is anybody brave who has no *audience?*" and "Is *any*body or any action ever unselfish? (Good theme for Club Essay)." [7] On February 19, 1883, he read to the Monday Evening Club "What Is Happiness?" [8] which, he later recalled, summarized a chapter in "my own gospel"—

. . . the chapter denying that there is any such thing as personal merit; maintaining that a man is merely a machine automatically functioning without any of his help. . . . I observed that the human machine gets all its inspirations from the outside and is not capable of originating an idea of any kind in its own head; and . . . that no man ever does a duty for duty's sake but only for the sake of avoiding the personal discomfort he would have to endure if he shirked the duty; also I indicated that there is no such thing as free will and no such thing as self-sacrifice.

In the final version of the "gospel" here rehearsed—"What Is Man?"—he called the outside inspirations "a man's *make*, and influences brought to bear on it by his heredities, his habitat, his associates." These, he said some years later, completely decide how a man *"secures peace of mind, spiritual comfort, FOR HIM-SELF"*—in other words, how he wins happiness.[9]

As I have shown, Mark has expressed these ideas in marginal arguments with Lecky perhaps as early as 1874 and in chapters of *Huck* in 1876. New, though, when he wrote later parts of the novel, was a deepened conviction. This had been fortified by wide reading—in history, travel books, ante-bellum humor, annals of crime—fortified, too, by observations of European life and of American politics and business. Moreover—a significant step [10] —he recently had written out his ideas. When club members strenuously disagreed and he hotly defended his thesis, out of sheer stubbornness (such was his "make") he hugged it more affectionately.

Alexander E. Jones has studied "What Is Happiness?" and "the gospel" as their author would have wished, considering how the writer's make or temperament and his circumstances shaped them. Jones (with many biographers) argues that an overactive conscience and a desire to escape its constant nagging by shedding responsibility figured importantly. So did "distaste with which [Clemens] viewed the smug self-righteousness of bourgeois Protestant society." [11] And surely if, in this instance as in others, personal circumstances affected his attitude, the sniffs of the reputedly most civilized members of society at him as a crude "Phunny Phellow"—and bedevilments of civilized life in the Hartford mansion—were influential.

Nagged by his conscience, irritated by "civilization," committed to his "gospel," the author must have been particularly irritated by man's "smug self-righteousness" because he considered it hypocritical. Here was man acting because of his "make," necessarily selfish, usually stupid and cruel. Mark's wise deckhand held "de Lawd taken en buil' up a man so he jes' boun' to kill people, en lie en sneak en embellish [embezzle]." [12] Here was man acting because of "forces brought to bear"—codes, creeds, patterns set by society. Yet man claimed with Lecky that "a natural power of perceiving" or with the religious that a supernatural power led him to righteous acts.

This would explain Twain's constant emphasis now and later on hypocrisy. An 1882 notebook entry explains why you can know a man better in a village than in a city: in the former you know the inner man; in the latter only his outside, "usually a lie." [13] In the passage excised from *Life on the Mississippi* Twain praises Mrs. Trollope for manifesting "prejudices . . . of an honest nature against humbug" and attacking " 'chivalrous' assassinations" and "sham godliness." Elsewhere in the same manuscript discussing cockfighting he wrote: "All the details of 'civilization' are legitimate matter for jeering. . . . It is made of about three tenths of reality and sincerity, and seven tenths of wind and humbug." "It seems to me that the civilization which is always preaching pity and humanity," he continued, and logically would have concluded, "is pitiless and inhuman," though without doing so he crossed out the passage.[14] In the midst of proofs for *Huck*, on August 21, 1884, chiding Howells for supporting candidate Blaine, he wrote, "*Isn't* human nature the most consummate sham and lie that was ever invented? Isn't man a creature to be ashamed of in pretty much all his aspects?" Within a year of *Huck*'s publication he considered writing another Monday Evening essay: "Club subject: the *insincerity* of man—all men are liars, partial or hiders of facts, half tellers of truths, shirks, moral sneaks." [15]

For various reasons Twain in early parts of *Huck* had played up disparities between professed creeds and actual deeds: jokes about lying and deceit were habitual for him as they were for all humorists in the tall-tale tradition. Routine as well as characterization accounted for Huck's saying, in his first paragraph, of the author of *Tom Sawyer:* "There was things which he stretched, but mainly he told the truth. That is nothing. I never seen anybody but lied. . . ." Incongruities between man's high pretenses and his ornery actions were staples of many humorists, Twain among them. The scene in chapter v where Pap professes he is reformed and then gets roaring drunk is a retelling of an 1867 anecdote. In some passages the writer had seen how, using such incongruities, he could state philosophical ideas. Most of the sporadic passages which had been inspired by Lecky involved such disparities. So Twain had prepared for the dramatizations of his theme which were to run from chapter xvii on.

From that point such dramatizations were practically continuous and their meanings were increasingly evident. Sherburn's speech stresses the average man's make—cowardice, dislike of trouble; it also stresses the way circumstances force a hypocritical show of bravery: "You didn't want to come. The average man don't like trouble and danger. *You* don't like trouble and danger. But if only *half* a man . . . shouts 'Lynch him! lynch him!' you're afraid to back down—afraid you'll be found out to be what you are—*cowards*—and so you raise a yell . . . and come raging up here, swearing what things you'll do." The mob's dispersal, as I have noticed, amply verifies Sherburn's claims.

So do folk whom Huck encounters beginning with the Grangerfords. That family subscribes to codes of aristocracy, chivalry, and sentiment, all results of influences brought to bear upon them; they are governed by such codes. But both high-sounding codes and the make of the Grangerfords turn them to ruthless murder. The Bricksville mob spirit is a sign that citizens are puppets of circumstance: laziness, sadism, morbidity, cowardice, lasciviousness, and stupidity are parts of their make. Sentimentality victimizes the Wilkses and their neighbors. But it does not prevent the neighbors from becoming a cruel mob bent on lynching or from being robbed of their fun by greed and curiosity. The duke and the king are perfect figures to exploit such villagers, since the former hides his villainy under a pose of sentimentality, the latter his under a pose of piety. Huck comments on both these pretenders and on bona fide privileged classes abroad: ". . . it's in the breed . . . kings is kings, and you got to make allowances. . . . It's the way they're raised."

Huck's last sight of his rascals comes in chapter xxxiii after he has gone to the Phelps' place to rescue Jim. They have become victims of the very mob spirit they have been "working." Once too often they have tried "The King's Camelopard" and ". . . here comes a raging rush of people with torches, and an awful whooping and yelling, and banging tin pans and blowing horns. . . . I see they had the king and the duke astraddle of a rail—that is,

I knowed it *was* the king and the duke, though they was all over tar and feathers, and didn't look like nothing in the world that was human—just looked like a couple of monstrous big soldier plumes." As heretofore the military metaphor, in "soldier plumes," betokens a mob. Huck, as he has so often recently, offers an explicit summary: "Well, it made me sick. . . . It was a dreadful thing to see. Human beings *can* be awful cruel to one another."

In several episodes, images exposing hypocrisy are drawn from religion, in part because the author was increasingly irritated by pretenses of Christianity, in part because historically riverside villagers had been religious folk. Grangerfords and Shepherdsons at church with guns in easy reach provide a forecast. The note which explodes the feud is hidden by Harney Shepherdson in Sophia Grangerford's New Testament. Huck ruminates on the greater sincerity of hogs than of human churchgoers. In Pokeville the women of the camp-meeting congregation lustfully caress the old king, and both male and female worshipers aid and abet the scoundrel. In Bricksville a pious bystander piles on Boggs' breast a huge Bible which hastens his death. In the town of the Wilkses the king's sanctimonious blathering inspires idiotic acts. The old coot himself is so in the habit of professing religion that in chapter xxv, alone with the duke and Huck whom he cannot hope to deceive, he praises the Lord for helping him defraud orphans: "Thish-yer comes of trust'n to Providence. It's the best way, in the long run. I've tried 'em all, and there ain't no better way." In the chapters to come, Silas Phelps, who imprisons Jim, is a part-time preacher.

Huck's debate about writing Miss Watson, as if to recapitulate, goes over this ground. Then it takes a turn which offers a highly significant contrast. Accordingly it falls into two parts. In Part I Huck decides not to write, but reverses his decision and writes the letter. In Part II he makes his final choice: he destroys the letter and accepts the consequences.

Part I follows the formula of "What Is Happiness?" Huck finds excuses for not writing: Miss Watson will be angered; Jim will suffer. Huck's next thoughts, however, show that his altruism is a pretense and that his real concern is not about Jim's but his own suffering: "And then think of *me!* It would get all around, that Huck Finn helped a nigger to get his freedom; and if I was to ever see anybody from that town again, I'd be ready to get down and lick his boots for shame." Fear of others' opinions is as operative here as when cowardly Bricksvillites march on Sherburn. But superimposed attitudes are at work here, and not what Mark would call Huck's "make." In vain Huck tries to excuse himself "by saying I was brung up wicked, and so I warn't so much to blame." For his thinking has been shaped by religion: ". . . Providence [was] slapping me in the face and letting me know my wickedness was being watched up there in heaven . . . showing me there's One that's always on the lookout. . . . It warn't no use to try and hide it from Him . . . my heart warn't right. . . ." So Huck writes the letter and feels "all washed clean of sin. . . ." The reasoning and the decision are like those of folk ashore—reasoning dictated by an outwardly imposed code leading to a cruel decision. Huck's style in reaching it and rejoicing about it has marks of insincerity. It is "the language of the official culture, a tawdry and faded effort that is the rhetorical equivalent of the ornaments of the Grangerford parlor" [16]—religious cant so often a token of hypocrisy ashore—the king's "hogwash."

But when Huck gets to "thinking over our trip down the river" he says:

. . . and I see Jim before me, all the time, in the day; and in the nighttime, sometimes moonlight, sometimes storms, and we a floating along, talking, and singing, and laughing. But somehow I couldn't strike no places to harden me against him, but only the other kind. I'd see him standing my watch on top of his'n, stead of calling me . . . and see how glad he was when I come back out of the fog . . . and suchlike times . . . and how good he always was . . . and then I happened to look around and see that paper.

It was a close place. I took it up, and held it in my hand. I was a trembling, because I'd got to decide, forever, betwixt two things. . . . I studied a minute, sort of holding my breath, and then says to myself:

"All right, then, I'll go to hell"—and tore it up.

The phrasings which precede this second decision are not mouthings of snippets from sermons. Their concreteness, their naturalness, their simplicity, their originality, indicate deep-felt emotion.

Both Huck here and Jim in his remorseful memories in chapter xxiii illustrate the concept which Mark had developed in 1876 when showing Huck's previous conflict with his conscience—the way "a sound heart" prompts a right decision. What makes both scenes more striking than the earlier one is, first, the author's clearer formulation and therefore his clearer articulation of the contrasts involved; second, his placing these sound and moral conclusions cheek-by-jowl with many stupid and immoral ones. The putting into words of his thought was influential; so was his recently defined technique of using juxtaposed scenes to embody "silent but eloquent comment."

The representations of Huck and Jim suggest that, for all his talk about believing man "merely a machine automatically functioning," Mark had not been completely converted by his own eloquence. Outlining that club paper in 1885 on "the *insincerity* of man" after saying "*all* men are liars" he would illogically propose discussing some who were not: "When a merely honest man appears he is a comet—his fame is eternal—needs no genius, no talent—mere honesty—Luther, Christ, etc." [17] Huck and Jim, like Christ and Luther, show that against all his logic Mark Twain was fighting for a faith.

Three years before, one of the most emotional passages in *A Tramp Abroad* had symbolically represented his struggle. In chapter xxxiv he had told of scrambling through a high Alpine pass, "a storm-swept and smileless desolation . . . masses, crags, ramparts . . . not a vestige or semblance of plant or tree or flower . . . ghastly desolation." But—

In the most forlorn and arid and dismal place of all . . . where the wind blew bitterest and the general aspect was mournfulest . . . and farthest from any suggestion of cheer and hope, I found a voluntary wee forget-me-not flourishing away, not a droop about it anywhere, but holding its bright blue star up . . . the only smiling thing in that grisly desert. . . . I judged she had earned a right to a friend who would respect her for the fight she had made . . . to make a whole vast Alpine desolation stop breaking his heart over the unalterable. . . .

Although the passage is marred when Twain has the flower chirrup inane advice about cheering up, by then it has embodied his dilemma pictorially. Otherwise its emotional freighting is a puzzle.

In chapter xviii of *A Connecticut Yankee in King Arthur's Court* in 1889 he stated the concept expounded in "What Is Happiness?" and his wish to fight against it quite explicitly:

We have no thoughts of our own, no opinions of our own; they are transmitted to us, trained into us. All that is original in us, and therefore fairly creditable or discreditable to us, can be covered up and hidden by the point of a cambric needle, all the rest being atoms contributed by, and inherited from, a procession of ancestors that stretches back a billion years. . . . And as for me, all that I think about in this plodding sad pilgrimage, this pathetic drift between the eternities, is to look out and humbly live a pure and high and blameless life, and save that one microscopic atom in me that is truly *me:* the rest may land in Sheol and welcome for all I care.

Again this passage, sandwiched as it is between humorous paragraphs, has an emotional tone which is inexplicable unless it speaks for the author.

These passages bracketing the final stage of writing *Huck* show Mark Twain's state of mind when he completed the novel. He was impelled toward the belief that his picture of folk on the shore represented the way humanity lived. Simultaneously he was pulled by the fervent wish that his picture of Huck and Jim represented a way some individuals at least might live.[18] As a result, contrasts and incongruities between Huck and Jim on the raft and the society on the shore (including emissaries from the shore to the raft—the king and the duke) embody a theme of great personal significance to the author.[19]

A striking thing about several of the most persuasive recent interpreters of the novel is not that they disagree about numerous points—this is a habit of critics—but that they agree that the contrast I have just noticed is vital to the book's meaning. Their formulations of the meaning in terms of this contrast, although phrased differently, have much in common. Lionel Trilling poetically describes Huck as "a servant of the river-god" and indicates what the boy and the shore folk represent for him: "After every sally into the social life of the shore [Huck] returns to . . . the god's beauty, mystery, and strength, and to his noble grandeur in contrast with the pettiness of men." Another poetic interpreter, T. S. Eliot, characterizes Huck similarly as "the spirit of the River," and finds that his "existence questions the values of America as much as the values of Europe." Edgar M. Branch notices "the conflict between individual freedom and the restraints imposed by convention and force." Gladys Bellamy sees a contrast between Huck, whose character rests on "moral intuition," and the village governed by "the mores of the folk." Henry Nash Smith writes of "a contrast between the raft—connoting freedom, security, happiness, and harmony with nature—and the society of the towns . . . connoting vulgarity and malice and fraud and greed and violence." [20]

That zigzags between raft and shore have become so significant has as its corollary that geographical movement has become less significant. I once argued that Twain considered the downriver journey his chief line of action and took care to provide causes for the movement of Huck and Jim from Jackson's Island to Phelps' plantation. [21] Well into the book, as working notes show, the author was interested in making the journey plausible and he did provide causation. But Smith revealed in 1958 that an alert and hitherto unsung proofreader helped greatly. Up into chapter xix Huck and Jim still cannot turn back upstream as they intend, because they still lack a canoe. But Smith discovered that in the proof of that chapter (hence in the manuscript) Mark has Huck say blithely, "One morning . . . I took the canoe. . . ." The proofreader wrote in the margin, "Qy see p. 129 canoe lost." Mark then revised to "I found a canoe. . . ." As Smith says, the indication is that by this time "the earlier plan has sunk from sight." Momentarily, while writing the Wilks chapters Mark recalled the broken thread and wrote on Note C-4, "And Jim can be smuggled north on [crossed out] a ship?—no, steamboat." But nothing came of this. So Smith sees "the linear movement toward freedom" supplanted by "a structural principle" which is "bipolar." He argues persuasively that this shift does not impair the basic unity, since "not only does the River connote freedom; the Shore connotes slavery, bondage in a more general sense than the actual servitude of Jim. . . . And the historical South itself . . . tended to become a metaphor for the human condition." [22]

My story of the writing of the book has suggested why, when he needed this metaphor, associations in earlier chapters had readied it. From the start, and more and more as time passed, the river and the raft had come to mean to Twain happy escape from what hurt and harassed him in civilization. By now inevitably he identified them with virtues which he had decided were all too rare in the world of man. Just as inevitably he identified the two cheating confidence men and the hypocritical folk ashore with his concept of civilization.

I believe that my account of the author's personal position also has suggested why in developing this contrast Mark Twain was able to do so with humor. From the start of the novel he had been of two minds about civilization and escape from it. Now his feelings were ambivalent about the things for which the shore and the raft stood: determinism on the one hand, freedom of choice on the other. Fierce though his attacks on shore folk were, his inability to condemn them brought mitigations. And his admiration for Jim and Huck was tempered by his envy of them and his skepticism about their state of grace. Both sinners and saints attracted and at the same time repelled him, and he was neither as rancorous toward the former nor as reverent toward the latter as he would have been if he were fully committed. He could make both groups comic. So the humor which makes *Huck* the funniest of all American books was vital to nuances of its meaning.

Two narrative stretches completed the book, an insertion telling about the visit of Huck and Jim to the wrecked steamboat *Walter Scott,* the talk with the ferryboat owner and the arguments about King Solomon and the French language (chapter xii, paragraph

12, through chapter xiv), and the account of Jim's rescue (chapters xxxii–xliii).[23]

When writing about the king and the duke, Twain probably thought of the insertion, for working note C-4 reads: "Back yonder, Huck reads and tells about monarchies and kings &c. So Jim stares when he learns the rank of these two." The same page has phrases worked into the discussion of Solomon.

"The wreck of the *Walter Scott*," says DeVoto, "exists solely to furnish Huck with books of history so that he can prepare for the coming of the vagabonds. . . ."[24] It serves other purposes. Twain was watching for chances to repeat motifs with variations. Picturing a real robber gang soon after Tom's romanticized gang afforded such a parallel. He encourages comparisons by naming the boat the *Walter Scott* after the author who for him summarized romantic excesses and by having Huck mention three times how Tom would enjoy the adventure.

DeVoto notices that "beginning with the *Walter Scott* the book moves purposefully."[25] He gives no reasons, but it might be argued that the episode shows the first encounter of the pair on the raft with folk living along the shore. Early in the trip, therefore, it announces the bipolar movement, and better than any other encounter with riverside dwellers before the Grangerford chapters it develops the thematic contrast.

On the boat Jim Turner, a murderer and a stool pigeon, has been trussed up because he is "the meanest, treacherousest hound in this country." He is "blubbering" and begging for mercy. His two captors want to kill him but compassionately decide simply to let him drown because they are "unfavorable to killin' a man as long as you can get around it; it ain't good sense, it ain't good morals." They start for the skiff and then decide to return to get Turner's share of the cash. As a result Huck and Jim take the skiff, leaving them and Turner behind. The trio have shown cruelty, treachery, hypocrisy, and greed—an assortment of shorefolk vices.

Too, the episode shows Huck's compassion: "We took out after our raft. . . . I begun to worry . . . to think how dreadful it was, even for murderers. . . . I says to myself, there ain't no telling but I might come to be a murderer myself yet, and then how would I like it?"[26] His sympathy—and empathy (shared by Twain)— cause him to get the ferryboatman to go to the rescue. This worthy has a frailty which Huck plays upon by telling a lie which persuades him to visit the sinking boat—greed for money.

Momentarily at the end of the incident the author sacrifices characterization to humor. Huck's inability to "rest easy till I could see the ferryboat start" is in keeping. So is his wish that the widow might know about his deed because "rapscallions and dead-beats is the kind . . . good people takes the most interest in." It also enforces the satire against the sentimental judge and anticipates the king's working the camp meeting.[27] But when Huck sees the boat drifting downstream so deep that it is evident the gang has drowned, he says merely, "I felt a bit heavy-hearted about the gang; but not much, for I reckoned if they could stand it I could." Such selfish indifference even toward rascals, though characteristic of shore folk, is not like Huck.

But in parts of the novel written that summer—the last stages perhaps—the author was often too interested in the broadest comedy. The arguments in chapter xiv are examples. True, Huck's talk about privileged classes prepares for Jim's astonishment.[28] When he tells about the dauphin, Jim's sympathetic remarks introduce evidence of his goodness of heart. Jim's explanation of Sollerman's callousness comically anticipates later serious indictments: "It lays in de way Sollerman was raised. You take a man dat's got on'y one or two chillen; is dat man gwyne to be waseful o' chillen? No . . . but you take a man dat's got 'bout five million chillen. . . . *He* as soon chop a chile in two as a cat." Huck's concluding words in the argument about the French language concern Jim's "make": "I see it warn't no use wasting words— you can't learn a nigger to argue"—and the comment is laughable since Jim has just outargued Huck. The laughter provoked by the arguments (for they are funny, favorite readings on the lecture platform) doubtless increases our liking for both disputants.

But the interlude is minstrel-show stuff which does little to develop the book's theme. It makes Huck a reader of history and an instructor, thus putting him uneasily into Tom's role.

Most readers find the Phelps chapters vulnerable to similar criticism. Learning where Jim is imprisoned, Tom Sawyer, who (thanks to a whopping coincidence) has joined Huck, conducts an escape with style to it, i.e., one following "all the best authorities" on prison breaks.

It is true that the chapters terminate some narrative threads and develop some modulations of themes. The picture of the one-horse plantation—strongly influenced by new memories of the Quarles place—enlarges Twain's panorama. Huck again satirizes ante-bellum morals and comically formulates his creator's ideas about mankind when, in chapters xxxiii and xxxiv, he marvels because Tom—"a boy that was respectable and well brung up . . . and not mean, but kind"—with such a make and such an environment "stoops to this business" of freeing a slave. In chapter xlii, on learning that Jim (very fortuitously) has been freed by Miss Watson, he says: "I couldn't understand before. . . ." but makes clear that he can understand now. Huck's acting despite danger to free Jim concretely proves the sincerity of his "All right, then, I'll go to hell." When Jim, in chapter xl, at great personal risk abandons his escape until a doctor attends Tom's wound he shows some of his finest qualities. And Huck climaxes his love and respect for Jim which has been developing through the book by paying a compliment astounding for a poor white: "I knowed he was white inside." It seems pretty clear what Twain had in mind: he would do for silly romances about prison escapes what Cervantes had done for silly romances in his day. More important, he would juxtapose with a serious narrative about a flight to achieve freedom, which develops certain themes, a burlesque narrative touching upon similar topics.[29]

These and other values, some poetically conceived,[30] have been cited by advocates of the Phelps chapters in an argument which continues. But even some approving the terminal chapters admit they "fall off." And I have seen no convincing argument that they are not overlong.

As burlesque the end jousts at an impressive number of writers about prison life and escapes—Baron Trenck, Casanova, Cellini, Henri IV, Dumas, Carlyle, Dickens, as well as more obscure writers such as X. B. Saintine and Baring-Gould.[31] Unfortunately, few readers ever have recognized references to the literature being satirized. Chapters, endlessly it seems, show Tom complicating things to follow bookish authorities while Huck offers commonsensible protests. The comedy is chiefly that of the Sut Lovingood school: hound packs streaming through Jim's cabin; menageries of bugs, spiders, caterpillars, and snakes discomforting Jim; snakes dropping from rafters onto Aunt Sally; butter melting atop Huck's head. Working notes show that Mark delighted in the elaboration; but few adult readers will. The chief crimes are against characterization: Jim, whom the reader and Huck have come to love and admire, becomes a victim of meaningless torture, a cartoon. Huck, who has fought against codes of civilization, follows one of the silliest of them.

Why did Mark write thus? On July 20 he told Howells, "I wrote 4000 words today and I touch 3000 and upwards pretty often, and don't fall below 2600 any working day." At summer's end he bragged about his prodigious output during six or seven eight-hour days per week. In addition to other writing, before the Phelps chapters he had rushed through two Bricksville chapters, the Wilks chapters, and probably the *Walter Scott* insert. Into episodes as powerful as anything he ever wrote he had poured much life and deep conviction. Perhaps even the ebullient Mark Twain was tired to the point of reckless improvisation. Also the book was a tough one to finish and he was postponing the end.

Apparently he did not hit upon the way the book had to end until after all his horsing around he reached the very last sentences: "I reckon I got to light out for the Territory . . . , because Aunt Sally she's going to adopt me and civilize me and I can't stand it. I been there before. THE END. YOURS TRULY, HUCK FINN." Here is Huck's true voice. The book-long condemnation of "civilization" continues. Properly the condemnation is not direct nor is it in abstract terms. For Huck himself has never formulated the generalizations his story has implied. His condemnation takes the form of a characteristic concrete action. Again he is lighting out in search of freedom.

Though Twain finished the manuscript late in August, 1883, he did not send it off until the third week in April, 1884.[32] During more than seven months—with and without help from the family[33]—he apparently revised the partly typed partly holograph manuscript thoroughly. This guess is justified by the holograph, about three-fifths of the novel, in the Buffalo Public Library. It shows that not only did he make many revisions while writing, he also made three later revisions. Numerous changes also were made—some doubtless by Howells—between manuscript and book. About a thousand changes testify that he revised with great care. Nor do these tell the whole story. Handwriting, cancellations, and pagination show that many pages were inserted and many passages rewritten.

Collations have been reported by DeLancey Ferguson, Bernard DeVoto, and Sydney J. Krause.[34] DeVoto's great concern is with the question of Livy's, Howells', or Mark's bowdlerization. He finds thirty-seven "softenings," "changes . . . made in the direction of contemporary good taste," most of which "either diminish a violence or avoid unpleasantness"—"a sizable sum." My feeling is that proportionately the sum is small. Also I question that several he cites necessarily show queasiness. He feels that at one point the changes from "drunk" and "drunken" to "tighter" and "mellow" lessen their impact. I suggest that if this were so elsewhere Mark would not have allowed Pap, the circus rider, and Boggs all to continue to be blatantly "drunk." Again "the specific 'gin-mill,' " he says, "becomes the euphemistic 'doggery.' " I have trouble believing that "doggery" is euphemistic; the temperance crusader's term "gin-mill" would seem to be more appropriate for Carrie Nation than for Huck. DeVoto holds that overnicety makes Huck say "hawking and sp——" instead of "hawking and spitting": I hold that "spitting" is still suggested and that the curtailed word in the context is funnier. Ten more alleged softenings seem to me equally questionable. But extended argument seems unjustifiable, since in the end DeVoto concedes that such changes were "trifling" and "not important." After all the changes, passages from the novel had to be prettied up before publication in *Century Magazine* and the novel was barred from many libraries because it offended taste.

Much more important than signs of censorship, as Ferguson and Krause hold, are revelations (to quote the former) of "a skilled craftsman at work." Revisions and rewritings in practically every episode prove on examination to have artistic justification. They range from minute shifts in wording to extensive readjustments in the action and the tone.

The *Walter Scott* visit, for instance, Mark works hard to make less lurid and melodramatic. He removes a gag which—sensationally but purposelessly—has been stuffed into Turner's mouth; he excises theatrical details about a murder which Turner has committed; he scratches out a violent threat; he replaces with more characteristic understatements exaggerated remarks Huck makes about his fear and excitement. The removal of the gag makes possible the robbery of Turner and therefore emphasis upon the greed of his companions. And the insertion of all of Huck's recollections of Tom Sawyer causes the reader to compare real robbers with Tom's romanticizations.

The Wilks chapters also show much tinkering. By constantly making the king's language more vulgar and slangy, Mark makes the cheat's pretense that he is an English clergyman more transparent, his victims' gullibility more stupid. The king's two "tears and flapdoodle" speeches are changed to indirect discourse, though Huck still repeats all their clichés: the change enables the boy to characterize them and voice his disgust. The author inserts two pages which prepare for Huck's stealing of Peter's gold; later he inserts five which take care of important details about its disappearance.

The most interesting revisions are in three key passages: Sherburn's speech, Jim's remorseful recollection of his treatment of 'Lizabeth, and Huck's final struggle with his conscience.

In Sherburn's speech from the sentence "I know you clear through *to your chicken hearts*" and from the phrase "cast-out women . . . *lowering themselves to your level to earn a bite of bitter bread to eat,"* the metaphorical and (in the second passage) alliterative words which I have italicized are deleted. "I know the average man of the country, and the average man of the world" becomes "I know the average all around." "The average man of the world is a coward" becomes "The average man's a coward." "You are" is changed to "you're"; "courage" to "grit"; "broad daylight" to "the daytime." As Ferguson claims, these changes make passages which were "excessively rhetorical" less so. Colloquial phrasing is in character for even the leading citizen of Bricksville. More important, as revised the speech loses the highfalutin diction which in the book is a mark of insincerity.

Twain had finished chapter xxiii with general statements about Jim's love for his family and had moved into the next chapter when the inspiration came to use the story about "L. A." as a dramatic and concrete instance. Thus Jim's tale about his unjust punishment of 'Lizabeth, so important for illustrating and deepening the characterization and for developing the thought of the novel, represents backtracking.

It is clear that Huck's ultimate struggle with his conscience in chapter xxxi has been completely rewritten. In the rewriting Twain has given it increased emphasis by expanding it by about 150 words. Although most revisions consequently have disappeared, an instance which remains is revealing. A part of the original version which has been replaced but is still readable under lines scratching it out is the first draft of Huck's mournful lament: "I would take up wickedness again, which was in my line, being brung up to it." "What I had been getting ready for," it perhaps began. The canceled words are: "for, and longing for and pining for; always, day and night and Sundays, was a career of crime. And just that thing was the thing I was a-starting in on, now, for good and all." If this was representative, the original passage was in a burlesque vein and was frivolous in tone. The impressive quality of this memorable scene apparently was missing from its first writing, but was supplied by thorough revision and rewriting.[35]

Throughout the manuscript as throughout most of the book there is evidence of craftsmanship. Even the inferior escape chapters at the end, in general flowingly written, show frequent revisions and some rewritings. The most interesting of the latter is in chapter xliii—the testimony of the doctor to Jim's fine character. Again a canceled earlier passage shows the author overcoming an impulse to include broad comedy and instead having the doctor give a straightforward account, free from jests, which emphasizes Jim's nobility.

The testimony of the revisions, then, is that during the summer of 1883 and for seven months thereafter Mark was both writing and revising with affection and care. Perhaps this should not surprise us, for Mark Twain would not have been likely to put so much of himself into a book in which he took small pride. As his own publisher he could have published everything he wrote, but the scores of abandoned manuscripts which he left unpublished prove that he withheld issuance of those that did not satisfy him. Then there is the fact that his last two novels, comparatively, had not sold at all well—not *The Prince and the Pauper*, not even *Tom Sawyer*, which was in a vein similar to that of *Huckleberry Finn*.

There was a certain defiance in his letter to Howells on July 20, 1883, about this "big one": "And *I* shall like it, whether anybody else does or not." He soon found that Howells liked it very much, but he had to wait more than a year to learn whether the public did.

25

PUBLICATION

There is no date *for the book. It can issue the 1st of December if 40,000 have been sold. It must wait till they are sold, if it is seven years.—S. L. C. to Charles Webster, April 12, 1884.*

Considering how busy he was and how determined to supervise every step in the publication of *Huckleberry Finn,* one wonders that Clemens managed to get the book published in England and Canada on December 10, 1884, and in the United States on February 18, 1885.

Even before finishing the manuscript he had vaulted with typical enthusiasm into the invention and perfection of a History Game which, played on a sort of cribbage board, would help cram children's minds with names and dates. He was still perfecting this and writing letters about it when the book was published. In the fall of 1883 he inveigled Howells into coming to Hartford and collaborating on a very bad play about Colonel Sellers, and he then sent Webster traipsing around to try to get it staged. He told Webster "if the book business interferes with the dramatic business, drop the *former,* for it doesn't pay salt; and I want the latter rushed." [1] In this mood he dramatized *The Prince and the Pauper,* had a second try at dramatizing *Tom Sawyer,* and started Webster peddling the scripts. He began a story about a character called Bill Ragsdale, piling his billiard table with books about Bill's homeland the Sandwich Islands, and plastering his walls with notes. He had a sequel to *Huck* in mind, *Tom and Huck among the Indians;* he did some reading for it and may have written some of it.

He tried to perfect a patentable clamp which would keep infants from kicking off bedclothes. He negotiated with Ulysses S. Grant concerning the publication of Grant's memoirs. He continued to help Paige perfect and finance his typesetting machine. He learned to ride a bicycle. He angrily switched political parties and campaigned for Cleveland. He helped manufacture and sell some grape shears invented by Howells' father. He entertained Matthew Arnold and a Hindoo prelate named Protap Chunder Mazoomdar. And on November 5, 1884, he went on a wide-ranging lecture tour with George Washington Cable which did not end until after *Huck* was being distributed.

Publishing this book required even more supervision than previous ones because the author's own company issued it. Persuaded that the American Publishing Company had been cheating him for years, in 1881 Clemens had switched to Osgood as a publisher. Although *The Prince and the Pauper* had been hailed by critics as a triumph of scholarship, refinement, morality, and artistry, it had sold badly. Clemens had been stoical about this. But he had had such high hopes for *Life on the Mississippi* that he had arranged to turn publishing procedures for it upside down: he put up money to print and sell the book and paid Osgood a royalty. Nevertheless he blamed Osgood because the book cost him $50,000 and sold too few copies. "The publisher," he said, "who sells less than 50,000 copies of a book for me has merely injured me, he has not benefitted me." [2]

The unsatisfactory sales led Clemens to decide, soon after finishing *Huck,* that with all its faults the American Publishing Company was preferable to Osgood for the new book. So in September, 1883, he had Webster prepare to visit Hartford "as soon as shall seem wise" to arrange a contract.[3] On January 20, 1884, he decided that the time was ripe and had his agent negotiate.[4] Probably hoping to get back in one swoop what he believed the company had bilked him of, he demanded 60 per cent of the profits and was refused.[5] In February, therefore, after toying with the idea of using Osgood's imprint but publishing the novel himself, he made plans which Webster proudly told his mother-in-law and her son: "The next book ('Adventures of Huck Fin' [sic]) will be published by me and will bear the imprint Chas. L. Webster & Co. New York. This Co. is S.L.C. please say nothing of this at present." [6]

The author had written his English publishers Chatto and Windus on March 3 about his plans to publish in the fall. On March 18 the company urged that early proof sheets be sent to them so that they might "make a much better canvas with the booksellers" and "make several better bargains for various continental editions." The writer told Webster to oblige.[7]

Of course the manuscript had to go to good old Howells for editing. Howells had scrutinized all Twain's book manuscripts since 1875, except for *Life on the Mississippi* written when he was abroad, and even that the author regretted not having sent to him "to be edited, as usual." On April 10 Howells agreed, looking forward, he said, to enjoying a microscopic examination of a piece of writing he liked.[8] Not only did he read it: he arranged for a typist to make two copies up to a point "where another duplicate begins." The new copies too he read carefully, for on sending them to Webster he said, "You can work from either, for both are ready to go to the printer's hands." [9]

Meanwhile Webster had seen the manuscript, had counted the words, and had suggested an important change: "The book is so *much* larger than Tom Sawyer would it not be better to omit the old [Life on the] Mississippi matter?" [10] The author showed no disinclination: "Yes, I think the raft chapter can be left wholly out, by heaving in a paragraph to say Huck visited the raft to find out how far it might be to Cairo, but got no satisfaction. Even *this* is not necessary unless that raft-visit is referred to later in the book. I think it is, but am not certain." [11] Thus casually he deleted a chapter which one modern psychoanalytical critic has argued offers the best clue to the author's chief concern in the novel.

Webster tried two illustrators on some pictures. Reluctantly he gave up the idea of using Hooper, "a *very* cheap man," and signed E. W. Kemble, whose work Clemens had seen and liked in *Life*. Kemble, though only twenty-three years old, and eager for an assignment which would be the making of him, was not cheap: his price was $1,200.[12] Webster hurried him with drawings some of which he made from unedited manuscript, some without manuscript, and some from the copy after Howells had edited it.[13]

Clemens demanded that he see all the drawings and at first complained about them. Concerning the cover portrait of Huck he wrote: "All right and good, and will answer; although the boy's mouth is a trifle more Irishy than necessary." The frontispiece, which many consider a perfect picture of the boy, he thought had "an ugly, ill-drawn face." "Huck," he said, "is an exceedingly good-hearted boy, and should carry a good and good-looking face." In other illustrations "the people are forbidding and repulsive." Webster assured him that he thought the pictures would "come out all right" but promised that he would keep trying "to get better work out of Kemble." On July 1 Clemens admitted that "Kemble's pictures are mighty good, now." With such guidance the artist eventually came up to expectations. "I knew Kemble had it *in* him," wrote the author, "if he would only modify his violences and come down to careful, painstaking work. This batch of pictures is rattling good." About chapter xv the pictures of characters in general get handsomer, and Huck as a rule is rather prettier and younger than most modern readers will feel he should be. Clemens' puritanism led him to decide that, although the illustrations were admirable, one of them would not do. "But you must knock out one of them—the lecherous old rascal kissing the girl at the campmeeting. It is powerful good, but it mustn't go in—don't forget it. Let's not make any pictures of the campmeeting. The subject won't *bear* illustrating. It is a disgusting thing, and pictures are sure to tell the truth about it too plainly." [14] Another illustration needed correcting: "misled by some of Huck's remarks about the boat's 'texas'—a thing which is a part of *every* boat," Kemble had labeled the *Walter Scott*

"TEXAS," and this should be changed.[15] This ended Clemens' comments on the art work.

Webster had estimates on printing costs by May 29 and, though he consulted his employer about the contract and every other matter of cost and timing, by mid-July he promised that he would soon have "everything, cuts and all, in the printers hands." By July 26 page proofs were coming along, although the printer still could modify the title page on that date.[16]

In her biography of her father Susie Clemens pictures the reading of proofs (which she calls the manuscript) at Quarry Farm:

Papa read *Huckleberry Finn* to us . . . just before it came out, and then he would leave parts of it with mama to expergate while he went off to the study to work, and sometimes Clara and I would be sitting with mama while she was looking the manuscript over, and I remember so well, with what pangs of regret we used to see her turn down the leaves . . . , which meant that some delightfully terrible part must be scratched out. And I remember one part pertickularly which was perfectly fascinating it was so terrible, that Clara and I used to delight in and oh with what despair we saw mama turn down the leaf on which it was written, we thought the book would almost be ruined without it. But we gradually came to think as mama did.

Susie's father recalled the occasion but not the sentence or phrase. It may have been one, he says, "cunningly devised and put into the book" to inspire discussion and without "hope or expectation that it would get by the 'expergator' alive."

Howells saw no need for either him or Mark to read proofs. "I read the copy so carefully that a good proof-reader's revision is all that is now necessary," he wrote Webster.[17] And he asked the author, "Why need *you* read Huck Finn proofs? . . . If I'd supposed they were going to send them to you I would have read them again myself." [18] The question was prompted by a wail about proofs in a recent letter. Mark said that while proofs were fairly clean, the mistakes that did occur made him curse his teeth loose. About five weeks later he was so distressed by the mere sight of a package of proofs that without opening it he readdressed it and shipped it to Howells, apologizing for the imposition and telling him not to read them unless he did not mind.[19] Good old Howells, accommodating as always, said, "If I had written half as good a book as Huck Finn, I shouldn't ask anything better than to read the proofs; even as it is I don't." He read two installments and by his count had read the novel "nearly all through" four times before it was published. But despite the groaning, the author depended upon Howells to read only a small portion of the page proofs and read the rest himself, finishing by the end of August.[20]

A few page proofs and plate proofs survive.[21] A run of the former with even-numbered folios seems to indicate that in response to Webster's request, through parts of the Bricksville chapters Twain proofread the running heads and the picture captions which—in addition to the table of contents—his nephew had written.[22] There are few revisions in the surviving page proofs, all in response to proofreaders' inquiries: on page 160 "I found a canoe" is substituted for "I took a canoe"; on page 164, "the duke" (who speaks a line) is substituted for "Baldy" (i.e., the king); on page 188 "stouping" is corrected to "stooping." On pages 143 and 157 realignments in the typesetting of the initial word in each of two chapters are indicated; then the marking is crossed out.

On September 13 the author airily concluded that he would like to add a portrait of himself. Karl Gerhardt, a young sculptor whom he had met in 1881 and whose study in Paris he had financed since that year, returned to America and proceeded to Elmira. There he made a bust of his benefactor, and the writer decided he would like to include a photograph of it at the start of the novel. Webster agreed that it would help the sale of the book and found that it would cost only 2.4 cents a copy. So he had a heliotype firm prepare a plate and the portrait was inserted.[23]

Unbound sheets exclusive of this portrait were available by September 19, since on that date Webster reported that he had sent a set to Chatto and Windus and was "getting up a set of plates the same as ours (because cheaper) for Dawson," the Canadian publisher.[24] The next day Clemens wrote that he hoped he would find "an *unbound* copy" awaiting him in Hartford on his return from Elmira so that he might mark "select readings from it for the platform." [25]

Meanwhile, pausing frequently to cope with the barrages of letters and commissions with which his employer bombarded him, Webster was making the intricate preparations necessary for issuing "a subscription book." Like Mark Twain's most successful volumes since 1869, *Huck* was to be sold initially not by stores but by agents going from house to house. Circulars had to be prepared to inform such canvassers of the wonderful chance to mint money the book would afford. Then the lucky agents had to be chosen and prospectuses had to be readied for them to show potential customers.[26] To start virtually from scratch—simultaneously keeping the author satisfied—required prodigious energy and effort. Webster was prepared to furnish both.

He paid $55.60 for the printing of the circulars on August 8.[27] These contained as major headlines: "Mark Twain's Latest Book./ The Adventures of/ HUCKLEBERRY FINN,/ Tom Sawyer's Comrade," and, in other headlines between passages in smaller type, stressed these features: "Every Line Fresh and New;" "Written in Mark Twain's Old Style"; "A Book for the Young and the Old, the Rich and the Poor"; "A Mine of Humor." And the flyer assured agents that "Mark Twain's Books are the Quickest Selling in the World" having sold "Five Hundred and Twenty-Five Thousand (over Half a Million) in this Country alone . . ." and that the volume would be "sold only by subscription." Then the prices were listed: $2.75 in "fine cloth binding"; $3.25 in "leather library style"; $4.25 in "half morocco, marbled edges." (On the West Coast prices were $3.50, $4.00, and $5.50 for comparable bindings.) A sheet enclosed headed "Confidential Terms for Agents" offered a "Magnificent and Unparalleled Offer to Canvassers": on selling fifty books an agent would get five additional copies free and after that 10 per cent of the number sold free. Agents in the East would get profits of $1.10, $1.30, and $1.70 per book depending upon the type of binding.[28]

On September 1 Webster wrote that he expected prospectuses the following week.[29] Those which I have seen have green cloth bindings identical with that of the first edition and contain samples of back strips in other bindings, the frontispiece picture

(Form 3.)

CONFIDENTIAL TERMS TO AGENTS.

MARK TWAIN'S NEW BOOK:

"ADVENTURES OF HUCKLEBERRY FINN."

TOM SAWYER'S COMPANION.

MAGNIFICENT AND UNPARALLELED OFFER TO CANVASSERS.
A CHANCE TO MAKE MONEY, FOR ALL.

To every Canvasser selling *fifty* copies of the book, we will send *five* additional copies *free*.
To every Canvasser selling *one hundred* copies of the book, we will send *Ten* additional copies *free*.
To every Canvasser selling *one hundred and fifty* copies of the book, we will send *fifteen* additional copies *free*.
To every Canvasser selling *Two Hundred* copies of the book, we will send *twenty* additional copies *free*.

For all sales above two hundred copies, agents will receive *five copies free* for every *fifty* copies sold.
To take advantage of the above unprecedented offer, the books must all be sold to bona fide subscribers, at the full retail price.

The above Premiums are entirely in addition to the liberal discounts offered below.

HARD FACTS!

Five Hundred and Twenty-five Thousand (over Half a Million) Copies Mark Twain's Books

Have been sold in *this country alone ; to say nothing of the immense* sales in England and Germany.

MARK TWAIN'S BOOKS ARE THE QUICKEST SELLING IN THE WORLD.

AGENTS! SECURE EASY WORK AND SURE PAY BY GETTING A MARK TWAIN AGENCY.

HOW TO GET AN AGENCY.

Among the circulars sent, you will notice one in blank, headed "APPLICATION FOR AGENCY." You will fill this out, naming the amount enclosed and the book and territory wanted. To each agent is given a certain field, and he must not canvass outside the prescribed limits. His first choice of territory is given him if it is not already assigned ; if it is, his second or third choice is given : provided he gives us satisfactory evidence of his ability and experience to work the territory, and conduct the agency successfully—we reserving the right to cancel the agency if not so conducted. Upon the receipt of this "APPLICATION FOR AGENCY," properly filled out, with proper amount inclosed for outfit, the territory asked for is assigned, the outfit forwarded, and the applicant informed that he has an agency and the sole and the exclusive sale of the book in the territory assigned. If he is a new agent, advice is given him how to get to work and such other instructions as will guarantee success.

OUTFIT FOR CANVASSING.

This consists of a Bound Prospectus book, fully representing the work. Showing the Style of Binding, Paper, Size of Page, Type, Engravings, etc., etc., also Circulars, Blanks, Notices, and a Private Instruction-Book, teaching the agent how to proceed with the business.

THESE ARE SENT POST-PAID FOR 75 CENTS,
Which must invariably accompany all orders for Canvassing books.

☞ POSITIVELY NO PROSPECTUSES GIVEN AWAY. ☜
The amount paid for outfit deducted on first order of ten or more copies.

WE FURNISH BOOKS TO AGENTS AS FOLLOWS :

			Retail Prices.	To Agents.	Agents' Profit.
In Fine English Cloth Binding, Plain Edges,			$2.75 style,	$1.65	$1.10
Leather Library	"	Sprinkled "	3.25 "	1.95	1.30
Half Morocco	"	Marbled "	4.25 "	2.55	1.70

Although this is a companion book to "Adventures of Tom Sawyer," yet *each* book is *complete* in itself.

Some parties however wish both books. In order to accommodate all such, we offer to supply them in *blue* cloth bindings *only*, at the greatly reduced price of $4.75 per set retail ; furnishing them to the agent at $2 80 per set; agent's profit $1.95. We also furnish "The Prince and The Pauper," and "Adventure of Huckleberry Finn," in *green* cloth *only*, at $5.00 per set retail ; furnishing them to the agent at $3.00; agents profit, $2.00.

☞ SPECIAL ADDITIONAL INDUCEMENTS ☜

We will charge you nothing for *packing boxes.*
We will pay exchange on drafts when amount is over $20.00.
We will pay charges on money sent us by Express when amount is over $20.00.
We will furnish all books given to editors for notices at one-half Agents' prices, but in every instance a copy of the paper containing the notice, for which a book is wanted, must be received by us.
We allot Agents certain specified territory to canvass. No other Agent is allowed to go into that territory, so long as the Agent to whom it is assigned canvasses satisfactorily and abides by our rules and regulations.
We sell the book exclusively by subscription, and every Agent pledges to do the same.
Finally, we give you a book the people want, by the greatest living humorist in the world.
If you can act as Agent for us, please signify your willingness at your earliest possible convenience. If unable to do so, *please oblige us* by handing this to some *intelligent person* of your acquaintance, whom you think might be willing to act for us in your stead. The *very reasonable price* of this work brings it within the reach of all classes. Those applying immediately, with remittances, will secure a choice territory.
When you write us, please give your POST OFFICE address in full, naming the TOWNSHIP as well as the COUNTY in which you live Please name the territory that you prefer to canvass ; also say where or in what paper you saw the advertisement that induced you to send for this circular.
Hoping that you will at once engage with us in the sale of this most valuable and popular work, we remain very respectfully yours.

CHAS. L. WEBSTER & CO., Publishers,

(OVER.)

658 Broadway, New York.

of Huck, tables of contents and of illustrations, and seventy-three pages of text meant to whet but not appease the appetite. The passages are brief (none longer than four consecutive pages) and they play up sensational and comic scenes.[30] The gorier scenes include the visit to the house of death, the adventure on the *Walter Scott*, the feud, the death of Boggs, Sherburn's speech to the mob, the lynching of the king and the duke. Comic selections include Huck's experiences at the widow's, Pap's reformation, Hank Bunker's story, the chat about Sollerman, Emmeline's pictures and her ode, the introductory speeches of the king and the duke, the comic undertaker, and several passages about Jim's escape. The booklet ends with two pages of advertising mostly lifted from the circular and some blank pages hopefully supplied for subscribers to order books.

A year before these were ready both Clemens and his manager had started making plans for the great final step—the selling of the book. Upon completing the novel the author had thought of issuing it in May, 1884, but this proved to be a typical unreasonable estimate of the time it took either to write or publish a book. He did not send the manuscript to Webster until April 12, 1884. By that time, he claimed, he had repeated thirty times to his manager a rule for publishing *Huck:* "The book is to be issued when a big edition has been sold—and not before. . . . There is *no date* for the book. It can be issued the 1st of December if 40,000 copies have been sold. It must wait until they *are* sold, if it is seven years." Two days later he himself mentioned dates—"the 10th (or 15th) of next December"—but repeated that regardless of the date 40,000 copies had to be sold; and May 23, July 15, and December 22 he went over the same ground.[31]

Webster reported on advance orders September 2, 1884. Despite the fact that this was a campaign year and consequently dull for business, "I think the book is going to sell well": "Watson Gill has agreed to take 4000 copies which is 500 more than he sold last year of Mississippi. Thompson & Co. of Boston have agreed to take 5000 copies which is 800 more than they have sold on Miss. to date. . . . The Gen. Agts. who have been in the office and who have seen the specimens of the book are confident that it will sell better than any recent one of yours. . . ."[32]

That fall Webster made a wide cross-country sweep "seeing the men, showing them the book [i.e., a dummy], and talking it down to them." He found that although prospective agents at first objected that the terms which the circular called "Magnificent" and "Unparalleled" were not—but "when I show them the book they itch for it, and then the [offer of a] rebate fixes them. I don't set the number to be sold [before the rebate starts] beyond the reach of possibility, if they attend to business, but the figures are much beyond last years sales I assure you. They all seem confident that they will reach the point, and if they do you will have cause to rejoice." [33] He took two weeks working out to Chicago, then went from there to St. Paul, Keokuk, St. Louis, Council Bluffs, Denver, Salt Lake City, and San Francisco, stopping two days in each. On the return trip he stopped in Galveston and New Orleans and probably other cities. "It is," he said believably enough, "*hard* work." [34]

Shortly before or after this trip Webster made a horrifying discovery: ribaldry, so carefully excluded by Mark Twain from his published works, had invaded the printed pages of *Huckleberry Finn*. A front-page headline in the New York *World* for November 27—Thanksgiving day, ironically enough—read: "MARK TWAIN IN A DILEMA [*sic*]—A Victim of a Joke He Thinks the Most Unkindest Cut of All." The long story which followed showed that "the Most Unkindest Cut" was a cruel pun, for the gist was that a cut illustrating the novel and included in the prospectus had been so altered as to contain "a glaring indecency":

The title of the cut was, "In a Dilema; What Shall I Do?"

When the plate was sent to the electrotyper, a wicked spirit must have possessed him. The title was suggestive. A mere stroke of the awl would suffice to give the cut an indecent character never intended by the author or engraver. It would make no difference in the surface that would be visible to the naked eye, but when printed would add to the engraving a characteristic that would be repudiated not only by the author, but by all the respectable people of the country into whose hands the volume would fall. The work of the engraver . . . passed the eye of the inspector and was approved. A proof was taken and submitted. If the alteration was manifested in the proof it was evidently attributed to a defect in the press and paper, which would be remedied when the volume was sent to the press. . . .

The cut, the story continued, was included in some 3,000 prospectuses with which agents were marching into pure American homes when—

At last a letter came from a Chicago agent calling attention to the cut. Then there was consternation in the office of the publishers . . . such an illustration would condemn the work. Immediately all the papers were telegraphed to, and the prospectuses were called in. The page containing the cut was torn from the book, a new and perfect illustration being substituted. Agents were supplied with the improved volumes and are now happy in canvassing for a work to which there can be no objection. . . . But the story leaked out. Several opposition publishers got hold of the cut . . . and they now adorn their respective offices.[35]

There are inaccuracies in this: the altered illustration is not described quite correctly; the title is wrong. It is hard to see why papers would be "telegraphed to" if, as the story implies, the publishers did not want the news to leak out. But the caption just above the illustration on page 283 was "In a Dilemma"; and J. J. Little, whose plant produced the book, in time verified other details.[36]

The New York *Tribune* of November 29 had a somewhat different story. Webster, it said, had his attention called to the defacement "in San Francisco a few days ago"; he telegraphed at once and stopped publication, and the discovery "saved the first edition of 30,000." The same day the New York *Herald* announced Webster's offer of a $500 reward "for the apprehension and conviction" of the jocose engraver. It reported an interview:

Mr. Webster said yesterday: "The book was examined before the final printing by W. D. Howells, Mr. Clemens, the proof-reader and myself. Nothing improper was discovered. On page 283 was a small illustration with the subscription 'Who do you reckon it is?' By the punch of an awl or graver, the illustration became an immoral one. But 250 copies left the office, I believe, before the mistake was discovered. Had the first edition been run off our loss would have been $250,000. Had the mistake not been discovered, Mr. Clemens' credit for decency and morality would have been destroyed.

Some statements in these stories are verifiable. Webster had been in San Francisco recently. The first printing numbered 30,000 copies.[37] If the 250 copies were prospectuses, supporting evidence is the fact that one of these containing the mutilated picture exists. And if only prospectuses had gone out, Webster might properly say the discovery "saved the first edition."

The facts were even more horrible than the *Herald*'s account indicates. Although engraver's proofs had not shown a defacement, Howells, Clemens, the proofreader, and Webster had seen page proofs or press proofs or both which did.[38] Almost certainly, some two months earlier, Clemens had received one or more sets of advance sheets containing it. One such set which G. W. Cable evidently received by October 13 is owned by Clifton Waller Barrett.[39]

The author was on tour in the vicinity of New York when the defacement was discovered.[40] If Webster hurried to him for a consultation (this would explain why no letter about the matter survived in the Mark Twain Papers), one would like to have a record of the profanity inspired by the revelation. Clemens' having his carefully nurtured reputation jeopardized by a prank and having publication postponed so that *Huck* would miss the Christmas trade [41] offered unparalleled justification.

The illustration showed Uncle Silas with his pelvis thrust forward, Aunt Sally looking sidewise at her spouse and grinning. The prankster with his awl or graver—surely with more than one stroke—drew a *penis erectus* (or was it a gosling with head and neck protruding from the man's fly?) at the appropriate place.[42]

J. J. Little told how his printing plant handled the problem: ". . . thousands of copies of the book were in the plant . . . a new sheet was run off with a reengraved plate to eliminate the damage, and . . . these sheets were tipped in, using a stub of the excised page. In the unbound copies whole signatures were printed and supplied in the regular manner of binding." [43] If taking these measures postponed publication in New York beyond the holiday period the huge size of the first printing must have been an important cause. In England advance sheets with the picture had to be changed before a cut was made; and in Canada the publishers, Dawson Brothers, had to reëngrave the plate.[44] But in both countries where initial printings were smaller *Huck* came out in time for the Christmas trade.

On December 6 Webster told Clemens: "I write to remind you that you must be in Canada on Wednesday Dec 10th from noon until 5 P.M. . . . Don't leave Canadian soil until 5 P.M. . . . I am going to Montreal Monday [December 8]."[45] This visit satisfied the requirement that an author be "domiciled" on British soil to secure a British copyright—a formula which Clemens had discovered in 1883. He was in Fort Erie, presumably until 5 P.M., when the novel was copyrighted "by Andrew Chatto,

REPAIRED ILLUSTRATION FOR

PAGE 283

in the Office of the Minister of Agriculture" on December 10. That same day the book was received at the British Museum. Certification of copyright was entered in Ottawa on January 7, 1885.[46]

In the United States ten copies were specially bound for copyright purposes by December 13 and copyright was secured.[47] But the book was not published until February 18, 1885.[48]

English and Canadian first editions of *Huck* therefore were the first. But the problem of determining "the first issue" of the New York first edition has stirred up the most tempestuous argument in which American bibliophiles have engaged. Printer's ink, vituperation, and complicated reasoning have flowed like water during attacks and counterattacks. At the height of the conflict during the 1930's "one of the contestants was so stirred that, in all seriousness, he offered to hire Carnegie Hall that he might publicly debate the bibliographic points. . . ."[49] Preferring to dis-

cuss the complex matter more privately I have placed a few remarks I have to make about it in an appendix.

Stories about the mutilated illustration publicized *Huck,* though
not in ways its author liked. On his lecture tour between November 13, 1884, and February 28, 1885, Mark was giving the book
more favorable publicity by reading excerpts with his inimitable
artistry in many parts of the United States and Canada. Favorite
passages included Huck's and Jim's talks about Sollerman and
French speech and the account of the rescue of Jim—often favorably mentioned in reviews.[50]

Portions of the novel suitably revised for genteel readers were
published in the *Century:* the feud chapters in December, 1884;
Jim's and Huck's Biblical discussion in January, 1885; and chapters about the king and the duke the following month.[51] The New
York *Tribune* of January 11 and the Chicago *Times* of that date
published excerpts, and perhaps other newspapers did.

In the winter of 1885 the author bethought himself of magazine
reviews and gave Webster varied instructions: send prominent
journals and magazines copies a day or two after the book issues,
perhaps unbound copies to "prominent *magazines* NOW" (January 23); send unbound copies "to the magazines, now" (January
26); send copies to newspapers only after the *Century* or the
Atlantic has reviewed the book (January 27); "we must talk over
the propriety of sending out 300 copies to the press *early*—say
Feb. 23rd—without waiting for the magazines" (February 8);
send out copies, bound and unbound, to selected newspapers and
if notices are favorable "send out your 300 press notices over the
land" (February 10). Webster replied on February 14: "In regard to the press notices of the book: That was not overlooked,
you remember you told me in the start that press notices *hurt*
the last book before it was out and that this year we would send
none until the book was out. I have sent the notices that you have
suggested." [52]

In the same letter Webster reported on a dozen other matters
including the Perpetual Calendar and the Historical Game. Also
he gave his latest information about a lawsuit concerning the

sale of *Huck* which had just terminated. Estes and Lariat, a book-selling firm, had advertised in their holiday catalogue copies of the novel for sale at from $2.25 to 50 cents less than agents were quoting as the price.[53] Clemens had received the catalogue, had torn out the offending page, and had penned an indignant letter in which he enclosed it to Webster: they were telling "a purely malicious lie" and should be sued or at least published "as thieves and swindlers"—preferably sued. He had proceeded to sue and had lost.[54]

What was involved was an old problem in the subscription book game. The publisher promised agents, as Webster had, that books must be sold "by subscription only." But some traitorous agents would peddle copies to the trade at discounts, and bookstore sales discouraged the canvassers. So subscription publishers fought to keep their volumes away from bookstores. It had been so with *Life on the Mississippi.* On August 16, 1883, Webster had reported that he and his staff were rushing to shops trying to buy all copies offered in New York by eight booksellers; on September 1 he had told of cleaning out trade copies in New York but of having heard that Western bookstores were selling copies; on September 6 he had suspended some Philadelphia agents for "putting books in the trade." [55]

A letter of October 25, however, offers a strange contrast: Webster then reported to his employer that he was trotting around to bookstores to ask them kindly how many copies of *Life on the Mississippi* they would like to buy; he was pleased to find a lively demand, and he urged delivery in December. And on October 30 he happily announced that he had signed Watson Gill "to act as my agent in the trade" "as far west as Kansas City and as far south as Washington for 7½% on all sales to bookstores." [56]

The reason for the turnabout was this: while publishers agreed to sell "by subscription only," they did so no longer when it ceased to pay; at the proper moment they "dumped" copies into trade channels. As Clemens explained to Osgood, "Yes, sir, I think a subscription book has just two lives: One drawn from the public *before* issuing; and one drawn from the trade. *after*." [57] A note-book entry shows that he planned to tell Osgood to "let the dump fall" at a specified time.[58] For a time therefore in the winter of 1884–85 Webster doubtless was selling all the copies of *Life on the Mississippi* he could to bookstores and simultaneously fighting tooth and nail to keep any dealers from getting copies of *Huckleberry Finn*. Then shortly—I have not learned how soon— *Huck* was being eagerly offered to bookstores.[59]

I have quoted Webster's figures on orders from general agents by September 2, 1884—9,000 copies. On December 13, 1884, he was less specific but still optimistic: "Reports from agents show good sales and the book is doing all that could be expected in these hard times." The next report I have found, dated March 14, 1885, shows that a few days short of a month after publication he had sold 39,000 copies; he had orders bringing up the total to 45,000; he planned to bring the total printed to 50,000. "We," he boasted, "are beating the old books." On March 18 he wrote: "We have sold *another* 1000 'Hucks,' making 42,000 sold to date and been out *just* a month today." On March 24: "We have sold about 1500 'Hucks' since [March 21]." [60] On May 6 he reported to his brother-in-law: "Sam I have already sold 51,000 of Huck." Somewhat less than fourteen months after publication, therefore, the sales in proportion to the population were roughly the equivalent of about 163,200 copies today. This is the last definite figure from Webster which I have found, although on April 22, 1886, he told his uncle, "Huck Finn is . . . selling right along a good steady sale." [61]

The book sales were off to a fine start.

26

HUCKA, KHŎK, HUNCKLE, GEKKELBERRI...

"Now which of your own books do you like best?"
"Well, I think 'Huckleberry Finn.'"
"I hope you have not killed Tom, Huck and Jim; we
long to hear of them again."
Mark Twain's eyes twinkled, and with a dry chuckle he
gave the English equivalent for the Spaniards' "Quen
sabe," who knows, as if the trusty trio were mighty hard
to kill.—The South Australian Register, *October 14, 1895.*

Impressive at the time, that initial sale of 51,000 copies of *Huckleberry Finn* during its first fourteen months now looks puny. For the book was destined to become one of the most popular American novels of all time in the United States and throughout the world. Any estimate of the world-wide circulation of a book is risky. Yet figures on editions, adaptations, and translations back up a guess that 10,000,000 copies of *Huck* in various forms have been published. And in its seventy-fifth year it was selling more briskly and attracting more readers than ever.

Only fragmentary returns on sales after that initial period are available for some time.[1] That sales were comparatively good is

indicated by a report of Fred Hall, manager of the Webster Company, on March 10, 1893, to Clemens that "certainly" sales of the
novel "for the past two years show that there is a field for your
books in the trade." [2] Since 1893 was a panic year this testified
to *Huck's* staying powers.

Also the Webster firm was in difficulties—not entirely because
of its operations: Clemens had drained away much money to
invest in the Paige machine. Then too the company, pioneering
in the sale of books by installment, was caught in the credit
squeeze. Sales of *Huck* and other books by Twain could not keep
the firm from executing assignment papers carrying the author
into bankruptcy with it on April 18, 1894. Luckily, H. H. Rogers,
Standard Oil financier, took charge of Clemens' snarled affairs
and at the start prevented him from assigning his copyrights to
creditors. When business returned to normal again this proved
wise: from 1903 until the author died in 1910 his annual royalties
never fell below $25,000 and sometimes reached $50,000. As late
as 1958 his annual royalties yielded $22,000 to the Estate.[3]

For a time two companies, American Publishing and Harper
and Brothers, were issuing *Huck*. Partial reports from both indicate that between January 1, 1899, and October 31, 1904, about
65,000 copies were sold.[4] These somewhat overlap another set of
figures. Beginning October 22, 1903, Harper and Brothers acquired all Mark Twain copyrights. In 1908 the author totaled
sales made by the firm during four years. *Huck,* second only to
Innocents Abroad, had sold more than 41,000 copies.[5]

The period may have been a good one for *Huck* despite the
fact that 1907 was the year of a formidable panic. When the Concord library banned the novel on its appearance Twain gleefully
predicted "that will sell 25,000 copies for us sure"; and James D.
Hart in *The Popular Book* awards the novel the honor of being the
first lifted to best sellerdom by being prohibited in Massachusetts.[6]
Between 1902 and 1907 libraries in Denver, Omaha, Brooklyn,
and other cities were publicizing the book by excluding it from
their shelves.[7]

There is another hiatus in statistics showing exact American
sales beginning in 1908. Figures on the number of editions issued,

however, indicate sales continued steadily until 1930 and then improved:

Period	Editions	Period	Editions
1885–1900	7	1931–1940	21
1901–1910	5	1941–1950	29
1911–1920	6	1951–1958	14
1921–1930	6	1885–1958	88

(These include fifteen abridgments, adaptations, and dramatizations between 1931 and 1958.) Probably in part because 1935 was Mark's centennial, the number jumped in the 1930's, and certainly the fact that the book went out of copyright in 1940 had much to do with the spurt during the following decade. Nevertheless the alacrity of the publishers testified to a continuing demand. The decrease in the number of editions during the 1950's does not necessarily indicate a decrease in sales: many editions of previous decades were being reprinted, and a number printed were inexpensive cloth or paperbacks. Fourteen editions at prices ranging from 15 cents to $1.75 were available in 1959, and a new paperback edition was announced.

The novel also appeared in volumes containing other works of Mark Twain. It was combined with *Tom Sawyer* in inexpensive formats in 1940 by the Modern Library; in 1940, 1943, and 1944 editions by Everyman (Dutton); in 1945 by Norton. The first has sold "between 2,500 and 10,000 copies a year," [8] a minimum of 52,500, and since the book is a best seller in its series a guess of 75,000 copies is reasonable. A costlier combination of the two books issued by Heritage in 1952 has totaled 20,000 copies. Circulation of an omnibus containing *Huck, The Family Mark Twain* (Harper and Brothers, 1935), was stimulated by publicity attending the centenary and by the sanction of the Book-of-the-Month Club: it remained in print in 1958. With about 300 pages lopped off as *The Favorite Works of Mark Twain* it was issued at a bargain price by Garden City and went through several printings. *Huck* also was included in *The Portable Mark Twain*, ed. Bernard DeVoto, printed by Viking in 1946, 1950, 1953, 1955 (when a second paperback edition was added), 1956, and 1958; and sales reached a total of 84,500 copies.[9] And it was included with novels by other authors in *Four Great American Novels,* ed. Raymond W. Short (Holt, 1946), still in print in 1958. When these editions are added to those of *Huck* alone the number containing the story complete or in adaptations is 113.

The demand for such collections reflects the general interest in Mark Twain, and that bears on interest in Mark's masterpiece. In 1935 to determine the humorist's popularity Charles H. Crompton collected figures on books and circulation in five scattered public libraries—approximate in Chicago and New York, exact in St. Louis, Newark, and Boston. In the last three Twain's works outnumbered those of runner-up Sinclair Lewis two to one. Examining the data and questioning librarians, Crompton decided that "if St. Louis is typical of other parts of America, Mark Twain is today the most widely read American author, living or dead." The book by Twain which in St. Louis in 1934 attracted the most readers was *Huckleberry Finn.*[10]

Another indicator of popular interest and also a stimulator of such interest is the motion picture. Paramount in 1918 released *Tom and Huck,* in 1920 *Huckleberry Finn* as silent pictures. Paramount did a version with sound in 1931, Metro-Goldwyn-Mayer one in 1939. In 1959 the newly formed Shenandoah Company planned *Huck* as its first release and Metro-Goldwyn-Mayer was readying a version. Since the latter company had improved on Mark Twain by eliminating Tom Sawyer from its script, had had the inspiration to sign a champion prizefighter to play Jim, and had readied some popular songs for insertion here and there, prospects for a faithful adaptation were bright. Television also once or twice has offered dramatizations purportedly of the novel.

The most concrete evidence of American interest in *Huckleberry Finn* is offered by a few publishers who have provided figures on copies printed. Harper and Brothers have made two estimates: in 1934 "more than a million," presumably including sales by other companies;[11] in 1958 (with figures on editions before 1914 unavailable) "584,000 copies since publication [by Harpers] in 1896," an estimate which the firm believes to be "fairly close."[12]

Several firms have been brisk competitors. Grosset and Dunlap for instance issued editions in 1939 and 1940 which by 1941 had totaled 118,000 copies; [13] data on later printings of these and on two 1948 editions if available would swell totals considerably. Goldsmith's 1940 edition by 1957 had achieved estimated sales of 500,000.[14] A Rinehart edition of 1948 within eleven years had seventeen printings totaling 292,293.[15] Beginning in 1950 Pocket Books, Inc., issued three editions adding up to 529,000 copies.[16] These last four editions were paperbacks at 65 cents, 25 cents, and 35 cents. For 15 cents in 1959 one could buy a comic-strip adaptation issued in the "Classics Illustrated Series" by Gilbertson Company—"not one of our best sellers . . . but a consistent one"— two editions of which (1945, 1956) have sold 1,800,000 copies.[17] At the opposite extreme in price was a Heritage Press edition of 1940 illustrated by Norman Rockwell which added up to about 60,000 copies before *Huck* was combined with *Tom* in 1952.

Excluding abridgments and adaptations I have very fragmentary figures on three editions, publishers' estimates or reasonably complete reports on forty editions. They total 2,472,632. This includes five limited editions averaging 1,800 copies. It does not include fifty-three moderately priced editions some of which probably sold very well (e.g., Grosset and Dunlap, Everyman, Whitman, Garden City). A total of 5,000,000 copies for all editions would seem a conservative estimate.

I have figures on six abridgments and adaptations of *Huckleberry Finn* published in the United States since 1931: they total 1,872,369 copies. I have no figures on nine such publications. A total of 2,500,000 copies for all these would seem conservative. How many should really count as publications of *Huck* it is impossible to say: they range from "atrocious" to "fair." Add the lot to legitimate editions and the total is 7,500,000 copies of *Huck* in one form or another issued in America.

Sales appear to be increasing. Of the Rinehart edition the first seven printings through that of October 31, 1952, averaged 9,642; the next three through October 28, 1954, were 15,000 each; the last seven through December 7, 1958, have averaged 25,572. Between 1946 and November 22, 1957, Viking had printed 55,000 copies of the *Portable Mark Twain;* by February 9, 1959, it had printed 29,500 additional copies. The 1950 Pocket Books edition was 99,000; the 1953, 100,000; the 1955, 300,000; and an official of the company writes, "This book is increasing in popularity each year. . . ."

Other evidence of mounting interest in the novel appears in critical magazines and learned journals. In 1932 in *Mark Twain's America* DeVoto complained that *Huck* had been almost completely ignored by critics and scholars. Beginning in the late 1940's this lack has been remedied with a vengeance. By the end of 1960 critics and scholars will have published within a fifteen-year period more than a hundred lengthy discussions of the novel.[18] At the moment no other book in American literature seems to interest so many teachers in high schools, colleges, and universities. A result is certain to be an increase in the number of readers in schools and colleges, some of course under duress.

Figures on English sales of *Huckleberry Finn* are scant since in England even publishers appear to be reticent. A few royalty statements which Clemens kept by chance show that published copies of the first English edition priced at 7/6 reached 13,000 by April, 1888. By 1909 an edition at 3/6 added up to 14,500 copies; one at 2/ 40,000; one at 6d 50,000. Having achieved a total of 118,000 before 1909, *Huck* had outdistanced other books by Twain issued by Chatto and Windus by sizable margins.[19] One other set of figures is available: George C. Harrup in 1924 published an edition which went through twenty-two printings totaling 107,800 copies by 1955.[20] Scant though they are, these figures indicate a continuing demand. Additional evidence of the appeal of the novel in the nineteenth century was its popularity in that very active pacifier of popular appetites, Mudie's circulating library.[21]

The number of English editions is indicative of continuing interest:

Period	Editions	Period	Editions
1884–1900	5	1931–1940	11
1901–1910	3	1941–1950	6
1911–1920	3	1951–1958	3
1921–1930	6	1884–1958	37

Again the author's centennial probably explains the boom in the 1930's. British publishers did not respond as American publishers did to news that the book was in the public domain: perhaps they were lacking in the American spirit of free enterprise; certainly recovering from World War II was more difficult for England than it was for the United States.

Still, if novelists and critics have been capable of stirring public interest in England the novel has done very well. Even before the book was published in the United States the London *Saturday Review* offered a discussion of *Huck* more laudatory than any which appeared in America for the next decade or so.[22] Kipling at a high point in his fame in 1899 published in a book an interview with Clemens full of praise which he had recorded when he was twenty-two; later he would acknowledge that *Huck* was the inspiration of his *Kim*. Andrew Lang in 1891 wrote at length about the American novel, calling it "a flawless gem"; Sir Walter Besant, another very influential critic, in 1900 named Mark Twain as his favorite novelist and *Huck* as Twain's finest book; William Archer in 1901 asserted that "if any work of incontestable genius . . . plainly destined for immortality" had appeared during the last quarter century, *Huckleberry Finn* was that book.[23] In 1907, when Oxford granted the humorist a Litt. D., his visit to England was a triumphant progress. In 1942, therefore, George Stuart Gordon had some reason to gloat because, before America did, England managed to recognize Twain as an "authentic man of genius" and to appreciate his masterpiece as belonging "among the greatest books of the world." [24] More recently such respected critics as V. S. Pritchett, T. S. Eliot, and W. H. Auden have given *Huck* high praise.[25] If such praise guides British readers the novel will continue to find readers in Great Britain.

Chatto and Windus took out copyright on *Huckleberry Finn* in Canada for the official publishers there, Dawson Brothers of Montreal. For the first time in Canada pirates were prevented from publishing one of Mark Twain's novels. No doubt the authorized edition benefited from the lively demand which had been created by the publishers of fifty-two editions of the author's previous works.[26] But figures on sales by Dawson, by Musson who rep-

German

Dutch

Russian

Huck Finn ABROAD

Norwegian

French

resented Harpers in Canada, and by Canadian representatives of British firms issuing the book are not available. And aside from finding a record of an edition of the novel published in Sydney, Australia, I have learned nothing about its circulation in other parts of the vast British Empire.

Vying with the British as enthusiasts about Mark Twain during his lifetime the Germans gave *Huck* a fine welcome and continued to read the book pretty steadily. Tauchnitz of Leipzig issued a two-volume paperback edition in English in 1885 in his series called somewhat inappropriately "Collection of British Authors." A translation by Henny Koch put out in Stuttgart in 1890 was frequently reissued—twelve printings by 1911, thirty by 1918. Three other editions of this translation were published: one in 1898 which reached its seventeenth printing in 1918 was still in print as late as 1921; one in 1899 reissued in 1900 (Eisenbahn-Ausgabe); one in 1904. A translation by H. Hellwag was published in Halle in 1902. A translation appeared in Berlin in 1909; one in Leipzig in 1910 reissued in 1910, 1911, and as late as 1925. A translation by Ulrich Johannsen and Marie Schloss was issued in Strassburg and Leipzig in 1913.

Grace Isabel Colbron reported in 1914 that in both Tauchnitz editions and inexpensive printings of translations, Twain as a best seller was outdistanced only by Bret Harte, while "in higher priced volumes by leading publishers" Twain was doing as well as Harte. *Huck* and *Tom* she found "outdistance all the other Twain books," and both were available in paperback libraries, "far and away the heaviest sellers in Germany." [27]

I have listed eight translated editions in Germany before 1914. Seven more had appeared after World War I: in 1921, 1922, 1925, 1926, 1930, and 1936 (two) when Edgar H. Hemminghaus made "a minimum estimate" of sales to 1936. *Huck*, he believed, was third among its author's works in Germany in sales with 190,000 copies.[28] As he wrote, Hemminghaus saw signs that Hitler's Germany might not be too appreciative of the humorist. "His aims and ideas," he said mildly, "do not in general accord with the psychology of the present generation."

The lack of rapport probably was responsible for no new edition appearing until 1948. But beginning with that year Germany showed revived interest. The 1948 edition was followed by thirteen others between 1950 and 1957. These, if one counts the Tauchnitz edition, bring the sum of editions in Germany to twenty-eight. If postwar editions on an average were only as large as those through 1936, "a minimum estimate" of sales of the book in German translations would be some 367,000.

Other northern European nations also liked the novel: I have recorded four editions in translation in the Netherlands, a Flemish translation in Belgium, two German translations in Switzerland. A Danish translation came out the year the book appeared in the United States—1885—and has been followed since by at least four others. Sweden had translations in 1896, 1898, and 1918, the last of which reached its fifteenth edition in 1940; and since 1940 three new Swedish editions have appeared to bring the total to twenty. A visitor in 1940 noticed that copies of the novel in English in the Stockholm library had been read often enough to make frequent rebinding necessary.[29] Finland has had ten translated editions, Norway two. In central Europe Hungary has had ten editions, Austria four.

Latin countries lagged in appreciating Mark Twain. In 1935 Maurice le Breton testified that the American humorist was practically unknown in France;[30] and evidently Italy and Spain shared France's lack of enthusiasm. Nevertheless an authorized translation by William L. Hughes, *Les Aventures de Huck Finn* appeared in France in 1886 and sold well enough to be reprinted in 1887 and to justify new editions in 1914 and 1926. Four other editions of translations were dated 1929, 1948, and 1950 (two). *Le Aventura di Huckleberry Finn,* translated by Teresa Orsi, appeared in Italy in 1915, 1918, 1930, and 1935; editions by other translators in 1934, 1935 (two), 1949, 1952, 1953 (three), and 1955. Spain had one undated edition, four editions between 1943 and 1952; Portugal five between 1934 and 1952. In Latin America Argentina has had eleven translated editions, Brazil seven.

Priklyuchenia Finna Gekkelberri made its Russian debut in 1888. Five times before World War I, sets of Twain's writings including this novel were issued—in St. Petersburg (1896–1899, 1898, 1910–

1913, 1911) and in Moscow (1907). The 1898 and 1907 sets as supplements to popular magazines had wide circulation. Russians, says Professor Albert Parry, placed Twain "among the world's most celebrated writers." Among a generation of Russian schoolboys at the start of the century, Professor George V. Bobrinskoy testifies, Huck was the favorite hero; among oldsters he was the most popular American fictional character.[31]

Since the revolution *Huck's* fame probably has increased. In Soviet Russia before 1939, Twain led all foreign authors in sales; today he is second only to Jack London in popularity.[32] A six-volume edition of Twain's collected works appeared in 1926, an omnibus volume in 1937: both included *Gekkelberri*. There were also editions of the novel alone in 1926, 1927, 1930, 1933, 1934, 1936 (reprinted in 1937), 1937, 1942, 1955, 1956 (two), 1957 (four). Translations into Ukrainian (2) and into Lettish dialects also have been published. Official figures on twelve editions published between 1926 and 1942 show them totaling 362,325 copies. These did not satisfy the demand: in 1945 whole evenings were devoted to reading Mark Twain's works on the Russian radio.[33] In 1959 plans called for issuing new translations of the author's complete works on the fiftieth anniversary of his death in 1960.

I have no figures on editions issued since 1942. But if they averaged as large as those of the 1930's and one of 1942 on which I have figures, they have brought the total number of copies of *Huck* issued in the Soviet Union since 1927 to at least 637,425. (They probably averaged larger.)

Soviet critics, after condemning Mark Twain for a period as "a petit-bourgeois writer," eventually discovered that he was a critic of American capitalism, imperialism, and racism. (A 1926 translation was titled *Adventures of Huckleberry Finn and a Runaway Negro*.) In another Iron Curtain country, Czechoslovakia, the library card which steers readers to *Dobrodružstvi Hucka Finna* assures them that the book preaches acceptable doctrines: "Mark Twain, the well-known American humorist, rejected in this work the false romanticism of worthless murder stories and sharply criticized American racism and the excesses of Puritan morality." [34] Czechoslovakian editions appeared in 1935, 1953,

1955 (combined with *Tom Sawyer*), 1956, and 1958. In Poland translated editions were published in 1898, 1900, 1901, 1923, 1936, 1937, and 1956. Yugoslavia issued two editions in translation in 1948, others in 1949 and 1952.

Listings show translations in several other countries: Greece, three celebrating Khŏk Phinn, O Philos Tou Tom Söger; Israel, two about Huckleberry Finn; Indonesia, one; Japan, one; China, five; Romania, four; Serbia, one. These listings are quite incomplete, since good compilations of books in translation run only from 1932 to 1940 and 1948 to 1958,[35] and even these are unsatisfactory. Professor D. M. McKeithan finds that *Huck* has been read extensively in Iceland, Lebanon, Turkey, Egypt, Java, and Siam,[36] though I have found no titles of translated editions in these countries.

Incomplete though it certainly is, my compilation of translations for which bibliographic data are available reaches an impressive total of 189 editions published in widely scattered parts of the world. With forty-two editions in English on which information is available—the Tauchnitz edition plus those issued in the British Empire—the foreign total is 231. Since some foreign editions have been printed thirty times and one at least totaled 120,000 copies, even if some were small the average size probably was fairly large. A minimum estimate of the number of copies printed abroad might be 2,500,000. If this is so, *Adventures of Huckleberry Finn* has few competitors for popularity among American novels.

Precisely why publishers have thought it worth while to print at least 7,500,000 copies of *Huckleberry Finn* in various forms in the United States and 2,500,000 or more abroad no one can be sure. Quite probably an important reason has been the wide variety of the book's appeals. Many children and adults in America enjoy it simply as a good story which provides hilarious comedy or exciting adventures or escape or all three: the same appeals are effective abroad. Other readers respond to different attractions. Not the least of these, as scores of affectionate comments prove, is the charm of Huck as a character who becomes vivid even in translations and inept adaptations. The frequent statement that the book is "America's epic" suggests other interests—the symbolic meanings which the raft, the river, and the shore come to have; the mythic quality of Huck's initiation; and the panoramic view which the novel affords. Beyond doubt the theme or themes, interpreted though they are variously, attracted readers. The life, the thought, the complex personality of Mark Twain, given immortality here as nowhere else, also have tremendous fascination. Separately or in combination these varied attractions must account for many readers.

In 1885, irritated and—though he swaggered it off—hurt by Concord's ban on *Huck,* Mark had a look at sensational headlines and stories in the New York *World:* ". . . Mother-in-law and wife shot by a man who then shoots himself . . . betrayed girl's father kills the betrayer . . . the poor girl's family now admit that this was not the first time she had been betrayed." He took pencil and estimated the number of words each issue of the paper contained. He calculated that "In a week they spread a full Huck before 1,000,000 families, 4,000,000 in a month, . . . 50,000,000 . . . in a year—while 100,000 have read Huck Finn and forgotten him. Moral. If you want [people] just right sweet and pure here and Paradise hereafter, banish Huck Finn from the home circle and introduce the N.Y. World in his place." [37]

He probably overestimated the number reading the *World;* he certainly (and very uncharacteristically) greatly underestimated the number who would read and remember his novel. I have been tempted to imagine Mark Twain in 1960, seventy-five years later, lolling alongside his old friend Captain Stormfield on a cloud, sardonically contemplating Huck's pervasive (and presumably pernicious) adventures in the world. Only briefly though. On further imagining the way Mark would blister with a blast anyone who engaged in such sentimentering I managed to refrain.

APPENDIX

FIRST NEW YORK EDITION, FIRST ISSUE

The establishment of the points of the first issue of the first New York edition of *Adventures of Huckleberry Finn* has been discussed often and vehemently. The chief published discussions are: Merle Johnson, *A Bibliography of the Works of Mark Twain* (New York, 1910), pp. 59–60; Revised Edition (New York, 1935), pp. 43–50; Irving S. Underhill, "An Inquiry into Huckleberry Finn," *Colophon*, Part VI (1931); Irving S. Underhill, "Two Interesting Letters Pertaining to 'Huckleberry Finn,'" *American Book Collector*, II (November, 1932), 282–289; John K. Potter, *Samuel L. Clemens: First Editions and Values* (Chicago, 1932), pp. 38–39; Irving S. Underhill, "Tempest in a Teapot or Notes on Huckleberry Finn," *American Book Collector*, IV (September–October, 1933), 153–156; Irving S. Underhill, "The Haunted Book: A Further Exploration Concerning Huckleberry Finn," *Colophon*, I (Autumn, 1935), 281–292; Jacob Blanck, *A Supplement to "A Bibliography of Mark Twain"* (New York: Privately Printed, 1939); Norman Clarke, *Huckleberry Finn Again* (Detroit, 1941); Whitman Bennett, *Practical Guide to Book Collecting* (New York, 1941); Merle Johnson, *American First Editions*, revised by Jacob Blanck (New York, 1942), p. 106; Jacob Blanck, "In Re *Huckleberry Finn*," *The New Colophon*, III (1950), 153–159; George H. Brownell, "Sam Webster Adds to the Mystery of That Cut on Page 283 of *Huckleberry Finn*," *The Twainian*, IX (January–February, 1950), 3; Walter Harding, "A Note on the Binding of the First Edition of *Huckleberry Finn*," *Bibliographical Society of the University of Virginia News Sheet*, No. 20 (March, 1952), 1–2: Jacob Blanck, *Bibliography of American Literature, Compiled . . . for the Bibliographical Society of America* (New Haven, 1957), II, 199–200.

An amateur hesitates to enter the bewildering labyrinths of bibliographical controversy. But since my study has revealed some facts concerning the publication of *Huckleberry Finn* in New York I feel that I should consider their bearing on the dispute.

Merle Johnson, his avowed disciple Jacob Blanck, and his severest critic Irving S. Underhill agree on one important matter— that the plate for page 283 was not damaged until after some copies of the book were printed. "In this case," says Johnson, "the first state would be printed from a perfect plate and the page would be *bound* in; the second published stage would be *tipped in*. . . ." [1] Although he has wavered, Blanck now accepts Johnson's hypothesis and therefore specifies as the first stage the illustration before defacement, not tipped in but conjugate with 18_3. This he calls "a well established and universally accepted point." [2] And Underhill, the most vociferous disputant and for me at least in general impossible to understand, says, "the tipped-in leaf [283] as a point of the first edition . . . to me is inconceivable." [3]

Several facts lead me to doubt this generally accepted hypothesis: both the London and the Montreal versions of page 283 in first editions appear to my eye to differ from any in a New York edition. (They do not duplicate Blanck's state "A," which he believes is the first version to come from the presses.) This suggests that the British firm noticed the defaced illustration in the advance sheets shipped to it before September 19, 1884, and repaired it or made a new one—independently. It suggests that the Montreal firm found the defaced illustration on page 283 of "plates the same as ours," sent it shortly after September 19, and repaired the plate or made a new one—independently. And there is more direct evidence: page proofs and press proofs for the New York first edition show the defaced illustration. Prospectuses which were paid for September 2, 1884, contained it. Advance sheets which George Washington Cable received, evidently, before October 13 contained it. All these facts support a belief that no copies of the novel could have been printed before the illustration was defaced.

Evidently when the defacement was discovered in New York the situation was this: "Thousands of copies," as Little testified to Johnson, "of the book were in the plant." Some were bound, some were unbound. But all contained the defaced illustration. These, as Little testified, were handled in two ways. 1. A reëngraved plate was made and was used to run off new sheets, and such sheets were tipped into bound copies. 2. "In the unbound copies whole signatures were printed and supplied in the regular manner of binding." Conceivably books of both sorts may have been sold simultaneously on the date of publication, February 18, 1885, some with page 283 tipped in, some with page 283 conjugate with 18_3.[4] Or books in one of the two categories may have been readied and therefore issued first. I see no way to determine certainly, on the basis of evidence I have seen, which procedure was followed. One bit of evidence arguing for the priority of copies with page 283 tipped in is the fact that "one of three cloth copies first bound" which was presented by Webster to his father as a Christmas present had the page in this state.[5]

Tho fact that the Montreal publishers used for their first edition plates made in New York and identical with those of the United States first edition is relevant to another disputed point.[6] The folio of page 155 exists in three states: (1) with the final five lacking, (2) with the final five present but set above the first five, (3) with the final five present but larger than the first. Blanck, though he has some doubts about the order of the first two of these stages, believes that they were in this order and that the third was the last stage.[7] But the Canadian edition has the folio with the final five present but larger than the first five. So do Barrett's advance sheets. Therefore the folio in this form would seem to be a point for the first issue of the first edition.

Otherwise—except for one which can easily be explained [8]— points in the Canadian first correspond with those which are generally accepted as points of the New York first.[9]

NOTES

CHAPTER 1: "THE END. YOURS TRULY, HUCK FINN."

(Pages 3–12)

[1] The Boston *Transcript's* assertion is in the issue of March 19, 1885. "Mark Twain's Blood-Curdling Humor" is in *Life*, V (February 26, 1885), 19. The quotation ending the paragraph is in Alexander Nicolas DeMenil, "A Century of Missouri Literature," *Missouri Historical Rev.*, XV (October, 1920), 97; De-Menil also remarks that "'Mark Twain' lacks the education absolutely necessary to a great writer; he lacks the refinement which would render it impossible for him to create such coarse characters as Huckleberry Finn." The changes in the reputation of Mark Twain and of *Huck* are traced in detail in Arthur L. Vogel-back, "The Literary Reputation of Mark Twain in America, 1869–1885" (unpublished doctoral dissertation, University of Chicago, 1939); Bernard DeVoto, "Mark Twain: The Ink of History," *Forays and Rebuttals* (Boston, 1936), pp. 348–372; Roger Asselineau, *The Literary Reputation of Mark Twain from 1910 to 1950* (Paris, 1954); E. Hudson Long, "Mark Twain's Place in Literature," *Mark Twain Handbook* (New York, 1957), pp. 399–414.

[2] Boston *Transcript*, March 17, 1885; *Critic*, VI (May 30, 1885), 264.

[3] Cablegrams to S. L. Clemens, August 12 and August 23, 1902, Mark Twain Papers, University of California Library in Berkeley (hereafter designated as *MTP*), © copyright 1960 by Mark Twain Co. Notes or text will indicate all materials drawn from *MTP* and from most other sources. The following books are not cited in the notes: Albert Bigelow Paine, *Mark Twain: A Biography* (New York, 1912); *Mark Twain's Letters*, ar. Albert Bigelow Paine (New York, 1917); *Mark Twain's Autobiography*, ed. Albert Bigelow Paine (New York, 1924); *Mark Twain in Eruption*, ed. Bernard DeVoto (New York, 1940); and Dixon Wecter, *Sam Clemens of Hannibal* (Boston, 1952). For pages on which the first two are quoted see footnote on p. x.

⁴ For details about the decision in Brooklyn see *Mark Twain's Autobiography* (New York, 1924), II, 332–339; E. L. Pearson, "The Children's Librarian versus *Huckleberry Finn*," *Library Jour.*, XXXII (July, 1907), 312–315.

⁵ New York *Times*, September 12, 1957. The general belief was that the action was taken because Huck, using the language of the 1830's and 1840's in Missouri, used the word "nigger." Interestingly, one adaptation which was barred did not contain the word, the adapter Verne B. Brown having carefully removed every racial reference.

⁶ March 15, 1881, *MTP*.

⁷ "Mark Twain's Life on the Mississippi," *Atlantic Monthly*, LII (September, 1883), 406. The "raftsmen chapter" was returned to the manuscript but because of space limitations was not included in the printed novel.

⁸ London *Saturday Rev.*, LIX (January 31, 1885), 153–154.

⁹ Bernard DeVoto, *Mark Twain at Work* (Cambridge, 1942), p. 87. Hereafter cited as *MTaW*.

¹⁰ Leo Marx, "Pilot and Passenger: Landscape Conventions and the Style of *Huckleberry Finn*," *American Literature*, XXVIII (May, 1956), 129. Hereafter cited as *AL*.

¹¹ See my bibliography for an extensive list.

¹² William Van O'Connor, "Why *Huckleberry Finn* Is Not the Great American Novel," *College English*, XVII (October, 1955), 6–10.

¹³ T. S. Eliot, "American Literature and the American Language," *Washington Univ. Studies in Lang. and Lit.*, n.s. XXIII (St. Louis, 1953), 16–17.

¹⁴ Associated Press dispatch, "This World" section, San Francisco *Chronicle*, August 5, 1956, p. 20; George Mayberry, "Reading and Writing," *New Republic*, CX (May 1, 1944), 808; Ben Hecht, *A Child of the Century* (New York, 1954), pp. 67–68; Henry Miller, *The Books in My Life* (Norfolk, Conn., [n.d.]), p. 41, also Appendix; William Saroyan, *The Twin Adventures* (New York, 1950), p. 55. Saroyan testifies that in *The Adventures of Wesley Jackson* he was trying to create "a kind of older Huck Finn—contemporary and therefore a little neurotic."

¹⁵ Ernest Hemingway, *Green Hills of Africa* (New York, 1935), p. 22; interview with William Faulkner by Jean Stein, *The Paris Review* (Spring, 1956), pp. 46–47.

¹⁶ *The Portable Mark Twain*, ed. Bernard DeVoto (New York, 1946), pp. 773–775, 9. The letter was written to an unidentified person in 1890. The bracketed sentence, a postscript, was crossed out.

¹⁷ See *Autobiography*, II, 175; *Life on the Mississippi*, chap. lvi.

¹⁸ In an uncompleted novel of 1877, "Autobiography of a Damned Fool," Twain uses the incident again and makes still other changes: the narrator, a professional reformer, gets drunk with a convert of his and the pair proceed in considerable disorder to the temperance parade arranged to celebrate the reformation. *MTP*.

¹⁹ Reprinted in *The Twainian*, November–December, 1948, p. 7. Henry Nash Smith called my attention to this passage.

CHAPTER 2: THE HANDSOMEST MANSION
IN HARTFORD

(Pages 16–32)

[1] S. L. Clemens, letters written during the autumn of 1874, *MTP*.

[2] Charles W. Burpee, *History of Hartford County, Connecticut* (Chicago, 1928), I, 451.

[3] London *English World*, January, 1878.

[4] William Dean Howells, *My Mark Twain* (New York, 1910), p. 7. Howells did not hear the remark but reported it. I suspect that Potter indicated partial discipleship to E. E. Viollet-le-Duc, a famous commentator on architecture of the 1870's, and that the name was misremembered or mispronounced.

[5] Charles H. Clark, "Mark Twain at Nook Farm (Hartford) and Elmira," *Critic*, VI (January 17, 1885), 25; *English World*, January, 1878.

[6] Works previously cited and Kenneth R. Andrews, *Nook Farm: Mark Twain's Hartford Circle* (Cambridge, 1950), pp. 81–82.

[7] *Alta California* letters dated January 25 and "August, Recently," 1868, reprinted in *The Twainian*, September–October, 1948, pp. 3–4, November–December, pp. 6–7.

[8] The figures are drawn from Hamlin Hill, "Mark Twain and the American Publishing Company" (unpublished doctoral dissertation, University of Chicago, 1959).

[9] For details about humorous lectures see Melville D. Landon, *Eli Perkins' Wit, Humor and Pathos* (Chicago, 1883); J. B. Pond, *Eccentricities of Genius* (New York, 1900); Walter Blair, *Native American Humor, 1800–1900* (New York, 1937), pp. 114–117.

[10] *The Washoe Giant in San Francisco*, ed. Franklin Walker (San Francisco, 1938), p. 76.

[11] Although the popular version appeared in newspapers, it is most easily available in Mrs. Thomas Bailey Aldrich, *Crowding Memories* (Boston, 1920), pp. 152–154. Mark Twain in his *Autobiography*, II, 104–105, tells a more believable but less dramatic story. It says that Newton's fee was $1,500.

[12] *Crowding Memories*, p. 151.

[13] News items which the author clipped and saved are in scrapbooks and in the Clippings and Documents File, *MTP;* others are in scrapbooks in the Morse Collection, Yale University Library. An impressive though partial list is in Arthur L. Vogelback, "The Literary Reputation of Mark Twain in America, 1869–1885" (unpublished doctoral dissertation, University of Chicago, 1939).

[14] *Crowding Memories*, p. 152.

[15] *The Love Letters of Mark Twain*, ed. Dixon Wecter (New York, 1949), pp. 16–62.

[16] *Crowding Memories*, pp. 128–129, 150–151.

[17] Leon T. Dickinson, "Mark Twain's *Innocents Abroad:* Its Origins, Composition and Popularity" (unpublished doctoral dissertation, University of Chicago, 1945), pp. 136–146.

[18] Vogelback, "Literary Reputation," pp. 60, 71, 73.

[19] Howells, *My Mark Twain*, pp. 6, 46–47.

[20] The group included, in addition to Harte and Clemens, Ralph Keeler, "a vagabond adventurer," T. B. Aldrich, and J. T. Fields. These, with Charles Eliot Norton, Francis C. Child, and James R. Osgood, were the Boston-Cambridge men who "accepted" the humorist. But Harte, Howells, and Aldrich were not native Bostonians; Norton and Child, as Howells says, had been "unlocalized" by travel abroad; and Fields and Osgood were publishers rather than scholars or writers.

[21] Mrs. James T. Fields, *Memories of a Hostess* (Boston, 1922), p. 246.

[22] Andrews, *Nook Farm*, p. 86. This was an entry of November, 1876.

[23] Mody C. Boatright, *Folk Laughter on the American Frontier* (New York, 1949), cites many instances.

[24] *Crowding Memories*, pp. 143–144.

[25] *Ibid.*, pp. 146–147, 160.

[26] *Nook Farm*, pp. 1–24.

[27] Henry-Russell Hitchcock, "High Victorian Gothic," *Victorian Studies*, I (September, 1957), 50–56.

[28] July 11, [1874], *MTP*, © copyright 1960 by Mark Twain Co.

[29] *Mark Twain to Mrs. Fairbanks*, ed. Dixon Wecter (San Marino, 1949), p. 195.

[30] Hartford *Times*, November 1, 1935.

[31] Katharine Seymour Day, "Mark Twain's First Years in Hartford and Personal Memories of the Clemens Family" (unpublished master's thesis, Trinity College, 1936), p. 43.

[32] *My Mark Twain*, p. 7.

[33] Moncure Daniel Conway, *Autobiography* (Boston, 1906), II, 143–144.

[34] "In Defense of Harriet Shelley," chap. i.

[35] *Memories of a Hostess*, p. 253.

[36] *Mark Twain to Mrs. Fairbanks*, pp. xxvii, 165, 178.

[37] *Ibid.*, p. xxvii.

[38] Letters from Hartford, March 12, March 13, 1869, *MTP*, © copyright 1960 by Mark Twain Co.

[39] *Memories of a Hostess*, p. 265; *Life in Letters of William Dean Howells*, ed. Mildred Howells (Garden City, 1928), I, 187.

[40] Mary Lawton, *A Lifetime with Mark Twain* (New York, 1925), p. 4.

[41] *My Mark Twain*, pp. 10, 13.

[42] *Love Letters of Mark Twain*, p. 11. See also *Mark Twain to Mrs. Fairbanks*, pp. 112–113.

[43] *A Lifetime with Mark Twain*, p. 18.

[44] Clara Clemens, *My Father Mark Twain* (New York, 1931), p. 68.

[45] An incident from the Clemens' history is recounted about Susan and David; the author says several things about Susan which he says elsewhere about Livy; originally Gridley's first name was Sam; Gridley's best friend, a working note specifies, is modeled after Clemens' best friend, Joseph Twichell. DV 302g, 302h, *MTP*.

[46] DV 302g, pp. 52–54, *MTP*, © copyright 1960 by Mark Twain Co.

[47] DV 302g, pp. 55–58, *MTP*, © copyright 1960 by Mark Twain Co.

[48] DV 302g, pp. 58–61, *MTP*, © copyright 1960 by Mark Twain Co.

[49] DV 302h, p. 46, *MTP*, © copyright 1960 by Mark Twain Co.

CHAPTER 3: A SERIES FOR THE
ATLANTIC MONTHLY
(Pages 35–47)

[1] In notes for the unfinished novel cited in chapter ii, Mark Twain identified a character thus: "Rev. Bailey is Twichell handsome and a beautiful spirit whom a stranger takes to his heart at once." *MTP*, © copyright 1960 by Mark Twain Co.

[2] I am indebted to the detailed account of Twichell's life by Leah Strong, "Joseph Hopkins Twichell: A Biography of Mark Twain's Pastor" (unpublished doctoral dissertation, Syracuse University, 1953).

[3] Frank Luther Mott, *A History of American Magazines, 1850–1865* (Cambridge, 1938), II, 493–494.

[4] Howells, *My Mark Twain*, p. 19.

[5] Possibly he meant that he had not thought of it as *Atlantic* copy.

[6] Cited by Dixon Wecter, "Introduction," *Life on the Mississippi* (New York, 1950), p. ix.

[7] *MTP*, © copyright 1960 by Mark Twain Co.

[8] Mott, *American Magazines*, III, 47–48.

[9] *Scribner's Monthly*, VIII (October, 1874), 642.

[10] Letters of November 23 and 24, 1874, *MTP*, © copyright 1960 by Mark Twain Co.

[11] *MTP*, © copyright 1960 by Mark Twain Co.

[12] Bernard DeVoto, *Mark Twain's America* (Boston, 1932), p. 13.

[13] *Ibid.*, pp. 108–109.

[14] Louis C. Hunter, *Steamboats on Western Rivers: An Economic and Technological History* (Cambridge, 1949).

[15] Rather more than a quarter of the *Atlantic's* list, some 15,000 subscribers, had canceled.

[16] Robert Spiller, *The Cycle of American Literature* (New York, 1955), p. 156.

[17] Letter of December 4, 1874, *MTP*.

[18] Some passages sound like the predictions of Colonel Sellers of *The Gilded Age*, modeled after a relative of Clemens. See, for example, I, 370–371.

[19] Fred W. Lorch, "Mark Twain in Iowa," *Iowa Jour. of History and Politics*, XXVII (July, 1929), 433–434.

[20] In an interview with Paine, Bixby said that the boat was above the head of Island No. 35 when his talk with Clemens took place.

[21] This particular development was continued in the chapters immediately following those of the series in *Life on the Mississippi*—chapters xviii–xx. Here Twain tells of his encounter with the sadistic pilot Brown and of his brother Henry's death in a steamboat explosion. In chapter xviii he says that "in that brief, sharp schooling [on the river], I got personally and familiarly acquainted with all the different types of human nature. . . ."

[22] These aspects of "Old Times" are related in an interesting way to aspects of *Roughing It* pointed out by Henry Nash Smith. His analysis, "Mark Twain as an Interpreter of the Far West: The Structure of *Roughing It*," in *The Frontier in Perspective* (Madison, 1957), pp. 205–228, reached me after I had written

this chapter. Smith sees the first half of the book as describing "the processes by which the tenderfoot is transformed into the old-timer . . . an initiation." He sees the second half as the story of the young man "succeeding, then finding that success does not bring happiness, but disillusionment." He remarks that, "although the principal character . . . tells the story in the first person, it is evident that the pronoun 'I' links two quite different personae: the tenderfoot starting out across the Plains and the old-timer, the veteran, who has seen the elephant and now looks back upon his own callow days of inexperience."

²³ *Scribner's Monthly*, IX (December, 1874), 134–135. There is no likelihood that Twain's passage was influenced by this, although King may have been influenced by similar passages in *The Gilded Age*.

²⁴ Professor John Francis McDermott's report on the original sketch, letter of March 27, 1959. See also the lithograph in Lewis's *Das Illustrirte Mississippithal*, "the general impression of which," says McDermott, "is not too greatly different."

²⁵ Ernest E. Leisy, "Mark Twain's Part in *The Gilded Age, AL*, VIII (1937), 445–448.

CHAPTER 4: TOM SAWYER

(Pages 51–70)

¹ Brander Matthews, "Memories of Mark Twain," in *The Tocsin of Revolt and Other Essays* (New York, 1922), pp. 265–267. The conversation took place in 1890.

² Theodore Hornberger, "An Introduction" to *Mark Twain's Letters to Will Bowen* (Austin, 1941), pp. 3–4. Twain says that he himself played a trick ascribed to Tom and that, like Tom, he was often guilty of truancy. *Autobiography*, II, 91–92.

³ Notebooks 4–5, *MTP*, © copyright 1960 by Mark Twain Co.

⁴ DV 131, *MTP*.

⁵ *MTP*, © copyright 1960 by Mark Twain Co. See also *Letters to Will Bowen*, p. 19.

⁶ *Letters to Will Bowen*, p. 17; Twain's testimony is in a footnote, *Boy's Manuscript, MTaW*, p. 39.

⁷ *Letters to Will Bowen*, p. 19.

⁸ DeLancey Ferguson, *Mark Twain: Man and Legend* (Indianapolis, 1943), p. 175. On p. 29, however, Ferguson stated, more accurately, "*Tom Sawyer* is not autobiographical in its details, but in its personalities, altered or heightened for dramatic purposes, it is essentially lifelike."

⁹ DV 47, *MTP*, © copyright 1960 by Mark Twain Co.

¹⁰ J. W. Ayres, "Recollections of Hannibal," *Palmyra Spectator*, August 22, 1917.

¹¹ "Introduction" to Cyril Clemens, *My Cousin Mark Twain* (Emmaus, Pa., 1939).

¹² DeVoto, *Portable Mark Twain*, p. 33.

¹³ *Letters to Will Bowen*, p. 18.

¹⁴ *Ibid.*, pp. 23–24. This was the original draft; Clemens took the trouble to "rewrite [the letter], saying the same harsh things softly."

¹⁵ *MTaW*, p. 6.

¹⁶ Gladys Carmen Bellamy, *Mark Twain as Literary Artist* (Norman, 1950), p. 333, guesses that this "may have been begun as a sort of playful, whimsical love letter to Olivia"; and cites incidents in its early pages which parallel hap-

penings during the courtship. I tend to doubt this because the style and tone differ from those of most Clemens' courting letters, and I think that at that time he was too involved to make fun of his courtship.

[17] *Love Letters*, p. 56.

[18] Article VI, written and proofread, April, 1875, published in June, 1875.

[19] Howells, "Recent Literature," *Atlantic Monthly*, XXX (October, 1872), 487.

[20] "Unconscious Plagiarism" (1879), *Mark Twain's Speeches*, ed. Albert Bigelow Paine (New York, 1910), pp. 57–58.

[21] The statement refers to another manuscript in progress.

[22] The original letter, to Howells, in the Berg Collection, is cited with the permission of the New York Public Library.

[23] Clemens spoke on "Plagiarism" to the Saturday Morning Club in 1880. Katharine Seymore Day, "Mark Twain's First Years in Hartford," p. 130.

[24] Clemens' copy of the book is in *MTP*. Quotations © copyright 1960 by Mark Twain Co.

[25] Clemens is again rephrasing Holmes' letter of 1869, as he recalls it, but he completely agrees.

[26] Charles H. Clark, "Mark Twain at Nook Farm (Hartford) and Elmira," *Critic*, VI (January 17, 1885), 26. See also Howells, *My Mark Twain*, p. 15.

[27] The latest and most extensive is by Harold Aspiz, "Mark Twain's Reading— A Critical Study" (unpublished doctoral dissertation, University of California, Los Angeles, 1949).

[28] Notebook 19, TS p. 36, *MTP*.

[29] Aspiz, "Mark Twain's Reading," pp. 207–209.

[30] Franklin J. Meine, "Introduction," *Tall Tales of the Southwest* (New York, 1930); DeVoto, *Mark Twain's America*, pp. 79–98; Blair, *Native American Humor*, pp. 153–158.

[31] Notebook 15, *MTP;* J. D. Wade, *Augustus Baldwin Longstreet* (New York, 1924), p. 168.

[32] For additional parallels see Blair, *Native American Humor*, pp. 150–152.

[33] *Writings of Thomas Bailey Aldrich* (Boston and New York, 1897), pp. 67–70, 75, 82, 59, 159–170.

[34] *Ibid.*, pp. 240–245.

[35] *MTaW*, pp. 28, 36.

[36] The story, which appeared in a reader, is quoted by E. D. Branch in *The Sentimental Years* (New York, 1934), pp. 312–313. For other examples and documentation for the discussion in the rest of this section, see Walter Blair, "On the Structure of *Tom Sawyer*," *Mod. Philol.*, XXXVII (August, 1939), 75–88.

[37] "Sixth Study," *Backlog Studies*, in *The Complete Writings of Charles Dudley Warner* (Hartford, 1904), I, 249–250, originally published in May, 1872.

[38] Letter to Annie Taylor, May 25, [1856], Kansas City *Star Mag.*, March 21, 1926.

[39] *My Father Mark Twain*, p. 9. The account, somewhat abbreviated and amended, is on pp. 9–12.

[40] *Mark Twain of the Enterprise*, ed. Henry Nash Smith with the assistance of Frederick Anderson (Berkeley and Los Angeles, 1957), pp. 134–138.

[41] Reprinted in *The Twainian*, November–December, 1948, p. 5.

[42] Letter to Miss Noyes dated Hartford, February 23, 1882: "The Chapter in

Tom Sawyer which you refer to was suggested by that mournful experience . . . in your school." *MTP*, © copyright 1960 by Mark Twain Co.

⁴³ *MTaW*, pp. 6–7.

⁴⁴ Dictation August 19, 1907, *Autobiography*, *MTP*, © copyright 1960 by Mark Twain Co. This version apparently was written in the first person and was incorporated with changes to the third person in the manuscript at Georgetown.

⁴⁵ *Portable Mark Twain*, p. 33.

CHAPTER 6: "PEACE, QUIET, REST, SECLUSION"

(Pages 78–89)

¹ Samuel C. Webster, *Mark Twain, Business Man* (Boston, 1946), p. 599; letter from Clemens to Howells, May 22, 1875, Houghton Library, Harvard University, cited with permission.

² Hamlin Hill, "Mark Twain and the American Publishing Company" (unpublished doctoral dissertation, University of Chicago, 1959).

³ A. M. Broadley, *Chats on Autographs* (New York, 1910), p. 229. Paine, who thought his version of the remark too racy for anything but the small print of a footnote, erroneously assigned it to the first meeting of the pair.

⁴ *Life in Letters*, I, 212.

⁵ *MTaW*, pp. 10–14, remarks all the changes reported here.

⁶ *Memories of a Hostess*, p. 251.

⁷ For a stunning example see William G. Barrett, M.D., "On the Naming of Tom Sawyer," *Psychoanalytic Quar.*, XXIV (1955), 424–436.

⁸ *The Twainian*, January–February, 1956, p. 1.

⁹ Ferguson, *Mark Twain: Man and Legend*, pp. 151–152.

¹⁰ *Love Letters*, p. 190.

¹¹ Letter to Bliss, TS in *MTP*, © copyright 1960 by Mark Twain Co. In his *Autobiography* he spoke of the Buffalo period as "saturated . . . with horrors and distress."

¹² Letter of September 20, 1876, Hayes Memorial Library, Fremont, Ohio, quoted with permission.

¹³ *Portable Mark Twain*, p. 754.

¹⁴ *Mark Twain to Mrs. Fairbanks*, p. 137; letters to Elisha Bliss, September 19, 1870, March 10, 1871, May 3, 1871, TS in *MTP*.

¹⁵ *Love Letters*, p. 70.

¹⁶ *Nook Farm*, p. 4.

¹⁷ *Life in Letters*, I, 187. Conway, *Autobiography*, II, 144, says that during a visit he paid Clemens in 1876 the Warners came by every day and Twichell "in the evening."

¹⁸ *My Mark Twain*, p. 9. See also Mary Lawton, *A Lifetime with Mark Twain* (New York, 1925), pp. 39, 92–93; *My Father Mark Twain*, p. 43.

¹⁹ *A Lifetime with Mark Twain*, pp. 19–20. Kate Leary speaks of a period after 1880; but I believe that the description is accurate for 1876.

²⁰ *My Mark Twain*, p. 35; *My Father Mark Twain*, p. 27.

²¹ *MTP*, © copyright 1960 by Mark Twain Co.

[22] *Mark Twain to Mrs. Fairbanks,* p. 197.

[23] *A List of Members of the Monday Evening Club . . . 1869–1954* (Hartford, 1954).

[24] *A Lifetime with Mark Twain,* p. 38.

[25] *Ibid.,* pp. 41–42.

[26] Letter to Miss Noyes, February 23, 1882, *MTP;* W. W. Ellsworth, *A Golden Age of Authors* (Boston, 1919), pp. 223–224; Day, "Mark Twain's Early Years in Hartford," p. 130.

[27] *A Golden Age of Authors,* pp. 222–223.

[28] *A Lifetime with Mark Twain,* p. 71; *My Father Mark Twain,* pp. 35–40.

[29] *A Golden Age of Authors,* pp. 222–223.

[30] *MTP.*

[31] *Mark Twain to Mrs. Fairbanks,* p. 205.

[32] *MTP.*

[33] *Mark Twain: Man and Legend,* p. 183.

[34] *Mark Twain to Mrs. Fairbanks,* p. 191.

[35] *Ibid.,* pp. 198–200.

CHAPTER 7: QUARRY FARM, SUMMER, 1876

(Pages 90–99)

[1] Letter to Mrs. Susie and Lillie G. W[arner], June 17, [1876], *MTP,* © copyright 1960 by Mark Twain Co.

[2] Letter of August 1, 1876, TS in *MTP,* © copyright 1960 by Mark Twain Co.

[3] *My Father Mark Twain,* pp. 78, 61.

[4] Letter of March 14, 1882, in *A Study of Stimulants,* ed. A. Arthur Reade (Manchester, 1883), pp. 120–123.

[5] He had an agreement with Bliss to produce such a book. He and Howells had exchanged letters about a proposed trip on the river to collect materials. But a letter of August 4, [1876], shows that he had left this manuscript in Hartford. *Mark Twain to Mrs. Fairbanks,* p. 201.

[6] *Ibid.,* p. 118.

[7] *The Twainian,* March, 1943.

[8] *Mark Twain to Mrs. Fairbanks,* p. 218, indicates he worked on it about this time.

[9] Franklin J. Meine learnedly discusses some of these sources (though not D'Urfey's poem) in his edition of *1601* privately printed by the Mark Twain Society (Chicago, 1939), pp. 57–65.

[10] Clemens gave his consent for private printings only, although many unauthorized editions have appeared. See Meine's edition for a bibliography, admittedly incomplete.

[11] Norris W. Yates, *William T. Porter and the "Spirit of the Times"* (Baton Rouge, 1957), pp. 122–136. Mr. Yates has considerately omitted some details from the excerpt dealing with Squire Funk.

[12] *Mark Twain: Man and Legend,* p. 185.

[13] *Atlantic Monthly,* May, 1876, reprinted in *My Mark Twain,* p. 126. Italics mine.

[14] *Life in Letters,* I, 206; *MTaW,* p. 10.
[15] *Life in Letters,* I, 212.
[16] *MTaW,* p. 46.
[17] Letters to Elisha Bliss, July 22 and August 8, 1876; letter to Moncure D. Conway, August 1, 1876, *MTP.*
[18] Letter to Conway, August 14, [1876], *MTP.*
[19] Letter to Moncure Conway, August 1, 1876, TS in *MTP.* In this letter he estimated that he had written only a third of the book, however.

CHAPTER 8: HARTFORD, HANNIBAL, AND HUCK

(Pages 100–109)

[1] This included, evidently, chapters i–xvi of the novel as we now know it, with two exceptions. One exception was an insert written later, beginning with paragraph 12 of chapter xii and ending with chapter xiv. The other exception is a passage about Huck's visit to a raft which followed the second paragraph of chapter xvi.

[2] In *Tom Sawyer,* neither Tom's nor Huck's age is mentioned; and I believe that the omission is intentional. A few years later, writing *The Prince and the Pauper,* Twain studiously avoided mentioning any dates that would remind readers that his boys were less than ten years old when he was "making them too wise and knowing for their *real* age." Unpublished letter of March 9, 1881, to "Mr. Anthony," *MTP,* © copyright 1960 by Mark Twain Co.

[3] Between ten and twelve months after the action starts, Huck uses the phrase quoted in chapter xvii when he remarks that Buck Grangerford "looked about as old as me." Notice, though, that Huck's age still is not precisely indicated.

[4] For purposes of comparison I have made some changes in the order of the sentences.

[5] DV 47, TS p. 5, *MTP,* © copyright 1960 by Mark Twain Co.

[6] "Villagers," TS p. 4; "Autobiography of a Damned Fool," TS p. 40, *MTP,* © copyright 1960 by Mark Twain Co.

[7] This is Si Higgens, identified in working notes as Jimmy Finn. "Autobiography of a Damned Fool," DV 310, TS p. 25, *MTP,* © copyright 1960 by Mark Twain Co.

[8] "Recollections of Norval L. ('Gull') Brady," Hannibal *Courier-Post,* March 6, 1935.

[9] Norman Dwight Harris, *History of Negro Slavery in Illinois and of the Anti-Slavery Agitation in That State* (Chicago, 1906), pp. 112–115.

CHAPTER 9: THE LITERARY FLUX

(Pages 111–129)

[1] Andrews, *Nook Farm,* p. 201.

[2] In 1873 Mrs. Stowe had anticipated such books by Northern invaders with her book about Florida, *Palmetto Leaves.*

[3] F. L. Pattee, *American Literature since 1870* (New York, 1915); J. B. Hubbell, *The South in American Literature* (Durham, 1954), pp. 695–804. In April, 1873,

Clemens recognized an unconscious plagiarism from Miss Woolson by C. D. Warner.

⁴ *MTP*, © copyright 1960 by Mark Twain Co.

⁵ Page inserted in MS of *Tom Sawyer's Conspiracy*, *MTP*.

⁶ Bret Harte, "The Rise of the 'Short Story,' " *Cornhill Mag.*, n.s. VII (July, 1899), 3.

⁷ Blair, *Native American Humor*, pp. 29–31; Boatright, *Folk Laughter on the American Frontier*, pp. 24–33.

⁸ T. B. Thorpe, "The Disgraced Scalp-Lock," *Spirit of the Times*, July 16, 1842, p. 229, reprinted in two books by Thorpe, one in 1846, another in 1854.

⁹ Letter of February 6, 1879, *Letters to Will Bowen*, p. 18. This contains a quotation from the General used in one of the boasts in *Huck*, "Whoop! Bow your neck and spread!" An earlier letter dated January 25, 1868, uses a phrase from the other boast, without attribution, "Give me room according to my strength." *Ibid.*, p. 17.

¹⁰ Twain refers to Mike Fink specifically in a notebook of 1882, *MTP*, and in a working note for *Huckleberry Finn*.

¹¹ *Life on the Mississippi*, chap. iii.

¹² First published in *The Spirit of the Times* in 1841; reprinted widely and included in a book by Thorpe in 1854.

¹³ See also *A Treasury of Mississippi River Folklore*, ed. B. A. Botkin (New York, 1955), pp. 4–5.

¹⁴ Documentation for statements about Carlyle and Dickens in this chapter will be found in Walter Blair, "The French Revolution and *Huckleberry Finn*," *Mod. Philol.*, IV (August, 1957), 21–35.

¹⁵ Twain had cited this custom of Bird's Jibbenainosay in the initial "Old Times" article. Bird quotes several old-time humorous frontier boasts.

¹⁶ Olin H. Moore, "Mark Twain and Don Quixote," *PMLA*, XXXVII (June, 1922), 337–338.

¹⁷ Berg Collection, quoted with the permission of the New York Public Library.

¹⁸ In chapter iv Huck comes upon Pap's footprints in the snow, and in chapter viii he finds signs of Jim's co-tenancy of Jackson's Island. These incidents are reminiscent of Robinson Crusoe's thrilling discovery of Friday's footprint—and *Robinson Crusoe* was a book Clemens often read with his daughters. Yet there is not enough borrowing—or enough adaptation—to make a comparison of the source and the episodes of any interest.

¹⁹ C. Grant Loomis, "Dan De Quille's Mark Twain," *Pacific Historical Rev.*, XV (September, 1946), 336–347.

²⁰ Mark Twain, "Mental Telegraphy," *Harper's Monthly*, LXXXIV (December, 1891), 97. Letters which Wright exchanged with Clemens cast doubt upon Clemens' accuracy concerning dates, but otherwise do not invalidate this account. Searchers for a more mundane reason for the happening will note that "the Big Bonanza," the Comstock Lode, and Virginia City had been in the newspapers a great deal just before these newspapermen got their simultaneous inspirations.

²¹ Quoted by Oscar Lewis in "Introduction" to Dan De Quille, *The Big Bonanza* (New York, 1953), p. xix. Clemens' comment about the value of statistics offers an interesting insight into his method of writing humorous-factual books.

[22] *Ibid.*, pp. xxi–xxiii. De Quille tells about the one-week stay on the seacoast in a letter printed in the *Territorial Enterprise*, September 3, 1875.

[23] I omit consideration of repetitions and references back to these chapters, written later.

[24] Dan De Quille, *History of the Big Bonanza* . . . (Hartford, 1877), pp. 368–369. Hereafter cited as *Big Bonanza*. A note in Notebook 14 for February 26, 1879, to September 8, 1879, *MTP*, parallels this remark. The likelihood is that Twain, uncertain at this time about finishing *Huck*, thought of using it in another book. Compare "You have the worst ideas about heaven of any man I ever saw" with Huck's remark (chap. xiv): "he was the most down on Soloman of any nigger I ever see."

[25] De Quille, *Big Bonanza*, p. 555.

[26] I omit, as dubious, consideration of a parallel between the passage in *Big Bonanza*, p. 553, wherein Pike sees the men who have tricked him and believes that they are ghosts, and the similar scene in chapter viii wherein Jim, on first seeing Huck on Jackson's Island, thinks him a ghost.

[27] *Ibid.*, pp. 272–273.

[28] Clemens, evidently liking the comic appeal of such a childlike concept of wealth, in later working notes reminded himself to recur to it again: "40 for Jim—who says 'told you I'd be rich agin.' " In "Chapter the Last" Tom gives Jim the specified sum, and Jim harks back to his prediction.

[29] *Big Bonanza*, pp. 554–555.

[30] Probably only an overeager searcher for parallels would make much of the slim resemblance of the itinerant "peddlers, showmen, and quack doctors" of De Quille to the king and the duke and the possible relationship of their "wonderful spotted boy" (*ibid.*, pp. 392–394) to Twain's camelopard. Also of dubious relevance is a passage in De Quille (pp. 366–367) wherein an old man discusses "that old rancher down in the Valley of Galilee, that the Bible tells of . . . when he had a frolic he wanted to see things whiz! . . . I mean that jolly old cock that gave the big blow-out when his oldest gal got married." This, it is true, is in the style of Jim's and Huck's talk about King Sollerman. But Mark had already exploited the incongruity between secular and religious phrasings in *Roughing It* and the passage about the Negro and the steamboat in *The Gilded Age*. Long before, he must have heard vernacular retellings of Biblical stories in Negro sermons.

[31] *Mark Twain's Autobiography*, I, 240. For an earlier account see "Unconscious Plagiarism," *Mark Twain's Speeches* (New York, 1910), pp. 56–58.

[32] A similar passage occurs in G. P. R. James, *One in a Thousand* (1836): a girl disguised as a page, on having a jackknife tossed into her lap, spreads her knees to catch it. Clemens may have read this; but it seems more likely that he encountered Reade's novel.

CHAPTER 10: "SO NOBLE . . . AND SO
BEAUTIFUL A BOOK"

(Pages 132–150)

[1] *Mark Twain to Mrs. Fairbanks*, pp. 208–209.

[2] *Loc. cit.*

[3] *Atlantic Monthly,* October, 1875.

[4] *Memories of a Hostess,* pp. 251–253. The awarding of votes, as Mrs. Fields recalled it, was slightly different.

[5] *What Is Man?* (Definitive Edition), XXVI, ix.

[6] Chester L. Davis, ed., "Mark Twain's Religious Beliefs as Indicated by Notations in His Books," *The Twainian,* May–June, July–August, September–October, November–December, 1956, describes an 1874 edition inscribed "F. W. Crane 1874" and "S. L. Clemens 1906." Except where indicated, my citations occur in these articles. Davis believes that the notations were made in 1906; but some clearly were written much earlier, and perhaps all were. Regardless, the markings show Clemens' reactions to Lecky's points. Paine does not cite the annotated edition which he has seen, but quotes comments by Clemens differing from those which Davis cites.

[7] Without reference to Lecky, Edgar Marquess Branch, *The Literary Apprenticeship of Mark Twain* (Urbana, 1950), pp. 200 ff., has pointed out the differences between the widow's and Miss Watson's "providences." He has gone on to argue that this contrast initiates a theme running through the novel: "the main action may be interpreted as Huck's faltering progress toward the widow's providence. . . ." This hypothesis leads Branch to several valuable insights, though, as will be seen, I do not believe that it is completely sound.

[8] A passage in Lecky which Clemens scored may have called his attention to this disparity between what was right and what the law sanctioned: in it Lecky notices "how widely the opinions of the philosophic classes in Rome were removed from the professed religion of the State" and that "the opinions of learned men never reflect faithfully those of the vulgar. . . ."

[9] Clemens did not mark this passage in I, 60–64, of his edition.

[10] © copyright 1960 by Mark Twain Co. Clemens' copy of the Tauchnitz edition, with his markings and insertions, is in *MTP.* Page references in Notebook 28a, kept between May 15, 1895, and August 23, 1895, *MTP,* indicate that this edition and the marked passages were used in lectures.

[11] In chapter xii Huck and Jim make the decision about borrowing. Huck says, "We warn't feeling just right before that [decision], but it was all comfortable now." In chapter xvi, after fooling Jim, Huck spends fifteen minutes deciding to apologize. In neither instance, though, are the workings of conscience explored.

[12] Clemens did not mark these passages, I, 62–64, of the 1874 edition.

[13] *My Mark Twain,* p. 34; Kipling, *From Sea to Sea* (New York, 1913), II, 170.

[14] All interpolated passages © copyright 1960 by Mark Twain Co.

[15] Notebook 28a, TS p. 21, *MTP,* © copyright 1960 by Mark Twain Co.

[16] Notebook 28a, TS pp. 35–36, *MTP,* © copyright 1960 by Mark Twain Co.

[17] "Introduction" to *Adventures of Huckleberry Finn* (Boston, 1958).

[18] *My Father Mark Twain,* p. 24.

[19] *Portable Mark Twain,* p. 776.

[20] *MTP.*

[21] Letter of August 25, 1876, *MTP,* © copyright 1960 by Mark Twain Co.

CHAPTER 11: MISTAKES AND MISFORTUNES

(Pages 152–166)

[1] Dixon Wecter, *Literary History of the United States* (New York, 1948), II, 933. The emphasis is not new: in 1912 Paine in his *Biography* confined his list of highlights of *Huck* almost entirely to later portions.

[2] *MTaW*, p. 56. DeVoto's statement actually concerns a longer period than I am considering here—1876–1882.

[3] *Loc. cit.*

[4] Quoted by George C. D. Odell, *Annals of the New York Stage* (New York, 1938), X, 194.

[5] *My Mark Twain*, p. 22.

[6] Quoted in *Mark Twain to Mrs. Fairbanks*, p. 206.

[7] Letter to Howells, January, 1879. In the same letter Clemens reports that he found the detective play, on rereading, "dreadfully witless and flat."

[8] *My Mark Twain*, p. 59.

[9] For this and other details about the banquet, see Henry Nash Smith, " 'That Hideous Mistake' of Poor Clemens's,' " *Harvard Library Bull.*, IX (Spring, 1955).

[10] Ferguson, *Mark Twain: Man and Legend*, p. 192.

[11] *Mark Twain to Mrs. Fairbanks*, p. 217.

[12] "Some Rambling Notes of an Idle Excursion," in *Tom Sawyer Abroad and Other Stories*. Despite the fact that the trip was defiantly "idle," the author kept a notebook and wrote it up in a series for the *Atlantic Monthly*.

[13] *Mark Twain to Mrs. Fairbanks*, p. 197.

[14] TS in *MTP*, © copyright 1960 by Mark Twain Co.

[15] Joseph F. Daley, *Augustin Daly* (New York, 1917), p. 147.

[16] Letter of August 6, 1877, *Mark Twain to Mrs. Fairbanks*, pp. 206–207.

[17] *Ibid.*, p. 210.

[18] *Ibid.*, p. 230. He first wrote "the intolerable expenses," then crossed out the phrase.

[19] *Ibid.*, pp. 210, 222.

[20] *Mark Twain's Notebook*, p. 131. Paine reversed the order of the paragraphs.

[21] Notebook 14, *MTP*, © copyright 1960 by Mark Twain Co. Clemens wrote similarly to Howells, May 4, 1878, in a letter in the Berg Collection, New York Public Library.

[22] *Portable Mark Twain*, p. 754.

[23] *Memories of a Hostess*, p. 246.

[24] *Mark Twain's Notebook*, p. 133.

[25] Letter of May 4, 1878, to Howells, Berg Collection, New York Public Library.

[26] Lucerne, August 20, 1878, Berg Collection, New York Public Library.

[27] TS in *MTP*, © copyright 1960 by Mark Twain Co.

[28] Hotel Normandie, Paris, April 13, 1879, Berg Collection, New York Public Library.

[29] Notebook 14, TS p. 41, *MTP*, © copyright 1960 by Mark Twain Co.

[30] June 10, 1878, *AL*, VIII (March, 1936).

[31] To Frank Bliss, Jr., from Heidelberg, TS in *MTP*, © copyright 1960 by Mark Twain Co.

[32] TS in *MTP*.

[33] Jervis Langdon, *Some Reminiscences*, p. 10; letter to Twichell, June 23, 1879, Morse Collection, Yale University.

[34] *Mark Twain to Mrs. Fairbanks*, p. 226. In his letter to Taylor his estimate had been 112 to 125 words per page.

[35] Letters to Frank Bliss, May 10; to Aldrich, May 15; to his mother and sister, May 29, *MTP*.

[36] New York *Herald*, September 3, 1879.

[37] TS in *MTP*, © copyright 1960 by Mark Twain Co.

[38] New York *Herald*, September 3, 1879.

[39] *Mark Twain to Mrs. Fairbanks*, pp. 232–233.

CHAPTER 12: ''I GENERALIZE WITH INTREPIDITY''

(Pages 168–184)

[1] In 1898 Clemens disqualified himself as a literary critic for similar reasons: "I often want to criticize Jane Austen, but her books madden me so that I can't conceal my frenzy from the reader; and therefore I have to stop. . . ."

[2] Some pages of manuscript about the early part of the trip in which the family appears survive in the *MTP*. August 20, 1878, Clemens wrote from Lucerne to Frank Bliss that he had had to invent a new plan for the book (Berg Collection, New York Public Library). This may have been when he decided to leave out the family.

[3] To Howells, Munich, January 30, 1879, in *Life in Letters*, I, 264.

[4] *Atlantic Monthly*, May, 1880, reprinted in *My Mark Twain*, pp. 130–132.

[5] Compare the passages quoted on pp. 71, 101–102, 189.

[6] Compare the passages quoted on pp. 102, 257, 258.

[7] Notebook 12, TS p. 14, *MTP*, © copyright 1960 by Mark Twain Co.

[8] Ferguson, *Mark Twain: Man and Legend*, p. 200.

[9] *Mark Twain's America*, p. 251.

[10] *Portable Mark Twain*, p. 750.

[11] DV 4, *MTP*.

[12] Letter of September 15, 1878, TS in *MTP*, © copyright 1960 by Mark Twain Co.

[13] *Mark Twain's Notebook*, p. 153.

[14] Notebook 14, TS pp. 16, 28, 30, 33, *MTP*, © copyright 1960 by Mark Twain Co. An interesting anomaly is the fact that in the midst of one stern discussion of French immorality, Clemens paused to translate a portion of a smutty French folk song, and then crossed it out. The comments, also, were current with his preparation of a famous unpublished speech, "The Science of Onanism," which was quite broad in its humor, and its delivery before a masculine group of artists, the Stomach Club, in Paris. I do not think that hypocrisy was involved here—simply the Victorian belief that smut was all right for men but degrading for women.

[15] The letter to Twichell is in *MTP*, © copyright 1960 by Mark Twain Co.; the description of the novel is in *Mark Twain to Mrs. Fairbanks*, p. 208; the French orthography is Clemens'.

[16] *Mark Twain to Mrs. Fairbanks,* pp. 207–209.

[17] Notebook 14, TS p. 27, *MTP,* © copyright 1960 by Mark Twain Co.

[18] DV 67, *MTP,* © copyright 1960 by Mark Twain Co.

[19] *Mark Twain's Notebook,* p. 380.

[20] Notebook 14, TS p. 37, *MTP,* © copyright 1960 by Mark Twain Co.

[21] *Mark Twain as Literary Artist,* pp. 315–316. Miss Bellamy has preceded me in noticing that the islanders "follow this Yankee [Stavely] like blind sheep, yielding themselves to be molded by his consuming desire for personal power," and that "finally some . . . lingering vestige of self-respect" prompts their rebellion. The part of her interpretation with which I disagree is that the theme of the story is that "a too-quick civilization brings disaster": the story is not so told, I believe, as to develop this moral.

CHAPTER 13: STRONG MILK FOR BABES

(Pages 186–196)

[1] These and additional aspects of his favorable attitude toward England are considered in Howard G. Baetzhold, "Mark Twain: England's Advocate," *AL,* XXVIII (November, 1956), 328–346.

[2] *Mark Twain to Mrs. Fairbanks,* p. 218.

[3] Among notes for *The Prince and the Pauper,* DV 15, *MTP,* is one reading, "Nobody in town—Bought Timbs—Walks—Stow—Leigh Hunt, and a lot of authorities and *read* about a thing, then went leisurely to see it." (© copyright 1960 by Mark Twain Co.) The three books mentioned are cited in footnotes to the novel.

[4] Letters to Orion Clemens, February 26 and March 5, 1880; to Howells, March 5, March 11, December 24, 1880; to Thomas Bailey Aldrich, September 15, 1880, *MTP;* to "Miss Annie," January 31, 1881, in *Mark Twain the Letter Writer* (Boston, 1932), p. 37.

[5] DV 15, *MTP,* © copyright 1960 by Mark Twain Co.

[6] *Mark Twain's Notebook,* p. 150. Immediately preceding this is a discussion of some reading, "that disgusting Tom Jones," Notebook 14, TS p. 4, *MTP.*

[7] *Mark Twain's Notebook,* pp. 156–157.

[8] Andrews, *Nook Farm,* p. 266.

[9] Letter of October 24, 1881, *MTP.*

[10] In the chapter for *Huck* "a woman in our town . . . loved her husband dearly but another man twict as well"; in this book, "She loved her husband dearilee, but another man he loved she." Clemens had sung it on his wedding trip, though, as an auditor remarks, it "does not seem particularly appropriate." Webster, *Mark Twain, Business Man,* p. 109.

[11] Roger Blaine Salomon, "Mark Twain's Conceptions of History" (unpublished doctoral dissertation, University of California, 1957), p. 157. Mr. Salomon, whose excellent study was brought to my attention after I had written this chapter and those which precede it, traces developments in Clemens' thinking in this period very similar to those which I have found, although he has other interests than mine. His chronology is different from mine in some important ways: he places at a later date than I do Clemens' complete disillusionment about American govern-

ment; he assigns Clemens' acquaintance with Lecky to a period much later than I do—not in 1874 (Paine's date) but in 1883–1889; and he puts Clemens' reading of materials for *The Prince and the Pauper* later than I do. Nevertheless, I was heartened to find so many elements of agreement.

[12] Salomon, pp. 163–165.

[13] Notebook 15, TS p. 2, *MTP.*

[14] As time passes Tom is tortured less and less by his conscience, and similarly his family "cease to trouble his thoughts wholly." In his discussion of conscience Lecky notes (I, 65–66) that some people are eventually inured against such pangs: "their repugnance simply ceases."

[15] Shortly before, Twain had written in chapter xxxvi of *A Tramp Abroad* an ironic passage about selfish motives. He tells about his disgust with Harris for being pleased because a young girl has been saved from a plunge into a stream: "He began straight off, and continued for an hour, to express his gratitude. . . . that was the kind of person he was; just so *he* was gratified, he never cared about anybody else . . . he cared not a straw for my feelings, or my loss of such a literary plum. . . . His selfishness was sufficient to place his own gratification . . . clear before all concern for me, his friend. Apparently, he did not once reflect upon the valuable details which would have fallen like a windfall to me. . . ."

[16] Bellamy, *Mark Twain as Literary Artist,* p. 310.

[17] Miss Bellamy errs, I think, in believing that Twain allowed his interest in Tom's story to take over the book: the two characters are equally important in three chapters; Edward's story is told in eighteen chapters; and Tom's in twelve. I place more emphasis than she does upon what happens to Edward.

[18] As Henry Nash Smith has noticed, they are related to the vagrants who had pretended to be venerated authors in the Whittier birthday speech.

[19] Compare "The boys jumped for the river—both of them hurt—and as they swum down the current the men run along the bank shouting at them and singing out, 'Kill them, kill them!' " *Huckleberry Finn,* chap. xviii.

CHAPTER 14: THE GRANGERFORDS

(Pages 198–219)

[1] In chapter xvii of *A Tramp Abroad,* Twain ended his and Harris's journey on the raft with a burlesque account of its wreck in a storm.

[2] This was first published as an introduction to the Limited Editions Club issue of the novel in 1942, later in *MTaW,* pp. 45–104.

[3] "When Was *Huckleberry Finn* Written?" *AL,* XXX (March, 1958), 1–25.

[4] Less specific, though relevant, is an interview Clemens gave, published in the Chicago *Times,* November 15, 1879. He is reported as saying that as soon as he finishes *A Tramp Abroad* "it is his intention to commence another book at once. The plot of this book," he told the reporter, "is now developing in his head. A third book is to follow this as soon as possible, and before he takes a vacation."

[5] The notes are printed in full in *MTaW,* pp. 64–78.

[6] Notebook 14, TS pp. 3–4, *MTP,* © copyright 1960 by Mark Twain Co.

[7] *Autobiography,* II, 73. Twain has inserted the phrase describing Emmeline in the original TS in *MTP,* © copyright 1960 by Mark Twain Co. See my p. 86.

[8] Franklin R. Rogers, "The Role of Literary Burlesque in the Development of Mark Twain's Structural Patterns" (unpublished doctoral dissertation, University of California, 1958), p. 195.

[9] MS in the Berg Collection, New York Public Library, pp. 15–16, 60, 322. Hank, unlike Bots, is revived.

[10] Robert J. Lowenherz, "Mark Twain Laughs at Death," *Mark Twain Jour.*, X (Spring–Summer, 1958).

[11] See Julia A. Moore, *The Sweet Singer of Michigan*, with an introduction by Walter Blair (Chicago, 1928).

[12] To John Hoover, January 12, 1906, TS in *MTP*, © copyright 1960 by Mark Twain Co.

[13] Caroline Matilda Kirkland in *A New Home—Who'll Follow?* (1839) pictured two sentimental poetesses whom Clemens may have read about. Similarly Frances Miriam Whitcher's Widow Bedott—mentioned three times in Clemens' 1880 notebook as a humorous character—engaged in sentimental versifying often marred by the intrusion of colloquialisms. These may have been influential, but I believe that Mrs. Moore was most influential on the picturing of Emmeline.

[14] MS in the Berg Collection, New York Public Library, pp. 6–7.

[15] Jane Louise Mesick, *The English Traveler in America, 1785–1835* (New York, 1922), pp. 67, 300. The quoted phrase is from William Newnham Blane, *An Excursion through the United States . . .* (London, 1824), p. 501.

[16] *European Magazine*, III (1825), 522.

[17] *Knickerbocker's History of New York*, Book IV, chap. ix.

[18] *North American Rev.*, XV (July, 1822), 252.

[19] F. P. Gaines, *The Southern Plantation* (New York, 1924), p. 64; Van Wyck Brooks, *The Times of Melville and Whitman* (New York, 1947), pp. 330–331; Paul H. Buck, *The Road to Reunion* (Boston, 1938), p. 208.

[20] Henry Childs Merwin, *The Life of Bret Harte* (Boston, 1911), p. 135.

[21] *Atlantic Monthly*, XXIX (March, 1872), 363. Italics mine.

[22] *Ibid.*, XXXIV (August, 1874), 228.

[23] *MTP*. A cryptic notebook entry of 1882 was "Kate Beaumont."

[24] *Heroines of Fiction* (New York, 1901), II, 155.

CHAPTER 15: THE FEUD

(Pages 220–238)

[1] "Villagers of 1840–3," TS p. 10, *MTP*, © copyright 1960 by Mark Twain Co.

[2] *Life on the Mississippi*, ed. Edward Wagenknecht (New York, 1944), p. 413. The passage was not included in the book.

[3] Notebook 15, TS p. 7, *MTP*, © copyright 1960 by Mark Twain Co.

[4] Compiled by George Francis Dawson (Washington, 1880), p. 173.

[5] Chicago *Times*, November 14, 1879.

[6] H. C. Thomas, *The Return of the Democratic Party to Power in 1884* (New York, 1919), p. 55.

[7] The quoted words are in *The Republican Campaign Text Book for 1880*, pp. 13, 113–126.

[8] Federal Writers Project, *In the Land of Breathitt* (Northport, N. Y., 1941),

pp. 61–67; Charles G. Mutzenberg, *Kentucky's Famous Feuds and Tragedies* (New York, 1917), pp. 278–279.

[9] Virgil Carrington Jones, *The Hatfields and the McCoys* (Chapel Hill, 1948), p. 69.

[10] Rogers, "The Role of Literary Burlesque . . . ," p. 199.

[11] Robert A. Lively, *Fiction Fights the Civil War* (Chapel Hill, 1957), p. 57.

[12] Cholmondely to Clemens, March 12, 1885; Clemens to Cholmondely, March 28, 1885, *MTP*, © copyright 1960 by Mark Twain Co.

[13] Notebook 16, TS p. 13, *MTP*, © copyright 1960 by Mark Twain Co.

[14] The secretarial notebook containing the reminiscences is Paine 259, *MTP*. All quoted portions © copyright 1960 by Mark Twain Co.

[15] A 12mo sheet containing this notation and 29 additional lines which are not quoted were included in a book offered for sale in 1911, *Anderson Auction Company Catalogue*, No. 892, p. 32.

[16] Wagenknecht, pp. 52–53. The first passage is in a letter, the second in an answer to Paul Bourget's attack on the United States.

[17] Pp. 27–28, New York Public Library.

[18] *Mark Twain to Mrs. Fairbanks*, p. 227.

[19] Mark Van Doren in a recent critical study, *Don Quixote's Profession* (New York, 1958), pp. 41–53, remarks that one long important series of adventures among three which "run through the entire work like a thread" is "the series of hoaxes, or pretended agreement on the part of others that Don Quixote is what ho says he is." After a point in the novel someone is constantly "humoring, indulging, or hoaxing" the knight. A climax is the deception of the duke and the duchess in Part II. Similarly Edward, clad in rags, is accepted by various groups who pretend that he is the royal personage he claims he is. Variants in *Huck* are Huck's and Jim's accepting and pretending to accept the king and the duke as what they claim to be.

[20] Paine 259, *MTP*, © copyright 1960 by Mark Twain Co.

[21] Lillian Ross, "How Do You Like It Now, Gentlemen?" *New Yorker*, XXVI (May 13, 1950), 44–45.

CHAPTER 16: "THE CHIEF (LOW-COMEDY) HUMORISTS"

(Pages 242–248)

[1] The story is reprinted in Blair, *Native American Humor*, pp. 330–333.

[2] *Mark Twain's America*, pp. 252–253. Mark Twain's version is called "The Invalid's Story."

[3] Interesting is the role the anecdote gives "that poor old ashcat," Gammer Hooker. Mrs. Isabella Hooker, a Nook Farm neighbor of the Clemenses, a religionist and a spiritualist, possibly was considered by some Philistines (including her long-suffering husband) to be possessed by devils.

[4] *Alta California*, July 14, 1867.

[5] Notebook 14, TS p. 10, *MTP*, © copyright 1960 by Mark Twain Co.

[6] Letters to Osgood, March 4, 1882, and to Howells, March 4, April 19, 1881, and March 27, 1882. *MTP*.

[7] Frances Whitcher's heroine wrote sentimental poems anticipatory of those by Emmeline Grangerford.

[8] Notebooks 14, 15, 16, *MTP*.

[9] Notebook 19, TS p. 24, *MTP*, © copyright 1960 by Mark Twain Co.

[10] *The Spirit of the Times*, XXI (June 28, 1851), 205. See the chapter, "All Sorts of a Stirring Place," in Boatright, *Folk Laughter* . . . , pp. 16–23, for comment upon similar picturings of the frontier.

[11] Salomon, "Mark Twain's Conceptions of History," pp. 110–112.

[12] *MTaW*, p. 65. Working notes mentioned later in this paragraph are printed on pp. 66, 67, 74.

[13] O. P. Fitzgerald, *Judge Longstreet, A Life Sketch* (Nashville, 1891), p. 164.

[14] *MTaW*, p. 69.

CHAPTER 17: BACK ON THE RIVER

(Pages 250–257)

[1] Rogers, "The Role of Literary Burlesque . . . ," p. 199.

[2] Letter to Howells, March, 1877, *MTP*.

[3] The working notes are with the manuscript, Berg Collection, New York Public Library.

[4] He calls Jim, who is Miss Watson's slave, "a slave of the widow's," and says that when Huck visits the raft he and Jim have begun to suspect that they have passed Cairo in the fog. The former inaccuracy may just possibly occur because he did not want to complicate his synopsis unduly, but I suspect that—as he has once before—he had forgotten about the widow's sister. Part of working note B-2 of 1879–1880 reads: "Widow Douglas—Then who is 'Miss Watson?' Ah she's WD's *sister*—old spinster." *MTaW*, p. 71. I can think of no reason for his second inaccuracy except his misremembering.

[5] October 21, 1882, *MTP*, © copyright 1960 by Mark Twain Co.

[6] March 16, 1880, *MTP*.

[7] New York *Sun*, December 16, 1939.

[8] March 1, 1883, TS in *MTP*, © copyright 1960 by Mark Twain Co.

CHAPTER 18: FRENZIED FINANCE

(Pages 262–269)

[1] *My Father Mark Twain*, p. 57.

[2] Letter to John Hay, March 18, 1882, *Life in Letters*, I, 311–312.

[3] *MTP*, © copyright 1960 by Mark Twain Co.

[4] Letter to Pamela Moffett, March 16, 1881, Webster, *Mark Twain, Business Man* (hereafter cited as *Bus. Man*), p. 150; *Mark Twain to Mrs. Fairbanks*, pp. 245–246.

[5] *Bus. Man*, p. 17.

[6] *Ibid.*, pp. 142–143, 147.

[7] *Ibid.*, p. 118.

[8] Letter to Osgood, February 12, 1875, Rogers Theatrical Collection, Houghton Library, Harvard University.

[9] Frank Bliss to Mark Twain, March 26, 1879, *MTP*.

[10] *Bus. Man,* pp. 139, 153, 239.

[11] Pamela Moffett to Samuel E. Moffett, March 20, 1881, *MTP.*

[12] Entries in Notebook 15, TS pp. 21–23, *MTP.*

[13] Pamela Moffett to Samuel E. Moffett, April 3, 1881, *MTP.*

[14] *Ibid.,* May 9, 1881, *MTP,* © copyright 1960 by Mark Twain Co.

[15] Pamela Moffett to Samuel E. Moffett, June 3, 1881, *MTP.*

[16] *Bus. Man,* p. 161.

[17] Pamela Moffett to Samuel E. Moffett, July 26, 1881, *MTP,* © copyright 1960 by Mark Twain Co.

[18] *Bus. Man,* pp. 204, 79.

[19] Charles L. Webster to Annie Webster, August 1, 1881, *MTP,* © copyright 1960 by Mark Twain Co.

[20] *Bus. Man,* pp. 153–154, 157, 160; Webster to Clemens, May 5–6, 1881, *MTP.*

[21] Webster to Clemens, August 11, 1881, *MTP,* © copyright 1960 by Mark Twain Co.

[22] Webster to Clemens, September 9, 1881; Pamela Moffett to Samuel E. Moffett, September 11, 1881, *MTP.*

[23] Webster to Clemens, August 11, 1881, *MTP.*

[24] *Bus. Man,* pp. 198–204.

[25] *Ibid.,* p. 192.

[26] Webster to Clemens, April 26, 1881, *MTP,* © copyright 1960 by Mark Twain Co.

[27] Pamela Moffett to Samuel E. Moffett, August 2, 1881, *MTP,* © copyright 1960 by Mark Twain Co.

[28] *Bus. Man,* p. 157.

[29] *Ibid.,* p. 183.

[30] *Ibid.,* p. 165.

CHAPTER 19: THE DUKE AND THE DAUPHIN

(Pages 271–283)

[1] *Speeches* (Stormfield Edition), XXVIII, 140–141.

[2] The name was spelled both "Lambton" and "Lampton."

[3] *MTP,* © copyright 1960 by Mark Twain Co.

[4] Letter of March 7, 1881, Rogers Theatrical Collection, Houghton Library, Harvard University.

[5] Notebook 3, TS p. 7, *MTP* and end paper in the original notebook, © copyright 1960 by Mark Twain Co. Luce Marieau I have not identified: Twain may have thought that these were good first names for a Bilgewater.

[6] Letter of [May] 10, 1869, *Mark Twain to Mrs. Fairbanks,* p. 95.

[7] *Mark Twain to Mrs. Fairbanks,* pp. 213–215; *Bus. Man,* p. 215.

[8] "The 'Duke's' Tooth-Powder Racket," *Mod. Lang. Notes,* LXI (November, 1946), 468–469.

[9] *Mark Twain's America,* pp. 318–319.

[10] "The Wild Man Interviewed," Buffalo *Express,* July 25, 1870.

[11] Yates, *William T. Porter . . . ,* p. 137.

[12] See James G. Harrison, "A Note on the Duke in *Huck Finn:* The Journeyman

Printer as Picaro," *Mark Twain Quar.*, VIII (Winter, 1947), 1–3. A passage about Singularity is in Burton's *Cyclopaedia of Wit and Humor* (New York, 1858), which Clemens read in part at least in 1880. (Notebook 15, *MTP.*) The "Wandering Typo" was created by John S. Robb for the St. Louis *Reveille* during Clemens' years in Hannibal.

¹³ Notebook 15, *MTP*, © copyright 1960 by Mark Twain Co.

¹⁴ *Mark Twain's America*, p. 255.

¹⁵ "Introduction" to *Adventures of Huckleberry Finn* (Boston, 1958), p. xix.

¹⁶ *MTP*, © copyright 1960 by Mark Twain Co.

¹⁷ Paine 259, *MTP.*

¹⁸ John Fox, Jr., *Blue-Grass and Rhododendron* (New York, 1901), p. 38.

CHAPTER 20: LIFE ON THE MISSISSIPPI

(PART II)

(Pages 286–299)

¹ *Love Letters*, pp. 210–213.

² Arlin Turner, "Mark Twain in New Orleans," *McNeese Rev.*, VI (1954), 10–13.

³ St. Louis *Post-Dispatch*, May 12, 1882; *Rollingpin's Humorous Illustrated Almanac* (New York, 1883). Carter was river editor on the St. Louis *Times.*

⁴ *Mark Twain's Notebook*, pp. 163, 165.

⁵ Notebook 16, TS pp. 12, 14, *MTP*, © copyright 1960 by Mark Twain Co.

⁶ On January 15, 1883, he told Cable he had "just finished." Guy A. Cardwell, *Twins of Genius* (East Lansing, 1953), p. 89. The same letter says that his secretary had been downed with scarlet fever "2½ weeks ago." A letter to Osgood inserted in the manuscript in the Morgan Library indicates that this happened when all but the "8th batch" had been copied, and that he expected it to be copied and forwarded presently. The letter to Webster is in *MTP*, © copyright 1960 by Mark Twain Co.

⁷ Paper and ink as well as the nature of the material indicate this source of parts of chapters xxxvi and liv.

⁸ See Henry Nash Smith, "Mark Twain's Images of Hannibal," *Univ. of Texas Studies in English*, XXXVII (1958), 11–13, for a description in somewhat different terms of the author's emotional conflicts.

⁹ *Atlantic Monthly*, LII (September, 1883), 407.

¹⁰ For refutations see H. J. Eckenrode, "Sir Walter Scott and the South," *North American Rev.*, CCVI (1917), 595–603; G. Harrison Orians, "Walter Scott, Mark Twain, and the Civil War," *South Atlantic Quar.*, XL (1941), 343–359.

¹¹ Six-page manuscript dated October 29, 1882, Rogers Theatrical Collection, Houghton Library, Harvard University.

¹² In a deleted passage he lists sixteen books, and elsewhere he quotes these and others. See *Life on the Mississippi*, ed. Edward Wagenknecht (New York, 1944), p. 402. This text (hereafter *LoM*) contains the deleted material, ed. Willis Wager.

¹³ On the upper left corner of the first page of the typescript, Rogers Theatrical

Collection, Harvard University, Osgood wrote: "I should suggest omitting this chapter."

[14] *LoM*, p. 392.

[15] *Ibid.*, pp. 402–407.

[16] *Ibid.*, pp. 407–411.

[17] *Ibid.*, pp. 412–416.

[18] Letter to Osgood, January 15, 1883, Morse Collection, Yale University.

[19] *LoM*, p. 395.

[20] *Ibid.*, p. vii.

[21] Robert Hunting, "Mark Twain's Arkansaw Yahoos," *Mod. Lang. Notes*, LXXIII (April, 1958), 264–267.

[22] *LoM*, p. 392.

[23] In chapter xxiii of *Domestic Manners* . . . Mrs. Trollope quotes the remark, "Cervantes laughed Spain's chivalry away," a point which Mark develops at some length when scolding Scott, who, he holds, had a very different sort of influence.

[24] If they had planned the performance in chapter xx as it was originally written, I believe that the duke would have printed advertisements for it when in that chapter he took over the Pokeville print shop. Instead, the printing is not taken care of until chapter xxi, when Huck says, somewhat inaccurately, "The first chance we got the duke he had some show-bills printed. . . ."

[25] *Love Letters*, p. 212.

[26] *LoM*, pp. 404–405, 406.

[27] Jane Louise Mesick, *The English Traveler in America, 1785–1835* (New York, 1922), p. 72. Miss Mesick cites passages by twelve different writers, one of them Mrs. Trollope.

[28] New York *Constellation*, July 14, 1832.

[29] Alexander Mackay, *Western World* (London, 1850), III, 33–37. Clemens may have read this before the trip, for it recounts the lynching of some gamblers in Natchez. In Notebook 16 he wrote: "Natchez . . . Hanging of (the gamblers)," TS p. 13, *MTP*.

CHAPTER 21: LIVELY TIMES IN BRICKSVILLE

(Pages 300–308)

[1] (*a*) If, as scholars agree, the trip reawakened Mark's interest in *Huck*, he would have been likely to return to it as soon as possible. (*b*) Sometime before the summer of 1883 he evidently had a typescript of the novel made, and notes on it as far along as chapter xx show the author preparing to continue the novel. (*c*) There is evidence that he wrote an insert for chapter xxi during the very month he wrote to Howells. See "When Was *Huckleberry Finn* Written?" *AL*, XXX (March, 1958), 17–19.

[2] My guess is that at Quarry Farm he began with chapter xxii, the first chapter of the partial manuscript which survives.

[3] Sol. Smith, *The Theatrical Journey-Work and Anecdotal Recollections* (Philadelphia, 1854), pp. 118–119.

[4] Minnie L. Brashear, *Mark Twain, Son of Missouri* (Chapel Hill, 1934), p. 135.

[5] Howells to Clemens, September 1, *Life in Letters*, I, 300; Clemens to Howells, September 3, Houghton Library, Harvard University.

[6] *Twins of Genius,* ed. Guy Cardwell, p. 52.

[7] *MTP,* © copyright 1960 by Mark Twain Co.

[8] On October 18, 1856, in a humorous letter the author told about seeing a performance of *Julius Caesar* in St. Louis; on April 10, 1857, in the same series he quoted a line from Hamlet's soliloquy. *The Adventures of Thomas Jefferson Snodgrass,* ed. Charles Honce (Chicago, 1928), pp. 3–16, 37. For his experiences with Ealer see "Is Shakespeare Dead?" in *What Is Man?* (Definitive Edition), XXVI, 299–305. The account of Ealer's readings interrupted by orders and curses echoes a passage about Uncle Mumford in *Life on the Mississippi.*

[9] Among suggested readings from *Huckleberry Finn* (others are denoted by typescript page numbers) he has "—1—2 Hamlet's Soliloquy." Notebook 17, *MTP.* He often numbered manuscript interpolations —1, —2, —3, and so forth.

[10] See Shields McIlwaine, *The Southern Poor-White from Lubberland to Tobacco Road* (Norman, 1939).

[11] William Tappan Thompson, "The Mystery Revealed," first published in 1844, appeared in *The Chronicles of Pineville* in 1845 and in nine subsequent editions before 1880. I quote the 1858 edition, pp. 60–61.

[12] "The Burning Shame at Napoleon, Ark.," *MTaW,* p. 64.

[13] James R. Masterson, "A Dog with a Bad Name," *Tall Tales of Arkansas* (Boston, 1943), pp. 1–14.

[14] Edward S. King, *The Great South* (Hartford, 1875), pp. 278, 280.

[15] A full account is in Wecter's *Sam Clemens of Hannibal,* pp. 106–108. Parallels between the Hannibal episode and the novel: the man committing the murder was a leading merchant; he called out his victim's name before shooting; only two shots were fired; only one man was killed; the victim was carried to a nearby store to die; some fool tortured the dying man by placing a big Bible on his chest. None of these details occurs in the "newspaper item." In the typescript of his *Autobiography* Mark annotated his mention of the shooting in Hannibal thus: "See 'Adventures of Huckleberry Finn.'" *MTP.*

[16] In a letter to Will Bowen in 1870; "Villagers of 1840–3"; *Autobiography,* I, 131, and a manuscript notation: "Owsley and Smar [*sic*]—Bible on breast. Gave him spiritual relief, no doubt, but must have crowded him physically"; and six other lines, listed in *Anderson Auction Company Catalogue* No. 892 (New York, 1911), p. 31, as an insert in a volume from Clemens' library entitled, ironically enough, *God in His World.*

[17] Hannibal *Missouri Courier,* May 20, 1850. Wecter suggests that possibly Mark Twain wrote the story. Mark's penciled footnote to the portion of the *Autobiography* dealing with this: "Used in 'Huck Finn,' I think." *MTP.*

CHAPTER 22: THE BRICKSVILLE MOB AND
THE ORNERINESS OF KINGS

(Pages 310–320)

[1] Henry W. Fisher, *Abroad with Mark Twain and Eugene Field* (New York, 1922), p. 50. For citations of specific passages quoted in the present chapter see "The French Revolution and *Huckleberry Finn,*" *MP,* LV (August, 1957), 31–33.

[2] The passage in *Huck* closest in detail to that by Carlyle occurs in the first

paragraph, chapter xxii: ". . . every window along the road was full of women's heads, and there was nigger boys in every tree, and bucks and wenches looking over every fence." This is not close enough to indicate specific and noteworthy influence, though it has value for comparison.

[3] Before this "the front wall of the crowd" has "rolled in like a wave." In chapter xxix Huck was to tell how another crowd "swarmed into the graveyard and washed over it like an overflow." Imagery comparing a mob in motion with a tide or a relentless sea is so commonplace in books about the French Revolution as to appear to be mandatory.

[4] DV 47, *MTP*, © copyright 1960 by Mark Twain Co. Wecter says that the author's memory was faulty here: "Advertisements show that [Owsley] was still in business in Hannibal as late as 1853," seven years after his acquittal.

[5] In a Buffalo *Express* editorial, August, 1869, quoted by Philip S. Foner, *Mark Twain: Social Critic* (New York, 1958), p. 218; in *Ah Sin* (1877); in *A Tramp Abroad* (1880), chap. xlvii.

[6] James Elbert Cutler, *Lynch-Law* (New York, 1905), pp. 161–179.

[7] For an analysis of the prose style in this passage see George Mayberry, "Reading and Writing," *New Republic,* CX (May 1, 1944), 608.

[8] De Quille's "The Reckless Ride—Mazeppa" appeared in the *Territorial Enterprise,* April 21, 1867; Harris's story was in an obscure Tennessee newspaper in 1868.

[9] Thompson's books were *Major Jones's Courtship* (1843) and *The Chronicles of Pineville* (1845). Johnston's story was published in *Scribner's,* January, 1881, and in *Dukesborough Tales* (New York, 1883). A story from Thompson's first book and "The Expensive Treat . . ." are in *Mark Twain's Library of Humor.*

[10] Working note A-6 goes: "The Circus—Huck's astonishment when the drunkard invades the ring, scuffles with clown and ring-master, then rides and strips." *MTaW,* p. 66. Only in Thompson's version—though not in *Huck*—does the drunken man struggle with the clown. But Johnston's description of the riders is closer to Twain's; Thompson's drunk still pretends to be in trouble after mounting, while Johnston's and Twain's do not; Johnston's drunk "reeled back and forth from side to side . . . gathering up the reins," and Huck's "grabbed the bridle, a-reeling this way and that."

[11] *MTP,* © copyright 1960 by Mark Twain Co. Wecter cites a Hannibal *Journal* story, "The —— Troupe," March 27, 1852, about a similarly bad performance which he believes "beyond a doubt" was influential at this point. I believe that "just possibly" would be more accurate.

[12] *Life,* V, 119.

[13] The same version had appeared in the *Southern Watch Tower,* February 27, 1845, attributed to *Greens Patriot.*

[14] See B. J. Whiting, "Guyascutus, Royal Nonesuch and Other Hoaxes," *Southern Folklore Quar.,* VIII (December, 1944), 251–275; Yates, *William T. Porter and "The Spirit of the Times,"* pp. 181–182; Virginia City (Nevada) *Evening Bulletin,* December 7, 1863; J. W. DeForest, *Kate Beaumont* (Boston, 1872), p. 33.

[15] In "The Mystery Revealed," *The Chronicles of Pineville,* under completely different circumstances two dupes, "foreseeing the ridicule that was certain to be visited upon them by their fellow citizens, had recourse to the trick which

they so successfully practiced in order to involve their neighbors in the same dilemma as themselves."

[16] Buffalo manuscript, pp. 186–187, cited with the permission of the Buffalo Public Library.

[17] Whiting, "Guyascutus . . . ," p. 273.

[18] Poe so spelled it but some of his editors revised it to "camelopard." Mark Twain in the first edition of *Huck* spelled it "camelopard," but later his editors changed it to "cameleopard." Macaulay, whose writings the humorist knew well, spelled it "cameleopard." Either spelling is correct. The name is an ancient one for giraffe.

[19] He used the word "cameleopard" in a letter to Livy *circa* August 9, 1871. *Love Letters,* p. 160.

[20] Edward H. Davidson, *Poe, A Critical Study* (Cambridge, 1957), pp. 151–152.

CHAPTER 23: THE WILKS FUNERAL ORGIES

(Pages 322–333)

[1] The anthology of humor still unpublished was discussed now and then. The author's continuing interest in Southern writing of the past was evidenced by his delivering a paper, "Southern Literature," to the Monday Evening Club in February, 1884.

[2] "Make a kind of Huck Finn narrative on a boat—let him [i.e., the narrator, I take it] stay as a Cabin boy and another boy as a cub pilot—and so put the great river and its bygone ways into history in the form of a story." Notebook 18, *MTP,* © copyright 1960 by Mark Twain Co. Mark speaks, notice, not of "a narrative by Huck" but of "a kind of a Huck Finn narrative." The note evidently was written during the lecture tour with Cable, since an adjacent notation says that Cable has urged returning the raftsmen chapter to *Huck.*

[3] *MTaW,* pp. 64–67.

[4] *Ibid.,* pp. 73, 75.

[5] *Twins of Genius,* p. 76. For evidence that Clemens admired Cable's books before meeting him see *Talks in a Library with Lawrence Hutton* (New York, 1911), p. 416.

[6] *MTaW,* p. 67.

[7] In "Villagers of 1840–3" the author recalls two Nash sisters who became deaf and dumb because of scarlet fever. The entry is in Notebook 16 of 1882, *MTP.*

[8] *MTaW,* pp. 73–77. All these are insertions.

[9] *My Mark Twain,* p. 15.

[10] Anderson Auction Company, *Catalogue of the Library and Manuscripts of Samuel L. Clemens . . . to be sold Feb. 7 and 8, 1911.*

[11] The copy is owned by Franklin J. Meine. Precise citations of pages are given in "The French Revolution and *Huckleberry Finn,*" *Mod. Philol.,* LV (August, 1957), 27–28.

[12] "Introduction," *Adventures of Huckleberry Finn* (Boston, 1958), p. xiv.

[13] *Following the Equator,* chap. xxxvi. Later in the same book Mark has at the *Vicar* again. My thanks to Professor Smith for suggesting this parallel.

[14] Wecter cites a similar discussion of Greek etymology in a Hannibal newspaper of 1851 but does not claim it was a source. For the use of the device in ante-

bellum humor, see Yates, *William T. Porter* . . . , p. 101. Mark in 1866 had used the phrase "funeral orgies" in his description of islanders mourning "the late king." *Letters from the Sandwich Islands,* ed. G. Ezra Dane (San Francisco, 1937), p. 100.

[15] *Mark Twain's Notebook,* p. 58.

[16] Notebook 12; Notebook 17, TS pp. 7, 8, *MTP,* © copyright 1960 by Mark Twain Co.

[17] A detail in the conversation with Joanna preceding this decision relates to a passage in a notebook Clemens kept during his first trip to England about the American consulate's stupid requirement: "If you want to ship anything to America you must go there and swear to a great long rigmarole and *kiss the book* (years ago they found it was a dictionary). . . ." P. 117, *MTP,* © copyright 1960 by Mark Twain Co. Joanna asks Huck to place his hand on a book while making a statement: "I see it warn't nothing but a dictionary, so I laid my hand on it and said it." Huck's announcement after Mary Jane's departure, that she is visiting a neighbor with "the dreadful pluribus-unum mumps," echoes a like jest in *The Prince and the Pauper,* chap. xxiv.

[18] Working notes B-7 and B-8 show that the author had trouble working out details of this conclusion. *MTaW,* pp. 76, 78.

[19] See also Smith's "Introduction," p. xv.

CHAPTER 24: ''THE END. YOURS TRULY, HUCK FINN.''

(Pages 334–353)

[1] Note C-7 has: "Huck exposes k[ing] and d[uke] and makes them sell Jim?" This is crossed out.

[2] *LoM,* pp. 412–416.

[3] MS p. 165. Italics mine.

[4] Several revisions, this included, make the speech more colloquial.

[5] *Literary History of the United States* (New York, 1948), II, 937.

[6] Notebook 16, TS p. 27, *MTP.* Like Poe's "Four Beasts in One" and Huck's comments on church-going swine, the comments of the wiser Negro advantageously contrast beasts with men.

[7] Notebook 16, TS p. 44, *MTP,* © copyright 1960 by Mark Twain Co.

[8] Howell Cheney, *A List of Members* . . . , p. 37. Kenneth Andrews errs in believing that Clemens treated a similar topic on November 21, 1881, since on that date his paper was titled "Phrenology."

[9] *What Is Man and Other Essays* (Definitive Edition, New York, 1923), xxvi, 5, 15. This treatise was written in 1898 and after, published anonymously in 1906.

[10] Dictating his *Autobiography* in 1907 he said that "the idea of publishing [his gospel] always brought me a shudder."

[11] Alexander E. Jones, "Mark Twain and the Determinism of *What Is Man?*" *AL,* XXIX (March, 1957), 1–17. In chapter xxxiii (1883) Mark has Huck's conscience bother him as indiscriminately as it had in 1876 passages: "It don't make no difference whether you do right or wrong: a person's conscience goes for him *anyway."*

[12] Notebook 16, TS p. 42, *MTP,* © copyright 1960 by Mark Twain Co. Such

emphasis on the sinfulness of man probably was inevitable for one obsessed by worry about his own sinfulness.

[13] Notebook 16, TS p. 27, *MTP.*

[14] Willis Wager, *A Critical Edition of "Life on the Mississippi,"* p. lxvii.

[15] *Mark Twain's Notebook,* p. 181.

[16] Smith, "Introduction," p. xv.

[17] *Mark Twain's Notebook,* p. 181.

[18] As Jones points out, in "Mark Twain . . . ," pp. 15–16, even in "What Is Man?" Twain emphasized the belief that a man might train his ideals so that he might both content himself and confer benefits upon his neighbors and his community. Huck's moral decisions content Huck and benefit Jim.

[19] I have stated this too baldly. As Lionel Trilling warns, "we cannot make— . . . Mark does not make—an absolute opposition between river and human society." But absolute or not, he does make an opposition.

[20] For citations of these and other discussions see the Bibliography.

[21] Walter Blair, "Why Huck and Jim Went Downstream," *College English* (November, 1956), 106–107.

[22] "Introduction," pp. x–xi, and Smith's text of *Adventures of Huckleberry Finn,* p. 263.

[23] Between 1879 and the end of the summer of 1883 Twain wrote some briefer inserts. Notebook 13, *MTP* (© copyright 1960 by Mark Twain Co.), has: "When I get beyond 6 times 7 is 35 I'm done"—an accomplishment Huck mentions in chapter iv. Working note C-2 suggests his cogitations on bread cast upon the waters utilized in chapter viii.

[24] *MTaW,* p. 90. DeVoto adds that "the house of death, already in the book, was surely as likely a place to find them." It may be questioned whether the folk who drank, gambled, and murdered in this house had the time or the inclination to read much history.

[25] *Ibid.,* p. 91.

[26] A similar passage occurs in chapter xxxiii when Huck sees the king and the duke being lynched: "I was sorry for them poor pitiful rascals, it seemed like I couldn't ever feel any hardness against them any more in the world." Since Huck has good reason to be angry at the pair as betrayers of Jim, this is impressive.

[27] Mark Twain had cynically developed this theme in "Edward Mills and George Benton: A Tale," *Atlantic Monthly,* August, 1880.

[28] Canceled pagination in the manuscript indicates that chapter xiv from this point to the end was written separately.

[29] Interestingly, back in 1875 in an unfinished novel, "The Mysterious Chamber," Mark himself had attempted a serious novel about the ingenuities of a prisoner.

[30] An instance: ". . . it is right that the mood at the end of the book should bring us back to that of the beginning. . . . [Tom reappears] to provide a foil for Huck. . . . Huckleberry Finn must come from nowhere and be bound for nowhere. . . . He has no beginning and no end. Hence, he can only disappear; and his disappearance can only be accomplished by bringing forward another performer to obscure the disappearance in a cloud of whimsicalities." T. S. Eliot, "Introduction" to *The Adventures of Huckleberry Finn* (London, 1950), pp. viii–xvi.

[31] See O. H. Moore, "Mark Twain and *Don Quixote,*" *PMLA,* XXXVII (June,

1922), 324–346; Blair, "The French Revolution and *Huckleberry Finn*," *Mod. Philol.*, LV (August, 1957), 22–25.

[32] Webster to Clemens, April 21, 1884, DV 19a, *MTP*.

[33] In 1896 or 1897 he recalled that "every book from Huck Finn and Prince and Pauper on was read to household critics nightly as it was written." Albert E. Stone, Jr., "Mark Twain's *Joan of Arc*: The Child as Goddess," *AL*, XXXI (March, 1959), 3. This may be true, but the indication seems to be that he first read *Huck* to the family in galley proofs in the summer of 1884.

[34] Ferguson, "*Huck Finn* A-Borning," *Colophon*, n.s., III; *Mark Twain: Man and Legend*, pp. 219–227; DeVoto, *MTaW*, pp. 82–86; Krause, "Twain's Method and Theory of Composition," *Mod. Philol.*, LVI (February, 1959), 173–177.

[35] My thanks to Cecily Raysor for calling my attention to the implications of the canceled passage in a course paper in the winter of 1959.

CHAPTER 25: PUBLICATION

(Pages 355–370)

[1] January 2, 1884, *Bus. Man*, p. 230.

[2] December 21, 1883, Rogers Theatrical Collection, Houghton Library, Harvard University.

[3] *Bus. Man*, p. 221.

[4] Letter to Webster, January 20, 1884, *MTP*.

[5] New York *World*, November 27, 1884. A memorandum dated September 13, 1883, shows that at that time he thought of asking 20 per cent "if 20 represents ¾ profits." *MTP*.

[6] Webster to Clemens, New York, February 5, 1884; Webster to "Dear Ma and Sam," New York, February 26, 1884, *MTP*, © copyright 1960 by Mark Twain Co.

[7] Letter of March 3, 1884, C. Waller Barrett Collection; *MTP;* Item 71, AAA, *Anderson Gallery Sale*, No. 4086, February 15–16, 1934.

[8] Boston, April 10, 1884, *MTP*. The phrasing seems to indicate a prior reading.

[9] Howells to Webster, Boston, May 4, 1884; Webster to Clemens, September 2, 1884, *MTP*, © copyright 1960 by Mark Twain Co.

[10] Webster to Clemens, April 21, 1884, DV 19a, *MTP*, © copyright 1960 by Mark Twain Co.

[11] *Bus. Man*, pp. 249–250.

[12] DV 19a, *MTP*.

[13] E. W. Kemble, "Illustrating *Huckleberry Finn*," *Colophon* (February, 1930), Part I. The illustration on p. 279 of the first edition has some details in the manuscript but not in the book. See also Kemble's letter to Webster, June 2, 1884, which asks for "manuscript from XIII chapter on" so that he may check on "illustrations . . . which are described minutely." *MTP*, © copyright 1960 by Mark Twain Co. The original manuscript does not contain chapter demarcations.

[14] *Bus. Man*, pp. 253, 255–256, 260, 262; DV 19a, *MTP*, © copyright 1960 by Mark Twain Co.

[15] *Bus. Man*, p. 262.

[16] DV 19a, *MTP*. On July 26 Webster told Clemens that it would be possible to change the statement about the time of the narrative on the title page.

[17] Howells to Webster, June 16, 1884, DV 19a, *MTP,* © copyright 1960 by Mark Twain Co.

[18] Howells to Clemens, July 2, 1884, *MTP,* © copyright 1960 by Mark Twain Co.

[19] Letters of June 28 and August 7, 1884, Houghton Library, Harvard University.

[20] Clemens to Howells, August 31, 1884, Berg Collection, New York Public Library; Howells to Webster, August 11 and 28, December 27, 1884, *MTP;* Webster to Clemens, August 9, 1884, *MTP,* © copyright 1960 by Mark Twain Co.

[21] Page proofs include 128–160 and even-numbered pages from 180 to 196; plate proofs 36–50, 65–80, 325, 326, 329–336, 339–344. Some plate proofs are marked by the author for public readings. *MTP.*

[22] Webster to Clemens, July 22, August 6, 1884, *MTP.*

[23] Webster to Clemens, September 13 and 17, 1884, *MTP.* Several varieties of this portrait occur in the first editions.

[24] Webster to Clemens, *MTP,* © copyright 1960 by Mark Twain Co.

[25] *Bus. Man,* p. 277. On September 1 Webster had promised: "As soon as I get a set of sheets I shall send them to you." *MTP,* © copyright 1960 by Mark Twain Co.

[26] Arthur L. Vogelback, "The Literary Reputation of Mark Twain in America, 1869–1884" (unpublished doctoral dissertation, University of Chicago, 1939), pp. 43 ff.

[27] Entry in Webster's list of expenses dated September 2, 1884, *MTP.*

[28] A circular is reproduced in Jacob Blanck, "In Re *Huckleberry Finn,*" *New Colophon* (1950), III, 158. Webster enclosed a copy of the insert in a letter to Clemens, August 23, 1884, *MTP,* reproduced on my p. 362.

[29] *MTP.*

[30] I have seen Franklin J. Meine's copy. The pages: 17–19, 24, 31–32, 35–36, 42–43, 67, 72, 77, 79, 81, 87, 98, 101, 110, 126–128, 138–140, 145, 149, 153, 162–165, 172–175, 187, 191, 211–212, 232–233, 237, 241, 257, 261, 263, 274, 283, 287, 290–291, 293, 302, 304–305, 314, 318, 322, 324, 331, 333, 335, 341, 343–345, 347, 355, 357, 361–362, 364–366.

[31] *Bus. Man,* pp. 248–249, 255, 269, 285–286.

[32] *MTP,* © copyright by Mark Twain Co.

[33] Webster to Clemens, Chicago, October 6, 1884. The account rendered by Webster for expenditures May–August 23 contains "June 4 Binding 1 Dummy of 'Huck'—.25." *MTP,* © copyright by Mark Twain Co.

[34] To "Ma and Sam," Chicago, October 7; New Orleans, November 12, 1884, *MTP.*

[35] Arthur Lawrence Vogelback, "The Publication and Reception of *Huckleberry Finn* in America," *AL,* XI (November, 1939), 262–263.

[36] Merle Johnson, *A Bibliography of Mark Twain* (New York, 1935), p. 48.

[37] *Bus. Man,* pp. 255, 304. This is supported by a notation on an envelope containing one of the pages in the J. J. Little and Company files, and by Little's testimony, quoted by Johnson. Franklin J. Meine has a photograph of the envelope.

[38] George Hiram Brownell, *The Twainian,* January–February, 1950, pp. 2–3, quotes a recent letter from Samuel C. Webster, son of the publisher: "I have original proofs of the illustrations that went into the book. On one of these proofs there appears the notorious picture that was later to appear at page 283. . . ." A photograph of this sheet, which contains in addition to this illustration the one

captioned "One of the Best Authorities," later placed on p. 302, is in the possession of Franklin J. Meine, who received it from Webster.

[39] On the envelope containing these Cable wrote, somewhat inaccurately, "Proof sheets (complete) of 'Huckleberry Finn' given me in 1885 by 'Mark Twain' when we were nightly performing on the platform together. G. W. Cable." These are not proof sheets but unbound signatures and Cable should have said "in 1884" since, in a letter of October 13, 1884, he evidently speaks of reading these. (*Twins of Genius*, ed. Cardwell, p. 104.) Cable's daughter sold these to Scribner's. The next owner, Leigh Block of Chicago, sold them to Mr. Barrett. Mr. Meine has a photograph of the press proof containing the defaced illustration.

[40] His itinerary: New York, November 18–19; Newburgh, N.Y., November 20; Philadelphia, November 21; Brooklyn, November 22–23; Washington, November 24–25; Philadelphia, November 26; Morristown, N.J., November 27 (Thanksgiving); Baltimore, November 28–29. *Twins of Genius*, pp. 19–25; *Love Letters*, p. 366.

[41] Advance sheets and prospectuses bear the copyright date 1885, but when the plan to issue earlier was made, a cancel bearing the copyright date 1884 was prepared.

[42] Jacob Blanck has reproduced this in "A Supplement to *A Bibliography of Mark Twain*" (New York, 1939).

[43] Johnson, *A Bibliography . . .* , p. 48.

[44] The Canadian plates duplicated those of the New York edition. Franklin J. Meine was told by Dawson's son that a family tradition was that Canadian production was halted while the cut was modified.

[45] *MTP*, © copyright 1960 by Mark Twain Co. The Montreal *Daily Star*, December 9, 1884, reported Webster's being in Montreal to arrange for copyright.

[46] *Bus. Man*, p. 283, and information supplied by Professor Gordon Roper, Trinity College, University of Toronto.

[47] In a letter to his mother-in-law and her son on December 18 Webster said that he was sending as a Christmas present to the son, Samuel Moffett, "One of ten [copies] which we have got in advance to save our copyright." *MTP*, © copyright 1960 by Mark Twain Co. See also *Bus. Man*, pp. 303–304.

[48] The inscription quoted in *Bus. Man*, pp. 303–304, predicts publication of the first edition of 30,000 copies "Feby. 16th." But a letter from Webster to Clemens dated March 16 says the book had not been out quite a month, and a letter dated March 18 says the book had been published "just a month today." *MTP*.

[49] Jacob Blanck, "In Re *Huckleberry Finn*," *New Colophon* (New York, 1950), III, 159.

[50] *Twins of Genius*, pp. 12–64.

[51] Changes made by Gilder, the editor, are discussed by DeVoto, *Mark Twain's America*, pp. 213–216, and by Arthur Scott, "*The Century Magazine* and *Huckleberry Finn*, 1884–1885," *AL*, XXVII (November, 1955), 356–362.

[52] *Bus. Man*, pp. 284, 298, 299, 300, 303.

[53] Vogelback, "The Literary Reputation . . . ," pp. 46–47.

[54] *Bus. Man*, pp. 284–285; Boston *Transcript*, February 10, 1885.

[55] Letter to Clemens, *MTP*.

[56] Letters to Clemens, *MTP*, © copyright 1960 by Mark Twain Co.

[57] April 7, 1882, Rogers Theatrical Collection, Houghton Library, Harvard University.

[58] Notebook 17, May, 1883—August 12, 1884, *MTP*.

[59] Back in May, Clemens had thought that if 40,000 copies had been sold by then, December 5 would be the right time. *Bus. Man*, p. 255.

[60] DV 19a, *MTP*, © copyright 1960 by Mark Twain Co.

[61] *MTP*, © copyright 1960 by Mark Twain Co.

CHAPTER 26: HUCKA, KHŎK, HUNCKLE,
GEKKELBERRI . . .

(Pages 371–384)

[1] Accountings preserved by chance show that January 1, 1886—April, 1887, the book sold between 2,700 and 4,000 copies, probably nearer the latter; April 1–October 1, 1887, 168; February–August, 1889, 1,115. *MTP*.

[2] Hall to Clemens, *MTP*, © copyright 1960 by Mark Twain Co.

[3] New York *Times*, April 18, 1859.

[4] With half the accountings missing, total sales of 32,523 copies are reported. *MTP*.

[5] *Autobiography*, TS of dictation, May 22, 1908, pp. 2521 ff., *MTP. Innocents Abroad* sold 46,000; *Tom Sawyer*, 41,000; *Roughing It*, 40,334. Sales of all books, 489,000.

[6] James D. Hart, *The Popular Book*, p. 150.

[7] Frances Lander Spain, Coördinator, Children's Service, New York Public Library, says the novel "was banned at the time of its publication and for several years afterwards by most people concerned with children's reading." *Saturday Rev.*, March 22, 1958, p. 38. Edmund Lester Pearson wrote a plea for reinstating the book in the *Library Jour.*, XXXII (July, 1907), 312–315.

[8] Letter from Jess Stein, Random House, March 11, 1959.

[9] Letter from Elizabeth Eulass, Viking Press, Inc., February 9, 1959.

[10] *Who Reads What* (New York, 1935), pp. 15–17, 21. Readers of the leading five books: *Huck*, 657; *Tom Sawyer*, 455; *Connecticut Yankee*, 409; *Innocents Abroad*, 382; *Pudd'nhead Wilson*, 327.

[11] Edward A. Weeks, "The Best Sellers since 1875," *Publishers Weekly*, CXXV (April 21, 1934), 1506.

[12] Letter from Cass Canfield, Jr., Harper & Bros., January 14, 1959. Sets of royalty statements with a number of returns missing show sales of 80,825 copies by Harpers from 1896 through 1907.

[13] Letter from F. L. Mott, March 17, 1959.

[14] Letter from Richard J. Donahue, Goldsmith, November 27, 1957.

[15] Letters from Elizabeth Adams, Rinehart, November 27, 1957; March 19, 1959.

[16] Letter from John P. Ware, Pocket Books, Inc., January 30, 1959.

[17] Letter from Roberta Strauss Feuerlicht, Gilbertson Co., February 25, 1959. Best sellers attract 4,000,000 to 5,000,000 purchasers.

[18] See the list of such discussions in the Bibliography.

[19] *MTP.* Runners-up: *Tom Sawyer,* 112,500; *Tramp Abroad,* 104,500; *Life on the Mississippi,* 54,500; *The Prince and the Pauper,* 43,250.

[20] Letter from John O. Oliver, George C. Harrup, December 17, 1957.

[21] Clarence Gohdes, "British Interest in American Literature . . . ," *AL,* XIII (January, 1942), 356–362.

[22] The review, unsigned, appeared on January 31, 1885. The author was Brander Matthews, Columbia University professor.

[23] *Illustrated News of the World,* February 14, 1891; *Munsey's,* June, 1900; *America Today* (London, 1900). See also E. Hudson Long, *Mark Twain Handbook* (New York, 1957), pp. 409–414.

[24] George Stuart Gordon, *Anglo-American Literary Relations* (Oxford, 1942), p. 110.

[25] *New Statesman and Nation,* XXII (August 2, 1941); "Introduction" to Cresset edition, *The Adventures of Huckleberry Finn* (London, 1950); *Listener,* L (October 1, 1953), 540–541. Pritchett, however, has strong reservations.

[26] Information provided by Professor Gordon Roper, Trinity College, University of Toronto.

[27] Grace Isabel Colbron, "The American Novel in Germany," *Bookman* XXXIX (March, 1914), 46–48. She named three editions in paperback libraries.

[28] Edgar H. Hemminghaus, *Mark Twain in Germany* (New York, 1939), p. 143. He placed *Sketches* first, 425,000; *Tom Sawyer* second, 240,000.

[29] Ivan Benson, "From Our Swedish Correspondent," *The Twainian,* II (May, 1940), 4.

[30] Maurice le Breton, "Un Centenaire: Mark Twain," *Revue Anglo-Américaine,* XIII (June, 1935), 401.

[31] Bibliographical data were supplied by Albert Parry, letter of August 1, 1959. The quotation is from his "Mark Twain in Russia," *Books Abroad,* Spring, 1941, pp. 168–175. George V. Bobrinskoy's interview was carried in a number of newspapers, April 21, 1959.

[32] Statistics presented during the World's Fair, New York, 1939, indicated that "in a period of three recent years Mark Twain's works sold over a million and a half copies printed in various languages of Soviet peoples; Jack London's followed with 1,431,000 copies . . ." Parry, "Mark Twain in Russia," p. 168. Figures on sales are included in Glenora W. Brown and Deming B. Brown, *A Guide to Soviet Russian Translations of American Literature, 1917–1947* (New York, 1954).

[33] New York *Times,* September 2, 1945.

[34] Vaclav Mostecky, "The Library under Communism: Czechoslovak Libraries from 1948 to 1954," *Library Quar.,* XXVI (April, 1956), 110.

[35] Translations for the earlier period were published by the League of Nations, for the later period by the United Nations, in *Index Translationum.*

[36] Transcript of radio discussion of *Huckleberry Finn,* Radio House, Austin, Texas, February 24, 1959.

[37] Notebook 19, TS pp. 2–5, *MTP,* © copyright 1960 by Mark Twain Co. In a letter of November, 1885, the author thanked Joel Chandler Harris for saying a good word for "Huck, that abused child of mine who has had so much unfair mud slung at him." "Somehow," he continued, "I can't help believing in him. . . ." Julia Chandler Harris, *The Life and Letters of Joel Chandler Harris* (Boston, 1918), p. 566.

APPENDIX

(Pages 386–387)

[1] Merle Johnson, *A Bibliography of Mark Twain* (1935), p. 287.

[2] Jacob Blanck, "In Re *Huckleberry Finn*," pp. 155–156; *Bibliography of American Literature*, p. 200. In *American Editions* (1936), p. 106, Blanck says, "The question of p. 283 remains doubtful but copies with this leaf tipped in are deemed most desirable."

[3] Underhill, "The Haunted Book," p. 287.

[4] The latter would be the copies bound in sheepskin in which Blanck's state "A" or "1" of p. 283 occurs.

[5] *Bus. Man,* pp. 303–304.

[6] Franklin J. Meine has held for a number of years that the first Canadian edition figured importantly in the story of publication. He has the first copy sold of that edition with an autograph statement that it is, signed by Charles L. Webster dated December 10, 1884.

[7] *Bibliography of American Literature,* p. 200. Blanck notes that this stage "has been in copies of the book as late as 1891"—a fact which would seem to support his belief. It does not, however, establish it.

[8] Signature mark 11 occurs on p. 161; but the Canadian printers had reason to insert this and could have done so.

[9] In the list of illustrations the one titled "Him and Another Man" is listed as on p. 88; on p. 23 line 23 has the words "with the was" instead of "with the saw."

BIBLIOGRAPHY

Extensive bibliographies of the writings of Mark Twain and of material relating to him are in the following: Roger Asselineau, *The Literary Reputation of Mark Twain from 1910 to 1950* (Paris, 1954); Harry H. Clark, "Mark Twain," in *Eight American Authors* (New York, 1956); Philip S. Foner, *Mark Twain: Social Critic* (New York, 1958); Merle Johnson, *A Bibliography of the Works of Mark Twain* (New York, 1935); E. Hudson Long, *Mark Twain Handbook* (New York, 1957). I list below only studies which have been of particular value to me; materials in manuscript; and studies which discuss in some detail aspects of *Adventures of Huckleberry Finn*.

Particularly useful books for this study have included *Mark Twain's Autobiography*, ed. Albert Bigelow Paine (New York, 1924), 2 vols.; *Mark Twain in Eruption* (further excerpts from the *Autobiography*), ed. Bernard DeVoto (New York, 1940); *Mark Twain's Letters*, ar. A. B. Paine (New York, 1917), 2 vols.; Dixon Wecter, *Sam Clemens of Hannibal* (Boston, 1952); A. B. Paine, *Mark Twain: A Biography* (New York, 1912), published in 4 vols., 3 vols., and 2 vols. The last three are the best collections of facts concerning Mark Twain's life. Also useful were *Mark Twain's Notebook*, ed. A. B. Paine (New York, 1935); *Mark Twain to Mrs. Fairbanks*, ed. Dixon Wecter (San Marino, 1949); *The Love Letters of Mark Twain*, ed. Dixon Wecter (New York, 1949); Kenneth R. Andrews, *Nook Farm: Mark Twain's Hartford Circle* (Cambridge, 1950); Gladys Carmen Bellamy, *Mark Twain as Literary Artist* (Norman, 1950); Bernard DeVoto, *Mark Twain at Work* (designated as *MTaW* in the notes) (Cambridge, 1942); DeLancey Ferguson, *Mark Twain: Man and Legend* (Indianapolis, 1943); *Life in Letters of William Dean Howells*, ed. Mildred Howells (Garden City, 1928), 2 vols.; W. D. Howells, *My Mark Twain* (New York, 1910); Samuel Charles Webster, *Mark Twain, Business Man* (Boston, 1946).

Materials in manuscript which I have utilized included the Mark Twain Papers, University of California, Berkeley; the partial manuscript of *Huckleberry Finn* in the Buffalo Public Library; the private collection of C. Waller Barrett, New York; the Henry W. and Albert A. Berg Collection, New York Public Library; the

Boston Public Library; the Houghton Library, Harvard University; the Morse Collection, Yale University Library; the Pierpont Morgan Library, New York; Huntington Library; private collection of Franklin J. Meine. To these institutions and collectors I am very grateful for assistance.

Discussions of *Huckleberry Finn*, 1884–1944, include: Anon., reviews in *Critic*, V (November 29, 1884), 257; *Independent*, XXXVI (December 4, 1885), 171; *Christian Union*, XXX (December 5, 1884), 550; XXXI (February 5, 1885), 171; *Life*, V (February 26, 1885), 19; *Punch*, January 4, 1896, p. 5; "Tom, Mark and Huck," *English Jour.*, X (September, 1921), 403–404; Warren Beck, "Huckleberry Finn versus the Cash Boy," *Education*, XLIX (September, 1928), 1–13; Walter Besant, "My Favorite Novelist and His Best Book," *Munsey's*, XVII (February, 1898), 659–664; Sarah Bolton, *Famous American Authors* (New York, 1887), pp. 384–387; Van Wyck Brooks, "The Genesis of *Huckleberry Finn*," *Freeman*, I (March 31, 1920), included in *The Ordeal of Mark Twain* (New York, 1920, 1933); Bernard DeVoto, "Tom, Huck and America," *Sat. Rev. Lit.*, IX (August 13, 1932), included in *Mark Twain's America* (Boston, 1932); "Introduction" to *The Adventures of Huckleberry Finn* (New York, 1932), included in *MTaW*; A. D. Dickinson, "Huckleberry Finn Is Fifty Years Old," *Wilson Bull. for Librarians*, X (November, 1935), 180–185; Albert Erding, "Einleitung," *Die Abenteuer Huckleberry Finns* (Berlin, 1909); John Erskine, "*Huckleberry Finn*," *Delineator* (February, 1927), pp. 94–97, reprinted in *Delight of Great Books* (Indianapolis, 1928); James T. Farrell, "Twain's 'Huckleberry Finn,'" *New York Times Book Rev.*, XLVIII (December 12, 1943), 6, included in *League of Frightened Philistines* (New York, 1945); DeLancey Ferguson, "*Huck Finn A-Borning*," *Colophon*, n. s. III (Spring, 1938), 171–180; *Mark Twain: Man and Legend* (Indianapolis, 1943), pp. 217–230; Waldo Frank, *Our America* (New York, 1919), pp. 34–38, 129–130; Joel Chandler Harris, "Letter on Mark Twain's Semi-Centennial," *Critic*, VII (November 28, 1885), 253; Archibald Henderson, *Mark Twain* (London, New York, 1911); W. D. Howells, "Mark Twain, an Inquiry," *North American Rev.*, CLXXII (February, 1901), 306–321; Franz Kwest, "Einleitung," *Die Abenteuer Huckleberry Finns* (Halle, 1902); Andrew Lang, "Tribute to Mark Twain," *Illustrated News of the World*, 1891, and *Critic*, XIX (July 25, 1891), 43–46; Fred W. Lorch, "A Note on Tom Blankenship," *American Literature* (designated as *AL*), XII (November, 1940), 351–352; John Macy, *The Spirit of American Literature* (Garden City, 1913), pp. 248–277; Archibald Marshall, "Last Century's Literary Favorites: I, *Huckleberry Finn*," *Literary Digest Internat. Book Rev.*, II (January, 1924), 104–106; Brander Matthews, "'The Adventures of Huckleberry Finn,'" *Saturday Rev.* (London), LIX (January 31, 1885), 153–154; *Aspects of Fiction* (New York, 1896); "Mark Twain— His Work," *Book Buyer*, XIII (January, 1897), 977–979; "Introduction" to *The Adventures of Huckleberry Finn* (New York, 1918); Olin H. Moore, "Mark Twain and Don Quixote," *PMLA*, XXXVII (June, 1922), 324–346; Christopher Morley, "The Return of Huckleberry Finn," *Columbia Univ. Quar.*, December, 1935, pp. 370–378; "Introduction" to *Tom Sawyer and Huckleberry Finn* (New York, 1944); Vernon L. Parrington, *Main Currents in American Thought* (New York, 1930), III, 85–101; Edmund Lester Pearson, "The Children's Librarian versus *Huckleberry Finn*," *Library Jour.*, XXXII (July, 1907), 312–315, included in *The Library and the Librarian* (Woodstock, 1910), pp. 26–32; T. S. Perry, "Mark

Twain," *Century,* XXX (May, 1885), 171–172; William Lyon Phelps, "Mark Twain," *North American Rev.,* CLXXXV (July, 1907), 540–548; V. S. Pritchett, "*Huckleberry Finn* and the Cruelty of American Humor," *New Statesman and Nation,* August 8, 1941; Constance Rourke, *American Humour: A Study of National Character* (New York, 1931); Stuart Pratt Sherman, "Mark Twain," *Cambridge History of American Literature* (New York, 1921), III, 16–17; Booth Tarkington, "Introduction" to *Adventures of Huckleberry Finn* (New York, 1933); Carl Van Doren, *The American Novel: 1798–1939* (New York, 1921, revised—with title indicated, 1942); Arthur L. Vogelback, "The Publication and Reception of *Huckleberry Finn* in America," *AL,* XI (November, 1939), 260–272; Edward Wagenknecht, *Mark Twain: The Man and His Work* (New Haven, 1935); B. J. Whiting, "Guyascutus, Royal Nonesuch and Other Hoaxes," *Southern Folklore Quar.,* VIII (December, 1944), 251–275.

Discussions and studies of *Huckleberry Finn,* 1945–1959, include: Lucille Adams, "*Huckleberry Finn:*" *A Descriptive Bibliography* (Buffalo, 1950); Richard P. Adams, "The Unity and Coherence of *Huckleberry Finn,*" *Tulane Studies in English,* VI (1956), 87–103; Walter Allen, "Introduction" to *The Adventures of Huckleberry Finn* (Camden, Ill., 1949); Kenneth R. Andrews, *Nook Farm: Mark Twain's Hartford Circle* (Cambridge, 1950), pp. 210–215; W. H. Auden, "Huck and Oliver," *Listener,* L (October 1, 1953), 540–541; Frank Baldanza, "The Structure of *Huckleberry Finn,*" *AL,* XXVII (November, 1955), 347–355; Robert E. Bell, "How Mark Twain Comments on Society through the Use of Folklore," *Mark Twain Jour.,* X (Summer, 1955), 1–8, 24; Gladys Carmen Bellamy, *Mark Twain as a Literary Artist* (Norman, 1950), pp. 336–347; Walter Blair, "The French Revolution and *Huckleberry Finn,*" *Mod. Philol.,* LV (August, 1957), 21–35; "When Was *Huckleberry Finn* Written?" *AL,* XXX (March, 1958), 1–25; "Why Huck and Jim Went Downstream," *College English,* XVIII (November, 1956), 106–107; W. Blessingame, "The Use of the Lie in *Huckleberry Finn* as a Technical Device," *Mark Twain Quar.,* IX (Winter, 1953), 11–12; Edgar M. Branch, "The Two Provinces: Thematic Form in *Huckleberry Finn,*" *College English,* XI (January, 1950), 188–195, included in *The Literary Apprenticeship of Mark Twain* (Urbana, 1950); "Mark Twain and J. D. Salinger: A Study in Literary Continuity," *American Quar.,* IX (1957), 144–158; Van Wyck Brooks, *The Times of Melville and Whitman* (New York, 1947), pp. 297–300, 453–457; Frances V. Brownell, "The Role of Jim in *Huckleberry Finn,*" *Studies in English,* I (1955), 74–83; Asher Brynes, "Boy-Men and Men-Boys," *Yale Rev.,* XXXVIII (Winter, 1949), 223–233; E. H. Cady, Frederick J. Hoffman, Roy Harvey Pearce, "Notes on Reading *Huckleberry Finn,*" in *The Growth of American Literature* (New York, 1956), I, 856–858; Henry Seidel Canby, *Turn East, Turn West* (Boston, 1951), pp. 132–147; Guy A. Cardwell, *Twins of Genius* (East Lansing, 1953), pp. 68–76; Richard Chase, *The American Novel and Its Tradition* (Garden City, 1957), pp. 139–149; Alexander Cowie, "Mark Twain," *The Rise of the American Novel* (New York, 1948); James M. Cox, "Remarks on the Sad Initiation of Huckleberry Finn," *Sewanee Rev.,* LXII (Summer, 1954), 389–405; Bernard DeVoto, "Introduction," *The Portable Mark Twain* (New York, 1946); "Those Two Immortal Boys," *Woman's Day,* November, 1947, pp. 38–39; T. S. Eliot, "Introduction," *The Adventures of Huckleberry Finn* (London, 1950; New York, 1950); George P. Elliott, "Wonder for Huckleberry Finn," *Twelve Original Essays* on *Great American Novels* (Detroit, 1958); Clifton Fadiman, "A Note on *Huckleberry Finn*," *Party of One* (Cleveland, 1955); Clarence Faust, "Introduction," *The Adventures of Huckleberry Finn* (Chicago, 1950); Leslie Fiedler, "Come Back to the Raft Ag'in Honey!" *Partisan Rev.*, XV (June, 1948), 664–671, reprinted in *An End to Innocence* (Boston, 1955); P. S. Foner, *Mark Twain Social Critic* (New York, 1958), pp. 204–210; Ray William Frantz, Jr., "The Role of Folklore in *Huckleberry Finn*," *AL*, XXVIII (November, 1956), 314–327; Edwin Fussell, "Hemingway and Mark Twain," *Accent*, XIV (Summer, 1954), 199–206; Helmut E. Gerber, "Twain's *Huckleberry Finn*," *The Explicator*, XII (March, 1954), 1–3; Edward J. Gordon, "What's Happened to Humor?" *English Jour.*, XLVII (March, 1958), 127–133; Thomas Arthur Gullason, "The 'Fatal' Ending of *Huckleberry Finn*," *AL*, XXIX (March, 1957), 86–91; James G. Harrison, "A Note on the Duke in 'Huckleberry Finn': The Journeyman Printer as Picaro," *Mark Twain Quar.*, VIII (Winter, 1947), 1–2; Arthur Heiserman and James E. Miller, Jr., "J. D. Salinger: Some Crazy Cliff," *Western Humanities Rev.*, X (Spring, 1956), 129–137; John Hinz, "Huck and Pluck: 'Bad' Boys in American Fiction," *South Atlantic Quar.*, LI (January, 1952), 120–129; Robert Hunting, "Mark Twain's Arkansaw Yahoos," *Mod. Lang. Notes*, LXXIII (April, 1958), 264–268; Graham Hutton, "Hawkeye, Huck Finn and an English Boy," *Chicago Sun Book Week*, IV (May 4, 1947), 2; H. E. Jones, "Mark Twain and Sexuality," *PMLA*, LXXI (Summer, 1956), 595–616; Joseph Jones, "The Duke's Tooth-Powder Racket," *Mod. Lang. Notes*, LXI (November, 1946), 468–469; Jean Kanapa, "Preface," *Les Aventures d'Huckleberry Finn* (Paris, 1948); Charles Kaplan, "Holden and Huck: The Odysseys of Youth," *College English*, XVIII (November, 1956), 76–80; Rosemarie Klaus, "Mark Twain und die Negerfrage—*Huckleberry Finn*," *Zeitschrift für Anglistik und Amerikanistik*, V (1957), 166–181; Sydney J. Krause, "Twain's Method and Theory of Composition," *Mod. Philol.*, LVI (February, 1959), 167–177; Joseph Wood Krutch, "Speaking of Books," *New York Times Book Rev.*, May 23, 1954, p. 2; Lauriat Lane, Jr., "Why *Huckleberry Finn* Is a Great World Novel," *College English*, XVII (October, 1955), 1–5; Lewis Leary, "Tom and Huck: Innocence on Trial," *Virginia Quar. Rev.*, XXX (Summer, 1954), 417–430; Kenneth S. Lynn, "Huck and Jim," *Yale Rev.*, XLVII (1958), 421–431; *Mark Twain's "Huckleberry Finn": Readings Selected by Department of American Studies, Amherst College*, ed. and with introduction by Barry A. Marks (Boston, 1959); William C. McGraw, "Pollyanna Rides Again," *Saturday Rev.* (London), XLI (March 22, 1958), 37–38; Leo Marx, "Mr. Eliot, Mr. Trilling and *Huckleberry Finn*," *American Scholar*, XXII (Autumn, 1953), 423–440; "The Pilot and the Passenger: Landscape Conventions and the Style of *Huckleberry Finn*," *AL*, XXVIII (May, 1956), 129–146; Franciosa Massimo, "I meriti nascosti di Mark Twain narratore," *La Fiera Letteraria*, June 24, 1951, pp. 4–7; Wright Morris, *The Territory Ahead* (New York, 1957), pp. 79–90; William Van O'Connor, "Why *Huckleberry Finn* Is Not the Great American Novel," *College English*, XVII (October, 1955), 6–10; Walker Percy, "The Man on the Train," *Partisan Rev.*, XXIII (Fall, 1956), 478–494; George Reinfeld, "*Huckleberry Finn*: Candidate for Greatness," *Mark Twain Jour.*, X (Fall–Winter, 1957), 12–14; Carol Remes, "The Heart of *Huckleberry Finn*," *Masses and Mainstream*, XIII (November, 1955), 8–16; Sister Mary Teresa Rhoades, "Was Mark Twain Influenced by the Prolog to *Don Quixote*?" *Mark Twain Quar.*, IX (Winter, 1952), 4–6; Gilbert

M. Rubenstein, "The Moral Structure of *Huckleberry Finn*," *College English*, XVIII (November, 1956), 72–76; George Santayana, "*Tom Sawyer* and *Don Quixote*," *Mark Twain Quar.*, IX (Winter, 1952), 1–3; Friedrich Schönemann, "Mark Twain's *Huckleberry Finn* (Zum 70 Geburtstag 1885–1955)," *Archiv.*, CXCII (1956), 273–289; Edward Schwartz, "*Huckleberry Finn*: The Inward Thoughts of a Generation," *Mark Twain Quar.*, IX (Winter, 1952), 11–16; Arthur Scott, "*The Century Magazine* Edits *Huckleberry Finn*, 1884–1885," *AL*, XXVII (November, 1955), 356–362; "Introduction" to *Mark Twain: Selected Criticism* (Dallas, 1955); Joseph Slater, "Music at Colonel Grangerford's," *AL*, XXI (March, 1949), 108–111; Henry Nash Smith, "Origins of a Native American Literary Tradition," *The American Writer and the European Tradition* (Minneapolis, 1950), pp. 70–77; "Mark Twain's Images of Hannibal," *Univ. of Texas Studies in English*, XXXVII (1958), 3–23; "Introduction" to *Adventures of Huckleberry Finn* (Boston, 1958); Robert Ernest Spiller, *The Cycle of American Literature* (New York, 1955), pp. 150–162; R. W. Stallman, "Huck Finn Again," *College English*, XVIII (May, 1957), 425–426; Rudolf Sühnel, "Huckleberry Finn," *Anglo-Americana*, LXI (1955), 150–156; Donald T. Torchiana, "Will Huck Hang?" *Mark Twain Jour.*, X (Winter, 1956), 5–8; Lionel Trilling, "Introduction" to *The Adventures of Huckleberry Finn* (New York, 1948); Edward Wagenknecht, *Cavalcade of the American Novel* (New York, 1952), pp. 117–120; Edward Wasiolek, "The Structure of Make-Believe: *Huckleberry Finn*," *Univ. of Kansas City Rev.*, XXIV (December, 1957), 97–101; Dixon Wecter, "Mark Twain," *Literary History of the United States* (New York, 1948), II, 930–934; "One Word More," in *The Adventures of Huckleberry Finn* (New York, 1948), pp. xix–xxvi; Ray B. West, Jr., "Mark Twain's Idyl of Frontier America," *Univ. of Kansas City Rev.*, XV (Winter, 1948), 92–104; Robert A. Wiggins, "Mark Twain and the Drama," *AL*, XXV (November, 1953), 279–286; Stanley T. Williams, "Introduction" to *The Adventures of Huckleberry Finn* (New York, 1953); Herman Wouk, "America's Voice Is Mark Twain's," "This World," San Francisco *Chronicle*, August 5, 1956, p. 18; Philip Young, *Ernest Hemingway* (New York, 1952), pp. 181–212.

INDEX